生态语言学 第二版

语言、生态与我们信奉和践行的故事

ECOLINGUISTICS

LANGUAGE, ECOLOGY AND THE STORIES WE LIVE BY

[英] 阿伦·斯提比 著　黄国文 哈长辰 注

清华大学出版社
北京

北京市版权局著作权合同登记号　图字：01-2021-6292

图书在版编目（CIP）数据

生态语言学：语言、生态与我们信奉和践行的故事：第二版：英文 /（英）阿伦·斯提比（Arran Stibbe）著；黄国文，哈长辰注.—北京：清华大学出版社，2023.4

书名原文：Ecolinguistics: Language, Ecology and the Stories We Live By (Second Edition)

ISBN 978-7-302-60417-4

Ⅰ.①生… Ⅱ.①阿… ②黄… ③哈… Ⅲ.①语言学—生态学—英文 Ⅳ.①H0-05

中国版本图书馆CIP数据核字（2022）第047949号

责任编辑：曹诗悦　许玲玉
封面设计：子　一
责任校对：王凤芝
责任印制：杨　艳

出版发行：清华大学出版社
　　　　　网　　　址：http://www.tup.com.cn，http://www.wqbook.com
　　　　　地　　　址：北京清华大学学研大厦A座　　邮　　编：100084
　　　　　社　总　机：010-83470000　　　　　　邮　　购：010-62786544
　　　　　投稿与读者服务：010-62776969, c-service@tup.tsinghua.edu.cn
　　　　　质量反馈：010-62772015, zhiliang@tup.tsinghua.edu.cn
印　装　者：天津安泰印刷有限公司
经　　销：全国新华书店
开　　本：180mm×250mm　　印　　张：21　　字　　数：420千字
版　　次：2023年4月第1版　　印　　次：2023年4月第1次印刷
定　　价：118.00元

产品编号：092107-01

　　最近半个多世纪以来，在环境污染严重、全球气候变暖、海平面上升、生物多样性锐减等全球性生态环境问题频繁出现的背景下，"生态"一词不断应用在人类生产生活的各个领域。这不仅促使着生态学研究本身逐渐深化，也体现了生态问题的探讨不再只是生态学家和其他与地球地理和环境研究有关的科学家所关注的焦点；其他学科的专家学者也纷纷参与到与生态相关的研究中来，借助生态学的原理、框架、视角和路径，同时也借助其他学科的理论和方法来分析各种各样的与生态有关的现实问题。这类生态学与其他学科结合研究的现象被称为生态泛化或学科的生态学化（李继宗、袁闯，1988；黄国文，2016a；赵蕊华、黄国文，2017），推动了许多新兴交叉学科的发展，例如：城市生态学、环境生态学、教育生态学、人类生态学和语言生态学；在人文社会科学领域则形成了诸如生态文学、生态哲学、生态心理学、生态翻译学和生态语言学等跨学科研究。Stibbe（2021）撰写的《生态语言学：语言、生态与我们信奉和践行的故事》（第二版）[*Ecolinguistics: Language, Ecology and the Stories We Live By*（Second Edition）]（以下简称"《生态语言学》（第二版）"）重点讨论的是生态语言学问题。作为全书的导读，我们主要从生态语言学学科的概述、本书的基本情况简介和本书的阅读说明三个方面进行介绍。

1. 生态语言学概述

　　关于生态语言学研究的基本概述，我们沿着五个层面展开论述。首先，交代"生态语言学"概念的定义，并结合生态语言学的传统研究模式，分别归纳出各模式下的研究议题；其次，继续以研究模式为基础，对生态语言学的研究方法和前期成果进行梳理；再次，提出生态语言学的发展趋势和研究热点；紧接着，对当前国内的研究现状进行初步总结；最后，这个部分还特别说明了我们对"语言生态学"的一些新的认识。

1.1 "生态语言学"概念与研究议题

　　就生态学和语言学结合而成的交叉学科来说，有"语言生态学"和"生态语言学"两种说法。由于研究者学科背景、研究视角、理论指导和研究方法等方面的差异，生态学家和语言学家在这个学科上的研究重心是不同的（详见下面 1.5 小节）。在语言学领域，国内很多学者将语言生态学和生态语言学视为同一个学科（范俊军，2005；韩军，2013；肖自辉、范俊军，2017），认为它们代表着相同学科的不同研究路径，二者相互补充（Fill，2001；艾尔文·菲尔等，2004）。根据目前的研究情况，学界普遍认同"生态语言学"更能够涵盖这个学科的整体内容，故更倾向于使用"生态语言学"（ecolinguistics）这一术语来统称这个学科。

生态语言学主要是通过研究语言中的生态因素以及语言与生态环境的关系，揭示出语言与生态环境的相互作用（黄国文，2016a）。Stibbe（2021：203）将生态语言学定义为"有关语言在人类、其他物种和物理环境之间的生命可持续互动中的作用研究"。在生态语言学领域被广泛认同的传统研究模式有两个（Fill，2001），即豪根模式（Haugen，1970，1972）和韩礼德模式（Halliday，1990/2003，2007）；它们也分别被称为隐喻模式和非隐喻模式（黄国文，2016a），代表着不同议题的探讨。

豪根模式（Haugen，1970，1972）将语言生态看作是隐喻的。Haugen 把语言和言语社团的关系与生物和自然环境的关系作了类比，主要研究的是任何特定的语言和周围环境之间的相互作用。很多学者认为，该模式主要是围绕社会语言学的研究问题展开的，具体的研究内容包括：语言的生存和发展状况、语言演变、语言活力、语言接触、双语或多语研究、濒危语保护、语言政策与规划以及语言生活等与语言生态本身相关的研究。

韩礼德模式（Halliday，1990/2003，2007）将语言视为生态系统的一部分，关注的是语言在各种生态环境问题中的作用。它主要是从系统功能语言学的视角出发的，涉及对话语和行为的生态审视与批评，也就是对"我们信奉和践行的故事"（Stibbe，2015）的反思、推崇或批评。该模式特别强调了语言研究者的"社会责任"（social accountability），它的研究过程可以分为"生态话语"的分析（analysis of ecological discourse）（即对涉及生态问题的话语的分析）和话语的"生态分析"（ecological analysis of discourse）（即对所有话语进行生态分析）两个部分（Alexander & Stibbe，2014）。因此，在韩礼德模式的研究下，语言生态是非隐喻的。因为人类本身是自然界中不可或缺的一部分，而语言又是人类生存的重要组成部分和人类生活的一种重要方式；人类通过语言进行沟通、反映社会现象，并主动构建现实世界（Halliday，1990/2003：145）。因此，类似于等级主义（classism）、增长主义（growthism）等与环境有关的问题，不仅仅生物学家和物理学家要重视，应用语言学家也同样应该特别关注（Halliday，1990/2003：172）。

1.2　研究方法与前期成果

鉴于生态语言学是一门"以问题为导向"的学科（黄国文，2018a；黄国文、李文蓓，2021），在研究中所选择的理论、方法和视角都是以研究问题为前提和基础的。因此，从不同的研究模式出发，所使用的研究方法是不一样的。下面主要围绕生态语言学的两个传统模式，梳理生态语言学的主要研究方法，并对前期的研究成果进行归纳。

从现有研究看，豪根模式下最常用的研究方法是田野调查法（field research），又称实地研究法；同时，案例分析和语料库等研究方法在该模式下也是适用的（黄国文、赵蕊华，2019：124）。这一路径主要是在文献阅读的基础上，使用录音和录像等方式记录和研究语言，以获取调查内容的一手资料，并对这些资料进行转写、建档、分析和评估（何伟、高然，2019）。田野调查法属于定性研究的范畴，它旨在通过对目标对象的抽样后，对样本进行观察、问卷调查和访谈等过程来收集数据。基于豪根模式的生态语言学，由于研究视角和范围的影响，加之其与社会语言学的关系，使得它在学界的关注度仍有待提高。目前国内豪根模式中比较有代表性的论著包括：郑通涛（1985）、李国正（1991）、范俊军（2005）、王晋军（2005）、冯广艺（2013）、范俊军和肖自辉（2018）等；国外的可见 Fill & Mühlhäusler（2001）和 Fill & Penz（2018）等。

韩礼德模式下最典型的研究方法是话语分析法。由于该模式聚焦的问题是"我们的意指方式如何左右我们对环境的影响"（How do our ways of meaning affect the impact we have on the environment?）（Halliday，2007：14），而"语言"是"意指方式"中最重要的一部分，且语篇或话语是由语言体现的，所以话语分析在该模式的研究中具有重要位置。Matthiessen（2009：48–52；2014：140–143）指出语言理论模型的建构方法大致需分为四个阶段：第一阶段，通过应用某一理论的框架进行语篇分析；第二阶段，基于第一阶段的语篇分析，根据一定数量的语篇分析，在特定的理论框架中对语言进行描述；第三阶段，以第二阶段的语篇描述为基础，对语言进行类型的划分；第四阶段，建构语言理论模型。这个过程清晰地说明了语篇分析和话语分析法在韩礼德模式中的实践路径。近几年，国内学者关于韩礼德模式研究做得较多，具有代表性的论著包括：辛志英和黄国文（2013）、赵蕊华（2016）、何伟和魏榕（2017）、何伟和张瑞杰（2017）、黄国文（2018b）、黄国文和赵蕊华（2019）、Huang & Zhao（2021）、赵蕊华和黄国文（2021）等。

除此之外，当前还出现了生态语言学与其他更加广泛的研究领域的交叉，例如：生态语言学与认知语言学（王馥芳，2017）、生态语言学与生态心理学（黄国文、王红阳，2018）、生态语言学与语料库语言学（赵蕊华，2018a，2018b）、生态语言学与生态素养（黄国文、哈长辰，2021），甚至是更加侧重生态实践性的根性生态语言学（radical ecolinguistics）（魏榕、史蒂芬·考利，2020），这一视角主要讨论分布式语言（a distributed language）的观点（Li et al.，2020）。究其根源，这是由生态语言学的跨学科属性决定的。可以预测，生态语言学还会与其他更多的学科进行交叉融合，产生新的增长点。因此，必须采用"和而不同"（live and let live）的包容态度，这对语言研究者践行和促进"人与自然和谐共生"宏伟蓝图的实现更有裨益。

正如我们（黄国文，2018a：451）说过的，关于豪根模式和韩礼德模式的区分，主要是以文章中所采用的研究路径来判定的，而认知模式应该是一种视角，不限于某一个人的某一个观点或某一篇文章所提出的某种研究路径。各种理论或模式都有自己的特点，要根据研究的问题和以解决问题为导向来选择理论作为指导、选择恰当的研究方法和采取合适的研究视角。因此，可以说，无论是生态语言学研究还是话语的生态分析，通常都应该以问题为导向，根据所要研究的问题来选择研究的理论支撑和研究视角，研究的目的就是为了解决问题。

1.3 发展趋势与研究热点

从前期的研究成果可以看出，自 1970 年美籍挪威语言学家 Einar Haugen 在奥地利（Burg Wartenstein，Austria）召开的一次学术会议上做了题为《论语言生态学》（"On the Ecology of Languages"）的学术报告以来，生态语言学的豪根模式逐渐受到学界的重视。到了 20 世纪 90 年代，系统功能语言学家 M. A. K. Halliday 在希腊（Thessaloniki，Greece）举办的国际应用语言学会议上做了题为《意义表达的新路径：对应用语言学的挑战》（"New Ways of Meaning：The Challenge to Applied Linguistics"）的学术报告。Halliday（1990/2003）的这篇文章在学界反响很大，它开创了系统功能语言学视角下研究生态语境、语言和语言影响的先河（黄国文，2017a），促进了生态语言学韩礼德模式的形成和发展。

可以这样说，在韩礼德模式下，与语言生态本身相关的内容需要紧紧围绕"维护人类社会良好的生存环境"这一核心目标展开研究。由此，韩礼德模式所涉及的因素更加广泛，包含了豪根模式的部分内容（黄国文、赵蕊华，2019：33），是对豪根模式的补充和创新。这说明生态语言学在研究范围、研究角度、研究内容和研究方法等方面越来越呈现出多样化的发展趋势。在这种趋势的驱动下，生态语言学的研究热点集中在以下四个方面：

第一，生态语言学的学科属性和研究范围。由于"生态"和"语言"都是十分广泛的概念，所以有关生态语言学的学科属性和研究范围问题，在学界一直是一个研究热点（何伟，2018；黄国文、陈旸，2018a）。黄国文和陈旸（2018a）从"微观生态语言学"和"宏观生态语言学"两个方面区分了生态语言学的学科属性和研究范围；概括来说，如果微观生态语言学关注的重点是"什么是生态语言学？"，那么宏观生态语言学则倾向于关注"什么不是生态语言学？"。这个问题目前仍存在一定的争议，有待进一步探究。

第二，世界各地传统文化的生态智慧。本书作者在最后一章中指出，世界各地传统文化中蕴含的生态智慧是值得深入挖掘的一个发展方向，能够补充我们信奉和践行的可替代性新故事（Stibbe，2021：211）。例如：在中国语境下提出的和谐话语分析（详见下面 1.4 小节和本书第 11 章）以及巴西的生态系统语言学（见本书第 11 章）。

第三，从"生态话语"的分析到话语的"生态分析"。Alexander & Stibbe（2014）的文章《从生态话语分析到话语的生态分析》（"From the Analysis of Ecological Discourse to the Ecological Analysis of Discourse"）给学界带来了很大的启示，为生态语言学研究注入了新鲜血液，扩大了研究领域。生态语言学视角下的话语分析不仅要重视与生态问题直接相关的话语，还要研究所有类型话语的生态意义，比如：银行排队票号说明（黄国文，2016b）、姚明参与拍摄的公益广告（黄国文、肖家燕，2017）、写给"知心姐姐"的信件（黄国文，2018a）等案例就属于话语的生态分析范畴。只有同时重视生态话语的分析和话语的生态分析，才有可能从各个角度分析语言中的生态问题，实现生态语言学研究的更大价值。

第四，从不同的视角研究语言与生态关系问题。由于生态语言学研究主要是问题驱动的，所以研究的重心是解决问题，这样就鼓励不同学科领域的学者从各自学科的角度去研究问题和解决问题，因此也就出现了不同的理论支撑和研究方法（参见Fill & Penz，2018；黄国文、赵蕊华，2019）。

1.4 国内研究现状

国外的生态语言学研究由于发展相对较早，因此目前发展更为成熟，研究视角和方法多样化趋势相对明显。相比较，国内的生态语言学研究则初具雏形，正处于蓬勃发展的阶段。截至2022年4月9日，在中国知网（CNKI）上检索关键词"生态语言学"，文章数量已到887篇，比2015年12月12日的150篇累计增加了737篇。具体来看，已经有多家学术期刊发表了生态语言学论文、设置生态语言学专栏，甚至是出版专号（special issue）刊登生态语言学领域的文章（参见黄国文、赵蕊华，2019：11）。

这些情况都表明，国内的生态语言学领域受到越来越多学者的关注和支持。这样的成就还得益于中国学者发起和策划召开的"国际生态语言学研讨会"（已召开6届）、中国英汉语比较研究会生态语言学专业委员会主办的"全国生态语言学研讨会"（已召开7届）和"中国生态语言学战略发展研讨会"（已召开7届）、华南农业大学举办的"生态语言学讲习班"（已举办4期）、北京外国语大学组织的"生态语言学"系列讲座以及外语教学与研究出版社组织的"生态语言学"网络课程和"生态语言学研究研修班"等多项学术活动。这里需要特别提及的是2020年8月22—23日线上举办的第五届全国生态语言学研讨会，承办单位山东师范大学外国语学院在学校新闻网上公布了一组数据——本次研讨会有430余人参与到学术讨论中来，且会议全程在网络平台同步直播，收看人数达17 000余人，《中国社会科学报》还就此次研讨会作了报道（2020年8月27日）。这一切足以说明生态语言学研究当前在国内蓬勃发展的现状。

另一方面，国内的生态语言学研究也受到了国外学者的特别关注，乃至大力支持。例如：中国生态语言学研究会在国际生态语言学学会的支持下于2017年4月成立，《劳特利奇生态语言学手册》（*The Routledge Handbook of Ecolinguistics*）中提及了中国学者的学术贡献（Fill & Penz，2018）。Stibbe也在《生态语言学》第一版汉译本的前言（阿伦·斯提比，2019：vi）、第二版的致谢（Pxxviii）中感谢了华南农业大学的黄国文教授在生态语言学研究领域所做出的努力，并在第二版的结语（第11章）中充分肯定了和谐话语分析的意义和价值（P265）。说起和谐话语分析，就要谈到生态语言学的本土化研究，这是将生态话语分析研究应用到中国实践的一个尝试，也是发现中国传统文化生态思想内在价值的路径。近年来，国内有关和谐话语分析的研究已经有了很多的讨论，取得了阶段性的成果（参见黄国文，2017b；黄国文、赵蕊华，2017；赵蕊华、黄国文，2017，2021；Zhou，2017；周文娟，2017；Zhou & Huang，2017；黄国文，2018c；Huang & Zhao，2021等），但这一研究方向目前仍有很多问题需要深入探索，中华文化的精髓（包括儒家和道家思想）需要进一步挖掘和解读。

1.5 对"语言生态学"的新认识

与生态语言学紧密相连的是"语言生态学"。关于"语言生态学"的英文表述，常见的有 linguistic ecology、language ecology 和 the ecology of language。对于语言学家而言，无论是用"生态语言学"还是"语言生态学"，其研究重点首先是语言，而且所采用的研究方法也是来自语言学或其他的人文社会科学。有些语言学者偏好使用"语言生态学"，但其研究的理论指导和研究方法主要都不是来自自然科学学科。也许可以这样断言，到目前为止的语言学者（如 Haugen，1972；Makkai，1993；Garner，2004；冯广艺，2013）所做出的语言生态研究，并不是自然科学学科的学者心目中的"语言生态（学）"。

对于自然科学学科（包括生态学）的学者来说，要研究"语言生态（学）"问题，核心学科是包括生态学在内的自然科学，涉及的学科除了语言和语言学外，还有生态学、环境学、气候学、地理学、土壤学、森林学、园艺学、植物学、动物学、遗传学等学科。而对于语言研究者，"语言生态学"所涉及的学科则除了语言学和生态学外，还有历史语言学、语言人口学、社会语言学、语言接触、语言变异、语文学、语言规划和政策、语言政治学、民族语言学、语言类型学等（见黄国文、李文蓓，2021）。因此，黄国文和李文蓓（2021：597）说，"'语言生态（学）'这个游戏，语言研究者与生态研究者各有自己的玩法，但很难一起玩，因为大家对这个东西没有一致的看法，更多共同之处有待挖掘"。

从我们接触到的文献来看，从自然科学角度所做的与语言和生态关系的研究也不少，涉及的视角有生态地理学、生物学、动物学、气候学、生理学、生态教育学、景感生态学等（如 Zhao *et al.*，2016，2020；Pitman & Daniels，2020；Han *et al.*，2021）。华南农业大学的语言生态学研究团队这些年已经在这方面做出了一些成果，如张兰等人在景感生态学框架中所做的语言景感生态学（linguistic landsenses ecology）（Zhang *et al.*，2021a，2021b）、哈长辰等人在语言生态学框架中所做的生态教育研究（Ha *et al.*，2022）。

2.《生态语言学》（第二版）基本情况简介

2015 年本书的第一版出版后，学界反响很大。但随着社会的发展变革，我们身边的故事在不断地发生变化，有些原来的故事已经不复存在，而一些新的故事也随之涌现。这给人类为社会做出贡献提供了新的契机，推动了本书第二版（Stibbe，2021）的出现。目前，本书第二版已经在劳特利奇（Routledge）出版社出版，也正在被翻译成意大利语、波斯语、阿拉伯语和韩语等多种译本。在国内，本书的第一版被翻译成汉语，并于 2019 年由外语教学与研究出版社出版（阿伦·斯提比，2019），第二版由清华大学出版社原文引进出版（中文注释版）。在原书基础上，中文注释版增添了汉语的章节导读、理论延伸、补充文献和中英文术语对照等内容，供读者阅读参考。

2.1 作者简介

本书的作者 Arran Stibbe 是英国格鲁斯特大学（University of Gloucestershire）生态语言学教授，国际生态语言学研究领域的知名学者；同时，他也是目前国际生态语言学学会（The International Ecolinguistics Association）的召集人（主席）。

Stibbe 于 1970 年 7 月出生在英国伦敦。1991 年至 1996 年，Stibbe 分别在英国约克大学（专业：电脑系统工程）、英国爱丁堡大学（专业：计算语言学、语言处理）和英国兰卡斯特大学（研究课题：疾病的隐喻）获得学士、硕士和博士学位。其中，他的博士学位论文题目是《隐喻与可替换的疾病概念》（"Metaphor and Alternative Conceptions of Illness"），主要研究中西方与疾病隐喻有关的问题。随后，为了更深入地进行生态语言学研究，Stibbe 于 2004 年在英国开放大学就读人类生态学专业，并于次年顺利获得第二个硕士学位（研究课题：环境素养）。从 Stibbe 的整个教育背景能够看出，他具有多学科的学习经历，这对其研究生态语言学问题有着非常重要的作用。

Stibbe 在 1996 年获得博士学位后，到南非罗德斯大学（Rhodes University）就职，为该校学生讲授批评话语分析和系统功能语言学课程，并对批评话语分析产生了浓厚的兴趣（Stibbe & Ross, 1997）。1997 年，他开始在日本的广岛大学工作，并在研究中关注了生态的问题，特别是有关跨文化的环境教育研究（Stibbe, 2004）。2004 年，Stibbe 发起成立语言与生态研究论坛（Language and Ecology Research Forum）（现已更名为国际生态语言学学会）。2005 年至今，Stibbe 一直在英国格鲁斯特大学工作，于 2018 年晋升为生态语言学教授。在这 17 年里，Stibbe 全面展开对生态语言学的研究，建构自己的研究框架，并发表了多篇学术论文（如 Stibbe, 2010, 2014a, 2014b, 2018; Alexander & Stibbe, 2014），撰写和编辑出版了多部生态语言学专著和论文集（Stibbe, 2009, 2012, 2015, 2021）。

在生态语言学教学方面，Stibbe 特别强调生态语言学的教育意义，注重环境教育的实施与可持续素养（sustainability literacy）的提升。他在英国格鲁斯特大学担任生态语言学、批评话语分析、生态批评、语言与身份认同等课程的主讲教师，将生态语言学融入课程教学中，传播生态理念。Stibbe 凭借出色的教学和研究贡献，获得了英国国家教学奖（National Teaching Fellowship）、高等教育学院高级研究员（Senior Fellowship of the Higher Education Academy）等诸多奖项。有关 Stibbe 的生态语言学研究相关的详细内容，可参见《斯提比生态语言学研究述评》（黄国文, 2018d）一文以及我们对 Stibbe 的访谈录（Huang, 2016）。

综上所述，Stibbe 在生态语言学研究领域具有很深的造诣，并为此做出了突出的贡献。我们将他主要的生态语言学研究成果归纳为如下四个方面：(1)厘清生态语言学的学科定位和研究范畴，明确生态语言学的定义；(2)发展自己的生态语言学理论框架；(3)重视批评话语分析方法在生态语言学研究中的作用；(4)强调生态语言学理论与实践结合的重要性。这四个方面在本书的两个版本（Stibbe, 2015, 2021）中都有着明显的体现，读者可在阅读过程中详细地了解。

2.2 主要特点和章节介绍

本书基于话语分析的研究路径，构建了一系列具有可操作性的生态语言学理论框架，并以此为基础，分析我们所信奉和践行故事的各类语篇（故事），尤其是工业文明故事背后的语言形式。本书是反映生态语言学研究领域最新成果的一部力作，集中体现了生态语言学研究发展的前沿动向，对生态语言学学科的全方位推进具有重要意义。与第一版相比，本书第二版在内容上有了很多的改变：对第一版的内容进行了更新和拓展，将最新的生态语言学研究成果与新的理论和实践结合起来，有了新的理论框架和新的案例分析，并增加了一个关于"叙事"的章节。综观全书，第二版的主要特点有：

第一，故事更加新颖。自本书第一版的出版已有 7 年，这 7 年来，关于生态的故事在我们的生活中不断变化，浮现出很多需要我们关注或重新审视的新故事；因此需要以新的方式、新的视角来分析和研究这些故事，并凭借新的语言特征模式构建出新的现实，将新故事呈现在生态文明的大背景下。

第二，概念更加清晰。如果比较 Alexander & Stibbe（2014：105）给出的定义和 Stibbe 在本书给生态语言学下的定义（P256）就可发现，本书的定义中更换了一个很重要的单词，把"impact"换成了"role"。也就是说，本书所指的生态语言学已经不单单指"人类如何对待生态系统"，而是将"语言"视为生态系统的一个重要组成部分，考量"语言"在生态系统中的作用。这有利于在牢牢抓住"维系生命的生态系统"这一研究要点的同时，将不同的生态语言学研究方法结合起来。

第三，案例更加丰富。由于故事的发展变化，作者在第二版增添了最新的语篇案例来分析，例如：可持续发展目标、有关难民问题的报纸和政治新闻报道、Luther Standing Bear 的作品、否认冠状病毒的真实性、创世故事和小说等。这些内容都使书中的案例分析更具说服力。

基于上述特点，本书将"生态"与"语言"的关系贯穿于各个章节，论证了二者的相互交叉，同时涉及与社会学、心理学等多个学科的融合问题。其核心是在揭露社会和生活中不平等的、不可持续的故事之后，以和谐的话语形式重构一个生态和谐、环境友好的世界。具体来看，全书分为绪论、主干和结语三个部分，由 11 个章节组成。其中主干部分有 9 个章节，每个章节分析一个类型的故事。前面八个类型的故事是根据第一版的内容更新而来的，分别是：意识形态、构架、隐喻、评估、身份、信念、删略和凸显；而第九个类型的故事——叙事（第 10 章）是作者在第二版中新添加的一个重要故事。叙事是本书中最复杂、最为重要，也是最强大的故事。作者谈到了关于宇宙起源的创世叙事以及以科学为基础的叙事。这些叙事在人们如何看待"人类在生态系统、地球内部和宇宙中的位置"方面发挥着重要作用。

2.3 关于"story we live by"的理解

本书书名的副标题是"Language, ecology and the stories we live by"。关于"the story/stories we live by"的理解和汉语翻译，很多人的理解和翻译是"我们赖以生存

的故事"（张瑞杰、何伟，2016），这与把"metaphors we live by"理解和翻译为"我们赖以生存的隐喻"是一样的。我们认为，把"the story/stories we live by"翻译成"我们信奉和践行的故事"可能会更加准确（参见阿伦·斯提比，2019：263–264）。对于这个问题，我们查阅了一些英文词典对"live by"的解释。

（1）在《COBUILD 英汉双解词典》/ *COBUILD English-Chinese Dictionary*（上海译文出版社，2002）中的"live"词条下，有一条关于"live by"的条目，所给的解释是：

LIVE BY; If you live by a particular rule, belief, or ideal, you behave in the way in which it says you should behave. 身体力行（规则、信仰或理想）。

e.g. Many people proclaim adherence to a religious ethic but do not live by it. 许多人宣称坚守某种宗教伦理，可是并不身体力行。

（2）在《牛津高阶英汉双解词典》/ *Oxford Advanced Learner's English-Chinese Dictionary*（商务印书馆 / 牛津大学出版社，2004）中的"live"词条下，关于"live by"的解释与《COBUILD 英汉双解词典》基本一致：

PHR V; LIVE BY STH; to follow a particular belief or set of principles. 按照（某信念或原则）生活。

e.g. That's a philosophy I could live by. 那就是我所信奉的人生哲学。

（3）在《朗文当代高级英语词典》/ *Longman Dictionary of Contemporary English*（外语教学与研究出版社 / Longman，2004）中的"live"词条下，"live by"有如下的条目和解释：

LIVE BY A PRINCIPLE/RULE ETC 按照某种原则 / 准则等生活；to always behave according to a particular set of rules or ideas. 总是按某一套准则（观念）行事。

e.g. People who live by the Bible. 以《圣经》为行事准则的人。

在认真研读这三部英国专家学者编纂的词典中关于"live by"的解释和例证之后，我们认为，"live by"理解和翻译为"信奉和践行"更加准确。因此，这本书书名中的"the stories we live by"就翻译为"我们信奉和践行的故事"。

3.《生态语言学》（第二版）阅读说明

前面两节已经对生态语言学的主要内容和本书基本情况进行了简要的介绍。最后这个部分我们为读者提供一些阅读说明，具体涉及《生态语言学》（第二版）阅读中需要注意的核心要点和本书的阅读与使用建议，并尝试通过相关书籍的推荐，更好地协助读者学习和理解生态语言学这个新生学科。

3.1　核心要点补充

通过前面的介绍，如果一定要说 Stibbe 在本书中的研究是属于豪根模式还是韩礼德模式，那很明显是属于韩礼德模式，并且正朝着更广泛的路径实践。正如 Stibbe（2015）在第一版的简介中讲到的那样：生态语言学阐述了语言分析如何能够帮助人们揭示出我们生活中的故事，对不合理的故事提出质疑，并为新故事的探索做出贡献。同时，本书的分析路径是对 Matthiessen 语言理论模型的应用（处于该模型的第二阶段研究）。按照系统功能语言学的研究方法来说，是一种自下而上的研究路径（Matthiessen & Halliday，2009）。

本书的分析路径可以归纳为五个步骤：第一步，确定分析者的生态哲学观；第二步，结合话语内容选择话语分析的理论框架；第三步，应用所选择的理论分析话语中的语言模式；第四步，判断话语的类型；第五步，针对不同的话语类型实行不同的处理方式。从这一路径进行研究，需要注意的内容如下：

首先，注重生态哲学观的明确和更新完善。本书提出的生态哲学观较为全面，一个英文单词"Living!"（生活！）清晰明了地概括了作者的生态哲学观；这个生态哲学观的七个要素覆盖广泛，能够作为本书九个故事的考量标准。虽然作者明确指出，每个研究者会有自己独特的生态哲学观，本书的生态哲学观也不是唯一正确的；不过作者的确为我们提供了一种确定生态哲学观的可靠方法以及用于分析话语的路径。另外，作者也提醒我们要随着自身价值观和假定的变化，对自己的生态哲学观进行改进调整，以更好地服务于话语的分析，例如：第二版中生态哲学观的第七个要素——深度适应（deep adaptation）是由第一版的适应性（resilience）完善而来的。

其次，合理确定理论框架。本书构建了九类故事的理论框架，每类故事有自己独特的理论内涵和分析路径。但是，归根到底都是从语言学的角度出发，基于本书第 1 章提出的生态哲学观，运用某一理论进行话语分析。进一步来说，就是归纳语篇或话语中的语言特征模式、判断其话语类型，并将分析结果应用到可替代性话语的实践中去。而且，每类故事的分析中，通过大量的真实案例分析和探讨，验证了这类故事所采用的理论框架的合理性和可行性。

最后，强调理论与实践相结合。本书每个章节的故事都由理论和实践两个部分构成，将搭建的理论框架落到了实处。同时，实践中的案例语料不仅出处权威可靠，而且来源广泛、贴近生活。作者的实例分析过程也是紧扣理论框架展开的，为本书的严谨性奠定了基础。更重要的是，本书的理论建构和实例分析过程皆有迹可循，为读者的进一步研究乃至在更广泛的话语中实践提供了学术引导。

3.2 阅读与使用建议

本书特别适合作为对生态语言学、系统功能语言学、话语分析、认知语言学、环境科学、生态学和生态文明研究等相关领域感兴趣的本科生、研究生和研究人员的生态语言学入门读本；也可作为一本系统研究生态语言学的专业书籍。此外，本书的核心内容已经在 Stibbe 的带领下制作成了免费的网上在线课程（详见"Ecolinguistics | Stories We Live By"网站），供更多感兴趣的读者学习。

自 2015 年本书第一版出版以来，已经有 20 多万访客阅读了本书的网络资料，并有 2 000 多人报名参加了网络课程的学习，使得第一版图书在世界范围内得到了广泛的关注，并被顺利地翻译成汉语（阿伦·斯提比，2019）、韩语和波斯语（Stibbe，2021）。为了解该网络课程的实际效果，国际生态语言学学会也通过实证研究的方式报告了读者在课程学习后的反馈；结果显示，课程学习对学习者的生态技能、知识、态度、行为以及自身的工作方面都产生了积极的影响（Roccia，2019）。同时，还有许多相关领域的学者为本书的两个版本撰写了书评（Edney，2016；张瑞杰、何伟，2016；Ghorbanpour，2021；Zhou，2021 等）；我们也在研究基于话语分析的生态语言学过程中，以本书的两版内容为主线，探索生态语言学研究的新思想（哈长辰、黄国文，2022），进一步推动了此书的广泛传播。读者在阅读本书的过程中，如果发现难以理顺的内容，不妨结合各章节的中文导读、本书的网络课程以及相关学者的书评来理解，不失为一种有效的阅读方式。

值得注意的是，虽然本书优点很多，向我们提供了新颖的视角、丰富的内容，但仍存在一些观点有待商榷。例如：由于话语类型的划分存在很多不确定性，受到很多因素的影响，因此在把话语划分为三类的同时，还需要通过连续统（cline）的概念对话语进行评估（参见黄国文、陈旸，2018b）。另外，书中的分析多为定性的个案分析和经验性研究，缺少概括性和普遍性意义；虽然作者也提到基于语料库的生态语言学研究，并认为这种方法具有很大的研究潜力（Poole，2016，2017，2022），但有关定量的分析在本书中是缺失的。最后，关于多理论框架在实际案例分析中的应用问题，以及如何保证研究的系统性和科学性，仍值得更深层次的探索。

目前国内外市面上已经出现了多项关于生态语言学研究的论著，主要包括：Fill & Mühlhäusler（2001）、Mühlhäusler（2002）、Bang & Døør（2007）、Stibbe（2009，2012，2015，2021）、冯广艺（2013）、Fill & Penz（2018）、黄国文和赵蕊华（2019）、Huang & Zhao（2021）等。从研究观点和视角来看，黄国文和赵蕊华（2019）撰写的专著《什么是生态语言学》与本书最为接近。不过，如果说《什么是生态语言学》这本专著能够让读者系统掌握生态语言学大观，那么这里所介绍的《生态语言学》则能够将生态语言学领域的全貌在实践中得以落实。因此，读者若能将这两本专著结合阅读，将会对生态语言学理论与实践了解得更加全面和透彻。总而言之，本书是一本不可多得的生态语言学学术专著，读者可以从中获得意想不到的启发。

4. 结束语

本书在国内的重新出版，有助于进一步扩大中国学者对生态语言学研究最新进展的了解，这不仅对不同领域学者的学术研究有帮助，在生活方面也会有着不一样的影响。就像本书作者在前言（Pxxvii）中说的那样——生态语言学研究不仅仅是一个学术研究领域，它还是一种生活方式。因此，我们也建议本书的读者：思，以生态语言学为本；行，以生态语言学为道（think and act ecolinguistically）（黄国文，2016a）。同时，作为新时代的外语研究者，我们呼吁更多国内相关领域的学者加入生态语言学研究的队伍，关注外语教学与研究的生态化取向（黄国文，2016b），积极参与生态文明建设。我们也要一起努力，用世界语言讲好生态文明的中国故事，传播生态语言学的中国声音，共同践行人与自然和谐共生。

参考文献

阿伦·斯提比 . 2019. 生态语言学：语言、生态与我们信奉和践行的故事 . 陈旸，黄国文，吴学进，译 . 北京：外语教学与研究出版社 .

艾尔文·菲尔，范俊军，宫齐 . 2004. 当代生态语言学的研究现状 . 国外社会科学，（6）：5–10.

范俊军 . 2005. 生态语言学研究述评 . 外语教学与研究，（2）：110–115.

范俊军，肖自辉 . 2018. 生态语言学文选 . 广州：广东人民出版社 .

冯广艺 . 2013. 语言生态学 . 北京：人民出版社 .

哈长辰，黄国文 . 2022. 生态语言学新思想及其对生态话语分析的启示 . 当代外语研究，5：88–96.

韩军 . 2013. 中国生态语言学研究综述 . 语言教学与研究，（4）：107–112.

何伟 . 2018. 关于生态语言学作为一门学科的几个重要问题 . 中国外语，（4）：1，11–17.

何伟，高然 . 2019. 生态语言学研究综观 . 浙江外国语学院学报，（1）：1–12.

何伟，魏榕 . 2017. 国际生态话语之及物性分析模式构建 . 现代外语，（5）：597–607.

何伟，张瑞杰 . 2017. 生态话语分析模式构建 . 中国外语，（5）：56–64.

黄国文 . 2016a. 生态语言学的兴起与发展 . 中国外语，（1）：1，9–12.

黄国文 . 2016b. 外语教学与研究的生态化取向 . 中国外语，（5）：1，9–13.

黄国文 . 2017a. 从系统功能语言学到生态语言学 . 外语教学，（5）：1–7.

黄国文 . 2017b. 论生态话语和行为分析的假定和原则 . 外语教学与研究，（6）：880–889.

黄国文 . 2018a. 生态语言学与生态话语分析 . 外国语言文学，（5）：449–459.

黄国文 . 2018b. M. A. K. Halliday 的系统功能语言学理论与生态语言学研究 . 浙江外国语学院学报，（5）：31–40.

黄国文 . 2018c. 从生态批评话语分析到和谐话语分析 . 中国外语，（4）：39–46.

黄国文 . 2018d. 斯提比生态语言学研究述评 . 鄱阳湖学刊，（1）：42–47.

黄国文，陈旸 . 2018a. 微观生态语言学与宏观生态语言学 . 外国语言文学，（5）：461–473.

黄国文，陈旸 . 2018b. 生态话语分类的不确定性 . 北京第二外国语学院学报，（1）：3–14.

黄国文，哈长辰 . 2021. 生态素养与生态语言学的关系 . 外语教学，（1）：15–19.

黄国文，李文蓓 . 2021. 作为应用语言学的生态语言学 . 现代外语，（5）：592–601.

黄国文，王红阳 . 2018. 给养理论与生态语言学研究 . 外语与外语教学，（5）：4–11.

黄国文，肖家燕 . 2017. "人类世" 概念与生态语言学研究 . 外语研究，（5）：14–17，30.

黄国文，赵蕊华 . 2017. 生态话语分析的缘起、目标、原则与方法 . 现代外语，（5）：585–596.

黄国文，赵蕊华 . 2019. 什么是生态语言学 . 上海：上海外语教育出版社 .

李国正 . 1991. 生态汉语学 . 长春：吉林教育出版社 .

李继宗，袁闯 . 1988. 论当代科学的生态学化 . 学术月刊，（7）：45–51.

王馥芳 . 2017. 生态语言学和认知语言学的相互借鉴 . 中国外语，（5）：47–55.

王晋军 . 2005. 生态语言学：语言学研究的新视域 . 天津外国语学院学报，（1）：53–57.

魏榕，史蒂芬·考利 . 2020. 生态语言学的新型模式：根性生态语言学 . 北京科技大学学报（社会科学版），（1）：8–12.

肖自辉，范俊军 . 2017. 生态语言学的发展、创新及问题：2006—2016. 南华大学学报（社会科学版），（3）：94–99.

辛志英，黄国文 . 2013. 系统功能语言学与生态话语分析 . 外语教学，（3）：7–10.

张瑞杰，何伟 . 2016.《生态语言学：语言、生态与我们赖以生存的故事》评介 . 现代外语，（6）：863–866.

赵蕊华 . 2016. 系统功能视角下生态话语分析的多层面模式——以生态报告中银无须鳕身份构建为例 . 中国外语，（5）：84–91.

赵蕊华 . 2018a. 基于语料库的生态跨学科性及学科生态化表征研究 . 中国外语，（4）：54–60.

赵蕊华 . 2018b. 基于语料库 CCL 的汉语语言生态研究——以"野生动物"为例 . 外语与外语教学，（5）：12–20，147.

赵蕊华，黄国文 . 2017. 生态语言学研究与和谐话语分析——黄国文教授访谈录 . 当代外语研究，（4）：15–18，25.

赵蕊华，黄国文 . 2021. 和谐话语分析框架及其应用 . 外语教学与研究，（1）：42–53.

郑通涛 . 1985. 语言的相关性原则——《语言生态学初探》之一 . 厦门大学学报（哲学社会科学版），（4）：150–157.

周文娟 . 2017. 中国语境下生态语言学研究的理念与实践——黄国文生态语言学研究述评 . 西安外国语大学学报，（3）：24–28.

Alexander, R. & Stibbe, A. 2014. From the analysis of ecological discourse to the ecological analysis of discourse. *Language Sciences, 41*: 104–110.

Bang, J. C. & Døør, J. 2007. *Language, ecology, and society: A dialectical approach*. London: Continuum.

Edney, S. 2016. Book review: *Ecolinguistics: Language, ecology and the stories we live by*. *Green Letters*, (2): 225–226.

Fill, A. 2001. Ecolinguistics: States of the art. In: A. Fill and P. Mühlhäusler. *The ecolinguistics reader: Language, ecology and environment*. London: Continuum, 43–53.

Fill, A. & Mühlhäusler, P. (Eds.). 2001. *The ecolinguistics reader: Language, ecology and environment*. London: Continuum.

Fill, A. & Penz, H. (Eds.). 2018. *The Routledge handbook of ecolinguistics*. London: Routledge.

Garner, M. 2004. *Language: An ecological view*. Bern: Peter Lang.

Ghorbanpour, A. 2021. Book review: *Ecolinguistics: Language, ecology and the stories we live by* (2nd ed.). *Language & Ecology*.

Ha, C. C., Huang, G. W., Zhang, J. E. & Dong, S. M. 2022. Assessing ecological literacy and its application based on linguistic ecology: A case study of Guiyang City, China. *Environmental Science and Pollution Research*, 29(13): 18741–18754.

Halliday, M. A. K. 1990. New ways of meaning: The challenge to applied linguistics. *Journal of Applied Linguistics*, (6): 7–16. (Reprinted from *On language and linguistics, Vol. 3 in The collected works of M. A. K. Halliday*, pp. 139–174, by J. Webster, ed., 2003, Continuum)

Halliday, M. A. K. 2007. Applied linguistics as an evolving theme. In J. Webster (Ed.), *Language and education, Vol. 9 in The collected works of M. A. K. Halliday*. London: Continuum, 1–19.

Han, L. W., Shi, L. Y., Yang, F. M., Xiang, X. Q. & Gao, L. J. 2021. Method for the evaluation of residents' perceptions of their community based on landsenses ecology. *Journal of Cleaner Production, 281*, 124048.

Haugen, E. 1970. On the ecology of languages. Talk Delivered at a Conference at Burg Wartenstein, Austria.

Haugen, E. 1972. The ecology of language. In A. S. Dil (Ed.), *The ecology of language: Essays by Einar Haugen*. Stanford: Stanford University Press, 325–339.

Huang, G. W. 2016. Ecolinguistics in an international context: An interview with Arran Stibbe. *Language & Ecology*, 1–10.

Huang, G. W. & Zhao, R. H. 2021. Harmonious discourse analysis: Approaching peoples' problems in a Chinese context. *Language Sciences, 85*: 1–18.

Li, J., Steffensen, S. V. & Huang, G. W. 2020. Rethinking ecolinguistics from a distributed language perspective. *Language Sciences, 80*: 1–12.

Makkai, A. 1993. *Ecolinguistics: Towards a new paradigm for the science of language*. London: Pinter.

Matthiessen, C. M. I. M. 2009. Ideas and new directions. In M. A. K. Halliday & J. Webster (Eds.), *Continuum companion to systemic functional linguistics*. London: Continuum, 12–58.

Matthiessen, C. M. I. M. 2014. Appliable discourse analysis. In Y. Fang & J. Webster (Eds.), *Developing systemic functional linguistics: Theory and application*. London: Equinox, 138–208.

Matthiessen, C. M. I. M. & Halliday, M. A. K. 2009. *Systemic functional grammar: A first step into the theory*. Beijing: Higher Education Press.

Mühlhäusler, P. 2002. *Linguistic ecology: Language change and linguistic imperialism in the Pacific region*. London: Routledge.

Pitman, S. D. & Daniels, C. B. 2020. Understanding how nature works: Five pathways towards a more ecologically literate world—a perspective. *Austral Ecology, 45*(5): 510–519.

Poole, R. 2016. A corpus-aided ecological discourse analysis of the Rosemont Copper Mine debate of Arizona, USA. *Discourse and Communication, 10*(6): 576–595.

Poole, R. 2017. Ecolinguistics, GIS, and corpus linguistics for the analysis of the Rosemont Copper Mine debate. *Environmental Communication, 12*(4): 525–540.

Poole, R. 2022. *Corpus-assisted ecolinguistics*. London: Bloomsbury.

Roccia, M. 2019. Changing lives and professional practice: A report on the impact of ecolinguistics. *Language & Ecology*.

Stibbe, A. 2004. Environmental education across cultures: Beyond the discourse of shallow environmentalism. *Language and Intercultural Communication*, (4): 242–260.

Stibbe, A. 2009. *The handbook of sustainability literacy: Skill for a changing world*. Dartington: Green Books.

Stibbe, A. 2010. Ecolinguistics and globalisation. In N. Coupland (Ed.), *The handbook of language and globalization*. Malden: Wiley-Blackwell, 406–423.

Stibbe, A. 2012. *Animals erased: Discourse, ecology and reconnection with the natural world*. Middleton: Wesleyan University Press.

Stibbe, A. 2014a. Ecolinguistics and erasure: Restoring the natural world to consciousness. In C. Hart & P. Cap (Eds.), *Contemporary critical discourse studies*. London: Bloomsbury Academic, 583–602.

Stibbe, A. 2014b. An ecolinguistic approach to critical discourse studies. *Critical Discourse Studies*, (1): 117–128.

Stibbe, A. 2015. *Ecolinguistics: Language, ecology and the stories we live by*. London: Routledge.

Stibbe, A. 2018. Positive discourse analysis: Rethinking human ecological relationships. In A. Fill & H. Penz (Eds.), *The Routledge handbook of ecolinguistics*. London: Routledge, 165–178.

Stibbe, A. 2021. *Ecolinguistics: Language, ecology and the stories we live by* (2nd ed.). London: Routledge.

Stibbe, A. & Ross, A. 1997. The truth commission: At the crossroads of discourse. *Southern African Journal of Applied Language Studies*, (5): 14–28.

Zhang, L., Huang, G. W., Li, Y. T. & Bao, S. T. 2021a. The application of landsenses in language carriers. *International Journal of Sustainable Development & World Ecology, 28*(7): 653–660.

Zhang, L., Huang, G. W., Li, Y. T. & Bao, S. T. 2021b. A psychological perception mechanism and factor analysis in landsenses ecology: A case study of low-carbon harmonious discourse. *International Journal of Environmental Research and Public Health, 18*(13): 6914.

Zhao, J. Z., Liu, X., Dong, R. C. & Shao, G. F. 2016. Landsenses ecology and ecological planning toward sustainable development. *International Journal of Sustainable Development & World Ecology*, (4): 293–297.

Zhao, J. Z., Yan, Y., Deng, H. B., Liu, G. H., Dai, L. M., Tang, L. N., Shi, L. Y. & Shao, G. F. 2020. Remarks about landsenses ecology and ecosystem services. *International Journal of Sustainable Development & World Ecology*, (3): 196–201.

Zhou, W. J. 2017. Ecolinguistics: Towards a new harmony. *Language Sciences*, 62: 124–138.

Zhou, W. J. 2021. Book review: *Ecolinguistics: language, ecology and the stories we live by* (2nd ed.). *Discourse Studies*, (3): 420–422.

Zhou, W. J. & Huang, G. W. 2017. Chinese ecological discourse: A Confucian-Daoist inquiry. *Journal of Multicultural Discourses*, (3): 264–281.

ECOLINGUISTICS

Ecolinguistics: Language, Ecology and the Stories We Live By is a ground-breaking book which reveals the stories that underpin unequal and unsustainable societies and searches for inspirational forms of language that can help rebuild a kinder, more ecological world. This new edition has been updated and expanded to bring together the latest ecolinguistic studies with new theoretical insights and practical analyses.

The book presents a theoretical framework and practical tools for analysing the key texts which shape the society we live in. The theory is illustrated through examples, including the representation of environmental refugees in the media; the construction of the selfish consumer in economics textbooks; the parallels between climate change denial and coronavirus denial; the erasure of nature in the Sustainable Development Goals; creation myths and how they orient people towards the natural world; and inspirational forms of language in nature writing, Japanese haiku and Native American writing. This edition provides an updated theoretical framework, new example analyses, and an additional chapter on narratives.

Accompanied by a free online course with videos, PowerPoints, notes and exercises, as well as a comprehensive glossary, this is essential reading for undergraduates, postgraduates and researchers working in the areas of Discourse Analysis, Environmental Studies and Communication Studies.

Arran Stibbe is Professor of Ecological Linguistics at the University of Gloucestershire. He has an academic background in both linguistics and human ecology and combines the two in his research and teaching. He is the founder of the International Ecolinguistics Association, and author of *Animals Erased: Discourse, Ecology and Reconnection with Nature*. He was awarded a National Teaching Fellowship by the Higher Education Academy for teaching excellence and has published widely on discourse analysis of social and ecological issues.

Preface to the Chinese Edition

I am delighted that this Chinese edition of my book *Ecolinguistics: Language, Ecology and the Stories We Live By* will be published by Tsinghua University Press. Ecolinguistics is a great passion of mine and is something which has benefited my life in many ways. I hope that this edition of the book, with its very helpful Chinese introduction and notes, will help others to discover the benefits that I have. Ecolinguistics is primarily an academic pursuit, but people who study it find a new awareness of the world around them and how language shapes that world. They find inspirational forms of language which help them rethink the society that they are part of and imagine a new, more ecological civilization. This can transform their own lives, making them more appreciative of the ecological systems that life depends on and giving them the motivation to work with others to protect them.

There are many ways to tell the story of ecolinguistics. Traditionally, the story starts in the 1970s, with sociolinguists such as Haugen who use the term 'ecology' as a metaphor to describe the interaction of languages as if they were biological species (Haugen 1972). The metaphor has the advantage of encouraging sociolinguists to pay more attention to interaction and provides a political tool to represent languages that are declining in use as 'endangered' and threatened with 'extinction'. This may provide motivation to protect linguistic diversity, as a parallel to biodiversity. However, the metaphor has its limitations too — imposing the metaphor draws attention away from the many ways that the interaction of languages is different from the interaction of species, so can obscure as much as it reveals. More importantly, using 'ecology' as a metaphor erases the actual ecology — the humans, animals, plants, forests, rain, oceans, soil, and the ecosystems that life depends on. As it becomes clearer that those ecosystems are being destroyed, it becomes increasingly important for all subjects to focus attention not only on humans and human societies, but on the literal ecosystems that are necessary for their continued survival. This is the central goal of the 'ecological humanities' — ecocriticism, ecopsychology, ecofeminism and many others including, of course, ecolinguistics.

Rather than starting the story of ecolinguistics with the early explorations of 'language ecology', therefore, I prefer to start it with an inspirational speech given by Michael Halliday in 1990 (Halliday 1990/2001). This speech was a clear and strong call to linguists to start focusing on how language encourages us to behave in ways that protect or destroy the ecosystems that life depends on. It was quite natural that this call arose from Halliday because his approach, Systemic Functional Grammar, focuses attention on how language construes human experience, makes sense of reality, and builds relationships between people. Halliday was keenly aware of how language influences thought and behaviour and can encourage people to behave in ways that are racist, sexist or ecologically destructive. The following quotation from his speech is a useful demonstration of ecolinguistics:

> ...countless texts repeated daily all around the world, contain[s] a simple message: growth is good. Many is better than few, more is better than less, big is better than small, grow is better than shrink, up is better than down. Gross National Products must go up, standards of living must rise, productivity must increase. But we know that these things can't happen. We are using up ... the fresh water and the agricultural soils that we can't live without ... We are destroying many of the other species who form part of the planetary cycle ...

What makes this ecolinguistic is the connection between language and its impact on the ecosystems that support life. Halliday tended to focus on the language system, e.g., the markedness of the term 'growth' which gives it an inbuilt positivity. Subsequent approaches to ecolinguistics focused more on characteristic patterns of language use, i.e., discourses, since these are more amenable to change than the deep levels of the language system (e.g., Goatly 2000). And later work gave closer attention to the cognitive structures in people's minds which influence how they think, talk and act, which I call 'stories' in this book. In cognitive terms, Halliday is criticising the story that growth is good, which is an evaluation in people minds built through exposure to patterns of language in the texts which surround them.

For me, the key element which distinguishes ecolinguistics from other forms of linguistic enquiry is not a particular methodology, framework, or theory. Instead, it is just that a linguist has reflected on human relations with other species and the physical environment and taken the results of that reflection into consideration when coming to the conclusions of their study. Informally, I would express this as linguistic enquiry where the linguist notices and cares about humans, animals, plants, forests, rivers, and the ecosystems that life depends on and dedicates their work to improving their wellbeing. More formally, I would say that ecolinguistics is linguistic enquiry where judgements about whether findings are positive or negative are made with reference to an ecosophy (ecological philosophy). This is how Arne Naess describes ecosophy:

> By an ecosophy I mean a philosophy of ecological harmony … openly normative, it contains both norms, rules, postulates, value priority announcements and hypotheses concerning the state of affairs… (Naess 1995, p. 8)

We know that Naess was influenced by Eastern thought (Katz *et al.* 2000), and his use of 'harmony' to describe the goal of an ecosophy resonates with Chinese ecolinguistics, where harmony is a central concept. Similarly, Michael Halliday was influenced by Chinese thought — his B.A was in Chinese language and literature and his doctorate was entitled *The Language of the Chinese 'Secret History of the Mongols'*. Later he conducted various research into Chinese linguistics (Halliday 2009) and was a frequent academic visitor to China. I have also been influenced by Chinese ideas, which I explored in my own doctorate, which was entitled *Metaphor and alternative conceptions of illness*. I compared Western metaphors of fighting illness with metaphors of traditional Chinese medicine including balance, energy flows, and the elements. Later I widened my interest from the health of humans to the health of animals, and then to the health of the planet, but what I discovered during my doctorate about how different forms of language can tell radically different stories about the world has always been central to my work. This shows how Chinese ideas already had a beneficial influence on ecolinguistics in the West before the discipline travelled to China, where an important and distinctive form of ecolinguistics with Chinese characteristics was developed.

Tan Xiaochun (2020) describes the history of ecolinguistics in China, starting with how in the early days, engagement with ecolinguistics was done on an individual level where researchers cooperated with linguists in the West or conducted ecolinguistic research on their own. These researchers were often systemic functional linguists who were following the path of Halliday towards application of the theory to ecolinguistics (e.g., He Wei and Zhang Ruijie 2017). Key among these scholars was Professor Huang Guowen who established the Research Centre for Ecolinguistics at South China Agricultural University (SCAU) in 2016. The following year, 2017, the China Association of Ecolinguistics was established, and the first ecolinguistics PhD students were enrolled in SCAU. This was followed by outstanding research activity including the holding of very well-attended conferences and a great number of ecolinguistics publications in English and Chinese. The China Association of Ecolinguistics has held an annual national conference on ecolinguistics each year since its inception. All of this was done within the support and encouragement provided by the Chinese Government's policy of Ecological Civilisation.

The framework of Harmonious Discourse Analysis (HDA) has emerged as an important and distinctive form of ecolinguistics with Chinese characteristics (Zhou and Huang 2017, Huang and Zhao 2021). Huang and Zhao (2021, p. 2) describe how:

> Interpreting "discourse" as language use in the narrow sense and in a broader sense in the context of various systems of social praxis (Foucault 1972), HDA aims to work on two levels: the micro level, a text-based level, analysing features and patterns in language forms; and the macro level, a translinguistic level, analysing the language system and other systems, whether semiotic, social, or material, in terms of their interactions in social praxis. HDA does not merely confirm or criticize a phenomenon, ecosophy, or action, but also shows how various relations in the ecosystem are harmonized and how language and other systems contribute to harmonizing such relations.

The concept of harmony in Harmonious Discourse Analysis is based on the Chinese philosophical tradition of Taoism and Confucianism (Zhou and Huang 2017), incorporating 'the principle of conscience, the principle of proximity, and the principle of regulation' (Huang and Zhao 2021, p. 3). The analysis within this framework makes strong use of systemic functional linguistics as well as cognitive linguistics.

A promising new development is Zhang *et al.*'s (2021) synthesis of landsenses ecology with ecolinguistics. This helps bridge the divide between natural science ecology and linguistics because landsenses ecology considers both cultural ecosystems services and the forms of language which inspire people to benefit from them or neglect them. Zhang *et al.*'s study uses Harmonious Discourse Analysis to analyse representations of fur in China, describing beneficial, ambivalent, and destructive discourses. The conclusion (Zhang *et al.*, p. 660) refers to an important quotation from Halliday's speech, showing his enduring influence in Chinese ecolinguistics:

> … by associating three types of fur slogans with Maslow's hierarchy of needs and ecosystem services, we analyse different visions and social effects of beneficial discourse, destructive discourse, and ambivalent discourse from the perspective of humanism psychology. It is proved from both micro and macro levels that 'language does not passively reflect reality, but actively creates reality' (Halliday 1990/2001).

Harmonious Discourse Analysis is a significant development since it not only provides a framework that is perfectly tuned to conducting discourse analysis in a Chinese context but offers insights that can be used around the world.

I would encourage readers to use this book to gain a basic understanding of ecolinguistics, and then to build on this understanding by reading the literature around Harmonious Discourse Analysis. Ecolinguistics is an active pursuit, since it has clear goals of contributing to the protection of the ecosystems that life depends on. I would therefore encourage readers to take the next step and use ecolinguistics to analyse and resist destructive dominant global stories such as those of consumerism, unlimited economic growth, and stories which see nature as a machine or resource. Even more important is the promotion of new stories to live by — stories that can help inspire people to protect the ecosystems that life depends on. An important place to look for these new stories is within the discourses of traditional Chinese culture, as well as contemporary Chinese discourses such as those around 'ecological civilisation'. One goal of ecolinguistics in China is to promote ecologically beneficial behaviour within the country, but there is a larger goal too, of offering inspirational new stories to live by that can replace some of the dominant global stories and help build ecological civilisations around the world.

References

Goatly, A. 2000. *Critical reading and writing: An introductory coursebook.* London: Routledge.

Halliday, M. 1990. New ways of meaning: The challenge to applied linguistics. *Journal of Applied Linguistics*, (6): 7–16. (Reprinted from *The ecolinguistics reader: language, ecology, and environment*, pp. 175–202, by A. Fill & P. Mühlhäusler, Eds., 2001, Continuum)

Halliday, M. 2009. Methods–techniques–problems. In M. Halliday & J. Webster (Eds.), *Continuum companion to systemic functional linguistics.* London: Continuum, 59–86.

Haugen, E. 1972. *The ecology of language.* Stanford: Stanford University Press.

He, W. & Zhang, R. 2017. An ecological analytical framework for discourse. *Foreign Languages in China, 5*: 56–64.

Huang, G. & Zhao, R. 2021. Harmonious discourse analysis: Approaching peoples' problems in a Chinese context. *Language Sciences, 85*: 1–18.

Katz, E., Light, A. & Rothenberg, D. 2000. *Beneath the surface: Critical essays in the philosophy of deep ecology.* Cambridge: MIT Press.

Naess, A. 1995. The shallow and the long range, deep ecology movement. In A. Drengson & Y. Inoue (Eds.), *The deep ecology movement: An introductory anthology.* Berkeley: North Atlantic Books, 3–10.

Tan, X. 2020. Overview of the development of ecolinguistics in China during the 40 years of reform and opening up. *Ecolinguística: Revista Brasileira de Ecologia e Linguagem, 6*(2): 62–77.

Zhang, L., Huang, G., Li, Y. & Bao, S. 2021. The application of landsenses ecology in language carriers. *International Journal of Sustainable Development & World Ecology,* *28*(7): 653–660.

Zhou, W. & Huang, G. 2017. Chinese ecological discourse: A Confucian-Daoist inquiry. *Journal of Multicultural Discourses, 12*(3): 272–289.

PREFACE TO THE SECOND EDITION

Six years have passed since the first edition of this book was published. Those years saw a great kindling of ecological awareness globally, with millions of people taking to the streets to demand climate and ecological action, and widespread declarations of climate emergency. Strong voices emerged which demanded fundamental changes to society in order to avoid ecological collapse. However, the mainstream still clung to the old goals of perpetual economic growth, profit and material consumption, albeit with a nod towards achieving these goals with greater environmental responsibility. And then came the coronavirus pandemic which, at least temporarily, changed everything.

The initial months of the pandemic showed that dramatic widespread change is possible in response to a clear threat. There were huge practical changes, like the shutting down of most air travel and many shops and industries. In some countries there were political changes too, as free-market principles were moved aside for governments to directly support people who were struggling to meet their needs, and public health was put above economic growth. And there were community changes too, where groups spontaneously emerged to help local vulnerable people and refugees get by. Above all, there were personal changes, as some reduced unnecessary shopping and travel, bonded with family members, reconnected with local nature, helped neighbours, grew vegetables and rethought what was important in their lives. Arising from this there were environmental changes too as emissions fell and the air became cleaner. However, any positives have come at an enormous cost, in death and suffering of those who became ill, and the exacerbating of existing inequalities as those in poverty who were already suffering the most from ecological destruction were pushed to the brink of survival or beyond.

There were voices which described the changes that were occurring during the pandemic as temporary, something to endure until 'normality' returned. But there were others who pointed out that there was nothing normal about the time before the pandemic. The population had never been so high, consumption had never been so high, and the impacts of climate change, biodiversity loss, resource depletion and pollution were being felt in ways that they had never been felt before. As Sonya Renee Taylor (2020) describes:

> We will not go back to normal. Normal never was. Our pre-corona existence was not normal other than we normalized greed, inequity, exhaustion, depletion, extraction, disconnection, confusion, rage, hoarding, hate and lack ... We are being given the opportunity to stitch a new garment. One that fits all of humanity and nature.

According to this perspective, going back to 'normal' is not only impossible but also undesirable — we must move on to something new. Arundhati Roy (2020) writes that 'historically, pandemics have forced humans to break with the past and imagine their world anew. This one is no different. It is a portal, a gateway between one world and the next'.

This book describes how language structures the stories that cultures and societies are based on. It describes the stories of the pre-pandemic world that were not serving us well, that were leading society towards inequality and ecological collapse. These include stories of perpetual growth as the goal of society; profit as the goal of corporations; material accumulation as the goal of individuals; humans as fundamentally selfish; nature as a resource existing only to be exploited; migration as an invasion; environmental regulations as an attack on freedom; and climate change as a hoax. While some of these stories were paused, the great danger is that we return to them even stronger than before in the wake of the pandemic, abandoning environmental concern in order to grow the economy as quickly as possible. Instead of this, we need to find new stories to live by, which were emerging before the pandemic but have been brought into sharp perspective now: stories of communities coming together to meet their own needs, of humans as fundamentally altruistic, of equality and social justice, of gratitude to key workers, and of the value of other species and the ecosystems that life depends on.

The focus of the book is on the forms of language behind the stories that industrial civilisation is based on, and the search for new forms of inspirational language that can help rebuild a more ecological civilisation. What has changed from the first edition is that we are now in a situation where the old stories are crumbling, new stories are already coming to the surface, and we have an incredible once-in-a-lifetime chance to contribute to the fundamental social and political change that is necessary if we and countless other species are to have a future.

On a practical level, the book has been updated to include some of the recent emerging research in ecolinguistics, including insights from the *Routledge Handbook of Ecolinguistics*. The definition of ecolinguistics has been made clearer, with a shift to seeing language as part of ecosystems rather than just influencing how humans treat ecosystems. This move helps unite different approaches to ecolinguistics, while still keeping the focus firmly on the literal ecosystems which life depends on. As Tove Skutnabb-Kangas and David Harmon (2018, p. 11) state in the first chapter of the *Routledge Handbook of Ecolinguistics:*

> We use ecology in its literal sense (i.e., not merely as a metaphor) to refer to the biological relationships of organisms (including human beings) to one another and to their physical surroundings. There has been a tendency of many sociolinguists to pay only lip service to this literal sense of 'ecology' and to focus only on social concerns.

The second edition makes it clear that ecolinguistics, like all ecological humanities disciplines, focuses on the literal ecosystems which life depends on, and examines the role of language within these ecosystems. Any area of linguistics, from language diversity to rhetorical analysis, can be part of ecolinguistics so long as it considers not only human society but also the ecosystems that all species depend on for their continued survival. This is a departure from how ecolinguistics has sometimes been described in the past, but a necessary one.

The second edition also includes analyses of some new example texts, including the influential Sustainable Development Goals, newspaper and political coverage of refugees, the writings of Luther Standing Bear, coronavirus denial, creation stories and fiction. The representation of refugees is a standard topic in Critical Discourse Analysis (CDA) but has been included to stress that, like CDA, ecolinguistics places importance on social justice and the lives and wellbeing of humans. The difference is that ecolinguistics highlights the ecological context of social justice issues (e.g., the role of climate change in migration) as well as extending consideration to animals, plants, future generations and life-sustaining ecosystems.

Most importantly, there is a new chapter, Chapter 10, which explores narratives. Narratives are without doubt the most complex, important and powerful of all the types of story in this book. The book ends with an exploration of creation narratives and science-based narratives about the origins of the universe. These foundational narratives play an important role in how people see the place of humanity within ecosystems, within the planet, and within the universe.

Finally, it is useful to mention the impact of the first edition and the *Stories We Live By* free online course which accompanied it. More than 200,000 visitors accessed the materials and more than 2000 people registered to take the full course. To discover what impact ecolinguistics has on people's work and lives, Mariana Roccia (2019) carried out a detailed research project involving questionnaires and interviews with 272 people who took the course. Her research revealed significant impact in the five areas described in

Table P.1.

TABLE P.1	Summary of the findings of Roccia (2019)
Skills	Improved ability to analyse texts critically and use language effectively to address ecological issues.
	Example comments: 'It has allowed me to develop a more critical point of view of how things are phrased and framed in subtle ways, not just the obvious message that they are giving', 'I'm more selective of the language that I use'.
Knowledge	Greater awareness of how texts shape self and society; greater understanding of the root causes of ecological issues.
	Example comment: 'It has had a significant effect on my view of the natural world and how language shapes our understanding of the world in general, and of environmental and ecological issues in particular'.
Attitude	Greater appreciation of local nature; increased concern for the environment.
	Example comments: 'I am more aware of my surrounding environment, and more conscious in my interaction with nature', 'After taking the course, I am much more concerned about the ecosystem and my environment'.
Behaviour	Practical changes to live more sustainable lives.
	Example comments: 'I changed my lifestyle and am living a happier, more natural and positive life than before. These changes were purely due to the outlet that ecolinguistics gave me', 'It's positively life-changing'.
Work	Transformation of curricula to include sustainability issues in education; improved environmental communication practice in corporations and NGOs; inclusion of ecological factors in therapy.
	Example comments: 'In a nutshell, ecolinguistics makes me and my students more aware of how communication represents our world and the way we live', 'I have worked with the NOAA and helped to change their message', 'It feeds into my therapeutic work where I facilitate dialogue between different environmental groups', 'I have changed the editorial direction of the small press I run'.

These comments, and many more that appear in the report, demonstrate how ecolinguistics is not just an area of academic enquiry but a way of life. Those who are exposed to ecolinguistics question the texts which surround them, asking how they shape them as people and the society they live in. They reveal the underlying stories and consider their impact on people, animals, plants, forests, rivers and the ecosystems that life depends on. And they begin a search for new stories to live by to bring into being the kind of ecological society that they want to see.

ACKNOWLEDGMENTS

I would like to express my gratitude to the convenors of the International Ecolinguistics Association (IEA) — Charlotte Dover, Amy Free, Jessica Iubini-Hampton, Amir Ghorbanpour, Mira Lieberman-Boyd, Maddie Mancey and Mariana Roccia — who have helped me and the discipline of ecolinguistics in many ways over the years. Thanks also to the steering group members, volunteer tutors and all members of the IEA for creating a wonderful academic community. I am very grateful to Amir Ghorbanpour and Nina Venkataraman for proofreading the first draft and to Elena Valvason for providing her insightful analyses of the 2030 Agenda for Sustainable Development. I would also like to thank Huang Guowen for introducing my work to Chinese scholars, organizing the translation of the first edition into Chinese, and for facilitating the founding of the hugely successful China Association of Ecolinguistics. And many thanks to Kyoohoon Kim for translating the first edition into Korean, and to Amir Ghorbanpour for translating my work into Persian and contributing to ecolinguistics in many ways. Thanks too to Anthony Nanson and others for offering advice on the first draft.

I would like to express my appreciation to Hidenobu Suzuki, a superb photographer who gave permission to use his photo *The Quiet Blue Pond* as the cover. I would also like to express my appreciation to INBAR for permission to include Image 2.1, to Trengayor Wood Works for Image 3.3, Berrett-Koehler publishers for Image 4.1, Mark Achbar for Image 4.2, to the University of Nebraska Press for Image 6.1, to Compassion in World Farming for Images 9.1 to 9.5, to the Compassionate Farming Education Initiative for Images 9.6 and 9.7, to Sort of Books for Image 9.8 and to Robert Woodford from the Deep Time Walk for Image 10.2.

Some sections of this book have drawn from, updated, and adapted extracts from previously published work. I would like to express gratitude to the publishers of this material for granting permission to use it. Chapters 1 and 2 have drawn from Stibbe, A., 2014. An ecolinguistic approach to critical discourse studies. *Critical Discourse*

Studies, 11(1), 117–128. Chapter 4 has made use of extracts from Stibbe, A., 2014. The corporation as person and psychopath: multimodal metaphor, rhetoric and resistance. *Critical Approaches to Discourse Analysis Across Disciplines*, 6(2), 114–136. Chapter 6 has used examples and brief extracts from Stibbe, A., 2020. Towards a grammar of ecocultural identity. In: T. Milstein and J. Castro-Sotomayor, eds. *Routledge Handbook of Ecocultural Identity*. London: Routledge. Chapter 8 has drawn from Stibbe, A., 2014. Ecolinguistics and erasure. In: C. Hart and P. Cap, eds. *Contemporary Critical Discourse Studies*. London: Bloomsbury.

I am grateful to North Atlantic Books for permission to reproduce the epigraphs in Chapters 1 and 6, which are from *Sacred Economics: Money, Gift, and Society in the Age of Transition* by Charles Eisenstein, copyright ©2011 by Charles Eisenstein. Also to Bloomsbury for the epigraph in Chapter 7, which is copyright ©Martin and Rose (2007), *Working with discourse*, Continuum, an imprint of Bloomsbury Publishing Plc. Other epigraphs have been reproduced with the kind permission of Taylor & Francis, Chelsea Green and Sage.

Finally, I'd like to express appreciation for the support of my family and dedicate this book to Shirleen Stibbe, Philip Stibbe and a snow goose cherry tree.

CONTENTS

1

INTRODUCTION

章节导读

作者在第 1 章主要交代了书中的生态语言学研究涉及的一些基本概念和内涵，包括以下五个方面的界定：（1）我们信奉和践行的故事；（2）生态语言学中的"生态"；（3）生态语言学中的"语言学"；（4）生态哲学观和本书的生态哲学观；（5）本书的写作结构、语料和术语的说明。

（1）我们信奉和践行的故事。首先，作者在本章的引言中，通过广告语和自然文学的例子将"语言"和"生态"联系起来，让读者意识到二者并不是完全无交集的，它们是可以联系在一起进行研究的。随后，以 Berry（1988）的话语引出"故事"一词，并指出当今社会人们对于新故事的需求更为迫切。那么，本书讲到的故事究竟是什么意思呢？它与我们熟知的传统意义上的故事是不同的，作者在此将其定义为：故事是个体（人）头脑中的认知结构，会影响他们的所思所想、言语和行为（*Stories are cognitive structures in the minds of individuals which influence how they think, talk and act.*）。这里的认知结构指的是个体（人）头脑中的思维模式（mental models）。

这样来看，"我们信奉和践行的故事"是一个专业的表述方式，用来指某种文化环境中多个个体头脑中的故事（*Stories we live by* are stories in the minds of multiple individuals across a culture.）。故事会影响我们的行为，比如：我们如果把自然当作资源，就会对它开发利用；如果把首要的政治目的确定为经济增长，就会在一定程度上忽视人类的福祉和环境问题的解决。所以从这个角度来说，本书的作者就是要通过话语分析的方式了解话语背后的故事。对有益于生态环境的故事要广泛地推广，而对于破坏生态环境的故事要揭露和抵制，并从其他文化中发现有益于生态环境的新故事予以践行。

（2）生态语言学中的"生态"。过去几十年来，人们意识到生态与人类和人类社会是和谐共生的关系，在人文社会科学领域出现了"生态转向"（the ecological turn）。这使得人们不再将思想、人类、社会、文化和宗教等研究对象与自然世界割裂开，而是把它们看作是自然世界中必不可少的一部分。由此，在语言学领域，生态语言学应运而生。这门学科已经越来越与更广泛的生态人文学科融为一体。本书中的"生态"，作者将其用来指有机体之间、有机体与自然环境之间的相互作用（the interaction of organisms with each other and their physical environment）。这里的有机体是包含人类在内的，且人类的生态是该研究的一个重点。所以，作者在这一部分将生态语言学中的"生态"定义为：人与人、人与其他有机体、人与整个物理环境之间的生命可持续关系，并通过某种规范来保护生命的繁荣发展。

（3）生态语言学中的"语言学"。本书中涉及的语言学方面，主要是用语言学的分析方法说明我们信奉和践行的故事；具体的做法是，作者通过应用多种语言学理论建构了一个简化的语言学框架，用于故事的分析中。所以说，故事在本书中至关重要，它处于最基本的层次。由于故事是思维层面的内容，我们无法对故事直接分析，需要从人类的语言使用方式中获得分析的线索，这说明语言学的作用在分析中不可或缺。总的来说，生态语言学中的"语言学"范围较为广泛，可以指代语言在人与人、人与其他物种、人与整个物理环境之间的生命可持续互动中的作用。而本书作者特别强调将语言学的理论应用在揭示工业文明中不可持续的故事分析，并探索新的我们信奉和践行的故事，以实现可持续发展。

（4）生态哲学观和本书的生态哲学观。Naess 使用"生态哲学观"（ecosophy，ecological philosophy）这一术语来描述包括生态因素在内的哲学准则（Naess，1995）。每位生态语言学研究者的头脑中都有着自己的哲学准则（philosophical principles），并应用这些准则来评判特定的故事是否与他们自身的价值观相符。虽然不存在所谓唯一正确的生态哲学观，且对于同一个分析者来说，其生态哲学观也是会不断变化的。但是，作为生态语言学研究者，他们普遍会将人类与其他有机体、人类与整个生态环境之间的相互关系和相互作用考虑进来。同时，生态哲学观的确定还要遵循三个必备的标准，即：必须符合科学发展规律，必须是可行的，必须要有理有据。

根据上述标准，本书作者采用 Naess（1995）的做法提出了自己的生态哲学观，应用于后面章节案例的语言学分析。这个生态哲学观可以用一个英文单词"Living!"（生活！）来概括，具体包括七个要素：重视生活（valuing living）、福祉（wellbeing）、现在和未来（now and the future）、关怀（care）、环境极限（environmental limits）、社会公正（social justice）、深度适应（deep adaptation）。

（5）本书的写作结构、语料和术语的说明。在写作结构上，本书从第 2 章开始重点讨论了九种类型的故事，依次是：意识形态（ideologies）、构架（framing）、隐喻（metaphors）、评估（evaluations）、身份（identities）、信念（convictions）、删略

（erasure）、凸显（salience）和叙事（narratives）。每个章节的结构大体分为三个部分：第一部分，描述故事背后的概念和理论，并提出一些可操作性的定义或分析方法；第二部分，将理论应用在实际的文本分析中；第三部分，在每章的最后一个小节，对该章所探讨的故事展开更加详细的案例分析，其目的是通过语篇或话语中的语言和语言结构分析，揭示出我们信奉和践行的故事，并根据作者的生态哲学观对故事进行评价。

本书案例的语料多种多样，包括来自于新古典经济学教程、农业综合企业手册、生态学报告、报纸、环境运动、自然文学、日本诗歌、纪录片、政治文件、广告以及生活杂志中的内容。最后，作者也在这一部分说明了本书的语料和术语在书中的标记方式，既符合学术的规范，又方便读者的阅读。

> Stories bear tremendous creative power. Through them we coordinate human activity, focus attention and intention, define roles, identify what is important and even what is real.
>
> (Charles Eisenstein 2011, p. 2)

When first encountered, ecolinguistics is sometimes met with bafflement. It is about ecology, and it is about language, but these two initially appear to be entirely separate areas of life. A cursory explanation is that language influences how we think about the world. The language of advertising can encourage us to desire unnecessary and environmentally damaging products, while nature writing can inspire respect for the natural world. How we think has an influence on how we act, so language can inspire us to destroy or protect the ecosystems that life depends on. Ecolinguistics, then, is about critiquing forms of language that contribute to ecological destruction, and aiding in the search for new forms of language that inspire people to protect the natural world. This is a superficial explanation but at least starts to create connections in people's minds between two areas of life — language and ecology — that are not so separate after all.

Ecolinguistics is more than this, though. The analysis goes deeper than commenting on individual texts such as advertisements or nature books. Ecolinguistics can explore the more general patterns of language that influence how people both think about, and treat, the world. It can investigate the *stories we live by* — mental models which influence behaviour and lie at the heart of the ecological challenges we are facing. There are certain key stories about economic growth, about technological progress, about nature as an object to be used or conquered, about profit and success, that have profound implications for how we treat the systems that life depends on. As Thomas Berry (1988, p. 123) puts it:

> We are in trouble just now because we don't have a good story. We are between stories. The old story, the account of how the world came to be and how we fit into it, is no longer effective. Yet we have not learned the new story.

We are now in a position where the old stories are crumbling due to coronavirus and the increasingly harmful impacts of climate change and biodiversity loss. There has never been a more urgent time or greater opportunity to find new stories.

The link between *ecology* and *language* is that how humans treat each other and the natural world is influenced by our thoughts, concepts, ideas, ideologies and worldviews, and these in turn are shaped through language. It is through language that economic systems are built, and when those systems are seen to lead to immense suffering and ecological destruction, it is through language that they are resisted and new forms of economy brought into being. It is through language that consumerist identities are built and lives orientated towards accumulation, and it is through language that consumerism is resisted and people are inspired to *be more* rather than *have more*. It is through language that the natural world is mentally reduced to objects or resources to be exploited, and it is through language that people can be encouraged to respect and care for the systems that support life. In critiquing the damaging social and ecological effects of financial structures, Berardi (2012, p. 157) states that:

> Only an act of language can give us the ability to see and to create a new human condition, where we now only see barbarianism and violence. Only an act of language escaping the technical automatisms of financial capitalism will make possible the emergence of a new life form.

Linguistics provides tools for analysing the texts that surround us in everyday life and revealing the hidden stories that exist between the lines. Once revealed, the stories can be questioned from an ecological perspective: do they encourage people to destroy or protect the ecosystems that life depends on? If they are destructive then they need to be resisted, and if they are beneficial then they need to be promoted. This book aims to bring together theories from linguistics and cognitive science into a framework which can be used for revealing the stories we live by, judging them from an ecological perspective, and contributing to the search for new stories to live by.

The stories we live by

As evidence of the scale of the ecological issues we are facing emerges, and the scale of the response required becomes clearer, there are increasing calls to go beyond attempts to address isolated symptoms with technical solutions and instead consider the deeper social and cultural causes of the problems we face. Growing inequality, climate change, biodiversity loss, the pandemic, alienation from nature and loss of community are bringing into question the fundamental stories that industrial societies are based on. As Ben Okri (1996, p. 21) points out: 'Stories are the secret reservoir of values: change the stories that individuals or nations live by and you change the individuals and nations themselves'.

David Korten (2006, p. 248) describes four stories at the heart of western imperial civilisation which, he claims, have profound ecological implications. There is the 'prosperity story,' which promotes worship of material acquisition and money; the 'biblical story,' which focuses on the afterlife rather than the world around us; the 'security story,' which builds up the military and police to protect relationships of domination; and the 'secular meaning story,' which reduces life to matter and mechanism. These stories, he maintains, perpetuate injustice and lead to both alienation from life and environmental destruction. For Paul Kingsnorth and Dougald Hine (2009), the most dangerous story of all is 'the story of human centrality, of a species destined to be lord of all it surveys, unconfined by the limits that apply to other, lesser creatures'. Martin Lee Mueller (2017, p. xiii), in his thought-provoking book *Being Salmon, Being Human,* expresses the damaging consequences of current stories:

> We inhabitants of industrial civilisation still live inside a human-centred story ... it shapes our encounters with other-than-human living creatures, as well as with the larger planetary presence. This is the story of the human as a separate self. The human-centred story is causing the ecological web to come undone ... We are in the midst of a systemic ecocide ... This is the time to abandon humanity-as-separation, and to aid forth the emergence of entirely different stories to live by.

These are not, however, stories in the usual sense of narratives. They are not told in novels, read to children at bedtime, shared around a fire, or conveyed through anecdotes in formal speeches. Instead, they exist behind and between the lines of the texts that surround us — the news reports that describe the 'bad news' about a drop in Christmas sales, or the 'good news' that airline profits are up, or the advertisements promising us that we will be better people if we purchase the unnecessary goods they are promoting. Underneath common ways of writing and speaking in industrial societies are stories of unlimited economic growth as the main goal of society; of the accumulation of unnecessary goods as a path towards self-improvement; of progress and success defined narrowly in terms of technological innovation and profit; and of nature as something separate from humans, a mere stock of resources to be exploited.

To give an example of how a story can be told 'between the lines,' consider the BBC *Horizon* documentary 'What makes us human?,' summarised on the BBC website as:

- Professor Alice Roberts investigates exactly what makes us different from the animal kingdom. What is it that truly makes us human? (ML12 — see Appendix for reference)

Behind this phrasing are two stories. The first is that humans live outside the animal kingdom, i.e., that humans are not animals. The second is that what makes us human is to be discovered in our differences from other animals rather than our commonalities. In the documentary, Professor Roberts herself does not use the first story, but she does use the second:

- What is it about our bodies, our genes and our brains that sets us apart? What is it that truly makes us human?
- Michael has devised an experiment that he believes reveals a specific piece of behaviour that separates us from chimps, that defines us as a species, and truly makes us human. (ML12 — transcribed extracts from 'What makes us human?')

Neither of these extracts directly states that 'it is in our differences from other animals that we can discover what makes us human'; instead, it is just assumed as the background story necessary to semantically link the two questions in the first extract, and to link the three coordinated statements in the second. The story is a pervasive one, told between the lines by many people, in many contexts. Noam Chomsky (2006, p. 88), for instance, wrote:

When we study human language, we are approaching what some might call the 'human essence,' the distinctive qualities of mind that are, so far as we know, unique to man.

The idea that our humanity lies in our uniqueness from other animals is just a story, however, and there are other possible stories. The danger in focusing on difference is that it can obscure some of the important things that humans and other animals have in common: having emotions, being embodied, bonding socially with others, and, most importantly, being dependent on other species and the environment for our continued survival. Plumwood (2007) strongly criticises this story:

Arguably, the distinguishing feature of western culture, and perhaps also the chief mark of its ecological failure, is the idea that humankind is radically different and apart from the rest of nature and from other animals. This idea, sometimes called Human Exceptionalism, has allowed us to exploit nature and people more ruthlessly (some would say more efficiently) than other cultures, and our high-powered, destructive forms of life dominate the planet.

In seeking responses to the ecological challenges we face, we may have to explore and reconsider some of the fundamental stories that underlie our culture, including stories about who we are as humans.

The focus on stories we live by in this book is a way of bringing together a diversity of approaches to ecolinguistic analysis into a single framework. When ecolinguists examine ideologies, metaphors, frames and a variety of other cognitive and linguistic phenomena, what they are doing is revealing and uncovering the stories which shape people's lives and shape the society we live in.

In its traditional sense, the word 'story' refers to a recounting of linked events from the perspective of characters involved in the events. When engaging with a story in this traditional sense, readers can recognise it as a story by its structure and context, and hence treat it as just one possible perspective or interpretation of the world around us. The stories we live by are different, however. We are exposed to them without consciously selecting them or necessarily being aware that they are just stories. They appear between the lines of the texts which surround us in everyday life: in news reports, advertisements, conversations with friends, the weather forecast, instruction manuals or textbooks. They appear in educational, political, professional, medical, legal and other institutional contexts without announcing themselves as stories.

In commenting on the 'story of human centrality', Kingsnorth and Hine (2009) state that 'what makes this story so dangerous is that, for the most part, we have forgotten that it is a story'. Similarly, David Loy (2010, p. 5) describes how 'unaware that our stories are stories, we experience them as the world'. Macy and Johnstone (2012, p. 15) describe the 'business-as-usual' story that sees economic growth and technological development as the way forward for society, and comment that 'when you're living in the middle of this story, it's easy to think of it as just the way things are'. The stories we live by are embedded deeply in the minds of individuals across a society and appear only indirectly between the lines of the texts that circulate in that society. They are therefore not immediately recognisable as stories, and need to be exposed, subjected to critical analysis, and resisted if they are implicated in injustice and environmental destruction.

Midgley (2011, p. 1) calls stories in this sense the 'myths we live by'. By *myths* she means 'imaginative patterns, networks of powerful symbols that suggest particular ways of interpreting the world'. Indeed, Kingsnorth and Hine (2009) use the terms *myth* and *story* interchangeably: 'We intend to challenge the stories which underpin our civilisation: the myth of progress, the myth of human centrality, and the myth of our separation from "nature"'. Robertson (2014, p. 54) uses the term 'paradigm' in a similar sense to refer to 'a fundamental framework for understanding the world, a coherent set of assumptions and concepts that defines a way of viewing reality'. Of particular concern for Robertson is the paradigm of 'economic growth'. She describes how 'growth as the core economic paradigm has been developing for several hundred years and has become solidly entrenched since the last century'. Berardi (2012, p. 131) emphasises the rhythmic nature of patterns using the term *refrain*, to mean the repetitions of gestures and signs that pervade and discipline society such as 'the refrain of factory work, the refrain of salary, the refrain of the assembly line'. He states that 'now we need refrains that disentangle singular existence from the social game of competition and productivity' (p. 146), and turns towards poetry to discover such refrains (p. 151). Martusewicz *et al.* (2011, p. 66) write of *root metaphors*, which 'structure and maintain a "that's just the way it is" perception of the world ... a deeply ingrained set of ideas that structures how one sees, relates to and behaves in the world'.

This book uses the term *stories we live by* to convey a similar concept to what these authors refer to as myths, paradigms, refrains and root metaphors. Specifically, the terms *story* and *stories we live by* are defined as follows for the purposes of this book:

> *Stories* are cognitive structures in the minds of individuals which influence how they think, talk and act.
> *Stories we live by* are stories in the minds of multiple individuals across a culture.

Stories exist as mental models, i.e., simplified structures in the minds of individuals. For example, an individual might have a mental model of the world where humans are exceptional animals who are unique, separate from, and superior to other animals. Of key interest are mental models that are shared widely within a culture because these models are likely to have a strong influence on how the culture treats the ecosystems that support life. These are the stories 'we' live by, where 'we' refers to members of an interacting community who share ideas and information with each other. These communities could be small (a community centred around a particular village, for example), or they could be vast (the community of people who are exposed to the consumerist discourses of trans-national capitalism). Importantly, the stories we live by influence how we act in the world — if nature is seen as a resource then we may be more likely to exploit it, or if economic growth is seen as the primary goal of politics then people's wellbeing and environmental concerns may be overlooked. This book encourages analysts to be aware of the stories that exist in the communities they are part of, promote the beneficial ones far and wide, resist the destructive ones, and search for beneficial new stories to live by from other cultures around the world.

The 'eco' of ecolinguistics

The story of human distinctiveness has been central to humanities subjects since their inception. These areas of scholarly enquiry have traditionally studied and celebrated rationality, language, a sense of history, religion, culture and literature as aspects which distinguish us from, and, implicitly, make us better than, animals. Orr (1992, p. 145) goes so far as to claim that 'for the past five hundred years, our sciences, social sciences and humanities alike have been committed to extending and celebrating the human domination of nature'. However, as awareness of the ecological embedding of humans and human societies has risen to the level of urgent and immediate concern there has been an 'ecological turn' in humanities and social science subjects. No longer is the object of study — whether the mind, the human, society, culture or religion — seen in isolation, but as an inextricable and integral part of a larger physical and living world. This has helped these subjects become more accurate in their enquiry, since undoubtedly human minds, cultures and society are shaped by the natural world they arose from and are part of.

More practically, the ecological turn has helped give a role to humanities subjects in addressing some of the overarching ecological challenges that humanity is facing in the twenty-first century: biodiversity loss, food security, climate change, water depletion, energy security, chemical contamination and the social injustice which both causes and arises from all these issues. Or, put more positively, it enables humanities to contribute to building a more ecological civilisation where people meet their physical needs, their needs for wellbeing, and their need to find meaning, in ways which protect and enhance the ecosystems that life depends on. If that is too ambitious an aspiration given the current trajectory of society, then humanities subjects could at least help in the deep adaptation necessary to come to terms with and respond to the inevitable collapse of our current civilisation (Bendell 2018).

The ecological turn has seen the rise of ecocriticism (Garrard 2014), ecopoetics (Knickerbocker 2012), ecofeminism (Adams and Gruen 2014), ecopsychology (Fisher 2013), ecosociology (Stevens 2012), political ecology (Robbins 2012), ecocomposition (Killingsworth 2005), ecotheology (Deane-Drummond 2008) and environmental communication (Cox 2012). Environmental communication has a particular focus which unites researchers, which Milstein *et al.* (2009, p. 344) summarise as:

Research and theory within the field are united by the topical focus on communication and human relations with the environment. Scholars who study environmental communication are particularly concerned with the ways people communicate about the natural world because they believe such communication has far-reaching effects at a time of largely human-caused crises.

For ecocriticism, Glotfelty (2014) describes how, despite a broad scope of enquiry:

> Ecocriticism takes as its subject the interconnections between nature and culture ... Most ecocritical work shares a common motivation: the troubling awareness that we have reached the age of environmental limits, a time when the consequences of human actions are damaging the planet's basic life support systems.

Marine humanities is a more recently emerging ecological humanities subject, which Ooi (2017, p. 83) describes simply as:

> Marine humanities is a very recent term to characterise an interdisciplinary field that examines the continuing narrative and construal of underwater and ocean environments, with the ultimate goal of understanding and preserving these environments.

Broadly speaking, ecological humanities subjects have two things in common. The first is that the object of study, whether literature, communication, the human mind or religion, is viewed in the context of ecosystems and the physical environment. The second is a practical orientation towards using the study to help protect or restore those ecosystems and promote the flourishing of life.

But what of 'ecolinguistics'? Certainly, the term 'ecolinguistics' has been used since at least the 1990s (Fill and Mühlhäsler 2001, p. 1), and the word 'ecology' has been incorporated in linguistic accounts since (at least) Einar Haugen's work in the 1970s (e.g. Haugen 1972). The term 'ecolinguistics' has been applied to a wide range of approaches and interests, some more relevant than others to the 'ecological turn'.

The term 'ecolinguistics' has been used to describe studies of language interaction and diversity; studies of texts such as signposts which are outdoors; analysis of texts which happen to be about the environment; studies of how words in a language relate to objects in the local environment; studies of the mix of languages surrounding pupils in multicultural schools; studies of dialects in particular geographical locations; and many other diverse areas. The multiplicity of approaches arises from different understandings of the concept of 'ecology,' from a very broad concept of 'the interaction of some things with other things' to narrow concepts such as 'related to environmentalism'.

However, ecolinguistics has increasingly converged with the broader ecological humanities, and primarily uses the term 'ecology' in its biological sense, i.e., *the interaction of organisms with each other and their physical environment*. The focus on 'organisms' does not mean that the human is forgotten, as is sometimes the case in ecological science where the focus is on animals and plants in pristine environments remote from the influence of humans. Humans are, after all, the object of study for humanities and are organisms too. Another way of describing ecology, then, is *interaction among humans, other organisms and the physical environment*. Since language usage is one of the primary ways that humans interact with each other it can be considered part of ecology too, along with the calls and gestures that other animals use to interact, and the messages that trees send to each other along mycorrhizal networks.

There are many forms of interaction between organisms that could be studied, but ecology is concerned specifically with the literally *vital* ones, i.e., ones which are necessary for the continuation of life. It is because of the connection between ecology and the continuing survival of life that the term is often used with a normative (moral) orientation towards protection of the ecological systems that life depends on. Although some forms of ecology disguise their normative dimension, Robbins (2012, p. 19) argues that 'apolitical ecologies, regardless of claims to even-handed objectivity, are implicitly political'. Robbins' own form of ecology 'is simply more *explicit* in its normative goals and more outspoken about the assumptions from which its research is conducted'.

Ecolinguistic studies also have normative goals, whether or not they are expressed explicitly, in the same way that medical science has an orientation towards the goal of health, or conservation biology has a goal of saving species from extinction. The normative goals that this book are based on will be discussed later in this chapter, but for now we can say that the 'eco' of ecolinguistics refers to *the life-sustaining interactions of humans with other humans, other organisms and the physical environment,* with some kind of normative orientation to protecting the flourishing of life.

The 'linguistics' of ecolinguistics

The discipline of linguistics has branched out in a great number of directions, from psycholinguistics, sociolinguistics and anthropological linguistics, to cognitive linguistics, corpus linguistics, forensic linguistics and much more. Linguistic enquiry in any of these branches is ecolinguistic if it considers the role of language in the life-sustaining interactions of humans with other humans, other organisms and the physical environment. Language contact studies, for example, have revealed how knowledge of living sustainably in the local environment is embedded in endangered languages and threatened by the global spread of dominant languages. Because of the embedding of environmental knowledge in local languages there is a strong correlation between high levels of linguistic diversity and high biodiversity.

In this book, the focus is on those branches of linguistics which are most useful in revealing the stories we live by. The relationship between language and the underlying stories that societies and cultures are built on is a highly complex one, and subject to a great deal of debate within the literature on linguistics and philosophy. The approach of this book is to build a simplified framework for analysing the stories we live by through drawing together a number of linguistic theories. These include Critical Discourse Analysis (Fairclough 2014), frame theory (Lakoff and Wehling 2012a), metaphor theory (Müller 2008), appraisal theory (Martin and White 2005), identity theory (Benwell and Stokoe 2006), fact construction (Potter 1996), theories of erasure and salience (drawing on van Leeuwen 2008) and linguistic narratology (Toolan 2018). All of these theories can be seen as analysing language to reveal underlying stories, although they use a range of different terms to describe what they do. While these frameworks tended in the past to focus exclusively on human relations with other humans, they have been adapted and are increasingly applied to wider ecological issues (e.g. Larson 2011; Milstein and Dickinson 2012; Alexander 2018; Mey 2018; Cook and Sealey 2018).

In the linguistic framework of this book, the most basic level is the 'story' — a mental model within the mind of an individual person which influences how they think, talk and act. A story of 'progress,' for example, may consider the past negatively as a brute struggle for survival, the present as a great improvement due to technological innovation, the future as even more promising, and further industrialisation and technological innovation as the path toward building a better society. Each person will have their own collection of stories in their minds, but some stories, like that of progress, are shared by large numbers of people. They do not just exist in individual people's minds, but across the larger culture in what van Dijk (2009, p. 19) refers to as *social cognition*.

The stories we live by are, therefore, cognitive structures which influence how multiple people think, talk and act. The story of progress has a fairly simple structure — a direction (forwards or backwards), an evaluative orientation (forwards is good and backwards is bad), certain elements which are mapped onto 'forwards' (e.g. technological innovation or industrialisation), certain elements which are mapped onto 'backwards' (e.g. living closer to nature), and a sense that progress is inevitable and unstoppable. This structure could influence people's thinking, for example their reasoning when deciding whether or not to support industrialisation of a green area. It could influence how they talk, for example in using expressions like 'you can't stop progress'. And, most importantly, it could influence how they act, for example in purchasing the latest technology or agreeing to development of a green area. In this way, the story has an impact on people's lives and how they treat the ecosystems that support life.

Since the stories are mental models they cannot be analysed directly, but we can get clues to them through analysing common ways that people use language. For example, by examining what people represent as 'moving forwards' and what they represent as 'going backwards' it is possible to get clues to the underlying story of progress that exists in people's minds, and then question whether or not 'progress' is a beneficial story in terms of the actions it encourages.

Although this section has so far discussed language, there are also other semiotic modes such as visual images, gestures, clothing, music and video (Kress 2010). Stories are cognitive structures and so can manifest themselves just as easily in words, pictures, songs or choice of clothing. Furthermore, language often appears intertwined with images and other modes in ways where the meaning of the words depends on the images which accompany them. While the central focus is on language, ecolinguistics inevitably needs to consider other modes that stories manifest themselves in. In this sense, ecolinguistics is *transdisciplinary* (Finke 2018) — while it starts with language, its goals lie in the complexity of the real world and it goes where it needs to go to achieve those goals.

This book, then, uses a range of linguistic theories and applies them to the task of revealing the stories that our unsustainable industrial civilisation is based on and searching for new stories to live by. In general, however, the 'linguistics' of ecolinguistics can be much wider than this, and can refer to any area of linguistic enquiry that is being used to explore the role of language in the life-sustaining interactions among humans, other species and the physical environment.

Ecosophy

The reason for revealing, exposing or shedding light on the stories we live by is to open them up to question and challenge — are these stories working in the current conditions of the world or do we need to search for new stories? Whether or not the stories are considered to be 'working' depends on the ethical vision of the analyst, i.e., on whether the stories are building the kind of world that the analyst wants to see.

Clearly, all critical language analysts have an ethical framework that they use for evaluating the language they are analysing, whether or not it is made explicit. An analysis of racist language, for instance, is likely to be conducted within a framework which sees racism as something negative that needs to be worked against rather than just an object for disinterested analysis of the technicalities of language. Only sometimes is the ethical framework made explicit, however.

Gavriely-Nuri (2012, p. 83) makes her framework explicit when she calls for a Cultural

Critical Discourse Analysis that promotes *'values, attitudes and behaviours based on the principles of freedom, justice and democracy, all human rights, tolerance and solidarity'*. This form of analysis is explicitly directed at exposing mainstream discourses which work against these values, and searching for 'discursive tools that practically promote the "culture of peace"'. Like many philosophical frameworks used in linguistics, however, the framework does not specifically mention ecological issues. Democracy, justice and solidarity do not automatically lead to sustainable levels of consumption, and peace in a society that exceeds environmental limits will be short-lived. Indeed, contamination and the over-exploitation of natural resources is one of the key drivers behind war, as Hiscock (2012) shows.

The ecolinguist Jøgen Bang uses a similar philosophical framework to Gavriely-Nuri, but does include ecological consideration. For Bang (personal communication), ecolinguistics is based on:

> contributing to a local and global culture in which (i) co-operation, (ii) sharing (iii) democratic dialogue, (iv) peace and non-violence, (v) equality in every sphere of daily life, and (vi) ecological sustainability are the fundamental features and primary values.

If this framework were employed, then stories would be judged on the degree to which they encourage co-operation or competition, sharing or greed, peace or violence, and ecological sustainability or destruction. Each ecolinguist will have their own set of philosophical principles they use to judge stories against, reflecting their own values and priorities, but all will have in common a consideration of the interactions of humans with other organisms and the physical environment.

Naess (1995) uses the term *ecosophy* (a shortening of 'ecological philosophy') to describe a set of philosophical principles which include ecological consideration. He expresses it as follows:

> By an ecosophy I mean a philosophy of ecological harmony ... openly normative, it contains both norms, rules, postulates, value priority announcements *and* hypotheses concerning the state of affairs ... The details of an ecosophy will show many variations due to significant differences concerning not only 'facts' of pollution, resources, population, etc., but also value priorities.
>
> (Naess 1995, p. 8)

Ecosophies are not just statements of philosophical positions but can also include a vision of a better society and the concrete steps necessary to achieve that vision. Sedlaczek

(2016) suggests an approach based on '(1) a representational model of the (problematic) status quo of society; (2) a visionary model of the desired state of society; and (3) a programmatic model of the necessary measures which need to be taken in order to reach this envisioned society'.

Since the ecosophy includes 'norms', 'value priority announcements' and 'visions', there is no single 'correct' ecosophy that ecolinguistics *should* be based on. Ecosophies can, however, be judged by whether evidence confirms or contradicts the assumptions about the state of the world that they are based on, or whether there are any internal inconsistencies.

There are many possible schools of thought that can be drawn on in forming an ecosophy, and they tend to run along three spectra. The first spectrum is from anthropocentric (human-centred) to ecocentric (centred on all life, including humans). The second spectrum is from neoliberal at one end to either socialist, localist or anarchist at the other. The third spectrum is from optimistic to pessimistic. Interestingly, the three spectra broadly align with each other, so conservative neoliberal frameworks tend to be optimistic and anthropocentric, while politically radical approaches tend towards pessimism and ecocentrism.

It is useful to give a brief outline of some philosophical perspectives, to illustrate how the frameworks align along the spectra. At the most politically conservative end is 'cornucopianism'. This philosophy considers that human ingenuity and ever-advancing technology will overcome environmental and resource issues. Humans should therefore continue with and accelerate industrial progress for the sake of human (and only human) benefit (e.g. Lomborg 2001; Ridley 2010). Then there is a cluster of perspectives under the umbrella of 'sustainable development,' which attempt to combine economic growth with environmental protection and social equity (e.g. Baker 2006). Social Ecology (e.g. Bookchin 2005) is a more politically radical perspective which sees the roots of ecological destruction as existing in oppressive social hierarchies. According to this perspective, humans will continue dominating nature and treating it as a resource until they stop dominating each other and treating each other as resources. Ecofeminism (e.g. Adams and Gruen 2014) also locates the cause of ecological crisis in domination, but focuses on the parallels between the oppression of animals and the environment and men's domination of women.

Deep Ecology (e.g. Drengson and Inoue 1995) recognises the intrinsic worth of humans, animals, plants and the natural world, that is, their value beyond direct, short-term use for humans. Recognising worth in nature, it is argued, is likely to encourage people to protect and preserve the conditions that support all life, including human life. The Transition Movement (Hopkins 2008) is based on a philosophy of 'resilience' as a key goal, as both climate change and the depletion of oil lead to an inevitable decline in the ability of the Earth to support human life. Transition is localist in encouraging communities to regain the bonds and skills to look after each other and fulfil their own needs outside of a turbulent and unreliable international economy. The Dark Mountain Project (Kingsnorth and Hine 2009) sees even the hope of resilience as overly optimistic, and aims at generating new stories for survivors to live by after the inevitable collapse of industrial civilisation. Deep Adaptation (Bendell 2018) likewise calls for preparation for near-term societal collapse.

Deep Green Resistance (McBay *et al.* 2011) sees industrial civilisation as evil due to the damage and suffering it causes both humans and other species. Rather than waiting for industrial civilisation to destroy itself, Deep Green Resistance aims to hasten its destruction through carefully planned sabotage. At the far other end of the spectrum there is the semi-serious Voluntary Human Extinction Movement (VHEMT 2014), with a utilitarian philosophy that it would be better for one species (homo sapiens) to become extinct (voluntarily through a global decision not to have children) rather than the millions of species that humans are driving to extinction. This is radically ecocentric and highly pessimistic since it views any continuation of human life as a threat to the ecosystems that support life.

An individual ecolinguist will survey the wide range of possible ecosophies described in the literature, consider them carefully in light of available evidence and their own experience of human communities and the natural world, and build their own ecosophy through combining them, extending them or creating something entirely new. Gary Snyder, ecocritic, poet and philosopher, for instance, has built a personal ecosophy which combines and extends both Social Ecology and Deep Ecology (Messersmith-Glavin 2012).

The ecosophy has to be scientifically possible — for example, an extreme version of sustainable development that promoted economic growth everywhere, even in the richest of countries, could be argued to be impossible given environmental limits. It also has to be plausible, which the Voluntary Human Extinction Movement clearly is not since it relies on everyone in the world voluntarily agreeing not to have children. It also has to be aligned with the available evidence. Transition, for example, is dependent on evidence that oil production is due to peak and decline, that climate change is occurring, and that both will have a serious impact on human society.

The ecosophy of this book

This section briefly summarises the ecosophy that this book is based on. Ecosophies are complex and sophisticated, changing and evolving as the analyst is exposed to new ideas, discovers new evidence and has new experiences. The summary of an ecosophy is therefore necessarily partial and incomplete, but this section gives at least an indication of the framework used. The summary follows Naess (1995) in starting with one word that sums up the ecosophy and then adding explanatory detail as concisely as possible.

Ecosophy in one word: *Living!*

Explanation

Valuing living: The exclamation mark in *Living!* is normative, indicating 'to be valued / celebrated /respected/affirmed,' and it applies to all species that are living. This is a value announcement but is based on the observation that beings value their lives and do whatever they can to continue living. The 'valuing' takes place in different ways: consciously, instinctively, and almost (but not quite) mechanically, from a pedestrian watching carefully for cars, to a sparrow taking flight at the sound of a fox, or a snow buttercup following the arc of the sun to soak up life-giving rays.

Wellbeing: *Living!* is not the same as 'being alive' since there are conditions which reduce the ability to value being alive, such as extreme exploitation, enclosure in factory farms or illness due to chemical contamination. The goal is not just living in the sense of survival but living well, with high wellbeing.

Now and the future: The temporal scope of *Living!* is not limited to the present, so includes the ability to live with high wellbeing in the present, in the future, and the ability of future generations to live and live well.

Care: While respect for the lives of all species is central, continued 'living' inevitably involves an exchange of life. There will therefore be those who we stop from living, and those whose lives we damage in order to continue our own lives and wellbeing. The ethical aspect of the ecosophy deals with this through empathy, regret and gratitude, rather than an attempt to preserve moral consistency by considering those we harm as inferior, worthless, or just resources. Empathy implies awareness of impacts on others, regret implies minimising harm, and gratitude implies a duty to 'give back' something to the systems that support us.

Environmental limits: If human consumption exceeds the ability of natural resources to replenish themselves then this damages the ability of ecological systems to support life (and living) into the future. Equally, if consumption leads to more waste than can be absorbed by ecosystems, the excess waste will prevent beings from living or living with high wellbeing. To keep within environmental limits an immediate and large scale reduction of total global consumption is necessary.

Social justice: Currently, large numbers of people do not have the resources to live, or to live with high wellbeing. As global consumption levels drop (either voluntarily or through resource exhaustion) resources will need to be redistributed from rich to poor if all are to live with high wellbeing.

Deep Adaptation: In addition to wake of the pandemic, ecological destruction is already occurring, and significantly more is inevitable if industrial societies return to the trajectory that they were on. It is necessary to put in place measures to preserve life and wellbeing as far as possible as current forms of society collapse or undergo radical change.

The ecosophy draws from: (a) Deep Ecology in giving ethical consideration to other species as well as humans; (b) from Social Ecology in being orientated towards social justice; (c) from Sustainable Development in considering future generations; and (d) from Transition and Deep Adaptation in recognising and responding to inevitable further ecological destruction. The ethic of care is based on feminist ethics (Peterson 2001, p. 133).

Although ecosophies are a statement of the personal values and assumptions of the analyst, they also need to be based on evidence, and adapted as further evidence emerges. There is a significant amount of scientific evidence of environmental limits, the ecological damage already done which needs adapting to, and the scale of reduction in consumption necessary to minimise further damage (e.g., IPCC 2018; Díaz *et al.* 2019; UNEP 2019).

Importantly, this is just one ecosophy, and each ecolinguist will have their own ecosophy that they use for analysing language. No claim is made that this particular ecosophy is the right, correct or most suitable one for ecolinguistics as a whole to be based on. Instead, this book shows how texts and stories can be analysed linguistically with *an* ecosophy.

After linguistic analysis reveals stories, they are judged according to the ecosophy. For this book, stories which value and celebrate the lives and wellbeing of all species, call for a reduction in consumption, or promote redistribution of resources are appraised positively. On the other hand, stories which treat people or other species as resources to be exploited, promote inequitable distribution of resources, or promote accumulation of material possessions are challenged.

Organisation of this book

In 1980, Lakoff and Johnson published their seminal work *Metaphors We Live By,* which described metaphors as cognitive structures, existing in people's minds and influencing how they see the world. This book extends this idea to other kinds of cognitive structure: the *ideologies, framings, metaphors, evaluations, identities, convictions, erasure, salience* and *narratives* we live by. These, collectively, are the *stories we live by.* Each chapter covers one of these types of story, describing the underlying cognitive structure and the linguistic ways it manifests itself in texts, as summarised in Table 1.1.

TABLE 1.1   Nine forms that stories take and their linguistic manifestations

Ch.	Form of story (cognitive, i.e., in people's minds)		Manifestation (linguistic, i.e., appearance in texts)
2	ideology	a story of how the world is and should be which is shared by members of a group	discourses, i.e., clusters of linguistic features characteristically used by the group
3	framing	a story that uses a frame (a packet of knowledge about an area of life) to structure another area of life	trigger words which bring a frame to mind
4	metaphor (a type of framing)	a story that uses a frame to structure a distinct and clearly different area of life	trigger words which bring a clearly distinct frame to mind
5	evaluation	a story about whether an area of life is good or bad	appraisal patterns, i.e., patterns of language which represent an area of life positively or negatively
6	identity	a story about what it means to be a particular kind of person	forms of language which define the characteristics of certain kinds of people
7	conviction	a story about whether a particular description of the world is true, uncertain or false	facticity patterns, i.e., patterns of language which represent descriptions of the world as true, uncertain or false
8	erasure	a story that an area of life is unimportant or unworthy of consideration	patterns of linguistic features which fail to represent a particular area of life at all, or which background or distort it
9	salience	a story that an area of life is important and worthy of consideration	patterns of language which give prominence to an area of life
10	narrative	a structure which involves a sequence of logically connected events	narrative text, i.e., a specific oral telling, written work, or other expressive form which recounts a series of temporally and logically connected events

The chapters begin by describing the theory behind the story and providing some practical definitions. A key part of each chapter consists of practical analyses of a range of texts to illustrate the theory in action. These analyses are woven throughout the chapter, but with a more detailed analysis of a specific area in the final section of each chapter. The example texts are drawn from a wide range of sources including: neoclassical economics textbooks, agribusiness manuals, ecology reports, newspapers, environmental campaigns, nature writing, Japanese poetry, documentary films, political reports, advertisements and lifestyle magazines. The texts were chosen firstly because they were considered representative of larger patterns of language in society, and secondly because they were considered important, either in forging and perpetuating the ecologically destructive stories we live by, or in challenging those stories and providing new stories that we could live by.

A note about references to data and glossary

This book uses example data from a variety of sources, from economics textbooks to haiku poems. The data are catalogued using a tag consisting of two letters and two numbers, e.g. ET 5:7. The two letters refer to a type of data, e.g. ET = economics textbooks. The two numbers give further information such as a specific book or edition of a magazine, and the page number. The list below shows the labels and the kind of data they correspond to. The appendix has full details about the sources of the data.

AG	Agribusiness documents
EA	Ecosystem assessment reports
EN	Environmental articles, reports, films and websites
ET	Economics textbooks
HK	Haiku Anthologies
MH	Men's Health magazine
ML	Miscellaneous
NE	New economics books and reports
NR	Narrative texts
NW	New Nature Writing
PD	Political documents

Extracts from the data appear with bullet points to distinguish them from extracts from academic sources. Finally, there is a glossary at the end of the book which contains brief descriptions of most of the linguistic terms used.

补充文献

Berry, T. 1988. *The dream of the earth*. San Francisco: Sierra Club Books.

Naess, A. 1995. The shallow and the long range, deep ecology movement. In A. Drengson & Y. Inoue (Eds.), *The deep ecology movement: An introductory anthology*. Berkeley: North Atlantic Books, 3–10.

2

IDEOLOGIES

章节导读

第 2 章主要从对意识形态问题的探究出发，将意识形态视为构成话语最基本的故事。作者将意识形态定义为：社会某种群体成员所共有的意念体系，认同世界的过去、现在和将来的真实样子或应有的样子（*Ideologies* are belief systems about how the world was, is, will be or should be which are shared by members of particular groups in society.）。从生态语言学的角度看意识形态，重点是要看它是否能够带动人们维系生命赖以生存的生态系统。而话语是意识形态的表征。本书对话语的定义是：社会中的某种群体所使用的语言、图像以及其他表现形式的标准化方式（*Discourses* are standardised ways that particular groups in society use language, images and other forms of representation.）。作者根据自己第 1 章给出的生态哲学观，在这一章将话语分为三种类型。随后，他提出了话语分析的方法，并以新古典经济学话语为例进行了详细的分析。

（1）话语的三种类型。本书作者认为，话语有三种类型，分别是破坏性话语（destructive discourses）、中性话语（ambivalent discourses）和有益性话语（beneficial discourses）。

破坏性话语即某一话语中的意识形态与分析者的生态哲学观不一致，这类话语是最需要我们揭露和抵制的。有很多类型的话语属于破坏性话语，作者在此举出了几种典型的破坏性话语，例如：经济学话语、消费主义话语、广告话语和集约工业化农业（intensive industrial agriculture）话语等。这里值得一提的是，作者在谈经济学话语时引用了 Halliday（1990/2003）的观点，批评了把"经济增长"作为社会基本目标的表达方式，因为这在资源有限的地球上，不仅会导致资源枯竭，还会使维系生命的生态系统遭到破坏。

中性话语涉及某一话语的意识形态，在某些方面与分析者的生态哲学观相一致，而其他方面也有与分析者的生态哲学观不一致的地方。因为这一类型的话语有其积极的一面，所以我们不能直接抵制；应该努力采取更有建设性的方式，改善中性话语中存在问题的部分。到目前为止，生态语言学研究者主要分析过的中性话语有：环保主义话语、企业环保话语、自然资源话语、动物园话语和可持续性话语等多方面内容。在这一部分，作者也以动物园话语为例，将此类话语中的有益性和破坏性的部分全面揭示出来，让读者清晰地了解到中性话语的意义和优化方式。

有益性话语涵盖的范围是话语中所指的意识形态与分析者的生态哲学观完全一致，能够引导人们保护我们赖以生存的生态系统，所以需要鼓励、发扬、宣传这种类型的话语。而且，有益性话语也是我们在认识、了解破坏性话语和中性话语之后，要寻找的可替代性新话语，并要对这类话语进行广泛传播。本书中提到有关有益性话语的例子主要有：浪漫主义诗歌话语、自然文学话语、新自然文学话语、"适应文化的自然"（encultured nature）话语、俳句自然诗歌话语、美国土著文学话语等。但是，对于有益性话语，我们不是要推广某些特定的语篇，而是要传递一种能够书写或言说重要故事的方式，也就是要描绘某种故事的具体语言特征。例如：代词使用、语法结构、预设、参与者角色的位置，等等。当我们将有益性话语融入身边的主流话语时，我们信奉和践行的故事就会受到明显的影响。

（2）话语分析的方法。概括来说，生态语言学研究者要做的就是推广有益性话语、抵制破坏性话语、改善中性话语。话语分析的属性是跨学科的，所以它的分析方法具有多种路径，需要我们从不同学科中汲取精华，达到话语分析的真正目的。分析者要在收集好所分析的语篇之后，进行详细的语言学分析，探究话语的使用模式，以揭示出这些语言学特征集合所隐含和讲述的故事。

作者在这一部分以批评话语分析为例，提出了该视角下所要关注的语言学特征，其中包括：词汇（vocabulary）、词与词之间的关系（relationships between words）、语法结构（grammatical structures）、及物性（transitivity）、嵌入在小句中的假设和预设（assumptions and presuppositions embedded in clauses）、小句间的关系（relationships between clauses）、事件呈现形式（how events are represented）、参与者呈现形式（how participants are represented）、互文性（intertextuality）、体裁（genres）、修辞手法（figures of speech）等。与此同时，话语通常涵盖多个模态，它会将语言、音乐、静态或动态图像结合，全方位地传达意义，分析者仍需将这些模态考虑进来。例如"视觉图像分析"的步骤如下：第一步，分析语言特征的模式，其模式可以从矢量、景别、透视、摄影角度、凝视和照相写实主义等方面讨论；第二步，揭示话语潜在的意识形态，也就是视觉图像传达的是什么样的故事；第三步，将潜在的故事用自己的生态哲学观进行评估，确定话语类型；第四步，就话语类型决定最后的行动（推广、改进或抵制）。

（3）案例：新古典经济学话语。新古典经济学话语在话语分析中具有重要地位，它广泛存在于教育领域。该部分探讨的例子来自一套五本的微观经济学教程，核心目的是了解这套教程话语中的意识形态与本书的生态哲学观是否保持一致。

首先，作者找出了话语中的角色，并梳理他们的位置（动作者、思考者或感觉者）。作者发现，在这五本教程中，通过话语创造出了"消费者"这个角色，且消费者均被当作极其主动的角色，也就是心理过程中的感觉者或物质过程中的动作者。他们不仅仅是利己主义者，还把购买视为唯一得到满足的路径。从这点可以看出，这类话语所信奉和践行的故事是：否认那些无须花钱就能获得幸福感的方式（例如：与亲友的沟通、积极的心态等），认为只有消费才会改善人们的生活；但实际上，消费者的花费是无止境的，即使购买得再多也不会满足。

这样来看，此类话语潜在的故事与本书的生态哲学观是不一致的，属于破坏性话语，我们应该予以抵制。此时，出现了一种展示人类意义的新故事，被称为新经济学话语，这类话语是与新古典经济学话语完全不同的语言特征，其差异体现在词汇选择、语法特征、预设系统以及代词使用等多个方面。它能够作为一种可替代性的话语，给作为破坏性话语的新古典经济学话语探索出一个可信奉和践行的新故事。

Ideologies allow people, as group members, to organise the multitude of social beliefs about what is the case, what is good or bad, right or wrong, *for them*, and act accordingly.

(van Dijk 1998, p. 8)

The first of the nine types of story described in this book is *ideology*. The term 'ideology' is commonly used in Critical Discourse Analysis to refer to belief systems or worldviews that are shared by a particular group in society. It is sometimes used negatively to refer to racist, regressive or exploitative worldviews shared by powerful groups in society. However, other theorists use it in a more neutral sense where it can refer to belief systems of any group in society, whether negative or positive. Ideologies are cognitive, that is, they exist in the minds of group members, but they also have a linguistic manifestation in characteristic ways of speaking and writing used by those members.

Nationalists are an example of a group of people who share an ideology or worldview which manifests itself in particular forms of language. The following examples from the British National Party contain language choices which divide people into an ingroup (*British;*

English; indigenous; native) and an outgroup (*immigrant; alien; foreigner; African*):

- MASS IMMIGRATION CRISIS: Immigrant hordes heading for Soft-Touch Britain ... We will put British people first. (BNP leaflet, PD13 — see appendix for full reference)
- ... to hold back the hordes of Third World migrants clamouring to invade the British Isles ... (PD14)
- Multiculturalism is the eradication of the indigenous culture and being replaced by a hotchpotch of foreign and alien groups ... the BNP has campaigned for ... a return to the homogenous, indigenous British culture in Britain. (BNP chairman speech 2019, PD15)
- And if large numbers of Africans come to Britain, breathing English air or even being born in England can never make them or their descendants English. (BNP article, PD16)
- So-called 'white flight' from London [is] a result of successive governments favouring and putting foreigners first at the expense of native Londoners. (BNP London manifesto, PD19)

The outgroup in these examples is represented negatively through words with negative connotations such as *hordes, invade, alien* and *hotchpotch*. The idea that there is an identifiable group of native or indigenous British people which is under threat from an undifferentiated mass of foreigners is a story, that is, a version of the world among other possible versions. Stories influence how people not only think and talk, but also act. As climate change and other forms of ecological destruction displace increasing numbers of people, the danger is that nationalist ideologies encourage people to be less hospitable to environmental refugees and less willing to consider the culpability of richer countries in causing the environmental destruction which displaced them in the first place.

The characteristic forms of language which convey particular ideologies are called 'discourses', at least in this book, since there are 'a bewildering range of overlapping and contrasting theorizations' of discourse (Fairclough 2003, p. 124). For the purposes of this book, discourses are defined as follows:

Discourses are standardised ways that particular groups in society use language, images and other forms of representation.

Members of groups, whether economists, magazine journalists, agriculturalists, environmentalists, or nature writers, have characteristic ways of speaking, writing or designing visual materials that are common to the group. These include selections of vocabulary, grammatical choices, patterns of presupposition and other linguistic features, which, importantly, come together to tell a particular 'story' about the world. As Fairclough (2003, p. 124) puts it:

> Discourses not only represent the world as it is (or rather is seen to be), they are also ... imaginaries, representing possible worlds that are different from the actual world, and tied in to projects to change the world in particular directions.

There are various ways that critical discourse analysts refer to the stories that underlie discourses, including 'perspectives on the world' (Fairclough 2003, p. 124); 'particular constructions or versions of reality' (Locke 2004, p. 1); 'a coherent way of making sense of the world' (Locke 2004, p. 5); 'a practice ... of constituting and constructing the world' (Fairclough 1992a, p. 64); 'models of the world' (Machin and Mayr 2012, p. 5); 'meaning-resources ... to make sense of the world' (Kress 2010, p. 110) and 'ideologies' (Richardson 2007, p. 32).

What is key is that the stories are not just transparent descriptions of reality, but instead shape how we perceive reality. Locke (2004, p. 11) puts this even more strongly, stating that discourse 'actually shapes or constitutes the object denoted', which echoes Foucault's original formulation that discourses are 'practices that systematically form the objects of which they speak' (Foucault 2013, p. 54). The 'market', for example, is central to political life but is a creation of discourse that is based only loosely on the actual physical reality of people exchanging goods.

The stories that underlie discourses are, in this book, referred to using the term 'ideology', defined as follows:

> *Ideologies* are belief systems about how the world was, is, will be or should be which are shared by members of particular groups in society.

This does not imply that the ideologies are shared only by members of the groups — in many cases, groups are keen for their stories to spread out into the larger culture and become the normal way that people think about an area of life. Ideologies are cognitive, in the sense that they exist in the minds of individual people but are also common to all members of the group. As van Dijk (2011, p. 382) puts it, ideologies are 'a form of *social cognition*, that is beliefs *shared* by and *distributed* over (the minds of) group members'.

Fairclough (2003, p. 9) gives an example of a particular ideology — 'the pervasive claim that in the new "global" economy, countries must be highly competitive to survive'.

He goes on to say that the ideology is not necessarily untrue but 'is not the inevitable law of nature it is often represented as being, but the product of a particular economic order which could be changed'. This captures the essence of a 'story' — a version, perspective, or description of the world which is not necessarily false, but is just one possibility among many others. The stories are conveyed through the choice of lexical items, grammatical constructs and other linguistic features that are standardly used by a particular group. For example, an article in the right-wing newspaper *The Daily Mail* describes international competition as a race between countries, with words like 'pull away', 'streak ahead' and 'overtake':

- Britain will remain a dominant global economy and will *streak ahead* of France ... Long-term forecasts show the UK will continue to *pull away* from France as Europe's second-biggest economy. The Centre for Economics and Business Research (CEBR) said that 'despite Brexit, the French economy failed to *overtake* the UK'. On current trends, Britain's output should be 'a quarter larger than the French economy' by 2034. (ML21)

What is of interest in discourse analysis is not just specific texts such as this newspaper article, which are transient, but the patterns of linguistic features that run across multiple texts and subtly convey the same ideology over and over again. In ecolinguistic analysis of an ideology, the question is not whether it is true but whether it encourages people to preserve or destroy the ecosystems that support life. There is, of course, no objective algorithm for determining whether ideologies are destructive or beneficial, so what ecolinguists actually do is to assess whether the ideology resonates with their ecosophy or works against it. For example, the ecosophy in this book calls for a global reduction in consumption and a redistribution from rich to poor, so a story which sets up rich countries as competing with each other to have even bigger economic outputs stands in opposition to the ecosophy.

Since ideologies are presented as obvious truths about the world, it is possible not to notice that they are only stories. The aim of analysis is to investigate 'how ideologies can become frozen in language and find ways to break the ice' (Bloor and Bloor 2007, p. 12). Once it becomes clear that a particular story is not the only one possible, and that it is a story that is causing great harm, then it becomes possible to 'engage in acts of dissent — to take issue with these constructions and to *resist* the *storied meanings*' (Locke 2004, p. 6). Stories that are perceived to be causing harm because they oppose the ecosophy of the analyst are called *destructive discourses* in this book.

Destructive discourses

Of the many discourses which can be considered destructive, mainstream *economics discourses* are perhaps the most influential. Gare (2002, p. 132) goes as far as saying that 'the dominant discourse in the medieval world was theology, in the modern world, science, and now the discourse that defines reality for most people is economics'. Economics has become 'the prime interpreter of society to its members, providing them with the concepts in terms of which they were able to define and legitimate their relationships to each other, to society and to nature' (Gare 1996, p. 144). Although dominant economics discourses may not refer to nature in any way, they still set up relationships between people and nature, even if these are alienated and destructive ones.

Economics discourses have been an issue in ecolinguistics from early in the development of the discipline. Halliday (2001) discusses the way that language is frequently used to represent economic growth as the primary goal of society. He criticises these representations because unlimited growth on a finite planet can only lead to the exhaustion of resources and destruction of the ecosystems that support life. Chawla (2001, p. 120) describes how economics discourses orient 'all aspects of a person's endeavours for the achievement of personal satisfaction towards the consumption of commodities' (Chawla 2001, p. 120). This runs counter to the ecosophy of this book not only because it encourages unnecessary consumption, with all the environmental damage which ensues, but because it obscures all those paths to wellbeing that do not involve consumption.

The advertising industry plays a role in promoting consumerism by manufacturing dissatisfaction and suggesting that the dissatisfaction can be overcome through purchase — an ideology of PURCHASING PRODUCTS IS A PATH TO HAPPINESS. As Eisenstein (2013, p. 20) describes:

> [Advertisers are] selling sports cars as a substitute for freedom, junk food and soda as a substitute for excitement, 'brands' as a substitute for social identity, and pretty much everything as a substitute for sex, itself a proxy for the intimacy that is so lacking in modern life.

Another discourse which can be classified as destructive according to the ecosophy of this book is that of intensive industrial agriculture. There is extensive evidence that factory farming harbours pathogens that can become pandemic (McCarron 2017), consumes excessive resources, produces significant pollution and causes harm to the wellbeing of animals (Henning 2011; Poore and Nemecek 2018). Glenn (2004, p. 65) offers a critical analysis of how 'particular overlapping discursive strategies constructed by the factory farming industry help create, sustain and perpetuate a practice that is cruel and environmentally dangerous'. Her analysis shows how a range of linguistic devices construct animals as commodities, including the expression 'grain- and roughage-consuming animal units'. She investigates 'double speak', where cramped cages are called 'individual accommodation', and partitions that stop animals moving their bodies for their whole lives are described as being 'for privacy'.

Trampe (2018, p. 325) coined the term *euphemisation* 'to draw attention to lexical phrases that veil and justify acts depriving voiceless animals of their right to a natural life'. He describes a great range and variety of euphemistic phrasing in the animal industry which draws attention away from the ecologically damaging and inhumane aspects of the industry. Examples include referring to male chicks and calves as 'waste product'; the killing of rodents as 'pest management'; the forced injection of growth hormones as 'treatment'; and a general tendency to refer to animals in terms more usually used for engineering products. In general, the industry discourses that Glenn and Trampe analyse can have the effect of justifying inhumane and environmentally damaging farming methods through conveying ideologies such as FACTORY FARMING IS BENEFICIAL TO ANIMALS and ANIMALS ARE OBJECTS.

Particular discourses of economics, consumerism, advertising, and intensive agriculture can be labelled *destructive* discourses since the ideologies they convey oppose the principles of the ecosophy of this book. In this case, the ideologies work against wellbeing for all species, against a reduction in consumption or against staying within environmental limits.

The way of dealing with destructive discourses is through *resistance*. Resistance consists of raising awareness that the ideology conveyed by the discourse is just a story, and that the story has harmful effects — what Fairclough (1992b) calls *Critical Language Awareness*. It is most effective when those most responsible for using destructive discourses become aware of the damaging effects of the ideology they are unwittingly promoting. For example, resistance could focus on encouraging politicians to become aware that the ideology of economic growth as the key goal for society is just one possible story, and that there are other possible stories which may have a less destructive impact on the systems which support life.

An optimistic perspective is that, in general, people do not want to contribute to social injustice and ecological destruction — these are side-effects of ideologies which have a narrow focus on other goals. If aware of the potentially destructive effects of a story, some members of a group which has been promoting the story through common language choices may call for change. An example of this is the poultry industry publication *Poultry Science*, which published an article that extensively referred to ecolinguistic research and came to the following conclusion:

> Scholars (Stibbe 2003; Linzey 2006) have suggested that industry discourse characterises animals in ways that objectify them and obscure morally relevant characteristics such as animal sentience (p. 387) ... Although an analysis of discourse may seem odd and irrelevant ... this type of examination is illuminating in some potentially beneficial ways (p. 390) ... It may be necessary to reconsider several aspects of animal production relative to ideology, discourse, and practice. Transparency of contemporary animal production practices and a real ethic of care and respect for animals must be embodied not just in our practices but also in the internal and external discourse of animal agriculture.
>
> (Croney and Reynnells 2008, pp. 387, 390)

The importance of this extract is that it is from within the industry itself, and calls for a change not just at the level of language but also in 'our practices', i.e., the practices of the industry.

If those responsible for using destructive discourses are unwilling to change, then Critical Language Awareness can be directed at putting pressure on them through raising the awareness of key stakeholders such as customers or voters.

Ecolinguistics, then, can scrutinise the discourse of groups such as veterinarians, agribusiness executives, economists, lifestyle magazine journalists, politicians and advertisers to raise awareness of potentially harmful ecological impacts of the underlying ideologies. Resisting a dominant destructive discourse is calling for a decrease in the use of the discourse based on a convincing account of the harm it causes, opening up space for other, potentially more beneficial, alternatives.

Ambivalent discourses

The majority of discourse analysis in ecolinguistics has focused on the more positive, though still problematic, discourses of environmentalism, ecology, conservation, sustainability, and green advertising. While these discourses have a positive aim of dealing with some of the ecological problems caused by destructive discourses, they arise from the same society as the destructive discourses and may be influenced by political or commercial interests. A discourse which genuinely and persuasively calls for a reduction in consumption, for example, is unlikely to be funded by a government obsessed with economic growth or to appear in a newspaper or magazine dependent for its profit on creating a 'buying mood' for advertisers. Discourses which are genuinely ecocentric in encouraging care for other species may be avoided by governments which focus on the short-term interests of those beings who vote, i.e., humans. Mainstream 'green' discourses are often, therefore, *ambivalent* discourses, in that they contain some aspects which align with the analyst's ecosophy and some which oppose it.

Ecolinguists have analysed a range of ambivalent discourses, including the discourse of environmentalism (Benton-Short 1999; Harré *et al.* 1999), corporate greenwash (Alexander 2009; Ihlen 2009), natural resources (Kurz *et al.* 2005), zoos (Milstein 2009) and sustainability (Kowalski 2013). Harré *et al.* (1999) give the collective name of 'Greenspeak' to such discourses, which echoes George Orwell's sinister concept of 'Newspeak'. The discourses are criticised for aspects such as (a) representing plants, animals, rivers and forests as resources in the same way as the destructive discourses of agribusiness, i.e., as objects to be exploited; (b) representing solutions to environmental problems in small individual activities such as recycling or buying a hybrid car which people can accomplish without reducing their consumption; and (c) hiding agency to disguise blame for ecological destruction. Mühlhäsler (2003, p. 134) writes that 'once metaphorised into an object, a concept such as pollution can ... be studied in isolation from its makers or its effects and, as already has happened, it can become a commercial commodity'.

The discourse of zoos can be considered ambivalent because on the one hand it emphasises connection with nature and conservation, but on the other it tears animals away from their original ecosystems and offers them up in caged isolation as 'others' to be gazed at. Milstein (2009, p. 164) describes three main tensions:

> I argue that the three tensions within zoo institutional discourse, the dialectics of mastery-harmony, othering-connection and exploitation-idealism, may be found at the interpersonal and intrapersonal scale.

In her analysis, Milstein considers not just the linguistic messages given by zoos, but also the messages conveyed by the physical layout of the cages, finding that 'conservation messages also in many ways conflict with overall approaches to visual, spatial, and design messages of the zoo's built environment' (p. 38). Rather than simply condemning the discourse, Milstein praises some useful aspects of the discourse of progressive zoos and offers suggestions for how the discourse could be changed. One suggestion is that the discourse of zoos could better link the causes of extinction with imperialist government policies, the actions of transnational corporations, and overconsumption in the West.

In general, since ambivalent discourses frequently share some of the aims of the ecosophy, the way of dealing with them may not be direct *resistance* but a more constructive attempt to work with those responsible for the discourse. The aim is to preserve the positive aspects of the discourse while addressing any problematic aspects.

Beneficial discourses

An essential, yet underdeveloped, role for ecolinguistics consists of going beyond critiquing *destructive* discourses or pointing out the gaps in *ambivalent* discourses, to searching for new discourses that convey ideologies which can actively encourage people to protect the systems which support life. These can be called *beneficial* discourses. While destructive and ambivalent discourses are selected primarily on how widespread or dominant they are, the criterion for selecting which beneficial discourses to focus on is different. Clearly, in an unsustainable society, discourses which encourage more ecologically beneficial behaviour are unlikely to be widespread or dominant. The purpose for analysing beneficial discourses is to promote them as useful alternative ways of telling stories about the world and help them become widespread, even if they are currently relatively unknown. What is most important is how aligned the ideologies are with the ecosophy of the analyst, e.g. whether they value the lives and wellbeing of humans and other species, promote reduction in consumption and social justice, or work towards resilience.

Martin (2004) introduced the term *Positive Discourse Analysis* for analysis of useful discourses, where the aim is to promote the discourse rather than resist it, and the concept was further developed by Macgilchrist (2007) and Bartlett (2012, 2018). However, the term has proved controversial. Wodak (in Kendall 2007, p. 17), for instance, argues that the term 'critical' does not imply 'being negative' and that 'proposing alternatives is also part of being critical'. Clearly, though, the overwhelming majority of work in Critical Discourse Analysis is about raising awareness of how discourses can lead to oppression and exploitation. Its purpose is, on the whole, empowering people to resist the discourses which oppress them. The term 'Positive Discourse Analysis' is useful in emphasising the importance of the search for beneficial discourses that can help imagine and build new forms of society.

Goatly's (2000) book *Critical Reading and Writing* contained one of the first ecolinguistic studies to examine a destructive discourse in comparison with a beneficial one. This was a study of newspaper discourse (an edition of *The Times*) compared with the discourse of romantic poetry (Wordsworth's *The Prelude*). Goatly found that the discourse of *The Times* 'present[s] a domesticated, processed and relatively passive nature, mainly avoided apart from the impact of weather (and disease) and an interest in dogs and horses, and sometimes subordinated, as brand names or commodities, to economic interests' (Goatly 2000, p. 301). On the other hand, Wordsworth's discourse presents nature as much more active and alive by representing rivers as *Sayers* ('a river murmuring, wild brooks prattling'), animals and landscape as *Actors* ('the eagle soars', 'a huge peak ... upreared its head'), and nature as *Phenomenon* ('I spied a glow-worm'). Goatly (2000, p. 301) concludes that:

> the view of the natural world represented by Wordsworth, along with aspects of his grammar, provides a much better model for our survival than that represented by *The Times* ... to survive we had better take note of Wordsworth ... rethink and respeak our participation in nature before it rethinks or rejects our participation in it.

Wordsworth's work is an example of a particular discourse of romantic writing, and there are many discourses of nature writing from the past to the present in cultures across the world that can be explored by ecolinguistics in the search for beneficial discourses. One particularly important discourse is that of a group of authors who Macfarlane (2013, p. 167) calls 'imaginative naturalists', which includes Rachel Carson (whose lyrical writing is often credited with starting the environmental movement), Aldo Leopold and Loren Eiseley. Another promising discourse is what Macfarlane calls 'New Nature Writing', a contemporary British school including Kathleen Jamie, Elizabeth-Jane Burnett and Olivia Laing, which 'is distinguished by its mix of memoir and lyricism, and specialises in delicacy of thought and precision of observation' (Macfarlane 2013, p. 167). Bunting (2007) describes the discourse as follows:

> It doesn't quite fit to call it 'nature writing', because what makes these books so compelling — and important — is that they put centre stage the interconnections between nature and human beings.

Traditional and indigenous cultures around the world provide an important source for beneficial discourses: after all, there are cultures which have survived for thousands of years without destroying the ecosystems that they depend on for their survival. As Armon (2019, p. 246) describes, ecolinguistics can:

> honour and learn from the values, traditions, beliefs, and experiences of others who have developed sustainable ways of living, particularly those from marginalised groups, such as indigenous and traditional cultures, alternative communities that combine ancient and contemporary practices, and women, elders, farmers, and others who work with and care for the natural world.

IMAGE 2.1 Satoyama © INBAR

Dewi and Perangin-Angin (2020) analyse traditional Indonesian Pagu tales, which they describe as 'morality tales calling for people's care for and attention to the environment and all the ecosystems which have so far supported people's life' (p. 71). Their study concludes that 'not only do traditional tales enhance language research and character education, they also deliver transformative power to call for an ethic of care' (p. 71).

Knight (2010) analyses a beneficial discourse in an article entitled 'The discourse of "encultured nature" in Japan: the concept of *satoyama* and its role in twenty-first century nature conservation'. In the article she describes how the discourse of *satoyama* provides a way of representing 'a sphere in which nature and culture intersect' (p. 421) and how 'the model of *satoyama* and the harmonious human-nature relationship it embodies can be leveraged throughout the world' (p. 237).

Haiku nature poetry is another traditional Japanese discourse which can be considered beneficial in modelling a close, respectful and non-destructive relationship of humans with nature. In the discourse of haiku, ordinary plants and animals are represented as worthy of consideration in their own right rather than being metaphors for something else. They are referred to in concretely imaginable ways (e.g. 'frog' rather than 'fauna') and are represented actively through being given the role of *Actor* and *Senser* (Stibbe 2012, p. 145).

Machiorlatti (2010) examines indigenous cinema, which she describes as 'an activist endeavour that looks to the past in order to make visible the enduring effects of colonisation, to reclaim annihilated ways of being and to envision an affirmative future'.

Bringhurst (2008, p. 26) uses what he calls 'Ecological Linguistics' to explore Native American literature, which he similarly treats positively as a beneficial discourse:

> [Native American] stories and poems are often of great practical value as well as artistic merit. They are the legacy, after all, of peoples who knew how to live in this land for thousands of years without wrecking it ... If we do want to learn how to live in the world, I think the study of Native American literature is one of the best and most efficient ways to do just that ... the fundamental subject of this thought, this intellectual tradition, is the relationship between human beings and the rest of the world.

There is, of course, a danger of idealising cultures which may have had ecologically damaging aspects to them, or appropriating discourses that have been altered through faulty translation to a point where they no longer reflect the original story of the people they were taken from. It is important not to assume that a particular culture was sustainable and use that as proof that the discourse 'works', and not to assume that texts passed down from ancient cultures are authentic records of the stories of past civilisations. What can be done, however, for any discourse, is to analyse the language features and the ideologies they convey, compare those ideologies to the ecosophy, and promote aspects of the discourse which align with and further the ends of the ecosophy.

For beneficial discourses, the final stage is *promotion*. Promoting a discourse does not mean promoting specific texts such as Rachel Carson's lyrical yet scientific book *Silent Spring* (Carson 2000), a guide to Bhutan's 'Gross National Happiness', a set of Japanese haiku poems, or a powerfully evocative essay by a New Nature writer. Instead, what is promoted is *a way of writing or speaking that tells a useful story*. In other words, what is promoted is a specific cluster of linguistic features (pronoun use, grammatical structures, presuppositions, positioning of participants, etc.) which conveys a particular story. The story could be that the goal of life is to be more not have more; that the aim of society is wellbeing rather than economic growth; that humans are dependent on nature, or any other stories that are aligned with the ecosophy of the analyst.

The importance of promoting ways of writing (rather than texts) is that discourses can cross genre types. No matter how inspiring nature writing or haiku poetry is, there is always the danger it will be in a corner of the bookshop filed under its genre and serving a small niche. However, the *discourse* of haiku or nature writing (i.e., clusters of linguistic features that convey ideologies) could be adapted and incorporated across a wide range of areas of life — in weather forecasts, economics textbooks, biology guides, news reports, and in education. It is when beneficial discourses start finding themselves incorporated within the mainstream discourses that surround us that they can start to have an impact on the stories we live by.

Methods

Whether ecolinguistics is exposing and resisting negative discourses (such as those of consumerism, economic growth, or intensive agriculture) or investigating and promoting alternative, positive discourses (such as certain types of nature writing), the method of analysis suggested in this book is the same. Analysis begins by gathering together a range of prototypical texts produced and used by a certain group in society. This could be a selection of standard economics textbooks to represent a particular discourse of economics, a set of widely used industry handbooks to represent intensive animal farming, a collection of ecological assessment reports to represent ecological discourse, or a collection of books to represent a particular discourse of nature writing. The texts can never be fully representative of all texts produced by a particular group of people, but can expose discourses that are prominently used by a subset of key members of the group.

The next stage is detailed linguistic analysis to reveal patterns in the way that language is used within and across the texts. The focus is on linguistic features which combine together to tell stories about the world. A great deal of work in Critical Discourse Analysis has shown which features are useful to focus on when revealing the stories told between the lines of texts (see Fairclough 2003; Martin and Rose 2007; van Dijk 2011; Machin and Mayr 2012). The features of interest include the following:

- vocabulary (e.g. connotations of words, pronoun use, modals such as 'might' or 'must')
- relationships between words (e.g. synonymy, antonymy or hyponymy)
- grammatical structures (e.g. active vs passive, nominalisation)
- transitivity (the arrangement of processes and participants in a clause)
- assumptions and presuppositions embedded in clauses
- relationships between clauses (e.g. reason, consequence, purpose)
- how events are represented (e.g. abstractly or concretely)
- how participants are represented (e.g. as individuals or an aggregated mass)
- intertextuality (patterns of borrowing from other texts)
- genres (conventional formats of texts which serve a social function)
- figures of speech (e.g. irony, metaphor, metonymy)

Discourses are often multimodal, with language, still images, music or moving images coming together to convey meaning, so analysing discourse also requires consideration of other modes. For visual images, there are features that can be analysed such as vectors (lines of movement in images that suggest an action is taking place), *shot size* (which indicates close or distant relationships with subjects), perspective (which can show involvement), *camera angle* (which can show participants as powerful or powerless), gaze (which can show relationships between participants, or between participants and the viewer) and *photorealism* (Kress and van Leeuwen 2006; Kress 2010).

The next stage of analysis, after the patterns of linguistic (and visual) features are revealed, is to expose the underlying ideologies that these features convey. Within the discourse of advertising, for example, may lurk a story that self-fulfilment lies in accumulation of material goods; within the discourse of certain politicians may lie a story that the purpose of society is to maximise economic growth whatever the cost; within the language of the handbooks of industrial agriculture there may be a story about animals and nature being only objects and resources to be exploited for profit; and within certain discourses of nature writing may be a story of humans as being an integral part of ecosystems and dependent for their continued survival on the preservation of those ecosystems.

None of the ideologies that are revealed through Critical Discourse Analysis are objectively good or bad in their own right. They can only be considered 'good' in the sense that they are consistent with, resonate with, or promote the ecosophy of the analyst; and 'bad' if they are incompatible with, opposed to, or work against the principles of that ecosophy. The next stage consists of comparing the stories with the ecosophy to come to a judgement. It is likely that any discourse will have positive or negative aspects within it. However, pragmatically it is useful to consider whether discourses are on the whole *destructive* (i.e., predominantly work against the ecosophy), *ambivalent* (i.e., have similar aims to the ecosophy but some key differences too), or *beneficial* (i.e., resonate strongly with the ecosophy). The reason for making this distinction is that the final stage will depend on what type of discourse it is — destructive discourses are resisted through raising awareness of their harm, ambivalent discourses are improved through constructively working with those responsible for them, and beneficial discourses are promoted.

There are clearly a very large number of discourses which ecolinguistics can focus on. This section has just mentioned some — those of economics, advertising, popular media, agriculture, nature writing and traditional discourses from around the world. The next section is a case study of one of these discourses, neoclassical economics, which aims to reveal the ideologies that underpin it and the linguistic features which convey those ideologies.

The discourse of neoclassical economics

The discourse of neoclassical economics is one of the most dominant and enduring stories that we live by. It is so ubiquitous in education that a network called 'Rethinking Economics' was established to 'create fresh economic narratives to challenge and enrich the predominant neoclassical narrative' (RE 2014). *The Guardian* newspaper describes the network as follows:

> In June a network of young economics students, thinkers and writers set up *Rethinking Economics*, a campaign group to challenge what they say is the predominant narrative in the subject. Earle said students across Britain were being taught neoclassical economics 'as if it was the only theory'. He said: 'It is given such a dominant position in our modules that many students aren't even aware that there are other distinct theories out there that question the assumptions, methodologies and conclusions of the economics we are taught'.
>
> (Inman 2013)

This section briefly analyses the discourse of neoclassical economics through examples drawn from a set of five microeconomics textbooks (ET1–ET5, see Appendix for details). Although the books were written at different times and have a slightly different focus, all have in common that they describe neoclassical economics theory using the discourse of neoclassical economics itself, at least in one section of the book. Other sections in the books question, challenge or adapt the principles of neoclassical economics to various degrees, but the focus of this illustrative analysis is on the sections which are written purely in the discourse of neoclassical economics. From an ecolinguistic perspective, the key issue is whether the ideology embedded in the discourse is aligned with or contradicts the ecosophy, e.g. whether it promotes an overall decrease in consumption, and whether it encourages redistribution of resources to relieve poverty as total consumption falls.

A starting point for analysis is to ask who the characters in the story are, and what they are positioned as doing, thinking and feeling. The textbook ET1 sets out the characters clearly:

- Microeconomics deals with the behaviour of individual economic units. These units include consumers, workers, investors, owners of land, business firms ... (ET1:3)

All the books divide up humanity in similar ways, simplifying the world into categories of people such as 'consumers' or 'owners' who are all assumed to think and act in the same way. What people do is given by the name of their category: consumers consume, workers work, investors invest, owners own. This is described as 'functionalisation' by van Leeuwen (2008, p. 42), where 'social actors are referred to in terms of an activity, in terms of something they do'. Machin and Mayr (2012, p. 81) point out that functionalisation can 'reduce people to a role which may in fact be assigned by the writer'. Clearly, most people do not refer to themselves as 'consumers', and the classification is one imposed by the discourse of neoclassical economics.

It is possible to gain an initial idea of how consumers are represented through looking at the *transitivity* of clauses that they participate in. Transitivity concerns types of *processes* and *participants* which are represented in the clauses. Halliday (2013, p. 213) describes a number of processes, including *material processes*, which are physical actions in the world; *mental processes*, which involve thinking or sensing; and *verbal processes* which are processes of speaking, writing or communicating [see glossary for italicised terms]. Depending on the process, there are different participants involved, for example a material process involves an *Actor* (who is the one doing something) and the *Affected* participant (the one having something done to them). For mental processes, there is the *Senser* (the one thinking, feeling or perceiving) and the *Phenomenon* (what they are perceiving). Transitivity is useful in indicating the types of processes that participants are represented as involved in, and whether they are taking an active role (i.e., Actor or Senser) or a more passive role (i.e., Affected or Phenomenon).

In all the textbooks, consumers are represented highly actively: as Senser in mental processes (such as 'choosing', 'selecting', 'deciding', 'preferring', 'wishing') and Actor of material processes (such as 'buying', 'paying', 'purchasing', 'trading', 'switching', 'obtaining', 'responding' to prices, 'entering' the market). With very few exceptions, the mental and material processes revolve around deciding what to buy and then buying it, i.e., the consumer is represented as a pure economic actor rather than a multi-dimensional person whose economic behaviour is part of a larger context of life. The goals that consumers are trying to achieve through their mental and material processes are given in the words around the processes. The following examples contain typical goals that consumers are represented as pursuing in the textbooks:

- The consumer wishes to do as well as possible, to select that consumption pattern out of all those available that will yield the highest level of satisfaction. (ET2:22)
- consumers maximise utility. (ET1:149)
- [consumers] decide ... what goods and services to buy ... to achieve the highest possible level of satisfaction. (ET3:6)
- consumers, based on their preferences, maximise their wellbeing. (ET1:114)
- consumers usually select market baskets that make them as well off as possible. (ET1:69)
- [consumers] maximise their wellbeing by trading off the purchase of more of some

goods for the purchase of less of others. (ET1:4)

- the utility-maximising consumer obviously wishes to maximise this net gain. (ET2:77)

The goals that the consumer is represented as trying to achieve are 'the highest level of satisfaction', 'utility', 'wellbeing', 'being well off' and 'do(ing) as well as possible', which are treated across the textbooks as *synonyms*. The pronouns 'their' in 'maximise their wellbeing' and 'them' in 'make them as well off as possible' reveal whose wellbeing the consumers are aiming for: it is their own personal wellbeing rather than that of others. The expression 'utility-maximising consumer' wraps this up into a single noun phrase, representing the pursuit of personal satisfaction as the defining characteristic of a particular kind of person. The ideology, then, is that CONSUMERS MAXIMISE THEIR OWN SATISFACTION THROUGH PURCHASE. The problem with this story, as Daly and Cobb (1994, p. 87) point out, is that what happens to other people is of no interest to the consumer, and nor is the morale of the community of which they are a part. Gare (1996, p. 146) traces this form of representation back to Adam Smith, who 'was compelled to conceive people in abstraction from their social relations and therefore as egoists in order to have a single principle to explain the economic mechanism'.

The problem is not just that consumers are represented as egotistically trying to satisfy themselves without regard to anyone else, but that the *only path to satisfaction is represented as being through purchase*. In the above extracts, the means that consumers use to maximise their satisfaction are represented only as 'select that consumption pattern', '[buy] goods and services', 'select market baskets' and 'choose goods'. As Daly and Cobb (1994, p. 87) point out, 'the gifts of nature are of no importance'. The assumption is not just that, as one of the textbooks puts it, 'money (i.e., a higher income) can buy happiness' (ET1:97), but that money is represented as the *only* path to wellbeing and happiness. In fact, the discourse goes beyond 'money can buy happiness' to represent money and happiness as almost *the same thing*, through the concept of 'utility'. As Ekins *et al.* (1992, p. 36) point out 'for the conventional economist ... price *is* value'. For instance, ET5:62–63 defines 'utility' firstly as 'benefit or satisfaction', and then as an amount of money a person would be prepared to pay:

- Economists use the term 'utility' to refer to the benefit or satisfaction we get from consumption. (ET5:62)
- if you were prepared to pay 50p for an extra packet of crisps per week, then we would say the marginal utility of eating it is 50p. (ET5:63)

This runs counter to the ecosophy of this book because it downplays all the ways that people could find wellbeing without spending money, such as connecting with family and friends, being active, learning things, or working towards the common good (NEF 2008).

There is another story that runs through the discourse: CONSUMERS CAN NEVER BE SATISFIED, no matter how much they consume. This story is told explicitly in places, and more subtly through assumptions about what consumers 'want' or 'prefer':

- consumers will want to purchase more of a good as its price goes down. (ET1:24)
- We believe that these assumptions hold for most people in most situations ... More is better than less: Goods are assumed to be desirable — i.e., to be *good*. Consequently, *consumers always prefer more of any good to less*. In addition, consumers are never satisfied or satiated; *more is always better, even if just a little better.* (ET1:70, emphasis in original)
- the assumptions we have made about taste, namely that more goods are preferred to few ... (ET2:27)
- people, both rich and poor, want more than they can have. (ET5:22)
- ... a bundle with more of one good and no less of another is preferred. (ET2:22)

The *modality* (i.e., claim to truthfulness) in this discourse is mixed. On one hand, there are low-modality statements such as 'We *believe* that these *assumptions* hold for *most* people in *most* situations', while other expressions show very high modality through bald-on-record expressions such as 'will want to', 'are preferred' and categorical adverbs such as 'always prefer' or 'never satisfied'. In general, characterisations of consumers are initially introduced with low modality, merely as assumptions, but after that are then treated as highly certain facts that can be plotted in graphs and used in equations. Once the 'facts' are created, the discourse represents the story that CONSUMERS CAN NEVER BE SATISFIED as an obvious and certain truth rather than a contentious claim. This closes down the possibility that there is an *optimal* level of consumption where people have enough material possessions and can search for wellbeing through non-material means.

Overall, the discourse of neoclassical economics uses language in a way which creates a character labelled 'consumer', and represents consumers as egotists who are only interested in maximising their own wellbeing, who seek satisfaction only through purchasing products, who always want to buy more and, no matter how much they consume, are never satisfied. This could just be an unflattering story about what it means to be human, based on the assumptions and intuitions of analysts in the richest countries in the world. However, economics theories are drawn on by business and government policymakers to make real decisions that influence people's lives and behaviour.

There is a danger that in order to create a growing economy policymakers will encourage people to act like the selfish consumer of neoclassical economics. The expression 'greed, for lack of a better word, is good' (used by fictional character Gordon Gekko in the film *Wall Street*) turns the 'selfish consumer' from a description to an ideal to aim for, and is echoed indirectly in the words of politicians such as Boris Johnson, who stated '... inequality is essential for the spirit of envy and keeping up with the Joneses, that is, like greed, a valuable spur to economic activity' (PD18).

If people do not have insatiable wants and desires, then advertising can step in and try to manufacture them. Daly and Cobb (1994, p. 87) describe how:

> If nonsatiety were the natural state of human nature then aggressive want-stimulating advertising would not be necessary, nor would the barrage of novelty aimed at promoting dissatisfaction with last year's model. The system attempts to remake people to fit its own presuppositions. If people's wants are not naturally insatiable we must make them so, in order to keep the system going.

There is also evidence that just reading texts which describe extrinsic (self-centred) values such as 'utility maximisation' or 'profit maximisation' is enough to influence people's attitudes and behaviour, making them less compassionate and less likely to engage in volunteering or pro-environmental behaviour (Molinsky *et al.* 2012; Blackmore and Holmes 2013). Grant (2013) describes evidence from multiple sources that economics students become less altruistic and more selfish through studying traditional economics degrees, concluding that 'even thinking about economics can make us less compassionate'. Blackmore and Holmes (2013, p. 13) describe evidence that texts which appeal to economic benefit can:

> [erode] our environmental concern, our long-term thinking, our civic motivation and even our wellbeing. Such communications instead make us more materialistic, less likely to act environmentally (such as recycling or conserving water), and less motivated to volunteer or be politically active.

This is of great concern given that so many people in powerful positions (politicians and business leaders) have been trained in neoclassical economics or are advised by those who have. Lakoff (2010, p. 77) warns that '*the economic and ecological meltdowns have the same cause,* namely the unregulated free market with the idea that greed is good' [emphasis in original].

Resisting the ideology that HUMANS ARE FUNDAMENTALLY SELFISH requires firstly pointing out that it is just a story and that other stories are possible. This is something that Caroline Lucas, a Green Party MP, did during the COVID-19 lockdown in speeches broadcast on social media:

- For decades, our political leaders have told us we are greedy, selfish and out for ourselves, and that this is the natural order of things. Many of us had even begun to believe it. But today, we have shown this to be a lie. In a crisis we pull together. For every person panic shopping, there's a dozen of us shopping for a neighbour ... This is the best that human beings can be. And this could be the beginnings of a better future. As US writer Rebecca Solnit has said, disasters can give us 'a glimpse of who else we ourselves may be and what else our society could become'. (PD17)
- Despite the danger and fear and terrible sadness caused by this pandemic we can now finally demolish the miserable mythology of human selfishness. (PD17)

Lucas and Solnit are pointing towards a profound change in who we are and the society we live in, what this book calls finding 'new stories to live by'. Even some conservative politicians have changed the way they speak to distance themselves from individualist ideologies of the past. Boris Johnson, for instance, stated that 'we are going to do it, we are going to do it together. One thing I think the coronavirus crisis has already proved is that there really is such a thing as society' (PD10). This is a direct intertextual reference to and contradiction of Margaret Thatcher's famous 1987 statement that 'there is no such thing as society'.

To overcome the ideology of neoclassical economics it is necessary to find new forms of language that resist them. One place to search for these forms of language are the discourses of *New Economics*. Examples of New Economics texts are Tim Jackson's *Prosperity Without Growth* (NE1), Kate Raworth's *Doughnut Economics* (NE2), the reports of the New Economics Forum (e.g. NE3), Bhutan's Gross National Happiness reports (e.g. NE4) and Charles Eisenstein's book *Sacred Economics* (NE5). Eisenstein explicitly declares that a new story is necessary:

- Anonymity, depersonalisation, personalisation of wealth, endless growth, ecological despoliation, social turmoil and irredeemable crisis are built into our economic system so deeply that nothing less than a transformation of the defining Story of the People will heal it. (NE5:2)

The language that Eisenstein uses provides one possible alternative 'Story of the People'. His book makes strong use of contrasts, which place current neoclassical ways of describing the world in the spotlight, to be considered, rejected, and replaced. Some of the contrasts he makes in the book are as follows:

- scarcity/abundance. (NE5: xix)
- separation/reunion. (NE5:1)
- fractured/whole. (NE5:2)
- selfishness/generosity. (NE5:6)
- polarisation of wealth/equitable distribution of wealth. (NE5:13)
- anxiety/ease. (NE5:13)
- hardship/leisure. (NE5:13)
- competition/cooperation. (NE5:17)
- hoarding/circulation. (NE5:17)
- linear/cyclical. (NE5:17)

Eisenstein's new story is of an economic system built on abundance, reunion, wholeness, generosity, equitable distribution, ease, leisure, cooperation, circulation of money and cycling of materials. The story is reflected in the choice of vocabulary, grammar, presupposition and pronoun use that run throughout his book. To give just one example, Eisenstein speaks of:

- [moving] away from the mentality of struggle, of survival, and therefore utilitarian efficiency, and toward our true state of gratitude: of reverence for what we have received and of desire to give equally, or better, from our endowment. (NE5:434)

This uses the inclusive pronoun 'we' to engage the reader and presupposes that gratitude, reverence and a desire to give are the reader's true nature. It conveys a story that opposes the neoclassical ideology that HUMANS ARE FUNDAMENTALLY SELFISH with the new story that HUMANS ARE FUNDAMENTALLY ALTRUISTIC. If it is true that reading neoclassical economics texts can make people more selfish, then being exposed to discourses like this may encourage readers to become more generous.

One of the key tasks of ecolinguistics is to search for ideologies which resonate with the ecosophy of the analyst, discover the linguistic features which convey those ideologies, and then promote those features widely so that they can become part of mainstream economic discourse. Analysis of the discourses of new economics can potentially help in the task of building a very different economic system as society reinvents itself after the pandemic.

理论延伸

本章主要是以话语分析为主线展开的讨论。话语分析涉及多个学科领域，因此它具有多学科或跨学科属性。话语分析的发展可以与西方哲学界的"语言转向"（the linguistic turn）和人文社会科学的"话语转向"（the discursive turn）结合起来。19世纪末到20世纪中期，西方哲学界意识到了哲学中的思维和意识等问题实质上都是语言的问题，这促使语言成为哲学反思自身传统的基础，这就是西方哲学界的"语言转向"。而到了20世纪50年代，出现了从"语言转向"到"话语转向"现象的发生（Bhatia et al.，2008）。有关学者不再局限于关注语言的形式和结构，开始关注现实生活中的话语，探索语言的使用及其对社会产生的影响（黄国文、刘明，2016）。这种"话语转向"主要是因为社会生活的性质发生了较大的变化，社会生活的很多现象都受到话语的影响，话语成为社会实践的主要"中介"；换句话说，社会生活的本质是话语的。

就话语分析作为一门学科而言，黄国文和刘明（2016）将其发展历程归纳为四个阶段：（1）产生阶段：20世纪50到60年代；（2）发展阶段：20世纪70年代；（3）成熟阶段：20世纪80到90年代；（4）鼎盛阶段：21世纪以来。目前，话语分析的发展速度非常快，其影响力已经超越了语言学研究领域的其他任何一门学科。由于话语分析的本质是多学科或跨学科的，所以它的分析框架也是多种多样的，没有公认的话语分析路径和方法（黄国文，1988：7）。话语分析过程中使用的理论支撑和分析框架是由分析者的学术兴趣和研究背景决定的。例如：从批评语言学角度出发，可以有批评话语分析（critical discourse analysis）（Fairclough，1995）；从系统功能语言学角度出发，又有功能语篇分析（functional discourse analysis）（黄国文，2006：175）和功能话语研究（黄国文、赵蕊华，2021）；如果从生态语言学的角度出发，还出现了生态批评话语分析（eco-critical discourse analysis）、生态话语分析（ecological discourse analysis）、和谐话语分析（harmonious discourse analysis）等框架（赵蕊华、黄国文，2017；黄国文，2018a；黄国文、赵蕊华，2019；Huang & Zhao，2021）。

批评话语分析是20世纪70年代出现的，它试图把社会分析的批评传统应用到语言研究中来，通过话语审视社会中不公平的现象（Fairclough，1995，2003；Wodak，2011）。但是批评话语分析存在很多局限性（何伟、魏榕，2018）：（1）分析对象多数为社会冲突性话语；（2）缺少话语分析具体的评判标准；（3）在话语实践和社会实践中缺乏清晰系统的分析框架。因此，为了弥补批评话语分析的缺憾，Martin提出积极话语分析的研究路径（Martin，1999，2004）。所谓积极话语分析，主要是用积极友好的态度分析话语，促进人类社会的和解、共存和一致（Martin，2004）。从这点可以看出，积极话语分析是对批评话语分析的补充；积极话语分析是建构的，凭借话语分析来建构社会的美好，而批评话语分析则是解构的，目的是解构社会的不平等（Martin，2004；胡壮麟，2012；何伟、魏榕，2018）。

功能语篇分析是在第七届全国语篇分析研讨会上提出的（黄国文，2001：30），主张研究者根据自身的研究兴趣来选择并分析语篇（黄国文，2018b：101），它有六个分析步骤（黄国文，2006：175）。第一步是观察（observation）：通过观察了解所选择的语篇能否达到既定的研究目的所需要的条件以及是否具有研究价值（曾蕾，2012：299）。第二步是解读（interpretation）：这一步要对其中的话语意义、研究目标和内容进行解读，后面的步骤都是以解读为基准的。第三步是描述（description）：描述的目的是让话语中每个元素之间的关系更加清晰。第四步是分析（analysis）：分析这一步贯穿了每个步骤，甚至是在观察阶段，一些预先分析也是必要的；但就这一步骤本身，分析是指在观察、解读、描述基础上进行的分析。第五步是解释（explanation）：解释是在分析之后对分析结果的阐释，它也是评估的前提条件。最后一步是评估（evaluation）：评估是最后也是最难的一个步骤，是话语分析的最终目标。Halliday（1994/2000：F41）认为评估是语篇分析的最高层次，能够揭示出话语结构与功能为何如此表示的原因、目的以及交际的合适性。

上面的几种话语分析角度在生态语言学研究中都有一定的应用（Stibbe，2015，2018a，2018b，2021；黄国文、陈旸，2017）。随着话语分析"生态转向"的出现，当生态语言学研究者借助批评话语分析路径来研究话语时，就形成了生态批评性话语分析（Fill & Mühlhäusler，2001），主要研究与气候变化、环境污染、资源消耗严重等主题有关的话语。这实际上就是生态话语分析中的"生态话语"的分析。但像我们在全书导读中提到的那样，生态话语分析不仅局限于此，还要努力从生态的角度对所有类型的话语进行分析，揭示所有话语和行为中对生态系统造成影响的问题（Alexander & Stibbe，2014：109）。

基于此，在生态语言学的指导下，我们还尝试将话语分析与我国政治、经济、文化、历史等因素结合起来，挖掘语言系统与生态系统的和谐现象以及话语在特定的文化语境中的和谐现象（黄国文、赵蕊华，2017），这就是和谐话语分析。和谐话语分析的定义是：在中国语境下，"生态"不仅指"生命有机体与其生存环境间的关系以及它们之间的相互关系和相互作用形成的结构和功能的关系"，而且是用来表示"和谐"，包括"人与自然的和谐"和"人与人之间的和谐"（黄国文，2016：12）。赵蕊华和黄国文（2021）也进一步印证了和谐话语分析不只适用于中国语境，在其他语境中也是可行的。有关和谐话语分析的内容还可进一步阅读黄国文（2017）、赵蕊华和黄国文（2017，2021）、黄国文和赵蕊华（2019，2021）、Huang & Zhao（2021）等论著。

综上所述，与本章的话语分析相关内容，读者可重点阅读黄国文和刘明（2016）、何伟和魏榕（2018）、黄国文（2018a）、Stibbe（2018a，2018b）、黄国文和赵蕊华（2019，2021）、何伟（2021）等论著，以系统地把握话语分析的核心要点。

补充文献

何伟．2021."生态话语分析"：韩礼德模式的再发展．外语教学，（1）：20–27.

何伟，魏榕．2018. 话语分析范式与生态话语分析的理论基础．当代修辞学，（5）：63–73.

胡壮麟．2012. 积极话语分析和批评话语分析的互补性．当代外语研究，（7）：3–8，76.

黄国文．1988. 语篇分析概要．长沙：湖南教育出版社．

黄国文．2001. 语篇分析的理论与实践——广告语篇研究．上海：上海外语教育出版社．

黄国文．2006. 翻译研究的语言学探索：古诗词英译本的语言学分析．上海：上海外语教育出版社．

黄国文．2016. 外语教学与研究的生态化取向．中国外语，（5）：1，9–13.

黄国文．2017. 论生态话语和行为分析的假定和原则．外语教学与研究，（6）：880–889.

黄国文．2018a. 从生态批评话语分析到和谐话语分析．中国外语，（4）：39–46.

黄国文．2018b."解读"在典籍翻译过程中的作用——以"唯女子与小人难养也"的英译为例．英语研究，（1）：100–109.

黄国文，陈旸．2017. 自然诗歌的生态话语分析——以狄金森的《一只小鸟沿小径走来》为例．外国语文，（2）：61–66.

黄国文，刘明．2016. 导读：话语分析核心术语．北京：外语教学与研究出版社，ix–xiii.

黄国文，赵蕊华．2017. 生态话语分析的缘起、目标、原则与方法．现代外语，（5）：585–596.

黄国文，赵蕊华．2019. 什么是生态语言学．上海：上海外语教育出版社．

黄国文，赵蕊华．2021. 功能话语研究．北京：清华大学出版社．

曾蕾．2012. 功能语篇分析．黄国文，辛志英主编．系统功能语言学研究现状和发展趋势．北京：外语教学与研究出版社，294–330.

赵蕊华，黄国文．2017. 生态语言学研究与和谐话语分析——黄国文教授访谈录．当代外语研究，（4）：15–18，25.

赵蕊华，黄国文．2021. 和谐话语分析框架及其应用．外语教学与研究，（1）：42–53.

Alexander, R. & Stibbe, A. 2014. From the analysis of ecological discourse to the ecological analysis of discourse. *Language Sciences, 41*: 104–110.

Bhatia, V. K., Flowerdew, J. & Jones, R. H. 2008. Approaches to discourse analysis. In V. K. Bhatia, J. Flowerdew & R. H. Jones (Eds.), *Advances in discourse studies*. London and New York: Routledge, 1–17.

Fairclough, N. 1995. *Critical discourse analysis: The critical study of language*. London & New York: Longman.

Fairclough, N. 2003. *Analysis discourse: Textual analysis for social research*. London: Routledge.

Fill, A. & Mühlhäusler, P. 2001. *The ecolinguistics reader: Language, ecology and environment*. London: Continuum.

Halliday, M. A. K. 1990. New ways of meaning: The challenge to applied linguistics. *Journal of Applied Linguistics*, (6): 7–16. (Reprinted from *On language and linguistics, Vol. 3 in The collected works of M. A. K. Halliday*, pp. 139–174, by J. Webster, ed., 2003, Continuum)

Halliday, M. A. K. 1994/2000. *An introduction to functional grammar*. London: Edward Arnold / Beijing: Foreign Language Teaching and Research Press.

Huang, G. W. & Zhao, R. H. 2021. Harmonious discourse analysis: Approaching people's problems in a Chinese context. *Language Sciences, 85*: 1–18.

Martin, J. R. 1999. Grace: The logogenesis of freedom. *Discourse Studies*, (1): 29–56.

Martin, J. R. 2004. Positive discourse analysis: Solidarity and change. *Revista Canaria De Estudios Ingleses, 49*: 179–202.

Stibbe, A. 2015. *Ecolinguistics: Language, ecology and the stories we live by*. London: Routledge.

Stibbe, A. 2018a. Positive discourse analysis: Rethinking human ecological relationships. In A. Fill & H. Penz (Eds.), *The Routledge handbook of ecolinguistics*. London: Routledge, 165–178.

Stibbe, A. 2018b. Critical discourse analysis and ecology. In J. Flowerdew & J. E. Richardson (Eds.), *The Routledge handbook of critical discourse studies*. London: Routledge, 497–509.

Stibbe, A. 2021. *Ecolinguistics: Language, ecology and the stories we live by* (2nd ed.). London: Routledge.

Wodak, R. 2011. Critical linguistics and critical discourse analysis. In J. Zienkowski, J-O. Östman & J. Verschueren (Eds.), *Discursive pragmatics*. Amsterdam: Benjamins, 50–70.

3

FRAMING

章节导读

这一章节主要探讨的问题是故事的构架，它是以框架理论（frame theory）为根基的。本章的核心是在辨析"框架"（frame）、"构架"（framing）、"重构"（reframing）三个重要的概念之后探寻构架分析的方法，并通过一个典型的构架案例揭示出其中详细的运作机制。下面我们将从三个层次介绍第 3 章的内容：（1）理论内涵；（2）构架分析的方法；（3）案例："发展"的构架。

（1）理论内涵。框架、构架、重构这三个核心概念来自多个学科领域，包括：人工智能、社会学、语言学以及认知科学。通常情况下，构架的概念会频繁出现在社会变革方面研究的组织和个人的话语中，所以这几个概念对于生态语言学研究十分重要。

框架是与生活某个领域相关的知识集合（A *frame* is a package of knowledge about an area of life.），它有三个内涵：第一，知识、信念和实践模式的集合；第二，事实性和程序性的知识；第三，用来了解世界的思想结构。框架的构成中有一个很重要的因素，就是触发词（trigger word）。例如：当听到"购买"这个触发词时，就会触发形成交易框架。该框架蕴含了与交易有关的参与者、参与者之间的关系和参与者采取的一系列行为。所以我们可以说，不同框架下的参与者以及参与者的相互关系和所作所为是不一样的，他（它）们处于不同的关系中，各自讲述着不同的故事。

构架是一个故事，它使用一个框架来构建生活的另一个领域是如何被概念化的（*Framing* is a story which uses a frame to structure how another area of life is conceptualised.）。构架的现象通常出现在使用某一触发词去描述一个领域的情况，这实质上是在认知层面上将一个领域的框架强加在另一个领域上。例如：环保慈善机构如果将"购买""折扣""顾客"作为触发词的话，"保护自然"则会被构建为交易框架。这不仅会增强以自我为中心的消费框架，还会对自然产生影响。这与本书的生态哲学观是相违背的，属于破坏性的构架，需要我们抵制并进行重构。

重构是指以一种不同于文化中典型构架的方式对一个概念进行构架的行为（*Reframing* is the act of framing a concept in a way that is different from its typical framing in a culture. ）。这是对原本不合理构架的积极反馈，是一种新的构建方式。例如："气候变化问题"如果被视为"单纯的环境问题"来构建，那就仅仅会由环境和能源部门来处理，不会引起更多人重视；而若用"安全威胁"来重构它，就会让人们联想到突发事件、紧急情况等状态，使得人们能够更加客观、深刻地认识到气候变化问题的严重性，并积极应对它。

（2）构架分析的方法。作者在这一部分采用了一个与本书研究方法吻合的框架应用程序，它是由 Blackmore & Holmes（2013：42）提出的。在面对一个特定的框架时，分析者可以依次从以下四个问题入手：问题一，这个框架表达了什么价值？问题二，是否有必要对该框架做出反馈？问题三，这个框架是否会被质疑？如果会受到质疑，该如何对它提出质疑？问题四，是否能够（或者是否有必要）构建一个新的框架？但在这之前，分析者首先需要识别出源框架（source frame）和目标域（target domain）。这里的源框架是指受众者在听到触发词后，对某一生活领域产生的想法，这个领域是与目标域不同的；目标域则是人们所谈论的一般领域。

如果分析者能完成对上面这四个问题的有效回答，那就能够在这个框架上真正贡献出自己的力量。作者在这个部分举出的例子主要有："红带子挑战"（The Red Tape Challenge）倡议框架、国际发展相关的框架、环境问题和社会问题的框架，等等。通过大量的例子，作者想要表达的是生态语言学在这些框架中的应用情况，生态语言学研究者要以影响决策为导向，从生态的视角审视这些框架，对不合理的框架探索出一个能够保护我们赖以生存的生态系统的可替代性框架。

这里我们来看其中的一个例子："自然是一种资源"的构架。首先，这句话的源框架是一个资源框架，目标域是"自然"，书中这个构架的触发词包括：资源、资本，等等。这个框架的意思是把自然标记成一种资源，这样的做法会使得自然在某种程度上被剥削和利用。所以这个构架存在很大的问题，与本书的生态哲学观相违背，需要进行抵制。对此，自然文学提出了一种抵制该构架的方式，并努力探索一个更加有益的构架。从本质上看，语言学中的框架就像是建筑框架一样，倘若我们能够将"自然是一种资源"转变为"我们是自然中的一个生命网（web of life）"，那么这个话语结构将会发生根本的变化。

（3）案例："发展"的构架。"发展"这个概念在政治话语中出现得非常普遍，它的构成方式对社会公正以及我们赖以生存的生态系统的良性发展具有重要意义。因此，作者在这个部分的案例中，选择了一系列的政治文件来分析"发展"这个框架的起源、改进和替换，探究是怎样的运作机制让"发展"的构架有着如此巨大的变化。概括来说，该框架的构架在案例里经历了一个循序渐进的过程，从"发展"（development）框架到"公平发展"（equitable development）框架，进而到"可持续发展"（sustainable development）框架，再到"可持续增长"（sustainable growth）框架，最终到"持续增长"（sustained growth）框架。

这个过程被称为"框架链"（frame chaining），我们要在框架建构发展过程中时刻保持头脑清醒。如果某一框架遭到破坏（例如：从"可持续发展"框架到"可持续增长"框架），就要及时根据自己的生态哲学观考虑对该框架进行合理更新；当然，也要恰当地宣传那些与我们生态哲学观相符合的新框架，这样才能从根源上解决问题。

> Frames are mental structures that shape how we see the world. As a result, they shape the goals we seek, the plans we make, the way we act, and what counts as a good or bad outcome of our actions.
>
> (George Lakoff 2014, p. xi)

In an article in *The Guardian* newspaper, various public figures were asked for their views on how to deal with climate change. Caroline Lucas, Green Party MP, gave the following response:

- Instead of treating the climate crisis as an environmental issue, to be dealt with by environment and energy departments alone, we need to *reframe* it as the overwhelming threat to national and global security which it is. (EN1, emphasis added)

In this extract Lucas is explicitly attempting to reframe climate change, using the frame of 'security threat', with all its associations of urgency, military intervention, states of emergency, and temporary cessations of freedoms. This replaces a more docile frame of 'environmental issue', with its association of a diffuse and distant problem to be solved through environmental policies and individual actions like recycling. In the same article, Alan Knight, director of Virgin Earth Challenge, states:

- Let's *reframe* sustainability as the biggest and boldest supply chain challenge yet, to give the 9 billion people we expect to see on the planet quality and sustainable lives. Business is good at giving customers what they want, so let's get on with it. (EN1, emphasis added)

This reframing is very different from that of Lucas. The words 'supply chain', 'business' and 'customer' invoke a commercial frame, with associations of consumers desiring and purchasing products supplied by firms. The two different framings call on different sets of actors to take the lead in solving the problem — in the first case governments and the military, and in the second case, businesses. As Hulme (2009, pp. 266–267) writes:

> Framing climate change as a failure of markets, for example, implies that it is market entrepreneurs, economists and businesses that need to take the lead in 'correcting' the failure. Framing climate change as a challenge to individual and corporate morality, on the other hand, suggests that very different cohorts of actors should be mobilised.

It is not just the participants which are different in the different frames, it is also what they do and how they relate to each other. In other words, different frames tell very different stories about how the world is, or should be in the future.

The concepts of *frame*, *framing* and *reframing* derive from a number of academic disciplines including artificial intelligence (Minsky 1988), sociology (Goffman 1974), linguistics (Tannen 1993) and cognitive science (Lakoff 2014). They are of particular importance to ecolinguistics since the concept of framing is frequently used by organisations and individuals who are working towards social change. A framing approach has been used by the UK government and non-governmental organisations (NGOs) to explore and advise about the communication of biodiversity issues (Lindströ 2019), conservation (Blackmore and Holmes 2013), climate change (Brewer and Lakoff 2008), development (Darnton and Kirk 2011), and a range of other social and ecological issues (Crompton 2010).

The term *frame* is used in a wide variety of ways by academics in different disciplines, by those in the same discipline, and sometimes even by the same author. There are also a number of related terms like 'schemata', 'idealised cognitive models', and 'scripts' which have much the same meaning as 'frame'. The following definitions simplify and bring together a range of definitions and terminology:

A *frame* is a package of knowledge about an area of life.

Framing is a story which uses a package of knowledge about one area of life (a frame) to structure how another area of life is conceptualised.

Reframing is the act of framing a concept in a way that is different from its typical framing in a culture.

The term *frame* in this definition can be understood as 'packages of knowledge, beliefs, and patterns of practice' (Fillmore and Baker 2010, p. 314), 'factual and procedural knowledge' (Darnton and Kirk 2011) and 'structures of ideas that we use to understand the world' (Lakoff and Wehling 2012a, p. 4). So, for example, when people hear the word 'buy' this triggers a commercial transaction frame — a mundane and ordinary package of knowledge about a typical event where a buyer hands over money and receives goods in exchange. The package consists of participants (buyer, seller, goods, price, money), relationships between the participants, and a sequence of typical actions that the participants perform. These frames are cognitive, i.e., in individual people's minds, so may include memories of typical commercial transactions, and emotions associated with them (e.g. pleasure at receiving goods), and they may differ from person to person. However, since people have similar experiences in a community, frames can be shared across a large number of people as part of social cognition.

Framing is when a frame is employed to structure a particular area of life, and occurs when a trigger word is used in describing that area. It is the cognitive imposition of a package of knowledge from one area of life onto another area. As an example, Blackmore and Holmes (2013, p. 15) analysed online materials from conservation charities and found that protecting nature was framed using the commercial transaction frame through the use of trigger words such as 'shopped', 'discounts' and 'customer':

> We were told we could 'save nature' while we shopped, and offered 10% discounts as if the natural world were any other consumer good. We were even called 'valued customers' outright. The transactional frame presented conservation organisations as a business, selling a product (conservation) to a customer (members or the public).

Blackmore and Holms are highly critical of the framing NATURE CONSERVATION IS A COMMERCIAL TRANSACTION, since it reinforces the self-centred, consumerist frames that are implicated in the destruction of nature in the first place.

Reframing provides a new structure for conceptualising an area of life which has standardly been framed in a particular way. In the two examples which opened this chapter, reframing occurs explicitly using the expression 'reframe' — in one case 'we need to reframe it [climate change]' and 'let's reframe sustainability'. However, all that is needed to reframe a concept is writing about it using trigger words that call up the frame in the mind of listeners. As Lakoff (2010, p. 73) puts it, 'words can be chosen to activate desired frames'. For example, 'Gangsta Gardener' Ron Finley reframes gardening during a pandemic from being 'a hobby', with connotations of a trivial way to kill time, to something much more serious, in fact a 'revolution':

- People looked at my garden like 'your little hobby' or something, now people realise this is no damn hobby, this is life and death. This is our revolution ... (ML11)

This reframing occurs through the trigger words 'hobby' and 'revolution' which pull up very different frames, without using the word 'reframing' at all.

Like discourses, frames can be critically analysed with reference to the ecosophy. The framing of gardening as a revolution could be considered beneficial because it encourages people to meet their needs in ways which do not require overconsumption. A less beneficial framing occurs in the 'let's reframe sustainability' quote discussed above. In this quote the director of Virgin Earth Challenge suggested that sustainability should be reframed as a 'supply chain challenge' because 'business is good at giving customers what they want'. The framing SUSTAINABILITY IS A BUSINESS ISSUE could be criticised according to the ecosophy since it does not necessarily work towards a reduction in consumption with corresponding redistribution of wealth. After all, businesses are not good at giving people who have no money what they need, but *are* good at providing the rich with the unnecessary luxuries they desire.

Blackmore and Holmes (2013, p. 42) give a procedure for working with frames which accords strongly with the approach of this book. For a particular frame, the questions to ask are:

What values does the frame embody?
Is a response necessary?
Can the frame be challenged? If so, how?
Can (and should) a new frame be created?

They give the example of the UK Government initiative 'The Red Tape Challenge'. This initiative claims that excess regulations have 'hurt business, doing real damage to our economy', and aims to 'fight back — and free up business and society from the burden of excessive regulation' (PD7). Blackmore and Holmes (2013, p. 43) criticise the framing REGULATION IS A BURDEN because so much of the regulation due to be 'slashed' is environmental regulation, so the framing puts the short-term interests of business ahead of environmental considerations. Blackmore and Holmes suggest using a REGULATIONS ARE GREEN FOUNDATIONS framing instead of 'red tape', with a message along the lines of 'support our green foundations — laws that make sure people, landscapes and wildlife are properly looked after' (Blackmore and Holmes 2013, p. 43).

In a similar way, Darnton and Kirk (2011, p. 8) critically examine frames related to international development, categorising them as 'negative' or 'positive', with the aim of influencing policymakers. An example they give of a negative frame is the moral order frame, 'in which "undeveloped" nations are like backward children who can only grow up (develop) by following the lessons given by "adult" nations higher up the moral order'. More positive framings are, according to Darnton and Kirk, DEVELOPMENT IS FREEDOM and DEVELOPMENT IS RESPONSIBILITY since they do not patronise the so-called 'underdeveloped' countries.

These studies illustrate ecolinguistics in action: they analyse frames and framing which are in common use, find problems with them from an ecological perspective, and search for alternative framings that can encourage people to protect the ecosystems that life depends on. They are also practically orientated in aiming to influence policymaking.

An important report published in 2010 by the World Wide Fund for Nature (WWF) provides a useful way of judging whether frames are beneficial or destructive. The report, *Common Cause: the case for working with our cultural values* (Crompton 2010), was written by linguists and social scientists, and looked into the framing of environmental and social issues. The report warns against reframing altruistic (or 'intrinsic') values such as alleviating poverty with frames that draw on self-centred (or 'extrinsic') values such as economic growth, saving money, or increasing power or status. It describes how 'many environmental campaigns are aimed at motivating individuals to adopt different behaviours through appeals to thrift, financial success, or social status' (p. 20). In doing so, these campaigns may reinforce the values that contributed to environmental destruction in the first place:

> In campaigning on climate change, appeal may be made to opportunities for 'green growth' and increased national economic competitiveness or the need to achieve better domestic energy security ... But there are problems ... increased public pressure for national energy security may lead to increased investment in renewables, and yet it may serve as an argument for investment in oil shale extraction, or oil exploration in environmentally sensitive areas.
>
> (Crompton 2010, p. 20)

Another example of this is when environmental campaigns use the extrinsic value of 'saving money' to encourage people to reduce their carbon emissions. The following example is drawn from a pamphlet produced by CRed, a carbon reduction initiative:

- No cost, just savings! Just unplugging things when you're not using them can help us reach the CRed 60% challenge ... Fit low energy bulbs where you can. For an initial outlay of just £7 for each bulb you will save about 80kg CO_2 and £10 on your electricity bill ... Remember if it reduces the energy you need it will reduce the CO_2 that you are responsible for and it will also make you richer. Just imagine what you could treat yourself to with all that money you won't be spending on your energy! (EN3)

While this gives advice on carbon dioxide reduction, the words 'savings', 'save', 'richer', and 'treat yourself' trigger a consumerist frame, entrenching the extrinsic values of getting richer and spending money on 'treats'. If the reader simply spends the proceeds of more efficient technology on buying things that they would not have bought before, then there may not even be any saving in carbon dioxide emissions. This is known as the rebound effect or Jevon's paradox (Alcott 2005). The *Common Cause* report therefore proposes caution in the selection of frames to ensure that intrinsic goals are high-lighted rather than the kind of extrinsic goals that encourage environmentally destructive behaviour.

Even stronger than 'saving money' through environmental action is 'winning money'. The charity fundraising site *My Trees* uses a lottery frame to encourage people to plant trees, while simultaneously reinforcing a financial focus on getting rich. The following are example statements from the website:

* SAVE TREES WIN PRIZES
* Get rewarded for saving the planet every month!
* £50,000 Monthly Prize. Good Luck!
* Win a whopping £50,000 every month
* Weekend Winners
* Guaranteed Cash Winners — Every Friday afternoon!
* Weekly jackpot £100 Cash prize £10 Cash prize. (ML 22)

The trigger words here are 'win', 'reward', 'prize', and 'jackpot', which are repeated numerous times across the site in an ENVIRONMENTAL ACTION IS GAMBLING framing. This is a *trigger pattern*, where multiple elements of the frame appear together within a single text. The pattern brings to mind the frame of a lottery in a way that is stronger than if it had been just a single trigger word.

The following quotations from a British National Party article are another example of a trigger pattern:

* the British people are the *indigenous, 'first people'* of our islands and are entitled to recognition and respect ...
* immigration stops being about the rights of immigrants and becomes about the *colonisation* and *dispossession* of the *indigenous community*

- *Genocide* — the destruction of *a people* — does not have to involve mass murder. Its evil can also be accomplished through propaganda and social conditioning designed to encourage different populations to mix. (PD16, emphasis added)

The framing uses the word 'British people' in a narrow sense to exclude immigrants and people from ethnic minorities, and then frames this ill-defined group as an oppressed indigenous population. The trigger pattern consists of the words 'indigenous', 'first people', 'a people', 'colonisation', 'dispossession' and 'genocide'. The framing places immigrants and people from ethnic minorities in the role of oppressor and depicts their action as colonising the UK, oppressing 'British people' and threatening to annihilate them as a cultural group. This reverses the polarity of social justice and has the danger of encouraging an inhospitable and dangerous environment for refugees or anyone perceived as not being 'indigenous'.

Importantly, the use of different frames can structure areas of life in quite different ways. To illustrate this with an example, consider the framing CLIMATE CHANGE IS A PROBLEM in the following examples:

- The problem is simple. If we are to hold the rise in global temperatures to 2C above pre-industrial levels — the point at which global damage becomes potentially catastrophic — we have to stop increasing our carbon emissions by the end of this decade, and then reduce them. (EN4)
- The best solution, nearly all scientists agree, would be the simplest: stop burning fossil fuels, which would reduce the amount of carbon we dump into the atmosphere. (EN5)

The words 'problem' in the first example and 'solution' in the second example both trigger the problem frame. This frame has a simple structure — there are two elements, a problem and a solution, and a relationship between them: once the solution has been applied the problem no longer exists. The 'problem' in these examples maps onto 'climate change' and the solutions onto 'stop increasing our carbon emissions' and 'stop burning fossil fuels'. The relationship 'once the solution has been applied the problem no longer exists' *entails* that 'if we stop increasing our carbon emissions or stop burning fossil fuels then climate change no longer exists'.

The framing CLIMATE CHANGE IS A PROBLEM is so pervasive that it could be considered a story we live by. Like all framings, however, it emphasises some aspects while downplaying others. In particular, it can focus attention away from the 'adaptation' principle in the ecosophy of this book. If climate change can be 'solved' then there is no need to create resilient societies which can adapt to the harmful impacts that climate change has already started having. Cachelin *et al.* (2010, p. 671) argue that the problem approach will not result in deeper understanding because 'the false hope of solvable, discrete, problems is soon exhausted by the problem's complexity'. Hulme (2009, p. 326) explicitly rejects the problem frame by stating 'climate change is not a problem that can be solved ... climate change should be seen as an intellectual resource around which our collective and personal identities and projects can form and take shape'. The problem framing remains persistent, however, even though we are already locked into significant climate change because of previous emissions, and drastic cuts of emissions to near zero are very unlikely in the time available. What is starting to happen is simply that the 'solution' is being changed from reducing emissions to geoengineering the planet through interventions such as mirrors in space, which keeps the problem framing alive (Nerlich and Jaspal 2012, p. 134).

John Michael Greer reframes climate change and other overarching issues such as peak oil in a different way, as 'predicaments':

- many things we've conceptualised as problems are actually predicaments ... The difference is that a problem calls for a solution; the only question is whether one can be found and made to work, and once this is done, the problem is solved. A predicament, by contrast, has no solution. Faced with a predicament, people come up with responses. (EN6:22)

The predicament frame, like the problem frame, has two elements: a 'predicament' and 'a response'. The relationship between the elements is different though: people do the best they can to make the most of the situation they are in, but the predicament itself does not and cannot disappear. If climate change or other issues like peak oil are treated as predicaments rather than a problem to be solved, then efforts to deal with them will be very different. Changing the framing of a concept therefore changes the entire way that the concept is structured in the minds of readers/listeners. Albert Bates uses a PEAK OIL IS A PREDICAMENT framing in the following extract:

- peak oil is an opportunity to pause, to think through our present course, and to adjust to a saner path for the future. We had best face facts: we really have no choice. Peak oil is a horrible predicament. It is also a wonderful opportunity to do a lot better. Let's not squander this moment. (EN7:197)

Here the 'predicament' is mapped onto peak oil, and the 'response' is mapped onto a wide range of actions which are described throughout Bate's book: saving water, generating energy, growing food, storing food, changing needs, doing less while living better, and rebuilding civilisation. For peak oil, the 'predicament' frame may be preferable to the problem frame since if peak oil is seen as a problem then a 'solution' might be sought in new sources of fossil fuels such as tar sands or fracking which are ecologically damaging and only temporary.

The predicament frame fits with the adaptation principle of the ecosophy since it emphasises adaptation and responding to the inevitable disruption that climate change and peak oil will cause humans. A more pessimistic frame than predicament is the 'tragic apocalyptical' frame, where nothing can be done at all and life as we know it will end. Foust and O'Shannon Murphy (2009, p. 151) define the 'tragic apocalyptical' frame as 'a linear temporality emphasizing a catastrophic end-point that is more or less outside the purview of human agency', and show that it frequently appears in US newspapers. This frame only has one element — an apocalypse, with no solution or response required except perhaps resignation. If it is mapped onto climate change then it may make action to mitigate the impact of climate change, adapt to inevitable change, or create more resilient communities appear pointless.

Analysing framing from an ecolinguistic perspective firstly requires identification of the source frame and the target domain. The target domain is the general area being talked about, while the source frame is a different area of life that is brought to mind through trigger words. To illustrate this by example, consider the following ways that nature is referred to in ecosystem assessment reports (labelled EA1-6 — see appendix for details of the sources):

- natural capital ... which comprises sub-soil assets, abiotic flows and ecosystem capital. (EA5:7)
- stocks of natural ecosystem resources. (EA4:4)
- biodiversity and other ecological resources. (EA3:1)
- trade in commodities such as grain, fish, and timber. (EA1:59)

The *source frame* being used here is clearly a resource frame, which is triggered by the words 'capital', 'stocks', 'resources', 'commodities' and 'assets'. The *target domain* that is being talked about, however, is nature — biodiversity, soils, fish, animals, forests, seeds, water, etc. There is therefore a framing here of nature is a resource. The structure of the resource frame consists of an owner and an object, with the relationship that the owner has the right to do what he/she wants with the object. The pronoun 'our' in 'our ecological resources' maps the owner onto 'humans', showing ecological systems as belonging to humans rather than to all species who depend on them. The problem with this framing is that, as Schultz (2001, p. 110), points out, 'when something is labelled as a resource, it is implicit that it should or will be used or exploited in some way'.

Raymond *et al.* (2013, p. 536) point out numerous problems with economic framings of nature, including how the framings can favour the status quo, de-emphasise the intrinsic value of species, and fail to incorporate important moral and ethical concerns that humans have for nature. Keulartz (2007, p. 31) describes how economic frames 'view nature as a set of resources with cash value; they have transformed nature into a reflection of the modern corporate state, a chain of factories, and an assembly line'. In general, the resource frame is incompatible with the respect and celebration of the living of all species that is part of the ecosophy of this book.

Economic framings for environmental action can also operate visually. Image 3.1 is a visual framing that is often used in different forms in environmental campaigns. Typically, a tap is depicted as having coins flowing out of it and is accompanied by a message related to saving money by saving water. The coins are an element of the source frame (of finance) and they are mapped onto water, which is an element of the target domain of saving water. The mapping occurs through visual replacement as the coins are placed in a location where water would usually be expected, while the water is removed (Forceville 2016). The problem with equating water with money is that it erases the much more important value of water as the basis of all life. The image may encourage people to turn the tap off, but not to campaign against corporations which harm local communities through excessive water extraction.

IMAGE 3.1   Gold coins fall out of a golden tap.

Nature writing provides a way of resisting the framing NATURE IS A RESOURCE. Richard Mabey, in his book *Nature Cure* (NW5), for example, contains a discussion of swifts which begins with the application of a resource frame:

- And in a view of the world based on 'resource conservation', swifts are almost certainly irrelevant. They are not (yet) endangered. No important predator depends on them ... It would be stretching credulity to suggest that one day they might be the source of drugs against, say, airsickness. (NW5:16)

Mabey then uses the lyrical language of nature writing to resist the framing and express a value for swifts that goes far beyond resources:

- [Swifts] touch and connect with us in deep and subtle ways ... They are part of our myths of spring ... They are the most pure expression of flight ... our twenty-first century equivalent of the Romantics' nightingales — cryptic, rhapsodic, electrifying. (NW5:16)

Descriptions of nature as a resource are so widespread that the framing NATURE IS A RESOURCE could be described as a pervasive story we live by. Resisting this framing and opening up paths towards more beneficial framing is a huge task, but one which ecolinguistics could contribute to through systematic analysis of current framing and the search for new framings to fundamentally restructure how nature is conceived.

IMAGE 3.2 A picture frame

IMAGE 3.3 A building frame. Trengayor wood works

In ordinary language, the noun 'frame' has two main meanings — the border which surrounds a picture (Image 3.2), and the supporting structure which gives a building its shape (Image 3.3). If a picture is placed in a new frame it may change how we regard it (perhaps it seems more grand or ordinary), but the picture itself remains unchanged. However, if the frame of a *building* changes, then the building itself is fundamentally changed. The term 'frame' in linguistics is like the building frame. If we reframe nature from being 'a resource for us to exploit' to being 'a web of life that we are a part of', then this fundamentally changes the structure of the concept.

An example which demonstrates the importance of the two different kinds of framing can be seen in a blog post written by Rob Hopkins entitled 'Might peak oil and climate change outlive their usefulness as framings for Transition?' (EN8). Transition is a movement that Hopkins founded with the twin aims of responding to climate change and creating resilient communities in the face of the end of cheap oil. However, his blog post implies that peak oil and climate change are marginal 'framings' around the concept of Transition. Like a picture that can be separated from its original frame and placed in a new one, the climate change and peak oil frames can be discarded and replaced with something new. Later in the blog post he states that:

- At the moment, the outward focus of Transition Town Totnes's work is more explicitly about economic regeneration and social enterprise, rather than on promoting the issues of peak oil and climate change. We are ... about to start work on an 'Economic Blueprint' for the town ... (EN8)

In selecting these particular words, Hopkins is *reframing* the Transition movement using an economic frame triggered by the terms 'economic', 'regeneration', and 'enterprise'. In the same year, Hopkins put this frame into action in an article for *Permaculture* magazine (EN9), where he stated that Transition 'promotes the idea of "localisation as economic development"'.

However, the sense of framing described in this chapter is different from the frame around a picture. When a target domain is framed using a source frame it takes on the structure of the source frame. Like changing the frame of a building, the target domain has been transformed and is quite different. In this case, changing the frame of Transition fundamentally changes what Transition is. It is not just a marginal difference on the outside of what remains basically the same thing, but instead a new set of participants and relationships between those participants. The change in participants does, in fact, seem to be one of Hopkins's goals:

- Shifting the focus to localization as economic development offers the opportunity for those who felt excluded by the peak oil and climate change focus to step in ... People with great expertise and skills in business and livelihoods are coming on board ... who may well not have done so before. (EN8)

The problem is that there is no guarantee that the new participants, in pursuing 'economic development', will act in ways which reduce consumption, mitigate climate change and create resilient communities. The 'economic development' frame, after all, is strongly tied to economic growth and is widely regarded as having had an ecologically destructive impact on communities around the world. As Sachs (1999, p. 29) writes, 'to be sure, "development" had many effects, but one of the most insidious was the dissolution of cultures that were not built around a frenzy of accumulation'. Clearly, there is a danger the framing could lead to the exact opposite of the aims of the Transition movement. The framing of 'development' has a long and inglorious history which is explored in the next section.

The framing of development

The concept of 'development' is ubiquitous in political discourse, and how it is framed has a significant impact on social justice and the health of the ecosystems that support life. This section draws from a collection of political documents (labelled PD — see Appendix) to explore the origins of the development frame and how it has been transformed and replaced over time to become something very different from how it started.

Manji and O'Coill (2002) trace the origin of the modern development frame to the late 1940s. As African countries were becoming independent, NGOs started to use the term 'underdeveloped' as an alternative to the pejorative concept of 'uncivilised'. The word 'underdeveloped country' triggers a particular frame — a story about the world where some countries are in an inferior state (underdeveloped countries), some are attempting to improve (developing countries), and some have already reached the goal of the ideal state (developed countries). Although 'underdeveloped' sounds less pejorative than 'uncivilised', both frames share part of their structure, as Manji and O'Coill (2002, p. 574) point out:

> It was no longer that Africans were 'uncivilised'. Instead, they were 'underdeveloped'. Either way, the 'civilised' or 'developed' European has a role to play in 'civilising' or 'developing' Africa.

Setting up 'developed' countries as a goal for other countries to head towards is problematic since it encourages increases in consumption in poor countries without corresponding decreases in consumption in rich countries. According to the Happy Planet Index (NEF 2020), many of the countries that have been given the inferior label of 'underdeveloped' actually achieve high wellbeing with low environmental consumption, while many labelled 'developed' have a highly unsustainable ecological footprint as well as low wellbeing. In this case, the developed countries should try to become more like the underdeveloped ones rather than the other way round.

The development frame came to international prominence with the 1949 inaugural address by US President Truman. Truman stated that:

- we must embark on a bold new program for making the benefits of our scientific advances and industrial progress available for the improvement and growth of underdeveloped areas. More than half the people of the world are living in conditions approaching misery. Their food is inadequate. They are victims of disease ... With the cooperation of business, private capital, agriculture, and labour in this country, this program can greatly increase the industrial activity in other nations. (PD1)

This adds detail to the frame, setting up the path from developing to developed country as industrialisation, with the altruistic goal of helping the poor. It also sets up 'business' and 'private capital' as major participants in achieving this goal. Importantly, Truman offers an additional incentive to appeal to those participants:

- Experience shows that our commerce with other countries expands as they progress industrially and economically. Greater production is the key to prosperity and peace. (PD1)

From the start, then, the frame for development has twin goals of expanding commerce for rich countries and helping the poor — both prosperity and peace. As Crompton (2010, p. 20) points out, 'policies aimed at assisting the economic development of developing countries may focus on the imperative to help create new markets for developed country exports'. Interestingly, Truman predicts this danger and tries to counter it with:

• The old imperialism — exploitation for foreign profit — has no place in our plans. (PD1)

However, using this frame can potentially lead to unintended consequences because of an issue described by Lakoff (2014) in his book *Don't Think of an Elephant!*. The expression 'don't think of an elephant!' causes exactly the same response as 'think of an elephant!' because either way the frame for elephant enters the mind of the hearer. Even if it is denied, Truman's words still bring frames of imperialism and exploitation to the mind of hearers and link them with development. Trainer (2011) describes how this ended up as the reality of development:

> Conventional development can be regarded as a *form of plunder*. The Third World *has been developed into* a state whereby its land and labour benefit the rich, not Third World people.

Once it was clear that 'development' was pushing the majority of people in developing countries into poverty by using their resources and labour to make cheap products for export, while a tiny elite of local people became rich and consumed foreign goods, the term 'equitable development' was coined. As Sachs (2010, p. 28) describes:

> Every time in the last thirty years when the destructive effects of development were recognised, the concept was stretched in such a way as to include both injury and therapy. For example, when it became obvious, around 1970, that the pursuit of development actually intensified poverty, the notion of 'equitable development' was invented so as to reconcile the irreconcilable: the creation of poverty with the abolition of poverty.

'Equitable development' is a *frame modification*, which can be defined as modification of an existing frame to create a new frame that carries some of the structure and characteristics of the old one but also some differences. In this case, the frame modification occurs through the addition of an adjectival *modifier* to the primary trigger word.

This particular frame modification did not last, however, since by the 1980s it became clear that 'equitable development' was not equitable across generations. Development (whether equitable or not) was leading to massively depleted resources and damaged ecosystems, leaving a legacy of destruction for future generations. A new frame modification was therefore employed and 'sustainable development' was brought into being by the influential Brundtland report:

- Sustainable development is development that meets the needs of the present without compromising the ability of future generations to meet their own needs. There are two concepts: needs, in particular the essential needs of the world's poor, to which overriding priority should be given [and environmental limits] (PD2)

Although frequently criticised for providing 'false hope for belief in the myth that "we can have our cake and eat it too"' (Romaine 1996, p. 176), Brundtland's frame for sustainable development still prioritises the altruistic goal of helping the poor and brings in the concepts of environmental limits.

However, a significant shifting of frames is visible in the UK government's *Mainstreaming sustainable development* document (PD4). The document starts with the sustainable development frame stating that the 'government is committed to sustainable development' (p. 1) but then on page 4 the frame shifts to 'sustainable growth':

- The UK Government is committed to sustainable growth, economically and environmentally, and there are many opportunities for UK businesses in moving to a green economy ... Government will seek to maximise economic growth, whilst decoupling it from impacts on the environment. (PD4)

Within the 'sustainable growth' frame, developing countries and the billion people living in poverty play no part at all, and instead the aim is to 'maximise economic growth' in already rich countries. This is a major semantic change, since it moves from sustainable development as an attempt to bring developing countries out of poverty without destroying the environment, to an attempt to increase economic growth in rich countries which are already overconsuming resources.

It is only a small step from 'sustainable growth' to a 'sustained growth' frame. A UK government report states that:

- With many key natural resources and ecosystems services scarce or under pressure, achieving sustained economic growth will require absolute decoupling of the production of goods and services from their environmental impacts. (PD5)

While this is explicitly environmental, the word 'achieving' sets up 'sustained economic growth' as the desired goal. There is nothing within the frame 'sustained growth' itself which considers the environment or poverty in other countries. Perhaps inevitably, the term started to be used without the environmental caveats. The following example is from a UK government report:

- The UK faces a range of challenges as it seeks to return to sustained growth [including] increasing competition from rapidly industrialising economies. (PD6)

There is a progressive change, then, from a 'development' frame, to an 'equitable development' frame to a 'sustainable development' frame, to a 'sustainable growth' frame and ultimately to 'sustained growth'. As the frames change, the focus moves from relieving poverty in poor countries and protecting the environment, to maximising economic growth in rich countries by competing against those poorer countries. This is an example of what can be called *frame chaining* — a series of incremental modifications to a frame which result in a new frame which is significantly different from the original. In this case, the final frame is entirely opposite to the original one.

The report *Transforming our world: the 2030 Agenda for Sustainable Development* (EN2) uses frames from across the troubled historical chain, including 'inclusive growth', 'sustainable growth' and 'sustained growth'. It is a particularly important document since it lays out the 17 Sustainable Development Goals (SDGs), which are now widely used in environmental campaigns, in education, and in corporate sustainability (see Image 3.4).

The report is an example of an ambivalent discourse — there are many aspects which accord with the ecosophy, including gender equality, eliminating poverty and environmental protection. However, the primary framing is economic, as the following examples illustrate:

- We are committed to achieving sustainable development in its three dimensions — *economic*, social and environmental. (EN2:3)

IMAGE 3.4   The United Nations Sustainable Development Goals

- We will seek to build strong *economic* foundations for all our countries. *Sustained, inclusive and sustainable economic growth* is essential for *prosperity*. (EN2:8)
- Private *business* activity, *investment* and *innovation* are major drivers of *productivity*, inclusive *economic growth* and job creation. (EN2:29)
- We will adopt policies which increase *productive capacities, productivity* and productive employment; *financial* inclusion ... sustainable *industrial* development. (EN2:8 — emphasis added in each example)

The economy appears first in the list of the three dimensions — 'economic, social and environmental', and economic trigger words such as 'business', 'innovation', 'economic growth', 'productive capacities', 'financial' and 'industrial' are far more frequent in the document than environmental trigger words. The primary goal is expressed as 'sustained, inclusive and sustainable' *growth* for all countries and *increases* in productive capacity, without a hint that the richer countries may need to drastically reduce their production and consumption to protect the environment and allow poorer countries to meet their needs.

The icon for goal 8, *Decent Work and Economic Growth*, depicts the goal of economic growth visually with a line which goes up and down before shooting upwards at a steep angle (Image 3.5). This is a *vector* (Kress and van Leeuwen 2006, p. 42) — a line with a direction that conveys a particular narrative. In this case the narrative is that the goal is of unlimited growth going on into the future rather than a flattening or reduction in growth for countries which are already overconsuming. As Hickel (2015) describes:

IMAGE 3.5　Goal 8 of the United Nations Sustainable Development Goals

the goals are not only a missed opportunity, they are actively dangerous: they lock in the global development agenda for the next 15 years around a failing economic model that requires urgent and deep structural changes ... the core of the SDG programme for development and poverty reduction relies precisely on the old model of industrial growth — ever-increasing levels of extraction, production, and consumption.

Countering the tendency for sustainability framing to quickly slide into profit, wealth and economic growth even for the richest requires critical awareness of how frames structure concepts, and the exercise of caution when attempts are made to reframe intrinsic values into extrinsic values. If frames become corrupted, then it becomes necessary to resist them and consider introducing new frames which better accord with the ecosophy.

Greta Thunberg resists economic growth framings by shifting the frame from *growing* to *moving* and then changing the goal to stopping:

• You only speak of a green eternal economic growth because you are scared of being unpopular. You only talk about moving forward with the same bad ideas that got us into this mess, even when the only sensible thing to do is to pull the emergency brake. (EN 27)

David Selby (2008) provides a more direct opposite of growth in promoting a frame of 'sustainable contraction'. As rich countries contract their economies, either willingly in an effort to mitigate ecological destruction, or unwillingly as a consequence of it, then 'sustainable contraction' means shrinking the economy in a way that protects jobs and preserves people's wellbeing.

James Lovelock (2006) goes one step further with the concept of 'sustainable retreat': 'It is much too late for sustainable development; what we need is sustainable retreat.' Swapping a 'development' frame for a 'retreat' frame calls for a very different response. Rather than a focus on economic growth with a mild concern for natural resources, the focus becomes resilience and drastic action to protect the systems that life depends on:

- we need most of all to renew that love and empathy that we lost when we began our love affair with city life ... our goal should be the cessation of fossil-fuel consumption as quickly as possible, and there must be no more natural-habitat destruction anywhere.

Some of Lovelock's proposals, such as extensive use of nuclear power to desalinate water and synthesise food, may be controversial, but the reframing of 'sustainable retreat' at least draws attention to the impossibility of development in overconsuming countries in the face of ecological destruction.

In general, there seems to be a tendency for frames which originate in altruistic attempts to make the world a better place to be modified towards more extrinsic efforts towards self-enrichment and profit. This is partly through the reinterpretation of frames by powerful forces, for example when 'sustainable development' is appropriated by rich countries and used to mean maximising their own economic growth. It also occurs when well-intentioned organisations reframe their activities in more extrinsic terms in order to win funding or support from powerful forces. While this may be justified as necessary in order to have more influence in the world, it is self-defeating if that influence becomes so distorted that it achieves the opposite of the original intention. It is important, therefore, to be constantly aware of the tendency for frames to become corrupted by extrinsic forces, and, when necessary, promote new frames which refocus on the original intentions and goals.

理论延伸

我们曾提出生态语言学除了"豪根模式"和"韩礼德模式"，还应该有一个"认知模式"，它是从认知语言学的理论视角出发的研究模式（黄国文，2017，2018）。王馥芳（2017）也进一步强调，认知语言学和生态语言学是可以相互借鉴的，认知语言学能够为生态语言学提供相应的理论基础和分析工具。其中，政治生活中的认知框架是认知语言学所探讨的一个重要内容（Lakoff，2004）。这就是本章所运用的框架理论。

框架理论实际上也是多学科或跨学科的研究领域。框架理论最初出现在人类学领域，后来在社会学和心理学领域得以发展（袁红梅、汪少华，2017）。直到20世纪70年代，美国语言学家Charles Fillmore首次将框架作为理论工具引入到语言学研究中来，并逐渐形成了框架语义学理论，探讨语言的意义和理解的一系列问题（Fillmore，1975，1982，1985）。Fillmore（1982：111）给"框架"一词下了一个明确的定义："框架"是一个相互关联的概念系统；如果要对其中任何一个概念加以理解，必须对与这个概念相对应的整个系统进行了解；当概念系统中的某个概念应用在某个话语或语篇时，其他概念会被自动激活。

这里我们看Fillmore列举的一个典型案例——"商务事件"框架（"commercial event" frame）（Fillmore，1977）。首先想象一下动词"buy"（购买）所能够形成的情境。比如：当我们去商店购买某个物品，与店家在该物品的价钱上达成一致之后，我们一般就会成功购买到这个物品。这个过程就由"buy"这个框架激活了其他四个要素："buyer"（买方）、"seller"（卖方）、"goods"（物品）和"money"（金钱）。这个框架可以被称为"（关于）购买（的）框架"，它的重点倾向的是"买方"和"物品"之间的行为，而"卖方"和"金钱"在这个框架中属于背景信息。我们也可以换一个角度来看这个活动——将动词"buy"换成"sell"（出售）。从本质上说，这两个动词形成的情境是相同的，但是它们的关注点不同。"出售的框架"主要关注的是"卖方"和"金钱"之间的行为，而"买方"和"物品"对这个框架而言，就是提供了相应的背景信息。倘若我们再将动词换成"pay"（支付）、"cost"（花费）、"charge"（收取）等相关词汇，还会分别激活"商务事件"框架中的其他方面，完成不同的语义描述。

Fillmore所提出的框架语义学在学界影响很大，因而被Lakoff称之为"框架语义学之父"（Lakoff，2004：121）。基于此，随着认知科学的兴起与发展，21世纪初期，Lakoff结合了认知语言学和神经认知科学的内容，将社会学、新闻传播学、框架语义学等领域的框架概念引入到政治学领域，进一步发展了框架理论（Lakoff，2004，2006，2008）。根据袁红梅和汪少华（2017）的观点，目前国内的框架理论研究仍需要加强其系统性和深入度，同时学科之间的交叉和融合也有待加强。将框架理论研究引入生态语言学领域，既能够推动框架理论的跨学科发展，还能够为生态语言学增添新的理论基础和分析视角。

与框架理论和框架语义学研究相关的内容，读者可重点阅读的论著包括：李福印（2008）、弗里德里希·温格瑞尔和汉斯－尤格·施密特（2009）、陈忠平和白解红（2011）、德克·盖拉茨（2012）、周汶霏和宁继鸣（2015）、袁红梅和汪少华（2017）、张翼（2021）等。此外，认知语言学与生态语言学结合的内容，也可进一步参看王馥芳（2017，2019）、马俊杰（2018）、郑红莲和王馥芳（2019）等文献。

补充文献

陈忠平，白解红 . 2011. 框架、场景与视角：Fillmore 语义理论认知观探源 . 外语教学与研究，（5）：665–675.

德克·盖拉茨 . 2012. 认知语言学基础 . 邵军航，杨波，译 . 上海：上海译文出版社 .

弗里德里希·温格瑞尔，汉斯－尤格·施密特 . 2009. 认知语言学导论（第二版）. 彭利贞，许国萍，赵微，译 . 上海：复旦大学出版社 .

黄国文 . 2017. 从系统功能语言学到生态语言学 . 外语教学，（5）：1–7.

黄国文 . 2018. 导读：生态语言学与生态话语分析 . 外国语言文学，（5）：449–459.

李福印 . 2008. 认知语言学概论 . 北京：北京大学出版社 .

马俊杰 . 2018. 生态语言学研究中的"认知范式". 外国语言文学，（5）：472–481.

王馥芳 . 2017. 生态语言学和认知语言学的相互借鉴 . 中国外语，（5）：47–55.

王馥芳 . 2019. 话语构建的社会认知语言学研究 . 现代外语，（3）：306–315.

袁红梅，汪少华 . 2017. 框架理论研究的发展趋势和前景展望 . 西安外国语大学学报，（4）：18–22，66.

张翼 . 2021. 话语·认知·身份 . 外语研究，（1）：24–28，48.

郑红莲，王馥芳 . 2019. 环境话语构建所隐藏的生态认知问题 . 外语研究，（5）：26–31.

周汶霏，宁继鸣 . 2015. 语言学视域下的框架理论 . 江西社会科学，（3）：102–108.

Blackmore, E. & Holmes, T. (Eds.). 2013. *Common cause for nature: Values and frames in conservation*. Machynlleth: Public Interest Research Centre.

Fillmore, C. 1975. An alternative to checklist theories of meaning. In C. Cogen, H. Thompson, G. Thurgood, K. Whistler & J. Wright (Eds.), *Proceedings of the first annual meeting of the Berkeley Linguistics Society*. Berkeley: University of California Press, 123–131.

Fillmore, C. 1977. Topics in lexical semantics. In R. Cole (Ed.), *Current issues in linguistic theory*. Bloomington: Indiana University Press, 76–138.

Fillmore, C. 1982. Frame semantics. In The Linguistic Society of Korea (Ed.), *Linguistics in the morning calm*. Seoul: Hanshin Publishing Co., 111–137.

Fillmore, C. 1985. Frames and the semantics of understanding. *Quaderni di Semantica*, (6): 222–254.

Lakoff, G. 2004. *Don't think of an elephant!: Know your values and frame the debate: the essential guide for progressives*. White River Junction: Chelsea Green Publishing.

Lakoff, G. 2006. *Whose freedom: The battle over America's most important idea*. New York: Farrar, Straus and Giroux.

Lakoff, G. 2008. *The political mind: Why you can't understand 21st century politics with an 18th century brain*. New York: Viking Press.

4

METAPHORS

章节导读

　　隐喻理论（metaphor theory）和上一章运用的框架理论是有一定联系的，但是二者在研究路径上有区别。隐喻研究的根源可以追溯到亚里士多德（Aristotle）时期；而框架方面的研究是 20 世纪 70 年代在语言学、人工智能和认知科学等领域才开始出现的（Tannen，1993）。本章讨论的是一个分析隐喻和构架的理论机制，并据此分析语篇或话语，以探索生态语言学研究中的隐喻问题。本章的主要内容包括三个部分：（1）理论内涵；（2）隐喻分析的方法；（3）案例："公司是人"的隐喻。

　　（1）理论内涵。首先，本章通过"应对口蹄疫"的例子对比引出了隐喻的概念。作者发现，隐喻和构架的作用方式是一样的，但是隐喻是一种特殊的构架。所以，凭借隐喻和框架的这个关系，作者将隐喻的概念表示为：使用某个特定的、具体的、可想象的生活领域框架对另一个完全不同的生活领域进行构建，使得其概念化（*Metaphors* use a frame from a specific, concrete and imaginable area of life to structure how a clearly distinct area of life is conceptualised.）。但如果从认知科学的角度分析，隐喻的概念会有一些不同（Lakoff & Johnson，1999：58）。认知科学领域对隐喻的定义是：由源域到目标域的映射（a mapping from a *source domain* to a *target domain*.）。这个定义中的源域是为目标域提供词汇和结构上的对照领域；而目标域是当前话语中所讨论的问题领域。

　　上述两个隐喻的定义并不矛盾，结合来看，作者将隐喻视为从源框架到目标框架的映射。源框架指的是一个特定的、具体的、可想象的生活领域；目标框架则是与之完全不同的生活领域。实际上这个说法在非隐喻的构架中也是同样适用的。隐喻构架和非隐喻构架在认知作用上是相似的，不过隐喻还具有一些额外的特性。正如 Semino（2008：11）所说的，隐喻的源框架是明确的，也是具体的，它容易看得见、听得清、感受得到，等等，通常和身体的动作有关。其实，在这个过程下，隐喻构建了一种推理模式，作者将其称为"隐喻推理"，主要是基于源框架中提取出的概念结构，并穿插目标域对应的要素，以推理出目标域的结论。

（2）隐喻分析的方法。从生态语言学的角度来分析隐喻，最重要的是以分析者的生态哲学观为基础，考量隐喻的类型，即破坏性隐喻、中性隐喻和有益性隐喻。具体要实现以下四个步骤：第一步，识别源框架和目标域；第二步，通过语篇或话语的线索归纳出源框架中拟映射到目标域的因素；第三步，分析隐喻中潜在的推理模式；第四步，对该隐喻的优缺点进行评价。

作者指出，隐喻的语境很重要，分析者不能过于简单地判断隐喻的类型，而是要依靠各种各样的隐喻去理解人与自然的关系，并为该语篇选择出一种合适的语境隐喻（Raymond *et al.*，2013：542）。作者在这个部分讨论了一组与生态语言学分析最为密切的隐喻内容——"自然"概念的隐喻构建演进。其隐喻内容主要包括："自然是竞争""自然是机器""自然是生物""自然是图书馆""自然是网""自然是一个群落"，等等。这些隐喻的表述都有其特定的框架，前面两个隐喻对自然的破坏性较大；后面几个隐喻相对较好，但仍存在一些缺点。

此外，作者还建议分析者不仅要判断隐喻的类型，还要关注它的活跃性，按照其活跃程度可以划分为：死隐喻（dead metaphor）、生动隐喻（vivid metaphor）和休眠隐喻（sleeping metaphor）。这一点也是非常重要的。

（3）案例："公司是人"的隐喻。在这一部分作者聚焦两方面的内容：第一，探索该隐喻案例活跃程度的各种表现形式；第二，根据自身的生态哲学观判断并分析该隐喻案例的类型。作者在此为这个隐喻话语提供了很多类型的语篇或话语来分析，例如：微观经济学教程话语、法律话语和法律条文、电影话语等。不同案例类型的隐喻话语所表达的"公司是人"的隐喻活跃程度是不一样的，对人与自然环境造成的影响也是不一样的，所以产生了该隐喻的不同类型（破坏性、中性、有益性）。

比如书中分析的加拿大电影《公司》（*The Corporation*）的例子（P92–93）。很明显这个隐喻的源框架是"人"，目标域是"公司"。该电影将公司描述为精神病患者，并通过音乐、视觉资料、字幕、有声语言等方式，将"公司是人"的隐喻生动地体现出来，也就是将源框架和目标域连接起来，并描绘出该隐喻对社会和生态造成的破坏。这里的隐喻潜在的模式是：如果"公司是人（精神病患者）"，那它就具有人格特征，需要对其进行治疗才能使我们更加具有同情心。该电影对这个隐喻的描述由于是多模态的，能给观众呈现不同的模式，并留下深刻的印象，使得这个映射过程变得更加有力；所以这个电影所认为的"公司是人"属于生动隐喻，并且是破坏性隐喻。因此，我们应该探寻新的有益性隐喻对其进行替代，逐渐让替代后的有益性隐喻成为我们信奉和践行的新隐喻。

Researchers in various fields have begun to see the import of metaphorical thought as the key to understanding our universe, and as a means of dealing with it in our ecological praxis.

(Mey 2018, p. 214)

A metaphor, to put it simply, is a story that conceptualises something as if it were something else. Metaphors 'imply an identity between otherwise different things' (Martin 2014, p. 78), or 'work by applying one taken-for-granted field of knowledge and applying it to another' (Chilton and Schäfner 2011, p. 320). However, they form such an important part of cognition and understanding of the world that authors such as Nerlich and Jaspal (2012, p. 143) claim that choosing the wrong metaphor 'may arguably contribute to the extermination of our species'. Likewise, Romaine (1996, p. 192) writes that 'it matters which metaphors we choose to live by. If we choose unwisely or fail to understand their implications, we will die by them.' This chapter develops a single framework for analysing both metaphors and framings, and then applies this framework to a range of texts to explore metaphors relevant to ecolinguistics.

Theories of metaphor and frames have two distinct paths: metaphor has been studied theoretically since at least the time of Aristotle, while 'frame' is a more recent concept arising in linguistics, Artificial Intelligence and cognitive science in the 1970s (Tannen 1993). The two concepts overlap, however, and are frequently used interchangeably. Nerlich *et al.* (2002, p. 93), for example, use the expression 'frames and metaphors' when investigating the construction of foot and mouth disease:

In the face of Foot and Mouth Disease the UK government, the media, and citizens tacitly and almost unconsciously relied on a well-structured network of *frames and metaphors* to conceptualise the problem. [emphasis added]

The authors describe how when the UK experienced a severe outbreak of foot and mouth disease (FMD) in 2001, politicians and the press used words like 'battle', 'enemy', 'defeat', 'combat', 'front line', and 'task force', setting up a metaphor of dealing with fmd is war. This metaphorical construction led to drastic solutions such as the killing and burning of thousands of animals, with severe consequences for animal welfare and the environment: 'Although the war against FMD was metaphoric in nature, its consequences were real and tangible' (Nerlich *et al.* 2002, p. 93). An alternative way of conceptualising FMD would have been to use medical terminology such as 'cure', 'vaccination', 'quarantine', 'illness', 'care', 'recovery', and 'hygiene'. If FMD had been conceptualised in this way, the resulting action may have been very different, for example helping sick animals recover from the infection and develop natural immunity, and vaccinating healthy animals rather than killing them.

Cognitively, what is occurring in these two cases is similar: in one case the concept of FMD is being structured by a war (which has allies, enemies, weapons, killing, etc.), and in the other it is structured by veterinary medicine (where there are vets, patients, drugs, quarantine procedures, etc.). The difference is that veterinary medicine can accommodate FMD directly, so is not a metaphor, whereas conceptualising FMD in terms of war requires an imaginative leap because it is a very different area of life. As Schö (1993, p. 141) puts it:

> What makes the process one of metaphor making, rather than simply of redescribing, is that the new putative description already belongs to what is initially perceived as a different albeit familiar thing.

Metaphor therefore works in the same way as framing, but is a special type of framing since the source frame belongs to a specific and clearly different area of life — often one that we are familiar with from everyday interaction. It is possible to define metaphor in a way which shows the relationship between metaphors and frames:

> *Metaphors* use a frame from a specific, concrete and imaginable area of life to structure how a clearly distinct area of life is conceptualised.

This is somewhat different from the most common way of describing metaphor in cognitive science (Lakoff and Johnson 1999, p. 58), where metaphor is described as a mapping from a *source domain* to a *target domain.* The target domain is the area being talked about, while the source domain is the area that is been drawn on for vocabulary and structure. For example, in LOVE IS A JOURNEY, the target domain of love is talked about using words from the source domain of journey.

However, it is clear that what metaphor theorists refer to as a 'source domain' is actually made up of frames (Sullivan 2013, p. 23). Sullivan shows how a source domain such as 'the body' is made up of frames including exercising, ingestion and observable body parts. In a particular metaphor (e.g. 'mental exercise' or 'digesting an idea') it is the specific frame ('exercise' or 'ingestion') which is structuring the target domain rather than the more abstract source domain of 'the body'. It therefore makes sense to talk of metaphor as a mapping from a *source frame* to a *target domain*, a terminology which can equally be applied to other, non-metaphoric framings. According to the framework used in this book, then, metaphors are a type of framing — one where the source frame is from a specific, concrete and imaginable area of life which is clearly different from the target domain.

A *Guardian* article entitled 'Call climate change what it is: violence' by Rebecca Solnit illustrates the difference between metaphorical and non-metaphorical framings. Solnit writes:

- Climate change is global-scale violence, against places and species as well as against human beings. Once we call it by name, we can start having a real conversation about our priorities and values. Because the revolt against brutality begins with a revolt against the language that hides that brutality. (EN21)

This reframing of climate change from environmental problem to act of violence emphasises the causation of death and harm to people in poor countries by acts of overconsumption in rich ones. The framing is meant quite literally, as can be seen by the expression 'what it is' in the title 'Call climate change *what it is*: violence'. The source frame of violence is large enough to accommodate climate change since violence can be interpreted as acting in ways which physically harm others, even if in this case it is an indirect causation. Likewise, framing climate change as a 'problem', 'predicament', 'moral issue' or 'environmental issue' is not metaphorical since these frames are broad enough to include climate change directly.

On the other hand, framing climate change as 'a rollercoaster' uses a frame which clearly belongs to a specific and very different area. The source frame of 'rollercoaster'is too specific to accept climate change literally. It would be semantically anomalous to say 'Call climate change what it is: a rollercoaster', or 'Climate change is literally a rollercoaster'. Climate change can only be framed *metaphorically* as a rollercoaster, as in the following example from an environmental blog:

- The planet may have reached the peak of the climate change rollercoaster and it may be a fast and unpleasant ride from now on. It may possibly be a ride that we cannot live through. (EN22)

Russill (2010, p. 115) describes a wide range of other metaphors which are used to describe climate change:

Metaphor is ubiquitous in climate discourse. There are hothouses and greenhouses, atmospheric blankets and holes, sinks and drains, flipped and flickering switches, conveyor belts ... and even bungee jumpers attached to speeding rollercoasters.

Perhaps most famously, there is Wally Broecker's warning that the climate is an 'ornery' or 'angry beast', which humans are poking with sticks.

Metaphors such as these structure how climate change is theorised within scientific communities, how it is communicated to the public, and how people conceptualise it in everyday life. Words such as 'blankets', 'switches' and 'rollercoasters' trigger frames which are specific, familiar areas of everyday life, and they are used to structure the vaguer and less well-defined area of climate change.

In general, the source frames used in metaphors are concrete, easy to imagine, see, hear, feel, smell and taste, related to bodily action, and precise rather than vague (Semino 2008, p. 11). Metaphorical and non-metaphorical framings are similar in how they work cognitively, but metaphors have an extra dimension of difference which can make them powerful and vivid ('the climate change time bomb' vs 'the climate change predicament'). In most cases it is clear whether the frame is a 'specific and clearly different area of life' (e.g. climate change is a rollercoaster) or not (e.g. climate change is a problem), but there are some edge cases where the distinction is less clear. The examples above range from the clearest metaphor (e.g. 'angry beast') to more literal framings (e.g. 'sinks' and 'drains').

Importantly, metaphors set up reasoning patterns — what Johnson (1983) calls *metaphorical reasoning* and Martin (2014, p. 78) terms 'analogical reasoning': 'an inductive style of argumentation that works by presenting a particular case as "being like", or sharing features with, another case such that we should react in the same way'. Metaphorical reasoning involves coming to conclusions about the target domain based on concepts that are drawn from the source frame.

To give an example, the following is an extract of a piece written by an unknown author that was circulated widely during the 2020 pandemic lockdown:

- I heard that we are all in the same boat, but it's not like that. We are in the same storm, but not in the same boat. Your ship could be shipwrecked and mine might not be. Or vice versa. For some, quarantine is optimal. A moment of reflection, of re-connection, easy in flip flops, with a cocktail or coffee. For others, this is a desperate financial and family crisis.

The *source frame* is boat journeys, a frame which is made up of *elements* that include boats, passengers, storms and being shipwrecked. The *target domain* is the impact of the coronavirus pandemic. Of key importance is how elements of the source frame *map onto* elements of the target domain. The passengers in the source frame of boat journeys map onto 'we' in the target domain, but clearly that 'we' is split into two groups of people: 'some' and 'others'. The reference to 'cocktails', with its upper-class connotations, is enough to show that the 'some' group are socially advantaged, in opposition to the 'others' group. The boats map onto life situations under quarantine — one of relative comfort and ease and the other of desperate crisis. The shipwreck maps onto the fate of the 'others' group, and not being shipwrecked maps onto the fate of the 'some' group. And, of course, the storm maps onto the pandemic. This is represented in Table 4.1.

The metaphorical reasoning pattern consists of a piece of structure from the source frame (in this case 'People in different boats have different experiences in a storm') being carried over to the target domain. This results in an *entailment*, which is quite simply the structure with the elements replaced by those of the target domain (e.g., 'storm' is replaced by 'the pandemic'). So the metaphor results in a reasoning pattern which conveys the entailment 'People at different levels of social advantage have different experiences in the pandemic', an important message for promoting social justice.

A key question is why the metaphor? Why not just provide the message directly? In this example there are three reasons. The first is intertextuality — clearly, the metaphor is intended to resist those commentators who claim that the pandemic is a great leveller and use the metaphor 'we are all in the same boat'. The extension and contradiction of the metaphor is a way of referring back to those original commentators. The second is emotional impact (or pathos) — a shipwreck in a storm is a powerful image which encourages empathy with those affected most by the pandemic. Thirdly, the metaphor engages the reader by requiring them to do some work to retrieve the intended meaning and bring it into their minds for themselves, which reinforces the message.

TABLE 4.1 Analysis of the framing in 'We are in the same storm, but not in the same boat'

Source frame (boat journey)		Target domain (impact of pandemic)
Element	*maps to*	*Element*
Passenger group one ('some')	→	Socially advantaged people
Passenger group two ('others')	→	Socially disadvantaged people
Boat one	→	Comfortable life situation
Boat two	→	Crisis life situation
Storm	→	The pandemic
No shipwreck (of boat one)	→	Fate of the socially advantaged
Shipwreck (of boat two)	→	Fate of socially disadvantaged
Structure: People in different boats have different experiences in a storm	→	*Entailment:* People at different levels of social advantage have different experiences in the pandemic

In general, analysing metaphor consists of identifying the source frame and target domain, then working out (using textual cues) which elements of the source frame are mapped onto the target domain. It is then possible to work out potential reasoning patterns that could follow from the use of the metaphor and consider their advantages and disadvantages. From an ecolinguistics perspective, what is most important is whether metaphors are destructive, ambivalent or beneficial from the perspective of the ecosophy. Some theorists (Romaine 1996; Goatly 2001; Nerlich and Jaspal 2012) put this quite dramatically in terms of 'metaphors we live by' or 'metaphors we die by'. Raymond *et al.* (2013, p. 537) take a more measured approach, stating that it is necessary to 'systematically consider the merits of different metaphors during environmental decision making'. Certainly, it would be simplistic to say that a particular metaphor is destructive in all situations, since the context of use is important. Raymond *et al.* (2013, p. 542) therefore recommend considering 'multiple metaphors to understand human–environment relationships and adopt an appropriate metaphor to suit the ... context'.

As an example of multiple metaphors, Keulartz (2007, p. 45) criticises the metaphor of 'ecological restoration', which treats nature as a work of art, because it is often unclear what ideal state the ecosystem needs to be restored to. He concludes, however, that the metaphor is suitable for the context of ecosystems which are only slightly degraded, where the state to be restored to is quite clear, but that other metaphors (such as 'ecological health') are more suitable for highly degraded habitats.

The commonest metaphors analysed in ecolinguistics are those which structure our concepts of 'nature'. As Verhagen (2008, p. 1) points out:

> one of the major functions of the new science of ecolinguistics is to contribute to the unmasking of myths, assumptions, and ideologies that underlie ... notions of Nature ... It is particularly in the linguistic device of metaphor that these assumptions are communicated.

One metaphor that is condemned as destructive by Krementsov and Todes (1991) and Larson (2011) is NATURE IS A COMPETITION and its variants such as NATURE IS A BATTLE, NATURE IS A STRUGGLE or NATURE IS A WAR. Krementsov and Todes (1991, p. 71) describe how:

> [Darwin's *Origin of Species*] is permeated by combat imagery — by phrases like the 'great battle of life' and the 'war of nature' ... His metaphor of a struggle for existence drew upon the power of battle images while encompassing the great variety of natural relations.

While Darwin did describe cooperative relationships of mutual benefit between organisms, he did so under the overarching metaphor of struggle, competition for resources and survival of the fittest. Larson (2011, p. 75) describes how this metaphor not only echoed the competitive view of human nature previously espoused by economists such as Adam Smith, but gave it a new legitimacy:

> Once the metaphor was naturalised in this way, people could more easily defend it in the cultural realm: not only is competition found in societies, but we should actively promote it because it is the way the world works — it is natural.

The metaphor of NATURE IS A COMPETITION reinforces the assumption of neo-classical economics that people are inherently selfish and interested only in maximising their personal satisfaction. It downplays the cooperation and working towards mutual benefit that is so important for satisfying needs in ways that preserve the systems that support life. Larson (2011, p. 25) describes both 'progress' and 'competition' as 'powerful, ideological metaphors that justify how we act in relation to the natural world and toward one another. It is thus essential that we rethink them in the interest of long-term socio-ecological sustainability.' He later states that 'by balancing corporate liberalism with a more cooperative worldview, we may set ourselves more firmly on the sustainability path' (Larson 2011, p. 86).

Another metaphor which is widely regarded as destructive is NATURE IS A MACHINE. There are various kinds of machine that nature or the planet are equated with, including a clock, a factory, a computer, or a spaceship. The first problem with the metaphor is that machines consist of an assembly of parts, and can be fixed through repair or replacement of the defective part without having to consider the system as a whole. This allows for misplaced optimism that a techno-fix such as carbon capture and storage, nuclear fusion, hydrogen cars, or geoengineering could solve environmental issues without any change to the larger social and cultural systems which underlie all the issues. Nerlich and Jaspal (2012, p. 137) investigated metaphors of geoengineering that appear in a range of newspapers. They found expressions such as 'turning down the global thermostat', 'fix our atmosphere', 'fixing the climate', 'technological fix', 'toolkit', and 'tool-box', which represent the climate as 'an object, such as a car, that can be fixed or repaired using technological tools to do so ... fixing the climate is framed as easy or routine and within the grasp of scientists and engineers'. By placing scientists and engineers as responsible for finding a solution, the metaphor of NATURE IS A MACHINE potentially absolves the rest of the population from considering the social changes and cultural shifts necessary to adapt to inevitable environmental change and contribute to the preservation of the systems that support life.

Another problem with NATURE IS A MACHINE is that it does nothing to celebrate the lives of the myriad beings who live within, and are part of, nature — they just become components. As Verhagen (2008, p. 11) describes:

Nature as a machine and its variant *Nature as a storehouse* justifies the *exploitative and managerial character* of Western civilisation, making it seem natural, obvious and normal.

The EARTH IS A SPACESHIP metaphor is a form of machine metaphor which has some positive aspects, however, so can be considered an ambivalent metaphor. Like other machine metaphors, 'the technological metaphor of the spaceship, reflect[s] the image of humans as managers and controllers rather than stewards' (Mühlhäsler 2003, p. 180), but it can also highlight environmental limits. The metaphorical reasoning pattern is that *resources are limited in a spaceship*, so *resources are limited on Earth*, and *we depend on a life-support system in a spaceship* so *we depend on ecosystems on Earth*. One of the first uses of this metaphor was Boulding (1966, p. 9) who stated '[Earth is] a single spaceship, without unlimited reservoirs of anything, either for extraction or for pollution'. Romaine (1996, p. 184) describes how the metaphor 'emphasises the fragility of the environment and the precariousness of the human predicament. Life hangs in the balance because it cannot exist outside the protected environment of the ... spaceship'.

One step away from machine metaphors is the NATURE IS AN ORGANISM metaphor, which can also take many forms. Most abstract is the concept of 'ecosystem health', or 'ecosystem medicine'. Ecosystem medicine aims at developing 'a systematic approach to the preventative, diagnostic, and prognostic aspects of ecosystem management' (Rapport *et al.* in Keulartz 2007, p. 36). Potentially, this could lead to a more sophisticated approach to dealing with ecological issues, since organisms exist as systemic wholes with the power to self-heal, as opposed to machines which are assemblages of reparable parts which require intervention to be 'fixed'. As Sahtouris (in Larson 2011, p. 63) points out, 'Was nature at large not likely to be more like us naturally evolved creatures than like our machines?'

The metaphors of ecosystem or planetary health are more likely to generate respect and care than NATURE IS A MACHINE because at least organisms are alive. However, they still hand responsibility for medical care over to experts. In some cases, health metaphors can invoke a fairly simplistic problem/solution frame. Nerlich and Jaspal (2012, p. 139), for example, found the metaphor THE PLANET IS A PATIENT is used to justify a medical geoengineering 'fix', with geo-engineering represented as 'chemotherapy'. This maps climate change onto cancer, the planet onto a cancer patient, geoengineering onto medical intervention, and engineers onto doctors. There is no concrete role in this metaphor for non-experts.

Forencich (1992, p. 142) promotes the use of the same cancer metaphor, but with a different mapping which radically changes the reasoning pattern:

> if the Earth is a living body then what physiological role do humans play? What kind of cells are we? Given the state of the planet and exponential human proliferation, the answer is shocking and unavoidable: cancer.

This maps human beings onto cancer cells, and the patient onto the Earth. Forencich pushes away the most obvious reasoning pattern — that curing cancer consists of killing the cancer cells so therefore people must be killed, as 'not a viable option' (p. 144). Instead, he gives a series of interventions for curing the cancer, such as reducing consumption, redistributing wealth, slowing population growth, behaving like normal parts of the body of the Earth rather than cancer cells, and protecting healthy tissue such as forests. The metaphor encourages urgency — we are experiencing an 'oncological emergency' where the Earth as a whole may die. However, the negative placement of human beings as cancer cells may lead to disregarding people's intrinsic worth, particularly people in parts of the world where population is rising rapidly. It could therefore be considered an ambivalent metaphor, with advantages and disadvantages depending on how the mapping is made.

A more specific instantiation of NATURE IS AN ORGANISM IS NATURE IS A PERSON. James Lovelock, originator of Gaia theory, makes frequent use of this metaphor, for example: 'I often think of Gaia as if she was an old lady of about my age ... she has already lived nearly 88% of her life' (Lovelock 2009, p. 96). Romaine (1996, p. 183) considers the Gaia metaphor to be 'an anthropocentric view because it puts humans at the centre of things', but other analysts are more positive. Verhagen (2008, p. 8) writes:

> *By personifying the earth,* it implies that it has intrinsic value and that its interests as a whole are worthy of human consideration. By thus encouraging *a sense of reverence for life*, it is to be welcomed. [emphasis in original]

The Gaia metaphor is certainly anthropo*morphic*, but could be argued not to be anthropo*centric* since it gives a reason for the existence of forests, plants and nature beyond the narrow utilitarian goal of supporting human lives. Lovelock (2004, p. 109), for instance, describes how:

the natural ecosystems of the earth are not just there for us to take as farmland; they are there to sustain the climate and chemistry of the planet.

Rather than placing humans 'at the centre of things', then, the Gaia metaphor could be seen as placing the organism of the Earth as the centre.

While personification of nature has generally been accepted, the specific gendering of nature as female has proved more controversial because of parallels between the oppression of women by men and the oppression of the Earth by humans. Berman (2001, p. 267) writes:

> The association of women and femininity with Nature in environmental discourse perpetuates patriarchal traditions and domination. It can therefore be seen that uncritical gendering of Nature and the use of the rape metaphor re-creates the dominant ideology of oppression ...

One key criterion for judging metaphors of nature is whether they place humans *within* or *outside of* the natural world. As Cachelin *et al.* (2010, p. 671) write:

> The consistently expressed divide between humans and nature is indicative of the fundamental problem in the metaphors we live by ... if we humans consider ourselves apart from nature, we will not necessarily consider ourselves subject to nature's laws.

The NATURE IS A MACHINE and NATURE IS A STOREHOUSE metaphors create a strong separation of humans and nature — nature is inert and there for human exploitation. Another metaphor which places humans outside nature is NATURE IS A LIBRARY. Väiverronen and Hellsten discuss the following example:

> Conversion of rainforests for other uses has been likened to burning libraries full of volumes that have not even been read. And in reading through a genetic library, it is not just the painstaking mapping of genes that is revealing but elucidation of many varied and surprising interactions between species.
>
> (Murray in Väiverronen and Hellsten 2002, p. 236)

This metaphor maps scientists onto readers and the diverse species of the rainforest onto books. However, the humans are outside the burning library rather than perishing inside it as the systems that support life go up in flames.

A metaphor which does include humans within nature is NATURE IS A WEB. A frequently quoted expression of the metaphor is the following:

- Humankind has not woven the web of life. We are but one thread within it. Whatever we do to the web, we do to ourselves. All things are bound together. All things connect.

This is usually attributed to 19th-century Native American Chief Seattle, although, as Furtwangler (1997) points out, it comes to us only indirectly through recollections of a translated speech. Whatever the origin, the importance of NATURE IS A WEB is that it conveys the metaphorical entailment that 'humans are one part of a wider ecological system and have the responsibility to understand their impacts on the various components of the broader system' (Raymond *et al.* 2013, p. 540). The metaphor is frequently used in popular explanations of ecology, such as the following from a museum:

- Our planet is literally teeming with life. An amazing variety of habitats, people, plants, and animals — everything from penguins to peas and bacteria to buffalo — are all interconnected in a fragile web of life. (EN11)

It would have been possible to represent the 'web' as a web of plants, animals, fungi, etc. without humans, but in this extract 'people' are firmly included in the list.

A similar metaphor is NATURE IS A COMMUNITY, which can be used to place humans within nature as if humans are represented as part of the community. The ecologist Aldo Leopold (1979, p. 203) makes use of the metaphor in his description of a 'land ethic':

> All ethics so far evolved rest upon a single premise: that the individual is a member of a community of interdependent parts. His instincts prompt him to compete for his place in that community, but his ethics prompt him to cooperate ... The land ethic simply enlarges the boundaries of the community to include soils, waters, plants, and animals, or collectively, the land.

It therefore follows that 'a thing is right when it tends to preserve the integrity, stability, and beauty of the biotic community. It is wrong when it tends otherwise' (Leopold 1979, p. 224). Garrard (2012, p. 81), however, criticises this metaphor on the lack of ability to delineate who and what falls within or outside the biotic community: 'If the community cannot be properly delineated, and if the ideal stable condition for it cannot be established, then neither "integrity" not "stability" are the objective criteria we need for moral action.'

Certainly, something more than just this metaphor is needed to guide specific actions, but the metaphor itself at least places humans within nature and provides a moral orientation that extends beyond the human-only world.

Although the majority of ecolinguistic studies of metaphor have focused on the various metaphorical constructions of nature and their advantages and disadvantages, there are metaphors in other areas that are important for ecolinguistics. An example of a destructive metaphor is the frequently used metaphor of ECONOMIC GROWTH IS A TIDE. President Obama used the metaphor in saying that 'the promise of America [is] that our prosperity can, and must be, the tide that lifts every boat; that we rise and fall as one nation' (in Mieder 2009, p. 323). The metaphor has traditionally been used in the form 'a rising tide lifts all boats' to represent economic growth as a solution to the problem of poverty alleviation. Economic growth maps onto the tide, and the fortunes of rich and poor onto boats. A parallel metaphor which has exactly the same metaphoric reasoning behind it is 'a growing cake increases the size of everyone's slice' (to rephrase it in parallel with 'a rising tide lifts all boats'). These metaphors can be seen as destructive metaphors from the perspective of the ecosophy because they attempt to justify unlimited growth in a finite world. Given environmental limits, the economy cannot grow forever, the tide must fall at some point, and the ingredients for the cake will run out, but these entailments from the source frames are not made. The metaphor can be seen as an attempt to distract attention away from the only way to 'lift the boats' of the poor within a finite world, which is redistribution. As Kowalski (2013, p. 79) points out, 'growth frequently becomes a substitute for equality of income and as long as there is growth there is hope, which makes large differences of income tolerable'. The metaphor can be resisted, however, by using it with different metaphorical reasoning, as Stiglitz (2003, p. 78) does in the following highly extended metaphor:

- ... growth need not benefit all. It is not true that 'a rising tide lifts all boats'. Sometimes, a quickly rising tide, especially when accompanied by a storm, dashes weaker boats against the shore, smashing them to smithereens.

A more beneficial metaphor, from the perspective of the ecosophy of this book, is CONSUMERISM IS A DISEASE, which has been explored and promoted in a wide range of TV programmes and books. The most comprehensive treatment so far is in the book *Affluenza: The All-Consuming epidemic* (NE6). The entire book consists of an extended metaphor that starts on page 1 with 'A powerful virus has infected American society, threatening our wallets, our friendship, our communities, and our environment. We call the virus *affluenza*' (NE6:1). The metaphor runs all the way through to the final page, ending with 'affluenza is one disease that we can cure by spending *less* money' (NE6:247). The book gives a definition of affluenza at the start in dictionary format:

- affluenza, n. a painful, contagious, socially transmitted condition of overload, debt, anxiety and waste resulting from the dogged pursuit of more. (NE6:1)

The source frame for the metaphor is a contagious virus, and the target domain is consumerism. The book is divided into three parts: symptoms, causes, and treatment. Consumerism and its consequences are mapped onto various types of medical symptoms: shopping fever, a rash of bankruptcies, chronic congestion, and an ache for meaning. The cover of the book (Image 4.1) contains a visual metaphor where a couple are shown on a TV screen, their spotted faces representing the source frame of illness. The pile of rubbish that the TV sits on represents the target domain of consumerism. The treatments that the book suggests are primarily personal measures to 'live better on less income' (NE6:174), i.e.,

IMAGE 4.1   Cover of *Affluenza*, Berrett-Koehler publishers

discover more meaningful, fulfilled lives by earning and consuming less. The measures include voluntary simplicity, connecting with nature, being creative, spending time with people and community, and reducing transport needs. The measures also extend to social and political action, with a range of 'political prescriptions' such as campaigning for reducing working hours, redirecting inappropriate government subsidies, and generating new ideas about economic growth. The metaphor is a powerful way of resisting the construction of the self-centred consumer of neoclassical economics who always wants more of everything. By associating 'the desire for more' with illness, it not only represents consumerism negatively, but also represents a reduction of spending positively by mapping it onto the cure. It can be considered a beneficial metaphor in terms of the ecosophy of this book since it promotes both wellbeing and reduction in consumption.

In addition to how destructive, ambivalent or beneficial metaphors are, there is also the question of how active the metaphor is — if it is a dead metaphor it is unlikely to have much impact, whereas if it conveys a vivid image in the minds of hearers it could have far greater influence (Müller 2008). The following example from Arundhati Roy (2020) is a powerfully vivid metaphor which comes alive by combining numerous trigger words which bring the source frame of a gateway to mind.

- Historically, pandemics have forced humans to break with the past and imagine their world anew. This one is no different. It is a portal, a gateway between one world and the next. We can choose to walk through it, dragging the carcasses of our prejudice and hatred, our avarice, our data banks and dead ideas, our dead rivers and smoky skies behind us. Or we can walk through lightly, with little luggage, ready to imagine another world.

The source frame is triggered by the words 'gateway', 'portal', 'walk through', and 'luggage'. This creates a strong image of people (which maps to 'we') walking from one side (which maps to 'one world') to the other ('the next' world), dragging their luggage (which maps to hatred, environmental destruction and everything that is wrong with current society). The word 'drag' here is important because it represents the luggage as something inconvenient. In fact, the luggage is a 'carcass', a mixed metaphor using a different source frame which makes it highly unpleasant. The vividness of the metaphor provides strong encouragement to rethink post-pandemic society.

Between 'dead' and 'vivid', however, are metaphors which are 'sleeping'. Although these metaphors often go unnoticed they can be of great importance if they are pervasive metaphors that are standardly used to think about areas of life — the 'metaphors we live by'. Investigating the vividness of metaphors requires more detailed study of their use both generally in society and in specific contexts. The next section analyses one metaphor that is particularly important for ecolinguistics, THE CORPORATION IS A PERSON, tracing the metaphor in its dead, sleeping and vivid forms, and examining whether it is destructive or beneficial according to the ecosophy.

The CORPORATION IS A PERSON metaphor

The word 'corporation' already contains the metaphor of THE CORPORATION IS A PERSON through its derivation. The word comes from the Latin *corporare*, which means 'form into a body', which in turn comes from 'corpus', which has a range of meanings including body, flesh or person. This is a dead metaphor, of course, since speakers are unlikely to know the etymology, and even if they did they were unlikely to bring it to bear in understanding the term. If that were the only way the metaphor appeared then it would be of little interest to ecolinguistics. Much more important is how corporations are talked about in ways that make them appear to act like people. The following example, from the microeconomics textbook ET1 (first discussed in Chapter 2) places 'firms' as one of the 'economic units' it describes:

- Microeconomics deals with the behaviour of individual economic units. These units include consumers, workers, investors, owners of land, business firms ... (ET1:3)

This is an example of *hyponymy*, where the meanings of the specific words 'consumers', 'workers', 'investors', 'owners' and 'firms' are included within the meaning of the more general term 'economic unit'. Fairclough (2003, p. 101) describes how hyponymy can set up equivalencies between words which would not normally be seen as equivalent. In the example above, 'firms' are represented as being equivalent to 'workers', 'investors' and 'owners' in as much as all are 'economic units'. The textbook ET2 similarly uses hyponymy to place firms and people side by side as hyponyms of the general term 'individual agents': 'individual agents, be they actual people, families, capitalist firms, cooperative or state-owned enterprises ...' (ET2:4).

The same textbook positions firms as Sensers of mental processes, a slot usually taken up by humans, endowing corporations with a human-like ability to 'seek', 'consider', 'choose', 'wish', 'select', 'try' or 'determine'. In the following examples, corporations are the Sensers of various processes that have been emphasised in italics:

- [The corporation is] *seeking* to minimise the inputs used for any output. (ET2:175)
- [The corporation is] *considering* entering the market. (ET2:329)
- [The corporation] *chooses* price rather than output. (ET2:324)

- [Corporations] *wish* to sell X. (ET2:216)
- [Corporations] *select* simple criteria. (ET2:352)
- [Corporations] *try* to maximise their profits. (ET1:5)
- [Corporations] *determine* the best (profit-maximizing) mix. (ET1:7)

These are examples of *metonymy,* where the word 'corporation' is a substitute for the owner, manager or director of the corporation. Lakoff and Johnson (1980, p. 38) describe this kind of metonymy as INSTITUTION FOR PERSON RESPONSIBLE, writing that 'like metaphors, metonymic concepts structure not just our language but our thoughts, attitudes and actions' (p. 39).

When corporations are represented as acting like people, the discourse of neoclassical economics can treat them as having intentions and goals. In the same way that consumers were assumed to have a single-minded goal of seeking their own satisfaction through consuming as much as possible, the discourse sets up 'profit-maximising firms' (ET2:9), or 'firms that pursue ... the maximisation of sales revenue or of revenue per employee' (ET2:9) or firms that aim for 'growth maximisation' (ET5:141). There is only a narrow range of 'personalities' that the discourse of neoclassical economics represents corporations as having, and all are self-centred and focused on extrinsic values such as profit or revenue. If a manager chooses one of these models then the discourse indirectly gives instructions on how to achieve the goals that the discourse sets up. For example, ET5 describes how:

- maximum growth over the next two or three years might be obtained by running factories to absolute maximum capacity ... and backing this up with massive advertising and price cuts. (ET5:142)

If managers put actions like this into practice then the growth-maximising corporation that is described by the discourse could become real, with consequent ecological harm caused by overproduction of unnecessary goods and the advertising and price cuts to encourage people to buy them. While some of the textbooks do consider corporate social responsibility and environmental externalities, in general the discourse of neoclassical economics sets up the corporation as a particular kind of person: one self-centredly seeking to push up profits, sales or growth, whatever the impact on the environment. A danger of representing a corporation as a person who decides things for itself is that it becomes very difficult to locate responsibility for behaviour that damages people's wellbeing and the environment. Yeager (2009, p. 19) describes how 'the foundational concept of criminal responsibility — originally located in the wilful minds of offending individuals — has been broadened and (in cases) even nullified' by considering the corporation as a person.

The metaphor of THE CORPORATION IS A PERSON is subtly conveyed in the discourse of neoclassical economics through hyponymy and metonymy, in ways that readers would be unlikely to notice. It could therefore be considered a sleeping metaphor. There are certain ways, however, that corporations themselves draw on the sleeping metaphor of THE CORPORATION IS A PERSON and bring it to life again. Koller (2009, p. 45) describes how 'corporate brands are cognitively structured by the metaphor BRANDS ARE LIVING ORGANISMS, often specifically BRANDS ARE PEOPLE.' Following the BRANDS ARE PEOPLE metaphor, individual corporations attempt to shape how the personality of the corporation is perceived. According to internal documents analysed by Koller across a very wide range of corporations, the most common characteristics that the corporations attempt to associate with their 'brand person' are: 'innovation, respect, excellence, integrity, performance, trust, teamwork, responsibility, growth ... creativity, competitiveness, transparency, professionalism and fairness' (p. 52). These self-descriptions may serve various functions: describing the reality of what the company is like; presenting an ideal that employees can aim for that is not yet reality; or disguising negative aspects of the corporation to give a false impression to external stakeholders. Naturally, the characteristics are all positive, and there are large advertising budgets to spread them, sometimes through multimodal metaphors where the 'brand person' comes to life as, for example, Ronald McDonald, Joe Camel or the Michelin Man.

The metaphor dramatically comes to life within the legal discourse of corporate lawyers and in legislation itself. The latest version of the Code of Laws of the United States, produced in 2006, codifies the metaphor through its definition of a person:

- Person includes a natural person (including an individual Indian), a corporation, a partnership, an unincorporated association, a trust, or an estate, or any other public or private entity, including a State or local government or an Indian tribe. (PD9:1349)

This is a much more explicit and active use of the metaphor since it directly defines a corporation as a person. Lakoff and Wehling (2012b) describe how:

The Supreme Court is a remarkable institution. By a 5–4 vote, it can decide what metaphors we will live — or die — by. It is time to recognise, and speak regularly of, the Metaphor Power of the Court, the power to make metaphors legally binding. It is an awesome power. This is something the press should be reporting on, legal theorists should be writing about, and all of us should be discussing.

The event in which corporations became legal 'people' is usually identified as a Supreme

Court ruling in 1886 when the Southern Pacific Railroad claimed rights under the 14th Amendment (which proclaimed human rights) on the grounds that it is a person. As John Witt (2011), professor of law and history at Yale Law School, points out:

> The chief justice of the United States Supreme Court, Morrison Waite, stood up in January of 1886 and said what pretty much everybody in the courthouse thought, which was that corporations were persons for the purposes of the 14th Amendment.

The phrase 'what pretty much everybody in the courthouse thought' is significant here, because it shows that it was not a sudden shock decision but a logical consequence of the background sleeping metaphor.

The metaphor, once enshrined in legal code, allowed corporations to use *metaphorical reasoning* (Johnson 1983) along the lines of 'People have a right to privacy. Our corporation is a person. Therefore our corporation has a right to privacy' to gain rights and freedoms that were previously reserved for people. There are many possible entailments which could be drawn from the source frame of 'persons', but clearly entailments which benefit corporations are likely to be vigorously pursued by corporate lawyers, while others, like 'People have responsibilities. Our company is a person. Therefore our company has responsibilities', are less likely to be pursued. In this way, the metaphor is used ideologically to increase corporate power while disguising individual responsibility for ecological damage.

While the reawakening of the metaphor THE CORPORATION IS A PERSON within legal discourse gives it greater power to shape the world we live in, it also opens the metaphor up to resistance: 'when [a] metaphor is exposed as partial or inadequate [it] might then be contested and its accuracy or hidden prejudices laid bare' (Martin 2014, p. 79). This is done powerfully in the Canadian film, *The Corporation* (ML1), which investigates the global harm that large corporations cause.

The film introduces the metaphor by describing the 14th Amendment to the US Constitution which gives rights to people (natural, human people). An interviewee states: 'Corporations come into court and corporation lawyers are very clever and they say "oh, you can't deprive a person of life, liberty or property. We are a person, a corporation is a person"' (ML1:09m21s). This demonstrates the metaphorical reasoning pattern used by lawyers in corporate law discourse.

It is made clear that the filmmakers strongly disapprove of the metaphor of THE CORPORATION IS A PERSON, but they run with it anyway rather than simply rejecting it. The narrator asks the rhetorical question 'Having acquired the legal rights and protections of a "person", the question arises "What kind of person is the corporation?"' (ML1:12m09s);

then, a little later, 'we can analyse [the corporation] like a psychiatrist would analyse a patient' (ML1:18m18s). What follows is a series of case studies of destructive corporate behaviour punctuated by ticks on a list of personality characteristics — 'callous unconcern for the feelings of others', 'deceitfulness', 'incapacity to experience guilt', etc. The grand conclusion comes at 40m33s when psychologist Robert Hare, originator of the checklist, reveals that the corporation is a *psychopath*. While the discourse of neoclassical economics provides a model of the corporation as a narrowly focused profit-maximising person, and the corporate marketers represent corporations as friendly, trustworthy, exciting people, *The Corporation* documentary uses the metaphor to represent the corporation as a psychopath.

The metaphors in the film are particularly vivid because they use more than one *mode* — music, visuals, text-on-screen, and spoken language — to link the source frame and target domain. As Müller (2008, p. 86) describes, metaphors can exist according to a scale of *vitality*, from dead to alive or from sleeping to awake. Since metaphor is a mapping from a source frame to a target domain, the more the source frame and target domain are represented across different modes, the stronger the mapping is likely to become. The film *The Corporation* provides a good illustration of how multiple modes can be combined to create a very vivid metaphor indeed.

In the film, the target domain (the corporation) is represented metonymically through multiple images such as logos, buildings, offices, executives, etc. There is also a musical theme that signifies the corporation — a fast and clear drumbeat conveying efficiency and productivity with high synthesiser sounds conveying modernity and artificiality, over background base tones. The base tones hint at something sinister lurking underneath the light and modern façade. At the same time, multiple expressions spoken by the narrator map the source frame of a person onto the target domain, such as: 'a corporation is a person', or 'imperial steel, along with thousands of other legal persons ... is a member of our society'. Both the source frame and target domain also appear as text-on-screen in the caption 'The corporation: a legal person'. Visually, the source frame of a person is represented by clips of Ronald McDonald smiling, Kellogg's Crackle and Pop characters playing, and the Michelin Man dancing, while the narrator says (at 12m46s) 'the great problem of having corporate citizens is that they aren't like the rest of us ... they have no soul to save and no body to incarcerate'. In a particularly powerful visualisation, an office scene is shown (at 18m18s), with people walking around, swapping papers and looking efficient, overlaid by the corporate theme music. The camera then pulls out and the whole office is shown as being in a box sitting on a psychiatrist's couch with three giant men peering over it and taking notes (Image 4.2). The accompanying narration says 'we can analyse it [the corporation] like a psychiatrist would a patient'. In this way, the source frame (a person) and the target domain (a corporation) are brought together across multiple modes, building up the vitality of the metaphor to very high levels.

IMAGE 4.2   The corporation on the couch, from the documentary film *The Corporation*

Overall, the film effectively resists the metaphor of THE CORPORATION IS A PERSON by bringing it vividly to the attention of viewers with extremely high vitality, and describing the social and ecological harm the metaphor causes. It uses evidence (the leading checklist of psychopathic behaviour) to demonstrate that if the corporation is considered a person then the metaphor THE CORPORATION IS A PSYCHOPATH is an apt way to describe what kind of person it is. If the corporation is a psychopath, it follows that it is in need of treatment to become more altruistic and compassionate, although the film itself does not go on to explore practical ways that the patient could be treated.

The metaphorical granting of personhood to corporations is powerful and dangerous, but it is also possible to use the power of personhood in positive ways. There have been a number of attempts to grant legal personhood to nature, in the form of rivers, ecosystems, or wild rice (*manoomin*), with some success. In 2019, Ohio City voted to give Lake Erie personhood status to protect it from pollution. The New Zealand government passed a law in 2017 changing the legal status of the Whanganui River to 'provide for the river's long-term protection and restoration by making it a person in the eyes of the law' (NZ Government 2017). In 2019, the Yurok Tribe in North America declared rights of personhood for the Klamath River. Geneva Thompson, associate general counsel for the tribe, stated that 'by granting the rights of personhood to the Klamath River, not only does it create laws and legal advocacy routes, but it's also an expression of Yurok values'

(Thompson in A. Smith 2019). Beyond legal issues, recognising the personhood of nature resonates with traditional animistic values of indigenous cultures across the world and has the potential to inspire people to protect ecosystems for the simple reason that it is harder to hurt or damage 'some*one*' than 'some*thing*'.

In general, metaphors in texts can be powerful linguistic devices since they can convey vivid images directly to the minds of readers. Whether these images set up more permanent cognitive patterns in the minds of readers depends on the individual readers, what other metaphors they have been exposed to, and on the prevailing metaphors in the society they are part of. Ecolinguistics can play a role in exposing and questioning the metaphors we live by, searching for novel metaphors which encourage behaviour that protects the ecosystems that support life, and promoting those metaphors so that they can become new metaphors we live by.

理论延伸

传统的隐喻研究早在亚里士多德时期就有一定的关注，但通常将其作为一种修辞手段来使用（参见亚里士多德，1996）。亚里士多德在《诗学》（*Poetics*）中描述了有关"属"和"种"的问题，他说到"把隶属于其他事物的词语选择借来作隐喻（或者以属代种、以种代属、以种代种、进行比较等）"（束定芳，2000；参见赵彦春，2010），这个现象说明了隐喻的替代作用。直到 20 世纪 70 年代末，隐喻研究出现了"认知转向"。1979 年，Ortony 出版了代表性专著《隐喻与思维》（*Metaphor and Thought*）（Steen，2011；参见张松松，2016）。紧接着，Lakoff 和 Johnson 出版了专著《我们赖以生存的隐喻》（*Metaphors We Live By*）（Lakoff & Johnson，1980），将隐喻应用在人类的认知领域，使得认知语言学领域开始研究隐喻问题，隐喻理论也逐渐成为认知语言学最为重要的理论之一。

本章使用的隐喻理论，主要是从认知语言学视角出发的。Lakoff 和 Johnson 强调隐喻是从一个具体的概念域到一个抽象的概念域的映射；隐喻的本质是一种概念结构，注重思维方式和认知手段，而不是语言结构（Lakoff & Johnson，1980；Lakoff，1993；参见李福印，2008：131）。这个"具体的概念域"和"抽象的概念域"分别对应的就是本章中的"源域"（"源框架"）和"目标域"（"目标框架"）。由此可以看出，认知语言学中的隐喻更加关注概念结构，以揭示出概念域之间的隐喻映射，并解释这个隐喻映射是怎样影响人们的思维、认知和行为的，这就是认知语言学中所说的概念隐喻理论。

张松松（2016）将概念隐喻的发展归纳为三个阶段：第一，初期阶段（1980—1993 年），主要论证了隐喻是无处不在的，在我们的日常生活中隐喻也是普遍存在的；

第二，近期阶段（1993—1999 年），概念隐喻理论得到了一定的改良，包括：涉身体验命题和意象图式理论、恒定原则问题、基本隐喻理论等三个方面；第三，21 世纪阶段（1999 年以来），概念隐喻理论进一步整合发展，形成神经隐喻理论。在《我们赖以生存的隐喻》（第二版）中，Lakoff 和 Johnson 指出概念隐喻理论已经在多个方面得到发展，例如：话语分析、语言习得等领域（Lakoff & Johnson，2003：247–248），而不仅仅是该书第一版（Lakoff & Johnson，1980）所说的两个领域——系统多义现象（systematic polysemy）和推理模式概括（generalizations over inference patterns）。

关于隐喻的类型划分，Lakoff & Johnson（1980）将其分为三种类型：方向隐喻（orientational metaphor）、本体隐喻（ontological metaphor）和结构隐喻（structural metaphor）。方向隐喻是一种简单的映射，它将两个概念在空间上联系起来，通过一个（或以上）表达空间的概念（上下、左右、前后等）来描绘另一个概念；本体隐喻为"抽象的概念域"提供一定的描述，使其更易于理解；结构隐喻相对于前两种类型较为复杂，它将"具体的概念域"映射到"抽象的概念域"上，这样就能够通过对"具体的概念域"的理解，更加清晰地明白"抽象的概念域"。这个分类后来得到了 Lakoff & Johnson（2003）的进一步说明，他们指出，所有的隐喻都具有本体性和结构性，且许多隐喻具有方向性，因此隐喻的这三种类型划分是人为的（Lakoff & Johnson，2003：264）。

概念隐喻存在于大量的语言结构中，生态语言学通过对语言结构中的概念隐喻进行研究，能够挖掘人类在该语言内部的认知推理过程，并指出这个过程是如何影响人类行为的以及如何影响生态环境的。到目前为止，国内从生态语言学视角对隐喻问题的研究仍然较少（朱长河，2009；薛亚红，2020），存在较大的研究空间。对隐喻和概念隐喻理论等相关问题感兴趣或有意向从生态语言学视角研究隐喻问题的读者可进一步参看李福印（2008）、朱长河（2009）、德克·盖拉茨（2012）、张松松（2013，2016）、董娟和张德禄（2017）、薛亚红（2020）等论著。

补充文献

德克·盖拉茨 . 2012. 认知语言学基础 . 邵军航，杨波，译 . 上海：上海译文出版社 .

董娟，张德禄 . 2017. 语法隐喻理论再思考——语篇隐喻概念探源 . 现代外语，（3）：293–303.

李福印 . 2008. 认知语言学概论 . 北京：北京大学出版社 .

束定芳 . 2000. 隐喻学研究 . 上海：上海外语教育出版社 .

薛亚红 . 2020. 生态语言学视角的"自然"隐喻研究 . 山东外语教学，（1）：25–32.

亚里士多德 . 1996. 诗学 . 陈中梅，译 . 北京：商务印书馆 .

张松松 . 2013. 当代隐喻理论研究的回顾与分类思考 . 外国语言文学，（3）：145–152.

张松松 . 2016. 关于隐喻理论最新发展的若干问题 . 外语与外语教学，（1）：90–97.

赵彦春 . 2010. 隐喻理论批评之批评 . 外语教学与研究，（6）：418–423.

朱长河 . 2009. 隐喻多样性原则与隐喻研究的生态语言学视角 . 山东外语教学，（2）：102–107.

Lakoff, G. 1993. The contemporary theory of metaphor. In A. Ortony (Ed.), *Metaphor and thought*. Cambridge: Cambridge University Press, 202–251.

Lakoff, G. & Johnson, M. 1980. *Metaphors we live by*. Chicago: University of Chicago Press.

Lakoff, G. & Johnson, M. 1999. *Philosophy in the flesh: The embodied mind and its challenge to western thought*. New York: Basic Books.

Lakoff, G. & Johnson, M. 2003. *Metaphors we live by* (2nd ed.). Chicago: University of Chicago Press.

Raymond, C., Singh, G., Benessaiah, K., Bernhardt, J., Levine, J., Nelson, H., Turner, N., Norton, B., Tam, J. & Chan, K. 2013. Ecosystem services and beyond: Using multiple metaphors to understand human-environment relationships. *BioScience*, (7): 536.

Semino, E. 2008. *Metaphor in discourse*. Cambridge: Cambridge University Press.

Steen, G. 2011. The contemporary theory of metaphor—now new and improved!. *Review of Cognitive Linguistics*, (1): 26–64.

Tannen, D. (Ed.). 1993. *Framing in discourse*. Oxford: Oxford University Press.

5

EVALUATIONS

第 5 章的核心是应用评价框架（appraisal framework）来分析语篇或话语中的评价模式。本章开头首先引入了 Halliday 在 1990 年国际应用语言学会议（International Association of Applied Linguistics）上的一段发言，他在发言中谈到了"语言"与"生态"的问题，提出了应用语言学家也要关注"增长主义"（growthism）的有关内容（Halliday，1990/2003）。本书作者认为，Halliday 对"增长"的描述反映了一种评价模式。因此，本章主要讨论三个模块的内容：（1）理论内涵；（2）评价模式分析的方法；（3）案例："天气"的评价。

（1）理论内涵。评价框架主要关注作者（或说话人）是怎样表达支持或反对、热爱或讨厌、赞美或批评等态度，并探究他们是如何用这种方式影响读者（或听众）的（Martin & White，2005：1）。本章的两个非常关键的术语是"评估"（evaluations）和"评价模式"（appraisal patterns），它们也是生态语言学研究中十分重要的概念。在本书中，评估是关于人们头脑中对某个生活领域是非判断的故事（*Evaluations* are stories in people's minds about whether an area of life is good or bad.）。评价模式是一组语言特征的集合，它们共同体现了某个生活领域是好的还是坏的（*Appraisal patterns* are clusters of linguistic features which come together to represent an area of life as good or bad.）。其中，这组语言特征能够对生活领域做出积极或消极的评价，这里的语言特征被称为评价项（appraisal items）（Martin & White，2005）。

评价模式是一种语言模式，它能够对人们在某个生活领域上的态度和看法产生很大的影响。例如：本章导读第一段提及的有关"增长主义"的例子，如果生活中到处都在表述"经济增长是好事情"的话语，那么就会影响人们对经济增长的判断，这样的理念也会逐渐深入人心进而影响到人们的行为，最终影响到对我们赖以生存的生态系统的判断。

（2）评价模式分析的方法。上面的例子告诉我们，对语言中的评价模式分析有利于揭示出人们头脑中的故事，也就是发现该语言中潜在的评估意义，并对其进行判断（支持、质疑或挑战）。但是面对语言里各种各样的评价模式，想要收集到"有代表性的样本"（representative sample）来分析是比较困难的。本书提出的评价模式分析的方法如下：第一，研究不同话语和不同领域中典型案例的评价模式；第二，根据自己的生态哲学观，判断该评价模式中的评估类型；第三，描述评价模式的运作机制，对有益性评估要发扬，对中性评估作合理改进，对破坏性评估进行抵制，并在必要时发展新的有益性评估进行替代。

生态语言学在此的意义在于，通过分析某种文化里常见的评价模式，提高对破坏性评估的认识，进而寻求新的语言表达来抵制破坏性评估。我们再来看"经济增长是好的"这个例子。根据作者的生态哲学观，它是破坏性话语，在这里也是破坏性评估。作者还通过大量的例子分析了这一话语的负面作用并剖析了它的运作模式。那么，它的有益的可替代性评估可以是什么表达呢？作者从不同的出处为这一话语提出了可替代性的评估，可以用"繁荣是好的""幸福是好的"等有益的评价模式来替换。

其实，自然文学能够为我们提供很多有益的可替代性评估，它会让我们通过欣赏和赞美自然来更幸福地生活。但是，这些作品一般只能受到那些对自然有一定热爱的少部分读者关注，所以将自然文学的评价模式融入我们日常生活的话语中就成为生态语言学研究者的一个重要任务。

（3）案例："天气"的评价。作者以英国2018年的热浪（heatwave）天气现象和结果为例，引出热浪很危险的事实，鼓励人们对气候变化采取行动，降低热浪的危害。具体来说，作者在这一小节的案例中，主要摘取了2018年夏季英国广播公司（BBC）在热浪高峰期间播报的天气预报进行评价。

在英国文化中，天气的话题经常出现在人们日常的交流中。他们在潜意识里将炎热、晴朗的天气视为是好的，通常会以积极的方式进行评价；多雨、潮湿的天气则在潜意识里被视为是不好的，即不晴朗的天气是坏的，一般以消极的方式进行评价。这一评价模式在英国人的意识形态中根深蒂固。不过，热浪天气的危害是实际存在的。因此，"晴朗的天气是好的"（sunny weather is good）这一评价模式就不总是积极的，它明显还具有消极的一面。我们应该客观地对待这个评价模式，为其中的消极部分寻找可替代的有益性评估。作者在此提出，中国山水作家对自然之美的描绘、日本俳句对自然的赏析等语言特征所蕴含的评价模式与本书的生态哲学观是一致的，能够成为"晴朗的天气是好的"这一内容的可替代性评估。

> Appraisal is concerned with evaluation — the kinds of attitudes that are negotiated in a text, the strength of the feelings involved and the ways in which values are sourced and readers aligned.
>
> (Martin and Rose 2007, p. 63)

Michael Halliday's 1990 speech to the International Association of Applied Linguistics (reprinted in Halliday 2001) is often credited with launching ecolinguistics as a recognisable form of the ecological humanities. In the speech there were a number of important observations that were later followed up and developed by the emerging discipline of ecolinguistics. However, there is one key observation that remains to be more fully explored. Halliday (2001, p. 192) describes how a particular newspaper represented a projected increase in air travel as something positive, with expressions like 'a more optimistic outlook includes prolonged air travel expansion driven by continued growth'. He argued that:

> Everything here, and in countless texts repeated daily all around the world, contains a simple message: growth is good. Many is better than few, more is better than less, big is better than small, grow is better than shrink, up is better than down. Gross National Products must go up, standards of living must rise, productivity must increase. But we know that these things can't happen. We are using up ... the fresh water and the agricultural soils that we *can't* live without ... We are destroying many of the other species who form part of the planetary cycle ...

What Halliday is describing can be called an *appraisal pattern* — a linguistic pattern where something is consistently described as positive or negative in texts. Appraisal patterns are of key interest in ecolinguistics because of their power to influence whether people think of an area of life positively or negatively. As Martin and Rose (2007, p. 63) point out, 'appraisal is a huge resource for constructing communities of feeling, and a great deal of it is realised through lexis as well as grammar'.

If inundated with statements that economic growth is good then the message may penetrate deep into people's minds and become a story that they live by. This story, once in their minds, can influence their behaviour and how they treat the systems which support life. In this book the mental models in people's minds about whether something is good or bad are referred to as *evaluations*. The terms can be defined as follows:

Evaluations are stories in people's minds about whether an area of life is good or bad.
Appraisal patterns are clusters of linguistic features which come together to represent

an area of life as good or bad.

Analysing the appraisal patterns in language can reveal the underlying evaluations — the stories in people's minds — and open them up to question and challenge.

There are many linguistic features which can appraise areas of life positively or negatively — what Martin and White (2005) call *appraisal items*. There are explicit appraisal items, such as *good, right, wrong* or *bad*, and implicit expressions which have positive or negative connotations, such as *fresh, natural* or *smart*. A grammatical structure such as 'a threat of X' (e.g. a threat of landslides) is an appraisal item, negatively appraising X. Certain metaphors can also be appraising items. For example, if consumerism is described as an illness, then this automatically triggers a negative appraisal due to world knowledge about the negativity of the source frame of illness.

Words that are morphologically marked with *un-, in-* or *dis-* are frequently appraising items, e.g. *unhappy, unsatis*fied, *unappreciated, untidy, disillusioned, inconsiderate* or *inconvenient*. In most cases, *marked* words (e.g. 'unhappy') are negative and their *unmarked* opposites ('happy') are positive. Even when marking is not morphological, there are numerous pairs of contrasting words which can trigger positive/negative appraisal, such as 'more/less', 'big/small', 'tall/short', 'high/low', 'growing/shrinking', 'up/down', 'ahead/behind' and 'forwards/backwards'. There is nothing intrinsically positive about going forwards, but there is no doubt that things described as 'backward' are being evaluated negatively, and people are praised rather than condemned for 'forward thinking'. Feeling 'up' is better than feeling 'down', and when things 'look up' or 'pick up' that is good rather than bad. Likewise, getting 'more from life' sounds far preferable to getting 'less from life'.

The power of unmarked expressions to trigger positive appraisals is limited, however. When cancer 'grows' or crime figures 'rise' there is certainly no positivity implied. What we can say, however, is that certain words like 'rise', 'more', 'grow' or 'ahead' amplify the positivity of things that are already considered positive, and words like 'lower', 'less', 'shrink' or 'behind' can amplify the negativity of things already thought of as negative.

Alexander (2009, p. 140) describes how positive words can cluster together to have a cumulative effect:

> Purr-words (as non-linguists call them) are positively sounding or euphemistic words ... The use of such words and phrases, and particularly, their tendency to cluster, or their cumulative effect when used often with each other, reflects a self-assured, unquestioning and practically incontestable perspective.

When positive words cluster together like this, they form an appraisal pattern. One example that Alexander gives is the way that Monsanto builds a positive appraisal pattern for genetically modified (GM) crops. The corporation's website does this by putting the positive expressions 'beneficial', 'improve', 'help', 'solutions', 'sharing', 'integrated', 'stewardship' and 'new', next to the terms 'biotech' and 'biotech crops' (pp. 140–143). In other words, it consistently *collocates* its own products with positive terms. Guy Cook (2004) found similar patterns in his detailed analysis of the GM debate. He found that pro-GM voices use expressions with a positive *prosody* (i.e., expressions which tend to be used in positive contexts):

> Innovation, like progress, is a word denoting change but one with a very positive prosody ... Where there are hooray words like 'progress' and 'innovation' there will also be boo words to refer to their opposites. A key boo word in arguments for GM is 'Luddite'.
>
> (Cook 2004, p. 105)

However, the efforts of the biotechnology industry have not yet led to a widespread positive evaluation for GM since there are both positive and negative appraisal patterns circulating in society around this controversial issue. Cook found that opponents of GM built up a negative appraisal pattern through the use of terms like 'Frankenstein foods', 'mutant crops', 'interfering or meddling with nature' and 'unnatural' to represent GM. There are, in general, social struggles going on where different sides use opposing appraisal patterns in order to influence the wider *cultural evaluations* (i.e., evaluations that are widespread in the minds of people across a culture).

Evaluations can be investigated in ecolinguistics using *appraisal theory* (White 2004; Martin and White 2005; Martin and Rose 2007; Salvi and Turnbull 2010). Appraisal theory is concerned with 'how writers/speakers approve and disapprove, enthuse and abhor, applaud and criticise, and with how they position their readers/listeners to do likewise' (Martin and White 2005, p. 1). A key concept is how the patterns of appraisal across a text establish a tone or mood. Martin and Rose (2007, p. 31) call this a 'prosodic pattern of appraisal choices', or, in other words, an appraisal pattern:

> The prosodic pattern of appraisal choices constructs the 'stance' or 'voice' of the appraiser, and this stance or voice defines the kind of community that is being set up around shared values.

The 'community' here consists of the writer and the readers of a specific text, who are being positioned by the text as appraising an area of life either positively or negatively. Readers can, of course, be critical and refuse to accept the appraisal pattern, i.e., not allow it to become an evaluation in their minds that influences their lives. However, those who are undecided may be more receptive to the appraisal pattern and it may play a role in shaping their evaluations. For ecolinguistics, what is important is not just temporary communities formed by specific texts, but the larger communities that are formed by common appraisal patterns that appear in 'countless texts repeated daily all around the world' (to use Halliday's expression referred to above).

While appraisal patterns that run across large numbers of texts within a culture are too widespread to gather a 'representative sample' to analyse, they can be explored through studies of prototypical instances of the pattern across different discourses and areas. The evaluations revealed can then be judged according to the ecosophy of the analyst, and categorised as destructive, ambivalent or beneficial. The aim is to draw attention to potentially damaging evaluations, describe the detailed workings of their associated appraisal patterns, and examine ways that they can be resisted or replaced with more beneficial alternatives.

The *language system* itself gives words 'potential' positivity or negativity, and cultures can take up this potential to different extents and focus it in particular directions. The word 'convenient', for example, has positivity within the language system as the unmarked term of the pair convenient/inconvenient. The evaluation CONVENIENCE IS GOOD is therefore one which would directly align with, and be supported by, the language system. What is important, though, is the extent to which convenience is a pervasive aspirational goal in society, and exactly what is counted as 'convenient'. Cars, for example, are often described positively as 'convenient', but working for years in an unpleasant job to pay for the cost of cars (including insurance, tax, petrol and repairs) is very rarely represented as being 'inconvenient'. There are clearly ecological implications if, due to the prevalence of the cultural evaluation CONVENIENT IS GOOD, environmentally destructive 'labour-saving' devices are being bought without consideration of the labour necessary to pay for them.

Similarly, SUCCESS IS GOOD is an appraisal pattern that directly aligns with the language system, given the positivity of success in contrast to failure, but what matters is how success-oriented a society is, and how success is defined. If a 'successful businessman' is commonly thought of as someone who has a large salary rather than someone who has helped their company become more ethical, then this is clearly a problematic evaluation. The environmental educator David Orr resists the evaluation SUCCESS IS GOOD but not by asserting its opposite, 'success is bad', which would not make sense linguistically. Instead, he describes what is missing from conventional conceptions of success:

- The fact is that the planet does not need more successful people. But it does desperately need more peacemakers, healers, restorers, storytellers and lovers of all kinds. It needs people of moral courage willing to join the fight to make the world habitable and humane. And these qualities have little to do with success as our culture has defined it. (ML16:12)

Another evaluation, PROGRESS IS GOOD, also aligns with the language system because of the metaphor of going forward and the positive associations that forward has in relation to backward. The evaluation becomes problematic if progress is thought of narrowly in terms of innovative new technology based on the latest science. As Larson (2011, p. 65) points out, 'we cannot maintain a faith in scientific progress ... without careful attention to the mixed blessings it often provides'.

The evaluation FAST IS GOOD works with the language system since 'fast' is the unmarked term (in a neutral context we ask 'how fast is this car?' rather than 'how slow is this car?'). FAST IS GOOD is hazardous when it comes to the positive image it gives of fast food, fast cars, fast profits, or other areas where speed takes priority over preserving the ecosystems which support life. The evaluation SLOW IS GOOD, on the other hand, contradicts the negative marking of the term 'slow'. Describing a person or object as 'slow' is usually a negative remark. Establishing SLOW IS GOOD as a cultural evaluation therefore requires extra work to overcome the marking. The Slow Food Movement, established in Italy in 1989, does attempt to do this, and provides important resistance to the ecologically damaging concept of 'fast food'. The Slow Food UK website describes how the movement 'links the pleasure of food with a commitment to community and the environment' (ML14), and contains ways of representing 'slow' that resist its negative marking:

- In the fast modern junk food environment, Slow Food is the voice of calm, reason and quality. We work to promote the greater enjoyment of food through a better understanding of its taste, quality and production.

The pattern in this extract counteracts the positivity of the unmarked terms 'fast' and 'modern' by coordinating them with the negative 'junk', and then associates 'slow' with multiple positive appraising items: 'calm', 'reason', 'quality', 'enjoyment' and 'better'.

In his book *Small Is Beautiful*, E. F. Schumacher attempted a similar turn-around for the word 'small' in order to oppose the prevailing cultural evaluation LARGE IS GOOD:

- For his different purposes man needs many different structures, both small ones and large ones ... Today, we suffer from an almost universal idolatry of gigantism. It is therefore necessary to insist on the virtues of smallness — where this applies. (ML15:49)

Small is the negative, marked term in the language system so requires work to turn it into something positive. In *Small Is Beautiful* Schumacher does this work by extolling the virtue of small in a range of situations. The point is not that LARGE IS GOOD is problematic in itself, but that it is hazardous if it becomes so prevalent a cultural evaluation that it is automatically brought to bear in situations where it is entirely inappropriate. The pattern of LARGE IS GOOD is ecologically damaging at the point when an increase in size (whether of a meal, an intensive farming system, or an economy) consumes extra resources without creating any extra benefits. As Naish (2009) points out in his book *Enough: Breaking Free from the World of Excess*, in many areas of life there is an *optimum* size, a fact that does not sit well with the simplistic cognitive patterns that can only recognise things as positive or negative rather than positive up to a point and negative in excess.

Efforts to turn the evaluation SMALL IS GOOD into a more pervasive cultural evaluation are being continued by the activist Vandana Shiva. Alexander (2009) analyses a key public lecture that Shiva gave as part of the Reith Lectures series. He demonstrates that Shiva consistently gives positivity to the term 'small' through collocating it with terms that are either intrinsically positive or are given positivity by the context of the lecture, including 'biodiversity', 'women', 'farms', 'farmers', 'peasants', 'local', 'cottage industry', 'plants' and 'insects'. Alexander also reveals how Shiva represents 'large' negatively by collocating it with 'industrial monocultures' and 'trading companies'. He concludes that:

> Shiva re-invigorates ... devalued notions like smallness. 'Small farmers' is a positively loaded, affirmative term as used by Shiva. Shiva rewrites and reiterates a counter-current to structural metaphorical thought, namely: SMALL IS GOOD (and by implication LARGE IS BAD).
>
> (Alexander 2009, p. 124)

Eisenstein has an interesting way of working against the cultural evaluation MORE IS GOOD. Rather than arguing for LESS IS GOOD or LESS IS BEAUTIFUL, he runs with MORE IS GOOD while shifting what 'more' refers to:

- I disagree with those environmentalists who say we have to make do with less. In fact, we are going to make do with more: more beauty, more community, more fulfilment, more art, more music, and material objects that are fewer in number but superior in utility and aesthetics. (NE5:28)

Given the complexity of the world, the limited power of human cognition, and the fact that we have to make decisions all the time, it is to be expected that the world gets simplified into positives and negatives, and that certain evaluations of what is good or bad become shared widely across a society. However, there is a danger that the simplification leads to uncritical praise for things which are actually damaging, or have become damaging as the world changes. The clearest example is the evaluation ECONOMIC GROWTH IS GOOD. A paper written by ten distinguished scholars in the journal *Nature* (Costanza *et al.* 2014) describes how the evaluation ECONOMIC GROWTH IS GOOD originated after the Second World War with the institution of Gross Domestic Product (or Gross National Product) as a measure of national progress:

> When GDP was instituted seven decades ago, it was a relevant signpost of progress: increased economic activity was credited with providing employment, income and amenities to reduce social conflict and prevent another world war.
>
> (Costanza *et al.* 2014, p. 284)

They argue that now the world has changed and GDP is a 'misleading measure of national success' which leads to 'growing inequality and the continued destruction of the natural capital on which all life on the planet depends'. In saying this, they echo numerous commentators, such as Ekins *et al.* (1992, p. 61) who stated 'the use of the growth rate of GNP as a sign of being better off is probably the most misleading practice in economics today' and McIntosh (2004, p. 35), who remarked that 'the use of GNP to measure wellbeing is an astonishingly crude yardstick of national accounting'. The danger of a cultural evaluation like ECONOMIC GROWTH IS GOOD is that after it is established and becomes a standard way of evaluating an area of life, the original reasons for why it was established may be forgotten.

To give an example of how economic growth is appraised in newspapers, it is useful to consider the media response to an International Monetary Fund (IMF) announcement which predicted greater economic growth for the UK. ML27 is a corpus of seven articles from seven different newspapers which responded to this news. Within these articles there are a range of linguistic devices which convey positivity. Most obvious are expressions which explicitly express economic growth as positive: 'welcomed', 'good news', 'best', 'improvement', 'far better', 'hails' and 'exceeded expectations'. These are what White (2004, p. 231) calls *attitudinal terms* — 'specific words or fixed phrases which explicitly carry a negative or positive sense ... [which would] still be conveyed even if the wordings were removed from their current context'. Whatever the context, only things the speaker or writer considers good are 'welcomed', 'hailed' or 'exceed expectations'.

Another form of appraisal occurs through expressions of *affect*, which are 'concerned with registering positive and negative feelings' (Martin and White 2005, p. 42). When certain participants are represented as feeling good about economic growth this represents it positively, at least as far as those actors are concerned. The expressions of affect are overwhelmingly positive in the news articles: 'celebrated', 'optimism', 'delight', 'pleasure', 'encouraging', 'pleasing' and 'relief'. These are either attributed to particular public figures or are part of direct quotes. Clearly, the news sources have selected a narrow set of politicians, economists and IMF officials to react to the news, rather than a wider set which might include environmentalists who take a different view of economic growth.

Metaphor provides another source of positive appraisal for economic growth. The following are examples from the news articles of metaphors based on the source frame of a journey or race:

- The latest projection by economists puts Britain ahead of European rivals
- Britain powers ahead of the rest of Europe
- Britain still lags behind the US
- Global growth is expected to increase ... after having been stuck in low gear
- The brakes to the recovery are progressively being loosened
- The United States, UK, Germany and Japan, will actually be ... new locomotives of growth. (all from ML27)

In these examples, economic growth is associated with the positive aspects of the source frame, i.e., movement and speed, while a lack of economic growth is associated with the negative aspects of being stuck, stalled or in low gear. The problem is that a journey has a goal which it is desirable to get to, but unlimited economic growth can only lead, in the end, to ecological destruction.

As the pandemic hit, the evaluation ECONOMIC GROWTH IS GOOD was temporarily set aside in some countries as other priorities took over — saving people's lives, preventing hospitals being overwhelmed and ensuring that people had the basic necessities to live. The danger is that as the virus recedes, the calls will be to go straight back to growth at all costs while ignoring other priorities like ensuring that the Earth remains hospitable to life.

Alongside the key cultural evaluation of ECONOMIC GROWTH IS GOOD there are a number of related evaluations and appraisal patterns. Anything that is associated with economic growth, such as an increase in consumption, retail sales or corporate profits, tends to be appraised positively across a wide range of areas of social life, including the media. On the other hand, red tape, government regulations (including environmental regulations), decreases in consumption, falling retail sales or lower profits attract negative appraisal patterns.

When a company's profits go up, this is almost universally reported positively by the media in line with the cultural evaluation PROFIT IS GOOD, no matter how ecologically damaging or unnecessary the products produced by the company. When the luxury car manufacturer Jaguar made a record profit, the BBC news website reported this with positive appraising items such as 'resurgence', 'increase', 'success', 'fantastic', 'highest', 'achieved', 'benefitting' and 'remarkable' (ML9). There was no countering perspective representing the negative implications of an increase in luxury cars for the environment or social equity. When climate change is reported on, the BBC has been accused of an 'over-diligent search for due impartiality' (Jones in BBC Trust 2011, p. 72) because of the tendency to bring climate change deniers in to 'balance' the voices of scientists; but when it comes to glowing reports of increases in economic growth or profits, there is no search for balance. The cultural evaluation PROFITS ARE GOOD appears to be too entrenched to be noticed or questioned.

The converse of PROFITS ARE GOOD is FALLING PROFITS ARE BAD. When profits at three large retailers (Tesco, Morrisons and M&S) were lower than expected one Christmas, the newspapers reported it with negative appraising items, such as 'appalling', 'slump', 'horror show', 'decline', 'poorer', 'sobering', 'plagued' (*Daily Mail*); 'plunged', 'suffered', 'difficult' (*Independent*); 'fears', 'disastrous', 'turmoil' (*Telegraph*); 'dire', 'headache' (*Guardian*); 'hurt', 'deteriorating', 'disappointed' (*Financial .Times*); 'gloomy', 'worries' (*Reuters*); and 'worst', 'dismal', 'decline' (*Evening Standard*). Just six months before this, there was a heatwave which increased sales of footwear, alcohol, sun cream, meat for barbecues, and hay-fever remedies. Unsurprisingly, this was reported with the unequivocally positive appraisal pattern RETAIL SALES ARE GOOD. The appraising items in newspaper articles about the increased sales included 'highest', 'good news', 'welcome news', 'enjoyed' (*Guardian*); 'boom', 'promising', 'pick-up', 'excellent', 'uplift', 'reward', 'good', 'encouraging' (*BBC*); 'buoyed', 'improvement', 'boosted', 'welcomed' (*Express and Star*); and 'best', 'strongest', 'golden', 'buoyant' (*Telegraph*). This appraisal pattern is potentially confusing because in the environmental sections of newspapers people are told that excessive consumption is threatening the future ability of the planet to support life, and that lower consumption is an ethical imperative. On the other hand, the appraisal patterns in the economics news sections suggest that reduced consumption is a tragedy and increased consumption a triumph.

One role of ecolinguistics is raising awareness of destructive cultural evaluations such as HIGH RETAIL SALES ARE GOOD OR ECONOMIC GROWTH IS GOOD through analysing appraisal patterns that are common within a culture. The other important role of ecolinguistics is to investigate the ways that destructive evaluations are resisted through language. The New

Economics Foundation (in NE3) resists ECONOMIC GROWTH IS GOOD by providing evidence that increases in Gross Domestic Product (GDP) in developing countries have not brought increased levels of happiness or wellbeing, and that economic growth is associated with ecological destruction. They also introduce the term 'uneconomic growth', where 'beyond a certain limit growth becomes uneconomic; in other words, its costs outweigh its benefits' (NE3:6). The morphological marking of 'un' turns the appraisal pattern around — 'uneconomic growth' cannot possibly be something good because of the marking.

Another technique in resisting ECONOMIC GROWTH IS GOOD is to take the key indicator of economic growth (Gross Domestic Product or Gross National Product) and show that it not only includes undesirable things, but also excludes desirable ones. At a speech at the University of Kansas, Senator Robert Kennedy did this in a particularly eloquent way that is worth quoting in full:

- Gross National Product counts air pollution and cigarette advertising, and ambulances to clear our highways of carnage. It counts special locks for our doors and the jails for the people who break them. It counts the destruction of the redwood and the loss of our natural wonder in chaotic sprawl. It counts napalm and counts nuclear warheads and armoured cars for the police to fight the riots in our cities. It counts ... the television programs which glorify violence in order to sell toys to our children. Yet the gross national product does not allow for the health of our children, the quality of their education or the joy of their play. It does not include the beauty of our poetry or the strength of our marriages, the intelligence of our public debate or the integrity of our public officials. It measures neither our wit nor our courage, neither our wisdom nor our learning, neither our compassion nor our devotion to our country, it measures everything in short, except that which makes life worthwhile. And it can tell us everything about America except why we are proud that we are Americans. (NE8)

While the type of language used by Robert Kennedy undermines the cultural evaluation ECONOMIC GROWTH IS GOOD, it does not provide an alternative evaluation. Alternatives have been proposed, however. A book by Tim Jackson can be seen as proposing the alternative evaluation PROSPERITY IS GOOD. At first, this seems remarkably similar to ECONOMIC GROWTH IS GOOD — after all, prosperity is commonly seen as material success and financial flourishing. However, Jackson's book is entitled *Prosperity without Growth* (NE1), and within it he redefines the concept of prosperity:

- For at the end of the day, prosperity goes beyond material pleasures. It transcends material concerns. It resides in the quality of our lives and in the health and happiness of our families. It is present in the strength of our relationships and our trust in the community. It is evidenced by our satisfaction at work and our sense of shared meaning and purpose. It hangs on our potential to participate fully in the life of society. Prosperity consists in our ability to flourish as human beings — within the ecological limits of a finite planet. (NE1:5)

This is strongly aligned with the ecosophy of this book, so PROSPERITY IS GOOD can be considered a beneficial appraisal pattern, although its success in creating a widespread cultural evaluation is dependent on breaking the narrow association of prosperity with financial wealth. It remains vulnerable to reinterpretation along very similar lines to economic growth if it cannot break that association.

An alternative approach is the Kingdom of Bhutan's major efforts to replace the concept of Gross Domestic Product with Gross National Happiness (GNH), as described by the Centre for Bhutan Studies and GNH Research (NE4). The evaluation HAPPINESS IS GOOD is one that is already pervasive and ubiquitous — there is no need to do any work at all to promote it. Happiness is also a concept that is less vulnerable to reinterpretation in financial terms. There is a danger, however, that happiness as a goal could be perceived as a selfish pursuit of personal feelings of contentment, along the lines of the consumer in neoclassical economics who seeks to maximise his/her own satisfaction. The Prime Minister of Bhutan explicitly attempts to steer the definition of happiness away from this:

- We have now clearly distinguished the 'happiness' ... in GNH from the fleeting, pleasurable 'feel good' moods so often associated with that term. We know that true abiding happiness cannot exist while others suffer, and comes only from serving others, living in harmony with nature, and realising our innate wisdom. (NE4:7)

This rethinks the concept of happiness by drawing from the traditional other-centred values of Mahayana Buddhism, the national religion of Bhutan. This extended concept of happiness is coded into 33 indicators that are used to define GNH in official documentation (NE4:13). These indicators bear a strong resemblance to Kennedy's list of 'things that make life worthwhile'. They include: 'health', 'education', 'positive emotions', 'cultural participation', 'good governance', 'responsibility to the environment', 'psychological wellbeing' and 'mental health' (NE4:13).

Bhutan is just one country but, as Stiglitz *et al.* (2020) describe, there is a growing global movement to move away from the narrow evaluation GROWTH IS GOOD towards WELLBEING IS GOOD. This new consciousness is slowly finding its way into political discourse. In 2019, Jacinda Ardern, the Prime Minister of New Zealand, declared that:

- We're embedding that notion of making decisions that aren't just about growth for growth's sake, but how are our people faring? How is their overall wellbeing and their mental health? How is our environment doing? These are the measures that will give us a true measure of our success. (PD8)

One way to improve wellbeing and without requiring excess consumption is through direct interaction with local nature. There are, however, a number of cultural evaluations which might limit people's opportunities to spend time in nature. One of these is DARK IS BAD, which may prevent people from enjoying the natural world after sunset. Chris Yates's book *Nightwalk: A Journey to the Heart of Nature* describes how, when walking at night:

- the only birds I saw were owls, but there were all kinds of other creatures, each one casually going about its night-time business, a whole secret world coming alive in the undisturbed dark. (NW8:15)

In the book *Findings* (NW3), Kathleen Jamie explicitly describes the prevailing evaluation DARK IS BAD that is so frequently expressed in the appraisal patterns of literature and everyday conversation in the UK. The following examples drawn from her book *Findings* (NW3) show how she resists the evaluation:

- I'd had a notion to sail by night, to enter into the dark for the love of its textures and wild intimacy. I had been asking around among literary people, readers of books, for instances of dark as natural phenomenon, rather than as cover for all that's wicked, but could find few ... Pity the dark; we're so concerned to overcome and banish it, it's crammed full of all that's devilish, like some grim cupboard under the stairs. But dark is good. (NW3:3)
- I'd wanted dark. Real, natural, starry dark, solstice dark... (NW3:5)
- Some hours out, I saw three brash lights... (NW3:6)
- The natural, courteous dark, was too much maligned. We couldn't see the real dark for the metaphorical dark. Because of the metaphorical dark, the death dark, we were constantly concerned to banish the natural dark. (NW3:10)
- Inside [the cairn] was bright as a tube train, and the effect was brutal. (NW3:14)
- A gleam reflected on the bow rail dazzled us all the way home. (NW3:190)

Jamie uses the negative appraisal items 'wicked', 'devilish', 'grim', and 'death' to illustrate a common way of describing the dark in literature and conceptualising it in everyday life. She rejects the evaluation DARK IS BAD, however, and instead replaces it with

DARK IS GOOD. This is done both explicitly through the words 'dark is good' and through associating the dark with numerous positive appraising items: 'love', 'intimacy', 'natural', 'good', 'courteous', 'real' and 'starry'. Brightness, on the other hand, is associated with the negative appraising items 'brash', 'brutal' and 'dazzled' while the simile 'bright as a tube train' brings connotations of artificiality and noise.

There are many other overlooked or maligned aspects of nature beyond the dark that nature writers can, and have, resisted. Esther Woolfson, for instance, resists the cultural evaluation rats are bad in her book *Field Notes from a Hidden City* (NW7):

- The word 'rat' is in itself enough to bring about extraordinary reactions, shuddering revulsion, distaste, fear and only rarely appreciation of their adaptability, their intelligence, charm or beauty. (NW7:64)
- Intelligent, successful and interesting as rats may be... (NW7:65)
- Admired in some cultures for their qualities, their resourcefulness and success as a species, they are equally reviled for their destructiveness. (NW7:69)

The resistance to RATS ARE BAD begins by bringing the evaluation to the attention of the readers through the negative appraising items 'shuddering revulsion', 'distaste', 'fear', 'reviled' and 'destructiveness'. Woolfson then attempts to replace RATS ARE BAD with the opposite evaluation, RATS ARE GOOD, using the positive appraising items 'appreciation', 'adaptability', intelligence', 'charm', 'beauty', 'successful', 'interesting', 'qualities', 'resourcefulness' and 'success'.

In general, the more that nature writers can resist and replace the cultural evaluations which cause us to disregard or dismiss the natural world around us, the more we can find ways to reach wellbeing through appreciating nature rather than through consumption. The problem with nature writing, however, is that it tends to appear in its own corner of bookshops to be read by those who are already sensitive to the beauty of the natural world. To have a chance of making a difference to prevailing cultural evaluations, the appraisal patterns within nature writing need to be incorporated across a wide range of everyday discourses and conversation patterns. That is a big task, but one that ecolinguistics can contribute to through analysing appraisal patterns to reveal the underlying evaluations, questioning those evaluations, and, where necessary, searching for beneficial alternatives.

Appraisal and the weather

In 2018 there was a heatwave in England which resulted in the deaths of 863 people over the age of 65 (PHE 2018, p. 1). The report by Public Health England which investigated the deaths started with the following warning:

Heatwaves are predicted to increase in frequency and intensity as a result of climate change. The health impacts of these events can be significant, particularly for vulnerable populations.... (PHE 2018, p. 1)

This tells the story that CLIMATE CHANGE CAUSES HEATWAVES and that HEATWAVES ARE DANGEROUS, which combined together have the potential to encourage people to act on climate change to reduce the danger. Unfortunately, though, they run up against what is probably the most entrenched cultural evaluation of all in England, SUNNY WEATHER IS GOOD. When strangers meet on the street the words 'Lovely day, isn't it?' has a very specific meaning — the weather is dry, hot and sunny. A spot of rain and the greeting is 'Miserable day, isn't it?' While a stranger may have very different political or religious views, the one topic that it is safe to assume they will agree on is that hot, sunny weather is good.

The cultural evaluation SUNNY WEATHER IS GOOD also finds its way into weather forecasts, where it sets up a very strong pattern which positively appraises hot, sunny weather, with only occasional exceptions. A heatwave is a time when the weather forecast might be expected to make an exception and draw attention to risk and threat of the heat and the fact that climate change will make heatwaves in the future worse. The transcripts below are extracts from weather forecasts broadcast on BBC television on various days during the height of the heatwave in summer 2018. They have been selected as clear examples of what was a strong pattern that emerged during the coverage:

- The best of the sunny spells are in the south and east
- It's set to remain very warm or hot during the coming week with mostly dry and fine weather continuing
- For this evening we've got some nice sunny spells to round off the day
- Yesterday we had one of the warmest days of the year ... further east the best of the sunshine
- Well it's certainly looking like a super weekend if you're after something dry, sunny and certainly very warm if not hot
- And then a beautiful evening, it's looking stunning, no rain
- On Friday it's a decent start with some good spells of sunshine. (ML10)

Within these are the explicit appraising items 'best' and 'good' as well as the positive attitudinal terms 'nice', 'super', 'stunning', 'fine', 'decent' and 'beautiful'. All these positive terms are attached to 'sunny', 'warm', 'fine', 'hot' or 'dry' weather through collocation in the sentence. The term 'fine' is interesting because it is both a positive attitudinal term and the name of a particular kind of weather at the same time.

The days of searing heat were occasionally relieved with some rain. The following examples from weather forecasts during the heatwave show the response to this change:

- another hot day in the south but always more cloud in the north west with the threat of a few spots of rain
- It's looking fine for many of us but there is still a threat of showers
- We'll see more in the way of cloud building along with the risk of a few showers
- Very hot across this part of the world ... this is where we could see those nasty storms
- Sunday does not look pretty at all, now there are already a few showers just sneaking into the west of the region
- As we go through the day we will notice that cloud will linger, and we could see some outbreaks of patchy rain
- Then we're looking down the barrel of some rain. (ML10)

The first two examples use the word 'threat' ('threat of a few spots of rain' and 'threat of showers'), a term which presupposes that whatever follows it is both dangerous and bad. It is surprising that a few spots of rain are seen as the threat during the heatwave rather than the excess heat, despite the deaths it was causing. The third example uses the word 'risk' in 'risk of a few showers', which also has a presupposition of negativity: in general, there is a 'chance' of good things happening and a 'risk' of bad things. Presupposition is a powerful form of appraisal because unlike a truth claim (e.g., 'Actually, spots of rain are dangerous'), the danger of rain is taken as a completely obvious background fact that does not need to be explicitly stated.

Other negative appraising items are the attitudinal terms 'nasty' and 'not pretty', and words with negative prosody: 'linger', 'sneak' and 'outbreaks'. The negative prosody of these words arises from the typical situation of their use, where 'linger' and 'sneak' tend to be used when people are up to no good, and 'outbreak' tends to be used with infectious illness. The final example describes a particularly hot week when rain was forecast for the weekend and states 'we're looking down the barrel of some rain'. This is an extraordinary metaphor because it turns the rain into a gun pointed in our direction at close range, an escalation of the much milder presupposition 'threat'.

These few examples are just part of a larger pattern within the weather forecast which appraises hot, dry, sunny and bright weather positively and all other kinds of weather (misty, cloudy, rainy, overcast, thundery, muggy, showery, damp, breezy, wet, dull, or grey weather) negatively. The pattern seems to express a cultural hygrophobia (fear of moisture) and achluophobia (fear of the dark) as well as a love of heat and sun.

Ideally, those responsible for representations of weather in the media will become aware of the stories that their texts convey, consider them in the context of climate change, and make changes. This is exactly what happened in the case of *The Guardian* newspaper in 2019. Like most media, the way that *The Guardian* represented deadly heatwaves tended to be pictures of happy people out enjoying the sun — a visual appraisal pattern of SUNNY WEATHER IS GOOD. The danger of this kind of imagery is that it might lead to thinking that climate change is good since it brings desired weather. The newspaper stated that 'we need new imagery for new narratives' because science tells a 'sinister story of regular heatwaves and unseasonal weather being a defining indicator of the climate crisis' (Shields 2019). When Australia suffered a terrible drought, the newspaper refrained from images of people sunbathing on beaches or children playing in water fountains; instead, 'the environmental scenes of the scorched landscape were striking, as were the suffering animals, but the portraits and stories of the people battling the catastrophe really anchored the piece and drove the level of engagement' (Shields 2019).

Aside from drawing attention away from the dangers of climate change, the main problem with the cultural evaluation SUNNY WEATHER IS GOOD and its converse, NOT SUNNY WEATHER IS BAD, is that it can manufacture dissatisfaction. Despite the occasional heatwave, there are few hot, sunny days in the UK, so most days in the year are therefore deemed bad weather. Ingold (2010) describes how we are not 'exhabitants' living *on* the hard rock of Planet Earth, but 'inhabitants' living *in* what he calls the 'weather-world'. If we do not like the weather for most of the year then we do not like our home. Rather than enjoying their weather-world, then, the evaluation could encourage people to banish the weather 'to the exterior of their air-conditioned, temperature-regulated, artificially lit, and glass-enclosed buildings' (Ingold 2010, p. 131) and entertain themselves with consumer gadgets and advertisement-full media.

The dissatisfaction with everyday weather might also encourage people to fly abroad on low-cost airlines to chase the Sun. Travel companies and newspapers are quick to take advantage of (and further entrench) the evaluation SUNNY WEATHER IS GOOD in order to encourage them to do so. The following examples are extracts from a corpus of travel agent advertisements and newspaper travel articles:

- Fed up with wet summers and ice-cold winters? Take a break from the traditional British weather and get away to one of our destinations for all-year-round sunshine holidays.
- Fed up with wintry Britain? Here are ten destinations where you're likely to find more pleasant temperatures.
- As the cold, dark nights drag on, summer seems further away than ever ... but in Orlando fun-in-the-sun never stops.

- Autumn is a fantastic time to jet off somewhere sunny. You don't need to go far to find better weather than British clouds.

- Winter in the UK can be a depressing experience; freezing temperatures, grey skies and sleet that can keep you indoors for days. (ML3)

The pattern is clear: weather in the UK is represented negatively while the weather of the holiday destination is represented positively. The range of appraising items includes: (a) rhetorical questions — just asking whether the reader is 'fed up' presupposes that they are likely to be; (b) using the comparatives 'more pleasant' and 'better' which logically imply that UK weather is 'less pleasant' and 'worse'; and (c) using words with negative prosody — 'cold', 'dark', 'drag', 'depressing', 'freezing' and 'grey' about the weather in the UK. This contrasts with the positive appraising items 'fun', 'pleasant' and 'fantastic' which describe the weather in the destination. Overall, they set up a problem frame (UK weather) and provide the solution of jetting off to the Sun, rather than more obvious and environmentally friendly solutions such as wearing a coat.

If people in the UK could appreciate a wider variety of weathers they may be able to find health, mental health and wellbeing through exploring local nature all year round rather than flying off for short, environmentally damaging holidays in sunny countries or staying indoors being entertained by consumer goods. Clearly, there are weathers that have a genuinely negative impact on people's lives through damaging their property, livelihood, health or feelings of comfort. However, there are also a wide range of other weathers that are not damaging and could be explored, appreciated and enjoyed if they were not cognitively dismissed by the NOT SUNNY WEATHER IS BAD evaluation.

In searching for forms of language that positively appraise a wider range of weathers it is useful to look at traditional cultures across the world. Robert Macfarlane (2013, p. 32) describes Chinese Shan-Shui writers who did not talk of the 'threat' of mist, but valued mist and other weathers as a manifestation of the beauty of nature along with egrets and bamboo groves:

[Shan-Shui writers] explored their mountains in what they called the 'dragon-suns' of summer, in the long winds of winter and the blossom storms of late spring. They wrote of the cool mist that settled into valleys at dawn, of bamboo groves into which green light fell, and of how thousands of snowy egrets would take off from lakes like lifting blizzards.

Japanese haiku poetry about nature is similarly an example of a genre of writing that expresses appreciation of a great range of weathers from cool breezes in summer to the snow of winter, and particularly of the rain. The examples below of haiku, together with the English translations, are drawn from anthologies of classical haiku (HK1–HK6, see appendix for details).

- 夜はうれしく／昼は静かや／春の雨

  Joyful at night / tranquil during the day / spring rain. (Chora HK4:18)
- おもしろし／雪にやならん／冬の雨

  What fun / it may change into snow / the winter rain. (Bashō HK1:90)
- 唇に／墨つく児の／すずみかな

  Traces of school ink / on his lips, a child enjoys / the evening cool. (Senna HK2:22)
- 山陰や／涼みがてらの／わらぢ茶屋

  Mountain shade / while enjoying the cool air / straw sandals, teahouse. (Issa HK6)

IMAGE 5.1　A little cuckoo across a hydrangea by Yosa Buson

- 五月雨／ある夜ひそかに／松の月

  Summer rains / secretly one evening / moon in the pines. (Ryōta HK1:39)
- 春なれや／名もなき山の／朝霞

  Spring is here / morning mist / on a nameless mountain. (Bashō HK4:16)
- 梅の樹の／かたちづくりす／初時雨

  Sculpting the shape / of the plum tree / first winter rain. (Kitō HK1:91)
- 三たびないて／聞こえずなりぬ／雨の鹿

  Calling three times / then no more to be heard / the deer in the rain. (Buson HK3:23)

- 春雨や/木の間に見ゆる/海の道

  Spring rain / visible through the trees / a path to the sea. (Otsuni HK4:25)

The first two of these explicitly evaluate rain positively with the words うれしく(joyous) and おもしろし (translated as 'fun', but closer in meaning to 'interesting'). In the third and fourth examples, the translators have added the word 'enjoy' to the English translation, but the haiku themselves contain no explicit term like 'enjoy' — the fourth one is more literally 'mountain shade / at the same time as coolness / sandals, tea house'. There is no need for the haiku to explicitly contain the word 'enjoy' because it is a background assumption within the discourse of haiku that coolness is something that people enjoy on a hot summer day. The other haiku represent rain and mist positively by associating them with culturally treasured aspects of nature ('the moon', 'pines', 'mountain', 'plum tree', 'deer' and 'sea'). There is also an inbuilt positivity that arises just from cool, rain and mist appearing in the form of a haiku, since haiku typically express appreciation of the aspects of the natural world they describe.

The character for rain (雨) contains within it four strokes which signify water. And this character combines with other characters to create dozens of expressions for different kinds of rain. Among the many expressions there is 春雨 (*harusame*) which the Goojisho (2020) Japanese to Japanese dictionary describes as 春しとしとと静かに降る雨 (gentle, quietly falling rain in spring). There is 村雨 (*murasame*) which the dictionary describes as 'light stop-start rain between the end of autumn and the start of winter'; 時雨 (*shigure*) 'passing rain that falls in large drops between the end of autumn and the start of winter'; and 夕立 (*yūdachi*) 'cooling rain that falls on a summer evening'. These expressions are often used in haiku poems to represent and celebrate a great diversity of kinds of rain.

There is, however, a common association in haiku between weather that is cold or windy and loneliness. There is even a particular word, 冬ごもり(*fuyugomori*) that expresses the concept of 'winter solitude'. The following are examples of this association:

- 蜘蛛殺す/後の淋しき/夜寒かな

  Lonely / after killing the spider / evening cold! (Shiki HK2:60)
- 能なしは/罪も又なし/冬ごもり

  No talents / also no sins / winter solitude. (Issa HK2:69)
- さびしさに/飯をくうなり/秋のかぜ

  Feeling lonely / I eat my dinner / autumn winds. (Issa HK2:85)

IMAGE 5.2 Winter in Dazaifu, Japan

- 居眠りて/我はかくれん/冬ごも

  Taking a nap / I hide within myself / winter seclusion. (Buson HK2:99)
- 淋しさの/うれしくもあり/秋の暮れ

  Loneliness / also has its pleasure / autumn dusk. (Buson HK2:90)

At first, the association with loneliness may seem to be an appraisal pattern that represents cold weather negatively, although Buson in the last of these haiku does state that loneliness can also have its pleasure. In fact, the aloneness, loneliness or seclusion in these haiku is not straightforwardly negative, but rather a manifestation of the high aesthetic principle of *sabi*. Sabi is usually translated as 'sadness', 'loneliness' or 'melancholy' and is, according to Ueda Makoto, 'the concept that one attains perfect spiritual serenity by immersing oneself in the ego-less, impersonal life of nature. The complete absorption of one's petty ego into the vast, powerful, magnificent universe' (Ueda in Lynch 1998, p. 117).

The winter seclusion, therefore, is not negative, but a way of finding serenity through immersion in nature, or the weather-world. These are not simplistic evaluations along the lines of COLD IS GOOD or LONELINESS IS GOOD — both *sabi* and the related concept of *wabi* are aesthetic values that find something deeply meaningful within something that seems outwardly insignificant or negative. Suzuki (1970, p. 23) describes how *wabi* suggests an image of being 'poor, that is, not to be dependent on things worldly — wealth, power, and reputation — and yet to feel inwardly the presence of something of the highest value'.

Solitude and the coldness of winter may not seem significant or positive, but it is possible to find something deeply meaningful within them.

While economic growth depends on constantly building dissatisfaction with ordinary life to fuel consumerism, haiku and the aesthetic of *wabi* work to build satisfaction from what is already freely available in nature. In the following two haiku, the poets find value not through owing possessions but through enjoying coolness in summer and the season of spring:

- 何もないが/心安さよ/涼しさよ

  Owning nothing / such peace / such coolness! (Issa HK2:88)
- 宿の春/何もなきこそ/何もあれ

  In my hut this spring / there is nothing / there is everything. (Sodo HK5:12)

In general, cultural evaluations are of great importance to ecolinguistics because they are so widespread and such an ordinary part of life that they can go unnoticed and unchallenged. As ecological destruction intensifies, aspects which a culture once considered 'good' may no longer be good for the ecosystems that support life. Rethinking societies along more sustainable and humane lines will require close attention to the evaluation patterns at the heart of those societies. Traditional cultures across the world are a potential source for new evaluations which can shift the focus towards what matters most for the future.

理论延伸

评价框架是系统功能语言学领域的一个新的发展（Martin，2010：324；王振华，2001），是对元功能理论的扩展（辛志英、黄国文，2012：63）。因此，本章的评价框架探讨隶属于生态语言学韩礼德模式的研究范畴。系统功能语言学的评价研究最初出现在《功能语法导论》（*An Introduction to Functional Grammar*）（Halliday，1985）一书中，讨论语法层面的人际意义（情感、态度和判断）。随后，Martin 在此基础上发展了 Halliday 的人际意义研究，拓展到语篇语义的层面，将其归类为语篇语义的一个子系统（Martin & Rose，2003）。

2000 年，Martin 的论文——《交换以外：英语评价系统》（"Beyond Exchange: Appraisal Systems in English"）的发表标志着评价框架体系的正式形成（王振华，2012：210），也被称为评价系统（appraisal systems）理论。Martin & White（2005）进一步出版了专著《评价语言：英语的评价系统》（*The Language of Evaluation: Appraisal in English*），完善了评价框架的相关内容，推动了评价框架研究走向成熟。

虽然评价框架建构了一套完整的分析框架（房红梅，2014）；但实际上，评价框架并没有超越系统功能语言学的理论框架范畴，而是对系统功能语言学的继承和发展，是系统功能语言学学派的"内部分歧"（黄国文、辛志英，2012：11）。

评价框架的中心是"系统"，"语言"是系统中的手段，其目的是通过语言的意义分析对语言使用者的立场、观点和态度进行评价，挖掘其中的深层意义（王振华，2001）。评价框架是由三个部分组成的：态度系统（attitude system）、级差系统（graduation system）和介入系统（engagement system）（Martin & White，2005：25）。

态度系统进一步包括：情感（affect）、判断（judgement）和鉴赏（appreciation）三个子系统。情感系统是一种心理反应，强调评价过程中的感情表达，可以从正面（positive）、负面（negative）、直接（direct）和隐含（implicit）等四个角度来分析（姜望琪，2012：170），它是以评价者为导向的（appraiser oriented）（Martin，2000：147）。判断系统用于判断和评价语言使用者的行为，在判断和评价过程中，要按照一定的道德标准进行，因此判断系统属于道德伦理的范畴。评价者除了可以从正面、负面、直接和间接的角度判断，还可以从"公德"（moral）和"私德"（personal）的角度进行判断（姜望琪，2012：170）。鉴赏系统主要是对评价对象的价值进行评估鉴赏，是基于美学理念的一种评价，覆盖反应（reaction）、构成（composition）和估值（valuation）三个变量（Martin & White，2005：35–36）。级差系统强调的是语势（force）和聚焦（focus）。语势可以分为强势语势（raise force）和弱势语势（lower force）；聚焦又可分为明显聚焦（sharpen focus）和模糊聚焦（soften focus）（王振华，2001）。介入系统涉及的内容是自言（monogloss）和借言（heterogloss）。自言是说话人自己的评价；而借言是对其他人话语的引用。介入系统的评价需要与态度系统和级差系统结合进行，例如：当评价介入系统的自言内容时，需要对自言中的态度系统或级差系统进一步展开评价。

自评价框架正式形成（Martin，2000）至今已有 20 余年。这 20 年来，评价框架无论是在理论研究方面还是应用研究方面都取得了较大的进展，并呈现出积极与其他学科交叉研究的趋势。其中在应用研究方面，主要在话语分析、外语教学和翻译研究领域得到了广泛的实践（刘世涛，2010；王振华，2012：218–226）。与评价框架相关的内容，读者可进一步阅读王振华（2001，2012：210–238）、张德禄和刘世涛（2006）、姜望琪（2009，2012：127–182）、刘世涛（2010）、黄国文和辛志英（2012）、房红梅（2014）、李梦骁和刘永兵（2017）、董丹（2019）等论著。除此之外，有关评价框架在生态语言学研究中的应用，也有学者已经展开讨论，读者可参阅的论著主要有：何伟和张瑞杰（2017）、张瑞杰和何伟（2018）、何伟和马子杰（2019，2020）、黄国文和赵蕊华（2019：176–179）、苗兴伟和雷蕾（2019）等。

补充文献

董丹 . 2019. 评价理论视角下意大利主流媒体对十九大报道的积极话语分析 . 外国语文，
　（4）：17–23.

房红梅 . 2014. 论评价理论对系统功能语言学的发展 . 现代外语，（3）：303–311.

何伟，马子杰 . 2019. 生态语言学视角下的澳大利亚主流媒体之十九大报道 . 外国语文，
　（4）：1–9.

何伟，马子杰 . 2020. 生态语言学视角下的评价系统 . 外国语，（1）：48–58.

何伟，张瑞杰 . 2017. 生态话语分析模式构建 . 中国外语，（5）：56–64.

黄国文，辛志英 . 2012. 系统功能语言学研究现状和发展趋势 . 北京：外语教学与研究
　出版社 .

黄国文，辛志英 . 2012. 解读"系统功能语言学" . 黄国文，辛志英主编 . 系统功能语
　言学研究现状和发展趋势 . 北京：外语教学与研究出版社，1–25.

黄国文，赵蕊华 . 2019. 什么是生态语言学 . 上海：上海外语教育出版社 .

姜望琪 . 2009. 语篇语义学与评价系统 . 外语教学，（2）：1–5，11.

姜望琪 . 2012. 语篇语义学 . 黄国文，辛志英主编 . 系统功能语言学研究现状和发展趋势 .
　北京：外语教学与研究出版社，127–182.

李梦骁，刘永兵 . 2017. 评价理论视域下中外学者期刊论文评论结果语步词块比较研究 .
　外语与外语教学，（5）：73–80，121.

刘世涛 . 2010. 评价理论在中国的发展 . 外语与外语教学，（5）：33–37.

苗兴伟，雷蕾 . 2019. 基于系统功能语言学的生态话语分析 . 山东外语教学，（1）：
　13–22.

王振华 . 2001. 评价系统及其运作——系统功能语言学的新发展 . 外国语，（6）：13–20.

王振华 . 2012. 评价理论研究在中国 . 黄国文，辛志英主编 . 系统功能语言学研究现状
　和发展趋势 . 北京：外语教学与研究出版社，210–238.

辛志英，黄国文 . 2012. 系统功能语言学的发展阶段 . 黄国文，辛志英主编 . 系统功能
　语言学研究现状和发展趋势 . 北京：外语教学与研究出版社，56–83.

张德禄，刘世涛 . 2006. 形式与意义的范畴化——兼评《评价语言——英语的评价系统》.
　外语教学与研究，（6）：423–427.

张瑞杰，何伟 . 2018. 生态语言学视角下的人际意义系统 . 外语与外语教学，（2）：
　99–108.

Halliday, M. A. K. 1985. *An introduction to functional grammar*. London: Edward Arnold.

Halliday, M. A. K. 1990. New ways of meaning: The challenge to applied linguistics.
　Journal of Applied Linguistics, (6): 7–16. (Reprinted from *On language and linguistics,
　Vol. 3 in The collected works of M. A. K. Halliday*, pp. 139–174, by J. Webster, ed.,
　2003, Continuum).

Martin, J. R. 2000. Beyond exchange: Appraisal systems in English. In S. Hunston & G. Thompson (Eds.), *Evaluation in text: Authorial stance and the construction of discourse*. Oxford: Oxford University Press, 142–176.

Martin, J. R. 2010. Meaning beyond the clause: SFL perspectives. In Z. Wang (Ed.), *Discourse semantics*. Shanghai: Shanghai Jiao Tong University Press, 317–340.

Martin, J. R. & Rose, D. 2003. *Working with discourse: Meaning beyond the clause*. London: Continuum.

Martin, J. R. & White, P. R. R. 2005. *The language of evaluation: Appraisal in English*. London & New York: Palgrave Macmillan.

6

IDENTITIES

    语言建构身份的方式是身份理论（identity theory）的一个重要内容，也是生态语言学研究的重要议题之一。Crompton & Kasser（2009）指出，我们既要改变当前身份中环境破坏方面的社会特征，还要推进环境友好方面的身份替代合理进行；只有身份的改变，才能够让人们的行为发生本质的变化。就第 6 章而言，作者分析的问题如下：（1）理论内涵；（2）身份建构分析的方法；（3）案例：生活杂志中的身份、性别与身体。

    （1）理论内涵。该部分作者通过信息赤字模型假设（Information Deficit Model）、《商业生态学》（*The Ecology of Commerce*）教程等例子的解读，总结出"身份"（identity）和"自我身份"（self-identity）的定义，以发现身份的社会和个人特征。身份讲的是人们脑海中有关成为某类人的故事，包括：外貌、性格、行为和价值观等内容（An *identity* is a story in people's minds about what it means to be a particular kind of person, including appearance, character, behaviour and values.）。自我身份是一个不断演化的故事，人们会告诉自己和他人，自己是什么样的人（A *self-identity* is an evolving story people tell themselves and others about what kind of person they are.）。

    有些身份一旦被人们所接受，即习惯了那类群体说话和做事的思维模式，就会对人们的行为产生有益或有害的影响。生态语言学研究者可以对社会中语言如何建构生态身份（ecological identity）问题进行研究。这里生态身份的意思是一种与自然息息相关且以不破坏维系生命的生态系统的方式去寻求满足感的身份，这种身份建构是本书作者所提倡的。

    （2）身份建构分析的方法。身份建构的方式有很多，本书对身份建构的分析沿着以下路径进行：第一，研究社会话语怎样为不同类型的人创建标签，使得他们拥有某些特性、价值观以及行为；第二，用自己的生态哲学观考量身份建构的合理性；第三，以身份建构的类型为基础，决定下一步的行动（维护、建设或重构）。

下面先看一组书中探讨的广告话语的例子（P131）。有一种广告话语对商品价格因素的关注高于其他所有的因素，有的还会对产品的低价进行一定的描述，例如："特价""半价""最低价""降价"等（摘自报纸广告语料库）。这样的广告是将消费者建构成"用最少的钱买到最多商品的人"，其方式夸大了价格的因素，而忽视了产品生产过程中工人的待遇、对其他生命体的危害、对环境的破坏等因素。所以这些例子与本书的生态哲学观是不相符的，属于破坏性的身份建构。

作者通过对另一组广告话语的分析，探索了可替代性的身份建构，它出自《道德消费者》（*Ethical Consumer*）这本杂志（P131）。这组广告传递的是以他人利益为中心的价值观，为读者建构了一个关爱世界的身份。其对读者的定位是：希望购买到对环境产生积极影响的产品，包括公平交易、保护动物、可回收利用和可再生等；作者将这种定位视为有益性的身份建构。

从另一个角度，社会运动领域也出现了一些抵制消费主义的身份建构。例如：书中《可持续冲浪指南》（*Sustainable Surfing Guide*）的讨论（P133），这组例子揭示了冲浪团体中的消费主义问题，并讨论了抗污水冲浪者组织（Surfers Against Sewage）抵制这种消费主义的方式（Wheaton，2007：279）。具体来讲，该例子以环境保护的思想为依据，给"冲浪者"建构出让他们引以为傲的生态身份——通过对冲浪者所思所想、一言一行的描述，以及代词"我们"（we）和短语"作为冲浪爱好者"（as surfers）的使用，为"冲浪者"建构了一个贴近自然生活、对环境敏感以及环境恶化的受害者的身份。

在生态身份的建构过程中，核心是"归属感"（a sense of belonging）问题。这种归属感不仅包含了人类，还包括了与我们共同生存的其他生命体，甚至是我们赖以生存的整个生态系统。当我们将这些群体与人类真正平等地对待的时候，它们受到伤害或破坏的概率将会大大降低。

（3）案例：生活杂志中的身份、性别与身体。这部分的主要目的是研究生活杂志中建构消费者身份的方式。作者以《男性的健康》（*Men's Health*）杂志为例（P138），分析了七期该杂志中的语篇：具体了解了这本杂志是怎样给男性确立身份的，并讨论了所确立的身份对生态环境的影响。该杂志几期的封面基本都遵循同一个模式：首先，为男性提供健康建议；随后，讲述"作为一名理想的男性意味着什么"的故事。但实际上，与帮助男性提升健康水平相比，该杂志更多的是展示语篇背后的故事。它利用、夸大和巩固了霸权男性（hegemonic masculinity）的身份模式，并为其建构了新的性别身份——消费者的身份。

例如：该杂志的封面图片一般是一名健硕的男性模特，且没有任何具体的行为举止；但伴随着男性模特图片的语言，则表达了该杂志赋予（设定）男性的理想身材，具体以祈使句和名词短语的形式，让这些内容成为男性读者想要实现的目标。事实上，这是一种只追求自我利益的破坏性身份建构。本书作者提倡将男性要实现的目标转移到与他人沟通、与自然联系、为社区利益而努力工作等内在的目标上来，这才是生活杂志应该为男性建构的有益性身份模式。

> An actual transformation in the way we experience *being* is necessary ... a collapse of the old Story of Self and Story of the World, and the birth of a new one. For the self, too, is ultimately a story, with a beginning and an end.
>
> (Charles Eisenstein 2011, p. 153)

Moser and Dilling (2011, p. 163) describe a common, though flawed, assumption that is often made when communicating environmental issues. The assumption, known as the 'Information Deficit Model', is that a lack of information explains the lack of public concern and engagement on environmental issues. Years of research, they claim, has shown that the model is incorrect, that 'ignorance of the details about climate change is NOT what prevents greater concern or action' and 'at worst it assumes that people have to be "little scientists" to make effective decisions' (p. 164). They describe how the cause of inaction, or destructive actions, is far deeper than a lack of information, and involves deeply held values and beliefs that relate to a sense of self.

Crompton and Kasser (2009, p. 7) argue that it is at this level of values and identity that environmental communication must aim, since only change of identity can make a real difference to people's behaviour. Their aim is to 'change those features of society that currently support the environmentally problematic aspects of identity, and promote those alternative aspects of identity that are environmentally beneficial' (p. 25). This is an ambitious aim, but given that identities are primarily, or at least partially, forged and resisted in language, it is one that ecolinguistics can contribute to.

Darier (1999) and Gorz (1993) are suspicious of the information deficit model not just because it is incorrect but because of the power it gives to dominant forces to define reality. Darier (1999, p. 238) argues that:

> Reducing individual energy consumption in the North shouldn't be justified by an imperative/threat like 'global warming' defined by an 'expertocracy', but because one might not want the consumption of large amounts of energy to be a defining characteristic of oneself! In the context of rampant consumerism in the North, it is up to us to ... work on ourselves.

The expression 'work on ourselves' relates to the 'project of the self', which Giddens (1991, p. 224) defines as 'the process by which self-identity is constituted by the reflexive ordering of self-narratives'. In other words, 'we create, maintain and revise a set of biographical narratives — the story of who we are'. It is at this story, the story of who we are as people, that any cultural change towards more environmentally beneficial practices needs to be aimed.

An example of 'the project of the self' can be seen in the self-reflection of Ray Anderson, the former CEO of Interface Carpets. Anderson describes how he had no environmental vision at all until he read Paul Hawken's book *The Ecology of Commerce* and came across the expression 'the death of birth'. To continue in his own words:

- It was E. O. Wilson's expression for species extinction, the death of birth, and it was the point of a spear into my chest, and I read on and the spear became deeper, and it was an epiphanous experience, a total change of mind-set for myself, and a change of paradigm. (Anderson interviewed in ML1)

The book caused Anderson to reconsider how he saw himself as a person and reject his current identity:

- One day early in this journey it dawned on me that the way I'd been running Interface was the way of the plunderer. Plundering something that's not mine. Something that belongs to every creature on Earth. [I realised that] someday people like me will end up in jail. (ML1)

The shift is profound, moving from a societal identity which he expresses as 'by our civilisation's definition I am a captain of industry ... a modern-day hero' to taking on the self-identity of a plunderer — 'I stand convicted by me myself alone, not anyone else, as a plunderer of the Earth' (ML1). The negative self-identity of the plunderer was a *liminal state* — a transition between two identities rather than a solid new identity in itself. Goethe (in Meyer and Land 2005, p. 376) describes how in making a transition to a new identity, an individual 'must strip away, or have stripped from them, the old identity. The period in which the individual is naked of self — neither fully in one category or another — is the liminal state'. After his liminal period of self-doubt, Anderson took on the new identity of an ecologically sensitive business leader, which required reinventing himself as well as his company. Interface moved from selling carpets to providing a carpet rental service based on reusable, recyclable carpet tiles.

Benwell and Stokoe (2006, p. 10) describe how the ability of people to reinvent themselves is a central issue in identity theory:

> The issue here is to do with whether people are free to construct their identity in any way they wish (the 'agency' view, in which the individual *has agency,* is *an agent* or *agentive*) or whether identity construction is constrained by forces of various kinds, from the unconscious psyche to institutionalised power structures (the 'structure' view, in which 'subjects' are restrictively positioned within existing 'discourses'...).

Clearly, though, it is not one or the other: there are identities which are built into a society or culture, and often people are encouraged or forced into taking on these identities. In Anderson's case, the prevailing story was of a successful CEO as a 'modern-day hero', with social expectations and even fiduciary duties that define success narrowly in terms of profit-making or sales revenue. On the other hand, to different extents in different situations, people have the power to resist the narrow range of identities that society makes available, and 'in some cases, it is possible to remake ourselves, to remake our self-identity independent of the normalisation process' (Darier 1999, p. 26).

Ecolinguistics can therefore investigate how language in society sets up ecologically destructive identities, how texts like *The Ecology of Commerce* can help people to resist these identities, and what alternative, more ecologically beneficial possibilities there are for re-imagining self. The following definitions attempt to capture both the social and personal aspects of identity:

> An *identity* is a story in people's minds about what it means to be a particular kind of person, including appearance, character, behaviour and values.
>
> A *self-identity* is an evolving story people tell themselves and others about what kind of person they are.

Identities are models in people's minds, but manifest themselves in particular ways of dressing, writing, speaking and behaving. Some identities (e.g. the insatiable consumer) encourage behaviours that are ecologically destructive if people adopt them, i.e., if they accept that they are that type of person and conform to the mental model of what that kind of person says and does. On the other hand, different identities may encourage people to behave in ways which help protect the systems that life depends on.

Identities can be explored through examining how texts within society create labels (*subject positions* or *social categories*) for different kinds of people and imbue these people with certain characteristics, values or behaviour. Subject positions include labels and corresponding identities such as mother, CEO, feminist, Catholic, doctor, etc. Texts do not just describe pre-existing identities, but play a role in establishing, constructing and maintaining those identities over time. In other words, texts build and perpetuate a model in people's minds about what kinds of people there are in society.

As discussed in Chapter 2, the discourse of neoclassical economics defines a range of categories of people, including 'consumer', 'owner', 'manager', and (metonymically) 'corporation', and describes the kind of character these people have. In the following example, a microeconomics textbook (ET2) describes (and simultaneously establishes) the identities of 'owners' and 'managers':

- Thus a corporate governance problem arises when ownership is separated from control and the objective of owners — profit maximisation — has the potential to differ from that of managers, who are concerned instead with their own *private benefits* ... for example, the ability to make less effort or acquire more managerial power. (ET2:242)

In this description, owners are represented narrowly, as characters whose sole interest is profit maximisation, while managers are represented as having some agency to pursue other goals since they deal with the day-to-day running of the company. Although the text represents this negatively as a 'problem', it is something potentially valuable from an ecological perspective because managers have the agency to break free from profit maximisation and instead pursue different objectives, such as community wellbeing or protection of the environment. Unfortunately though, the textbook provides only two examples for the kind of goals a manager might pursue: 'make less effort' and 'acquire more managerial power'. The textbook ET5 makes a very similar point:

- Can the owners of a firm ever be sure that their managers will pursue the business strategy most appropriate to the owner's goals (i.e., profit maximisation)? (ET5:9)
- As a manager of a firm, what are you interested in? A higher salary, greater power or prestige, greater sales, better working conditions, or greater popularity with your subordinates? (ET5:12)

Again, there is a presupposition that the owner's goal is profit maximisation but that the manager has a range of other possible goals. In the second example, the textbook uses the pronoun 'you' to place the reader in the subject position of 'manager' by addressing them directly as such. Whether a manager in real life or not, the reader temporarily takes the position in order to make sense of the sentence. The text then directly questions them, encouraging them to think about how they would exercise their agency as a manager to pursue their objectives. Except again, the text provides only a very narrow range of possibilities to consider: the extrinsic values of salary, power, prestige and popularity. Underneath all the talk of agency, then, is a story that being a manager means being someone who is only interested in self-centred extrinsic values such as their own advancement, and not in larger issues of wellbeing or the environment. The same applies for the construction of the identity of an owner (profit maximising), the identity of a consumer (utility maximising), and a 'firm' (revenue maximising). Even politicians are represented as concerned only with extrinsic values in the following extract:

- Politicians are people too. It would be nice to assume that political leaders are always looking out for the well-being of the society ... Nice, perhaps, but not realistic. ... self-interest is as powerful a motive for political actors as it is for consumers and firm owners. Some politicians, motivated by a desire for re-election, are willing to sacrifice the national interest ... Others are motivated by simple greed ... Policy is not made by a benevolent king but by real people with their own all-too-human desires ... motivated by their own political and financial ambitions. (ET3:471)

This tells a story about the identity of a politician — that, like all the other kinds of people described by neoclassical economics, they are motivated by the extrinsic values of self-interest, greed, re-election and financial ambitions. Chilton *et al.* (2012) showed that people who are primed by reading extrinsic value words such as 'popularity', 'preserving public image' and 'wealth' were likely to show less concern for social justice and the environment in subsequent interviews than those primed with intrinsic values such as 'acceptance', 'affiliation' and 'being broad-minded'. If neoclassical economics materials, which are full of words denoting extrinsic values, are read by aspiring businessmen and politicians, they may become self-fulfilling prophecies and create the kinds of people they describe.

However, it is not just politicians who are being described as selfish in the above quotation, it is people in general. The expressions 'real people', 'all too human desires' and 'politicians are people too' presuppose that the selfish behaviour is a natural characteristic of being human. This is based on what Fairclough (2003, p. 123) describes as a highly pervasive 'individualist discourse of the self' which represents people as 'primarily rational, separate and unitary individuals, whose identity as social beings is secondary'. Eisenstein (2011, p. 22) argues that 'based on the story of separate self, both biology and economics have therefore written greed into their basic axioms ... in economics it is the rational actor seeking to maximise financial self-interest'.

In neoclassical economics, the concept of rationality itself, which in many discourses is fundamental to what makes people human, is represented as being identical to this self-centred individualism. Examples are:

- We assume that consumers make this choice in a rational way — that they choose goods to *maximise the satisfaction they can achieve.* (ET1:86)
- In short, for our consumer, Nutty-fruit must be cheaper than Fruity-nut before purchase becomes rational. (ET2:315)
- Rational decision making, as far as consumers are concerned, involves choosing those items that give you best value for money, i.e., the *greatest benefit relative to cost.* (ET5:24, emphasis in original)

Of course, only a small minority of people read economics textbooks, but the identity of the rational consumer who is only concerned with price appears across a wide variety of discourses in everyday life. There is a particular discourse of advertising, for example, which focuses on price above all other considerations when buying a product, with expressions like BARGAIN, DISCOUNT, SALE, ONLY £299, 30% OFF, LOWEST PRICES, 2 for £15, SAVE £400, great savings, great value, HALF PRICE, 3 for 2, JUST £89 (from ML23, a corpus of newspaper advertisements). If price is the only information available (as opposed to how well the workers were treated, whether animals were harmed, or whether the environment was damaged in the making of the product) then people cannot help but behave as the rational consumers described in the books.

There is, however, a different discourse of advertising which can be seen in the advertisements of the magazine *Ethical Consumer* (ML24). The following are some key examples from various issues of the magazine:

- You may be concerned about the environment, human rights, better employment practices or promoting third world development and cooperatives. Our financial planning [takes account] of your values. We and our clients aim to make a positive difference to the world in which we all live (investment company)
- Make your savings work harder. Financially, socially, culturally and environmentally. Follow your heart (bank)
- new Fair Trade iced teas (tea)
- animal-friendly footwear (shoes)
- low-energy homes, whether you are building your dream eco home from scratch or insulating your attic (building store)
- ethically sourced from organic farms in Asia (coconut milk)
- organic, ethically produced, made using renewable energy (mayonnaise)
- we source our energy from certified renewables (energy provider)

- a positive impact on the world around us (energy provider). (all from ML24)

These advertisements position the reader in a very different way from the rational consumer of neoclassical economics who wants to buy at the cheapest price. Instead, the reader is positioned as wanting their products to be Fair Trade, animal-friendly, organic, recycled, ethically sourced, renewable, and having a positive impact on the world — all intrinsic values that centre around the interests of others. The first of these uses the pronoun 'you' to reach out directly to the reader and gives a list of things that the reader is likely to care about, from environment to third world development. Like the economics textbook discussed above which gave the list 'a higher salary, greater power or prestige ...', the range of options is narrow, pushing the reader into a particular identity. This time, though, it is an identity of care for the world rather than selfishness. These advertisements are therefore forging the new identity of the 'ethical consumer', which is the title of the magazine, and placing the reader in the position of this ethical consumer. Readers can, of course, be critical and resist the positioning, but at least this discourse of advertising opens up a possible identity beyond that of the selfish consumer.

Benwell and Stokoe (2006, pp. 171–177) describe advertising as 'a crucial facilitator of consumption' and show how it appeals to identity through references to a 'real you', an 'inner self' or to group membership. They analyse how advertisements in *Cosmopolitan* magazine encourage unnecessary consumption by promoting an ideology of envy, using unobtainable beauty ideals to generate dissatisfaction, and representing small surface changes such as cosmetics or accessories as if they were deep changes of identify. An example they give is 'Celebrate *the new you* in the New Year with fabulous fashion and accessories'. Giddens (1991, p. 198) describes what can happen when advertisers conflate who we are with what we own:

> To a greater or lesser degree, the project of the self becomes translated into one of possession of desired goods and the pursuit of artificially framed styles of life. ... The consumption of ever-novel goods becomes in some part a substitute for the genuine development of self; appearance replaces essence as the visible signs of successful consumption come actually to outweigh the use-values of the goods and services themselves.

Benwell and Stokoe (2006, p. 174) identify a series of 'rules' underpinning the identity of consumer femininity in *Cosmopolitan*, which can also be seen as *evaluations*. These are AGEING IS BAD, FAT IS BAD, ACTIVITY/FITNESS IS GOOD, BODY HAIR IS BAD, NATURAL BODY ODOUR IS BAD, TRANSFORMATION IS GOOD, and NEW IS GOOD. These evaluations have ecological consequences since they set up women's current state of being as inadequate and in need of transformation through the purchase of products. Overall, they found that 'in almost all of the advertisements in *Cosmopolitan*, we identified a model of femininity characterised by self-indulgence and narcissism' (p. 173).

While there are numerous critical studies of consumerism, there are also some studies of identity in social movements that resist consumerism. Wheaton (2007, p. 279) analyses consumerism in the surfing community and how one particular organisation, *Surfers Against Sewage* (SAS), attempts to fight against it. She starts by describing how 'academic accounts of leisure activities like surfing tend to emphasise their individualist, hedonistic and commercialised qualities, seeing this as characteristic of leisure consumption in late capitalism'. However, she introduces SAS as 'a politicised trans-local collectivity based around their own localised environment' that is 'part of a broader wave of new social movements and direct action groups [where] the politics of identity take centre stage'. SAS attempts to reclaim the identity of 'surfer' from the advertisers who commercialise it and instead create a more environmentally beneficial identity for surfers. Overall, Wheaton (2007, p. 182) makes the more general point that while many see postmodern culture as characterised by narcissistic consumption, 'others observe postmodern processes leading to the emergence or intensification of new kinds of collectivities ... based around "alternative" lifestyle interests and their identity politics'.

While Wheaton does not look specifically at the language used by SAS, ecolinguistic analysis can help reveal the techniques that SAS uses to forge environmentally beneficial identities. A 'surfer', clearly, is more than someone who happens to be participating in a water sport at a particular moment — it is a particular kind of person, an identity. What it means to be that kind of person is constructed by texts of all kinds from surfing magazines and conversations with other surfers to advertisements for surfing accessories. Among the texts which play a role in forging the identity of a surfer are those of Surfers Against Sewage, including their website, social media sites, guides and campaigns. The following extracts are from SAS UK's *Sustainable Surfing Guide* (EN10):

- As surfers, we are interested in being able to continue to surf, and for our children and grandchildren to be able to surf. (EN10:8)
- Any alteration in the climate and its inevitable knock-on effects, particularly on such a fragile interface such as the coast, will be severely felt by surfers. (EN10:12)
- surfers ... were already living closer to nature. (EN10:3)
- as surfers we are sensitised incrementally to the environment around us and the damage done to it. (EN10:6)

The power of this guide is that it is written specifically for members of a group, so can tailor environmentalism to fit the prized self-identity of the 'surfer'. The first extract above is clearly a re-expression of the definition of sustainability in terms that appeal directly to the interests of surfers. The inclusive pronoun 'we' shows that the writers are part of the group they are addressing, giving them the inside information to authoritatively describe the characteristics of a 'surfer'. The expression 'as surfers, we ...' appears to express a pre-existing and obvious 'fact' about what surfers think, do, aspire to, or look like, but at the same time is trying to make that description become reality by influencing the reader. In the first example, surfers in general may not care about the ability of their future grandchildren to surf, but are being positioned as doing so by the sentence. Whether that takes hold and influences the identity of surfers more generally depends on how widely the guide is read and whether it is read sympathetically or with resistance.

The guide uses the pronoun 'we', the expression 'as surfers', and general descriptions of what surfers feel, think and do to nudge the identity towards someone who lives close to nature, is sensitised to the environment and environmental damage, and is a primary victim of environmental degradation. In many ways, the report sets up the identity of a surfer as already being an environmentalist identity, but still has to deal with the issue of consumerism which it admits is 'rife' in the surfing world. The following examples show how it does this:

- Nowadays, surfing has turned 'mainstream', and our obsession with the clothes we wear and the boards we ride has almost become more important to us than the actual waves we surf. (EN10:46)
- A surfer with a really fancy motor is ... more of a poser than a proper surfer. (EN10:32)
- As surfers, we ... recognise that it is possible to live happily without consuming too much energy. Surfing, stripped down to its bare essentials, actually consumes very little energy, and usually makes us extremely happy. (EN10:19)

Here caring about fashion is evaluated negatively with the word 'obsession', and instead 'the actual waves we surf' is positioned as what surfers should be caring about. The inclusive pronouns in '*our* obsession' and 'more important to *us*' keep the writer and reader on the same side and avoid being accusatory. In the second example, the category of 'proper surfer' is used to keep undesirable characteristics such as conspicuous displays of wealth outside the core identity of a surfer. Finally, the guide uses the expression 'as surfers, we ... recognise' to represent the fact that surfing provides fulfilment without using much energy as something that anyone who has the identity of a surfer would agree with. Overall, *Surfers Against Sewage* can be seen as not just resisting consumerism, but also building an ecological identity for surfers — one that is deeply connected with nature and seeks fulfilment in ways that do not damage the ecosystems that support life.

Thomashow (1995, p. 3) defines ecological identity as 'all the different ways people construe themselves in relationship to the earth as manifested in personality, values, actions and sense of self'. This is quite a general definition, but he refines it by saying that 'ecological identity broadens the concept of community so that it stretches beyond the limited sphere of human relations' (p. 94). It is not just any relationship to the Earth, then, but specifically one where the sense of self goes beyond, as Barrows (1995, p. 106) puts it, 'an "inside" bounded by our own skin, with everyone and everything else on the outside'. It goes beyond being a member of a family, a human community, or humankind, to being part of a larger community of life. The hope is that taking on an ecological identity will encourage people to notice the larger ecological systems that life depends on, increase their respect and care for life in all its forms, and, importantly, act.

The link between ecological identity and pro-environmental behaviour can be summed up by a quote from Leopold (1979, p. viii): 'We abuse land because we regard it as a commodity. When we see land as a community to which we belong we may begin to use it with love and respect'. Harding (2010, p. 41) similarly describes how, from a sense of ecological identity 'there arises a deep appreciation of the reality of interdependence, and from this comes the urge to be involved in opposing all sorts of ecological abuses'. Thomashow (1995, p. 4) examines evidence from psychological studies and concludes that 'there is evidence suggesting that people take action, or formulate their personality based on their ecological worldview'. This is confirmed by Crompton and Kasser (2009, p. 12), who describe how 'studies of environmental identity and connectedness with nature have indeed established that connectedness is strongly correlated with environmental attitudes and behaviours'.

An example of a text which constructs ecological identities is Luther Standing Bear's autobiographical book *Land of the Spotted Eagle* (NR16), originally published in 1933. Standing Bear grew up in the traditional oral culture of the Lakota in North America, then learned English and expressed insights from the traditional culture in English. He is one of a small group of Lakota writers who 'used autobiographical storytelling to preserve traditional values and to challenge their readers' preconceptions of what it meant to be "civilized"' (Eick 2013). Analysing the language of the book can reveal how Standing Bear uses the vocabulary and grammar of the English language to express ecological identity.

Central to ecological identity is a sense of belonging to a group which not only includes humans but also others from the wider community of life. If beings from other species, or even whole ecosystems such as rivers, are seen as being within the same in-group as humans then it becomes much harder to hurt or damage them. Standing Bear includes humans in wider groups through *hyponymy*, i.e., by creating a category and placing not just humans but other species into the category. The following is an example:

- The character of the Indian's emotion left little room in his heart for antagonism toward his fellow *creatures*. (ML205:195, emphasis added)

IMAGE 6.1 Cover of *Land of the Spotted Eagle* by Luther Standing Bear

This establishes 'the Indian' (referring to Native Americans in general) as a member of the category 'creatures', which also includes beings from the more-than-human world. The following are further examples:

- By acknowledging the virtues of other *beings* the Lakota came to possess them for himself. (NR16:204)
- In order to place himself in communication with the other *earth entities* the Lakota submitted to the purification ceremony. (NR16:204)
- To sit or lie upon the ground is to be able to think more deeply and to feel more

keenly; he can see more clearly into the mysteries of life and come closer in kinship to other *lives* about him. (NR16:192, emphasis added in each case)

From these examples we can see that humans are placed in categories that contain more than just humans through the use of the terms 'too', 'more than', 'other', and 'fellow'. The superordinate terms, i.e., the names of the categories, are 'creatures', 'beings', 'earth entities' and 'lives'.

Another way that Standing Bear constructs ecological identities is through kinship metaphor, where the target domain is *the earth* or *animals*, and the source frame is *a family*. The following are examples, with the trigger words highlighted:

- The Indian, as well as all other creatures that were given birth and grew, were sustained by the common *mother* — earth. He was therefore *kin* to all living things and he gave to all creatures equal rights with himself. Everything of earth was loved and reverenced. (NR16:166)
- For the animal and bird world there existed a *brotherly* feeling that kept the Lakota safe among them. And so close did some of the Lakotas come to their feathered and furred friends that in true *brotherhood* they spoke a common tongue. (NR16:193)

In the first example, the 'earth' maps onto the 'mother' and both 'the Indian' and 'all other creatures' map onto children. This not only places humans directly within the same category as other creatures, but also makes them siblings. The second example represents this explicitly with the term 'brotherhood' applied to the Lakota, animals and birds. There is an important entailment of this, which is explicitly drawn out in the first example: that if all living things are siblings then we must love, revere and protect them.

The story of human exceptionalism, which is so common in industrialised countries, finds separation and superiority in the differences of humans from other animals. Standing Bear, however, uses language in ways which express commonalities:

- The world was a library and its books were the stones, leaves, grass, brooks and the birds and animals that shared, *alike with* us, the storms and blessings of the earth. (NR16:194)
- From Wakan Tanka there came a great unifying life force that flowed in and *through all* things — the flowers of the plains, blowing winds, rocks, trees, birds, animals — and was *the same* force that had been breathed into the first man. Thus all things were kindred and brought together by *the same* Great Mystery. (NR16:193)
- [there is] a place *for all* things in the scheme of existence with equal importance *for*

all. The Lakota could despise no creature *for all* were *of one* blood, made by *the same* hand, and filled with the essence of the Great Mystery. (NR16:193, emphasis added in each example)

The commonalities are expressed through the words 'the same', 'alike with', 'through all', 'for all' and 'of one'. These examples are notable because they locate commonalities not just between humans and other animals, but also between humans and flowers, winds, rocks, trees, stones, leaves, grass, and brooks. Emphasising commonality in this way helps to expand the moral sphere to encompass all life and aspects of the physical environment. The third example explicitly draws out the entailment that sharing a morally relevant commonality entails equal treatment for other beings, that all beings have a place in the scheme of existence, and that there are no grounds for despising them.

In the end, exposure to events and texts of all kinds can influence the stories that people hold inside them about what kind of person they are in relation to other people and the natural world. As Giddens (1991, p. 54) describes:

A person's identity is not to be found in behaviour ... but in the capacity to keep a particular narrative going. The individual's biography ... must continually integrate events which occur in the external world, and sort them into the ongoing 'story about the self'.

Identity, gender and the body in *Men's Health* magazine

This section will investigate how consumer identities are set up in lifestyle magazines, specifically *Men's Health*. Gauntlett (2002, p. 248) describes how the media provide 'myriad suggestions of ways of living' and 'we lap up this material because the social construction of identity today is the *knowing* social constructing of identity. Your life is your project — there is no escape. The media provides some of the tools which can be used in this work'. One of those tools is *Men's Health,* a magazine which started in 1987 and has a 'brand reach' of 924,000 with 1.6 m social media followers according to the publisher (Hearst 2020). As such, the magazine has the power to entrench, resist and shape the stories that men live by, in ways that may encourage men to protect or destroy the ecological systems that support life. That does not mean, however, that readers are sponges who unquestioningly soak up whatever world-view they are presented with by the media. As Giddens (1991, p. 179) points out, 'yet powerful though commodifying influences no doubt are, they are scarcely received in an uncritical way by the populations they affect'. A key role that ecolinguistics can therefore play is in working with, encouraging and providing tools for readers to treat media texts even more critically, by considering the stories they tell within a larger ecological context. With this in mind, this section analyses seven editions of *Men's Health* magazine (MH1–MH7, see Appendix), examining how the magazine sets up identities for men and what the ecological consequences of these identities are.

It is clear from the cover of *Men's Health* that the magazine is doing more than just giving health advice — it is telling a story about what it means to be a man. Although each cover is unique they all follow the same pattern. All the covers (MH1–MH7) show a medium shot of a muscular man, either bare chested or in a tight T-shirt, against a white background. The white background gives an indication of low modality (Kress and van Leeuwen 2006, p. 166), showing that this is not just a photograph of an attractive man for the reader to look at but a symbol of something else. The angle of the images is straight on, indicating equality, and the eyes looking out at the reader form a *demand picture* (Kress and van Leeuwen 2006, p. 123), i.e., the picture demands a relationship with the viewer. A clue to this relationship is given by arrows pointing from text to the image: the expressions 'BUILD ARMS LIKE THIS' (MH1: cover), 'biceps like these' (MH5: cover), and '5 STEPS TO BIGGER BICEPS' (MH6: cover) all have arrows pointing to the huge muscles of the cover model. The subject of an imperative like 'build arms like this', although elided, is 'you'. The arrows, therefore, link 'you', the reader, with the image of the cover model. The *Men's Health* website provides another clue in the statement 'Build a cover model body: Craft the body you've always wanted' (MH8), which presupposes that the reader wants a body like that of the model. The model, then, is like a mirror showing the reader what he could become if he follows the advice of the magazine. As with women's lifestyle magazines, the cover provides a 'window to the future self' (McCracken 1993, p. 13).

IMAGE 6.2   Men's magazines.

The cover models are not represented as *doing* anything, except for one (MH3) who is punching towards the viewer. They are not reading, writing, walking in the countryside, growing vegetables, spending time with family, or volunteering. They are, in effect, just bodies to be admired in their corporality rather than their deeds. Giddens (1991, p. 218) describes how the body cannot just be 'accepted' anymore; it forms a fundamental part of the reflexive project of self-identity. He writes that in pre-modern times, 'the body was a "given", the often inconvenient and inadequate seat of the self ... [but now] the body has become fully available to be "worked upon" by the influences of high modernity'. For Giddens, this has positive aspects, since people have more freedom not only to become the person they want to be but also, within constraints, to gain the body they want. However, it does open men up to the traditional consumerist pressure that women have been subjected to for quite some time. Connell (2005, p. 49) describes how the media provide 'systems of imagery through which bodies are defined as beautiful or ugly, slender or fat. Through this imagery a whole series of body-related needs has been created: for diet, cosmetics, fashionable clothing, slimming programmes and the like'.

The body that *Men's Health* defines as ideal is revealed not just by the image of the cover models, but by the text on the cover, which consists primarily of imperative statements and noun phrases that appear in a variety of fonts, from huge, red, bold capital lettering to smaller black or blue fonts. The genre of lifestyle magazines holds that whatever appears in imperative statements or noun phrases on the cover is desirable — if the cover states 'Build a V Shape Back' or 'ADD 3IN TO YOUR ARMS' then the reader is positioned as viewing these goals as desirable, whether or not they had previously thought that a V-shaped back or enormous arms were necessary. The covers set up one particular goal as the most important of all — gaining large muscles:

- BUILD BIG ARMS. (MH4: cover)
- BUILD 6KG OF HARD MUSCLE. (MH3: cover)
- 6-PACK ABS. (MH2: cover)
- 20% More Muscle. (MH2: cover)
- MUSCLE POWER SPEED! (MH3: cover)
- MUSCLE DOUBLED! (And Body Fat Halved) (MH5: cover)
- BUILD ARMS LIKE THIS — 6 moves to add 3in by April. (MH1: cover)
- HARD ABS. (MH6: cover)
- PACK ON 10KG OF MUSCLE. (MH7: cover)

This tells a story that AN IDEAL MAN HAS HUGE MUSCLES, but this story was not invented by the magazine. Instead the magazine is drawing on and further entrenching the widespread identity of 'hegemonic masculinity', which Connell (1996, p. 209) describes as the 'expression of the privilege men collectively have over women'. Klein (1993, p. 5) writes that:

> Musculature and what it connotes — power, domination and virility — once again concentrates on the masculine side, its opposite traits on the feminine side ... The danger of such views lies in their artificially attaching all manner of power and privilege to biological differences.

In other words, hegemonic masculinity places prestige on muscles simply because it is biologically easier for men to gain larger muscles than for women, so men as a group gain more prestige than women. Certainly, the covers of *Men's Health* contain a range of psychologically positive unmarked terms such as 'bigger', 'harder', 'faster', and 'stronger' which rarely appear on the covers of the corresponding *Women's Health* magazine. If these are associated with prestige then this gives men an advantage since they are biologically adapted to having harder, stronger, bigger and faster bodies. The strong emphasis on increasing muscle size may be a form of compensation for placing men in the position of a reader of a lifestyle magazine full of fashion and slimming tips. Greenfield *et al.* (1999, p. 463) describe how the magazine *Men Only* 'embodied great risks, as it involved addressing men as consumers when this role was often disparagingly associated with women'. *Men's Health* embodies even greater risks since caring about health and appearance, reading recipes, looking at advertisements for fashion, fragrance and grooming products, and viewing pictures of attractive semi-naked men run against dominant images of masculinity.

The story that AN IDEAL MAN HAS HUGE MUSCLES has a number of ecological implications. The route that the magazine gives for gaining those muscles consists of indoor weight training requiring large amounts of equipment, and eating large quantities of meat, particularly red meat. The primary link the magazine makes between meat and muscle is protein:

- Sweet science of beefing up. Steak is a reliable weapon in the battle to bulk up, with protein and creatine arming your muscular growth when training. (MH4:114)

Ecologically, the production of meat in intensive farms tends to be resource-intensive, polluting and damaging to the wellbeing of countless animals (Poore and Nemecek 2018). It is also questionable from a health perspective too. Courtenay (2002) provides evidence that excess meat consumption is one of the reasons why men's lifespan is significantly shorter than women's. The promotion of meat, like muscle, may therefore be related to its symbolic value. Meat is, according to Adams (2010, p. 58), 'a symbol and celebration of male dominance', and 'men who decide to eschew meat eating are deemed effeminate; failure of men to eat meat announces they are not masculine' (p. 57). In addition to the link with protein and muscles, there are a number of other ways that meat is linked with masculinity. The following are examples:

- Build muscle faster. Thai beef on multi-grain bread. Lean beef packs a hefty punch of iron, zinc and creatine. (MH6:85)
- The POWER list ... THE 48-HOUR STENGTH SANDWICH ... Take aim at the Shooter's Sandwich ... Venison (400g) Packs 20% more protein than beef. (MH5:57)
- I eat a lot of meat. I'm not boasting ... I need the protein for muscular growth ... I eat animal protein at every meal. (MH7:137)
- STEAK AND ALE PIE — A manly comfort food classic that will keep you satiated from dinner till dawn, and build muscle. (MH2:103)
- Red meat's creatine will fire up your muscle power. (MH1:113)
- Man vs Food ... Take your meat like a warrior ... Raw power ... muscle fuelling steak tartare ... named after Attila the Hun's army of Tartar warriors ... (MH6:153)
- A seriously hot curry is one of the healthier ways to indulge your red meat craving. (MH4:174)

The lexical item 'manly' in 'manly comfort food' directly links men and meat, while 'power' and 'strength' link meat with the attributes that hegemonic masculinity holds up as properties of the ideal man. Meat is linked with the aggression of hegemonic masculinity through the vocabulary that triggers frames of war and fighting — 'shooter', 'warrior', 'army', 'punch', 'weapon' and 'battle'. The expression 'I eat a lot of meat. I'm not boasting' implies that eating a lot of meat is the kind of thing that men *could* boast about. The last extract presupposes, i.e., takes it to be obvious, that the reader has a 'red meat craving'. There are counter-examples, for example where (MH4:24) and (MH1:25) briefly mention the carcinogenic effects of meat, but overall the pattern entrenches the story of hegemonic masculinity that AN IDEAL MAN IS A MEAT EATER.

Another questionable story of hegemonic masculinity is that *real men do not cook*, at least not unpaid cooking at home. Fiddes (1991, p. 158) writes that cooking 'in routine and mundane situations ... is the drudgery that is delegated to women'. Ecologically, this is problematic because it could encourage men to turn to convenience food, which has environmental costs in terms of processing, packaging, transportation and the ecological damage caused by the fast-food industry. Overconsumption of convenience foods is also one of the behaviours that Courtenay (2002) links with men's excess mortality.

Rather than countering the story that AN IDEAL MAN EATS CONVENIENCE FOOD, *Men's Health* appears to entrench it by presenting convenience food as the natural food for men. The 'Man Food Special' (MH1:13) features burgers, fish and chips, cheeseburgers, meatball subs, and pizza, linking all these foods with masculinity through the title 'Man Food'. Hotdogs are directly described as 'energy boosting man fodder' (MH3:149). The 'Down-Size-Me Man-Food Menu' (MH3:65) includes BLT, cheeseburger, sausages, and steak and chips, which are presupposed to be 'our favourite foods' in the sentence 'The *MH* Nutrition Lab ... has re-engineered our favourite fatty foods'. Convenience foods are represented not only as 'man foods' but as healthy foods, for example in the following expressions:

- 3 Cheeseburgers the doctor ordered. (MH1: cover)
- Fat-burning burgers. (MH4:47)
- The bacon sandwich just got tastier and better for you. (MH4:91)
- You can eat burgers AND lose pounds. (MH4:176)
- Prepare a delicious hotdog that's actually *good* for you. (MH3:21)

All the convenience food promoted has a twist — the bacon sandwich uses flax seed bread, the hot dog has vitamin-rich salsa on it, the burgers have wasabi powder sprinkled on to cut fat, the pizza in MH6:21 has pepper on it to help fat absorption, the cheeseburgers and sausages in MH3:65 use buffalo and bison meat, and the burgers you can eat while losing pounds are 'Burger King Whoppers' since they have fewer calories than 'Big Macs'. While these may all be slightly healthier alternatives, the fundamental story that AN IDEAL MAN EATS CONVENIENCE FOOD not only goes unchallenged but is further entrenched.

One final story that is central to hegemonic masculinity is that THE IDEAL MAN IS COMPETITIVE. As Savran (1998, p. 16) points out, 'certainly, what appears to be paramount in the representation of masculinity in capitalist societies is an obsession with competition and achievement'. This story runs throughout the magazine, which presents warriors, boxers, athletes, cowboys, soldiers, bodybuilders and sportsmen as role models. The magazine suggests that readers can become like these role models by eating the same kind of food or undergoing the same kind of training:

- Harness the power of heroes: these four elite sportsmen have all had a world-beating year. (MH2:36)
- USE EXPLOSIVE POWER LIKE A NORMAN KNIGHT ... Norman knights used the high protein content of their meat to build the explosive power required for successful Saxon smashing. (MH7:30)

These use imperative statements to link the reader (as the implied subject of the verb) with elite sportsmen and Norman knights. The article that the second quote came from is entitled 'Alpha Male' and uses the same pattern to link the reader not only with knights but also 'Roman gladiators', 'Aztec warriors', 'Viking raiders', 'Japanese ninjas' and 'Mongol marauders'. The aggressive descriptions in this article may be a form of compensation for the fact that the 'six belligerent superfoods' include real health foods such as quinoa, barley, kale, buckwheat and tofu. So, while the article is beneficial in promoting food which is healthy and has a lower ecological footprint than meat, it is simultaneously entrenching the story that THE IDEAL MAN IS COMPETITIVE. The competition being set up in general by the magazine is to achieve extrinsic values — power, status, muscle, performance — rather than anything that could prove helpful to others or the ecosystems that support life.

If readers accept the competitive framing and compare themselves with the heroes and cover models of the magazine then they are likely to come out as losers. In one article (MH7:179), five overweight men with small muscles are pictured with the text 'Introducing five ordinary *MH* readers. Helping you to achieve your fitness goals'. The pronouns 'you' and 'your' make it clear that these men are representing the reader, and that the reader is 'ordinary'. The expression 'your fitness goals' presupposes that the reader already has certain goals, although one of the primary functions of the magazine is to set up goals for the reader.

The goals that the magazine sets up for the 'ordinary' reader, however, are very challenging indeed. The magazine's '12 step program' will 'take you from sofa to superstar' (MH7:11), you will 'pack on 10kg of muscles in just 6 weeks' (MH7: cover), 'become the ultimate athlete' (MH2: cover), 'join the athletic elite' (MH1:92), 'become one of the top 1%' (MH1:92), and achieve 'Olympic performance' in the bedroom (MH3:35). Clearly, for all but a tiny minority of readers these goals are unachievable. Giles and Close (2008) describe how 'existing research argues that the muscular male body ideal, often promoted in the media, is associated with male body dissatisfaction and increasingly problematic attempts to attain unrealistic body shape by young males' and they confirm this in their own research, which found that exposure to men's magazines was correlated with 'both drive for muscularity and eating disturbance'.

While the out-of-reach goals may lead to anxiety for the readers, they provide an opportunity for advertisers to step in and offer to relieve the anxiety through purchases. As McLoughlin (2000, p. 39) points out, magazines are 'a vehicle for promoting various commodities through advertisements because this is where the real revenue lies'. The reader may not be able to create a huge powerful body but could instead buy a powerful car to compensate. The Ford Ranger pick-up truck is pictured in one advertisement in a powerful position hurtling down towards the viewer with the caption THE ALL-NEW RANGER TAMES THE WORLD (MH5:69) in bold capitals; the Audi Avant is pictured next to 444 horses, emphasising only one of its characteristics: power (MH1:37). The huge Mercedes-Benz M-class 4x4 is 'Big on power' and represented from a low camera angle to highlight that power. The reader himself may not manage 'Olympic performance', but the advertisement for the Porsche 911 uses the same keyword 'performance', declaring that:

- each new generation has pushed the boundaries of performance ... As well as their legendary all-wheel drive handling, they feature broad shoulders, making for a striking presence. (MH2:54)

The metaphorical 'shoulders' of the car here confuses the line between the looks of the car and those of its owner. This may be because, as Barthel (1992, p. 144) points out, 'the male mode ... is most in evidence in car advertisements, where the keywords are masculine: power, precision, performance ... As the juxtaposition of shape and power suggests, the car is not simply the Other. It is also an extension of the owner'.

While the text of the magazine encourages readers to aspire to become warriors and Olympic champions by eating and training like them, the advertisements give readers an easier route: simply shopping like them. The advertisements are full of sportsmen, musclemen, and men who look like cover models displaying their purchases of particular products. For example, one advertisement makes it clear that 'Herbert Nitsch Airline pilot. Deep sea diver. Extreme record breaker' buys Breitling watches (MH7:7). More directly, there is a wide range of advertisements for protein powders and supplements to 'boost muscle development' (MH4:150) or for 'building hard, lean muscle' (MH4:164). Whether goods are being bought to achieve the goals set up by the magazine or to compensate for not being able to achieve them, the dissatisfaction of being 'ordinary' in comparison to the heroes described in the magazine could drive readers towards consumerism.

In general, then, while *Men's Health* magazine does include a range of useful health tips, and recommends some healthy food beyond its staple of meat and convenience food, its main purpose seems to lie outside of health promotion. Instead, it tells a story about what it means to be an ideal man that draws from, exaggerates and entrenches traditional models of hegemonic masculinity: an ideal man is aggressive, competitive, a meat eater, and a convenience food eater.

That is not the whole story, however. The magazine also constructs a new form of gender identity for men that echoes that previously reserved for women — that of a consumer compensating for their bodily inadequacies through the purchase of fashion products, grooming aids, supplements and powerful cars. From the perspective of the ecosophy, this is highly problematic, firstly because of the environmental impact of meat production, convenience food and consumer items. At a deeper level, the construction of masculine identity directs the energy, resources and efforts of men into an entirely self-centred mission to build a particular type of body in order to gain personal status. The activities promoted in the magazine are, in general, performed for personal gain and are conducted alone rather than with the company or cooperation of others. The only representations of genuine connection with other people are through sex. Even sex, though, is sometimes represented as a form of self-centred muscle-building exercise through expressions like 'bulk up, slim down ... with sex ... The coregasm: lie back and think of muscle ...' (MH3:77) or 'the dirty weekend that burns 10,000 calories' (MH4: cover). This fits in with the much larger story of the individual dedicated only to self-gain, which appears in neoclassical economics and is one of the defining stories of modernity. The time and energy which men put into building muscles and increasing status through consumption and competition could instead be directed towards intrinsic goals such as connecting with other people, connecting with nature, or working towards the benefit of the community.

理论延伸

　　20 世纪以来，"身份"的概念在各个领域中的作用越来越明显，逐渐被广泛应用在人类学、社会学、心理学和语言学等人文社会科学的多个领域。不同学科的研究者开始依据自身的研究背景和学术兴趣对身份问题的不同方面进行研究，推动了这门跨学科研究领域的发展。本章所运用的身份理论（具体是话语身份建构）与生态语言学研究领域最大的契合点是：借助语言这一交际工具来建构生态身份，努力通过语言的生态实现人与自然的和谐共生。

　　话语身份建构的相关研究是从社会学领域兴起的，而后拓展到语言学领域，它是社会发展的结果，但就其根源而言，可以追踪到哲学的范畴（范宏雅、宋锐，2021）。在哲学领域，存在两种身份观：本质主义（essentialism）身份观和社会建构主义（social constructionism）身份观。本质主义身份观强调的是身份的自然属性，认为身份是永恒不变的，人们表现出来的身份均具有其自身的本质，不受社会因素的影响；社会建构主义身份观注重对社会因素的关注，认为人们无法孤立地认识事物的本身，它具有一定的动态性（陈新仁，2018；范宏雅、宋锐，2021）。社会建构主义中的身份在社会实践中是会不断变化的，人们可以根据实际情况不断建构出新的身份，突出其在社会中的角色和特征。

　　因此，随着社会的发展，话语身份建构研究经历了从本质主义身份观到社会建构主义身份观的转变。基于社会建构主义身份观，著名社会学家 Tajfel & Turner（1979）提出了社会身份理论（social identity theory），最初用于探讨种群中心主义（ethnocentrism）的相关问题，区分了自我认同和社会认同。随后，Turner 在社会身份理论的基础上进一步完善，形成了自我分类理论（self-categorization theory），更加关注自我身份的群体归类，以体现出个体的社会身份（参见李春、宫秀丽，2006）。

在人文社会科学研究的"话语转向"驱动下，到 20 世纪后期，有关话语身份建构的研究出现了一种新的倾向（项蕴华，2009），即重视话语的作用，它是对社会建构主义身份观的继承和发展。从语言学的角度，对身份建构问题的讨论主要关注的是语言和身份之间的关系，探讨语言如何建构身份，强调通过话语的实践、挖掘和分析来建构人们的身份。由此可以看出，话语身份建构在语言学领域与我们在本书第 2 章所讨论的话语分析是分不开的，读者可将其与第 2 章的内容结合起来。换句话说，我们在话语分析的过程中，可以根据具体的研究问题，研究语篇或话语中的身份建构问题。

针对不同的研究个体或群体、从不同的理论视角可以建构出各种各样的身份类型，例如：个人身份、社会身份、集体身份、文化身份、民族身份等（Wodak *et al.*，2009；陈建平、王加林，2014；张玮、谢朝群，2016；郭旭，2021；史兴松、程霞，2021）。本章尝试建构的是生态身份。目前有关生态身份问题的研究较少，对生态身份问题研究感兴趣的读者可重点阅读王姗姗和宗秀蔡（2012）、苗兴伟和李珂（2021）的这两篇论文以及黄国文和赵蕊华（2019：138–140）有关生态身份内容的阐述。此外，读者可进一步阅读《话语与身份》（*Discourse and Identity*）这本专著（Benwell & Stokoe，2006），以便更加系统地了解有关语言与身份的理论与实践。

补充文献

陈建平，王加林 . 2014. 互文性与身份建构话语策略 . 中国外语，（2）：32–38.

陈新仁 . 2018. 语用身份论——如何用身份话语做事 . 北京：北京师范大学出版社 .

范宏雅，宋锐 . 2021. 话语身份建构研究的学理分析 . 长春理工大学学报（社会科学版），（1）：139–142.

郭旭 . 2021. 中医药跨文化传播的互文性与身份建构研究 . 天津外国语大学学报，（1）：105–119.

黄国文，赵蕊华 . 2019. 什么是生态语言学 . 上海：上海外语教育出版社 .

李春，宫秀丽 . 2006. 自我分类理论概述 . 山东师范大学学报（人文社会科学版），（3）：157–160.

苗兴伟，李珂 . 2021. 再语境化视角下企业生态身份的话语建构 . 外语教学，（2）：1–6.

史兴松，程霞. 2021. 基于语料库的中美银行企业身份话语研究. 现代外语，（2）：170–182.

王姗姗，宗秀蔡. 2012. 地方感与生态身份认同——梭罗生态观新读. 鄱阳湖学刊，（2）：85–92.

项蕴华. 2009. 身份建构研究综述. 社会科学研究，（5）：188–192.

张玮，谢朝群. 2016. 驾校冲突话语的规约化不礼貌程式与身份建构. 中国外语，（6）：45–52.

Benwell, B. & Stokoe, E. 2006. *Discourse and identity*. Edinburgh: Edinburgh University Press.

Crompton, T. & Kasser, T. 2009. *Meeting environmental challenges: The role of human identity*. Godalming: WWF-UK.

Tajfel, H. & Turner, J. C. 1979. An integrative theory of intergroup conflict. In W. G. Austin & S. Worchel (Eds.), *The social psychology of intergroup relations*. Monterey: Brooks Cole, 33–47.

Wheaton, B. 2007. Identity, politics, and the beach: Environmental activism in *Surfers Against Sewage. Leisure Studies*, (3): 279–302.

Wodak, R., DeCillia, R., Reisigl, M. & Liebhart, K. 2009. *The discursive construction of national identity* (2nd ed.). Edinburgh: Edinburgh University Press.

7

CONVICTIONS

章节导读

　　一般来说，几乎在所有的情形下，不管我们是对实际发生的事情进行话语描绘，还是对虚构的事情展开讲解，都是非常有效的语言表达策略，同时也暗示了语言的真实性程度。本章主要运用真实性理论（facticity theory），针对语言的真实性问题进行分析，探究语篇或话语的真实性模式是如何影响人们的信念的。此处我们对这一章节的主要内容按三个层次进行梳理：（1）理论内涵；（2）真实性分析的方法；（3）案例：否认"气候变化"和"冠状病毒"中的真实性。

　　（1）理论内涵。作者在这个部分围绕"人类导致了气候变化"这一表述的多个例子分析，例如：对不同国家人们的相关调查（Smith，2019）、IPCC 评估报告、Fraser报告、电影《奥巴马的欺骗》（*The Obama Deception*）等，引出了本章的两个核心概念——"信念"（convictions）和"真实性模式"（facticity patterns）。本书将信念定义为：人们内心中关于世界描述的真实性和确定性的故事（*Convictions are stories in people's minds about whether descriptions of the world are true, uncertain or false.*）。真实性模式的意思是：一组描述世界真实性和确定性故事的语言机制（*Facticity patterns are clusters of linguistic devices which come together to represent descriptions of the world as true, uncertain or false.*）。

　　针对这一章节的主题，生态语言学研究者要做的是，通过话语分析发现语篇或话语中是怎样增强或降低对人类未来至关重要的表述的。比如 IPCC 评估报告的例子（P152）中的情态副词（"极有可能"）的使用。这个词语不是"完全肯定"或"完全否定"的，而是降低了该句中话语的真实性。作者提出，如果将这个情态副词去掉，那么这句话的真实性将会增强很多。其实，这里的真实性说的不是话语表述是真的，而是指通过一组语言机制把它表达得有理有据，不受说话者的影响，反映世界的某一个方面。

（2）真实性分析的方法。批评话语分析为语言特征的真实性分析提供了分析的方法，分析过程中可聚焦的语言特征有以下几个：情态词语（Martin & Rose，2007：53）、权威的称呼词语（van Leeuwen，2008：107）、数量词语（Machin & Mayr，2012：192）、模糊词语（Machin & Mayr，2012：189）、预设词语（Martin & White，2005：101）。

在生态语言学的研究中，真实性模式研究涉及很多领域，其中突出的领域是有关气候变化问题的讨论。下面来看书中的一组例子（P156）——对英国核燃料公司（British Nuclear Fuels）手册的分析（Harré *et al.*，1999：85）。这个例子中蕴含着两种观点：首先是核产业本身的观点——在预设和可信度方面表现的权利较大；另一个是来自环保主义者的观点——被描述为不可靠、过于乐观、无权对核能的危害及未来做出科学的判断（Harré *et al.*，1999：86）。后来，这个公司被核工业协会（Nuclear Industry Association）取代，目前该协会在官网上分别引用了政治家、能源公司拥有者、科学家、环保主义者等代表的观点。这些引用都支持核工业的进行，且在发话者名字的后面都使用了同位语的方式，表示他们分别代表某一类群体说话。这种话语表述的语言特征为读者较好地平衡了不同群体间的利害关系，增强了这些话语的真实性。

（3）案例：否认"气候变化"和"冠状病毒"中的真实性。作者在这个部分讨论的案例主要来自存在争议的纪录片《全球变暖的大骗局》（*The Great Global Warming Swindle*）。该视频通过与来自不同学科领域的 17 名受访者交流，传递出"气候变化是人类造成的"观点是完全不正确的。而且，整个纪录片也尽可能以较高的真实性模式，向观众展现了"二氧化碳不是导致气候变化的原因"这一信念。具体方式主要体现在：第一，非情态化话语的使用，例如：通过"显然""任何"等词语增强话语的真实性；第二，描述部分群体与"气候变化是人类造成的"这个观点的利害关系；第三，运用已知信息或新信息坚持"气候变化是一个政治概念，而非科学概念"。总的来说，这部纪录片的真实性模式是：运用多种语言机制将"气候变化是人类造成的"的真实性降到最低；而将"气候变化是太阳造成的"的真实性放到了最高的位置。因此，这一纪录片是应该受到抵制的。

哈特兰研究所（Heartland Institute）的一名研究员 Naomi Seibt 分析了气候变化与冠状病毒的相似之处。Seibt 表示，在另一个视频中有人对冠状病毒的一系列问题表示怀疑——认为"死亡率的数据统计被夸大""冠状病毒的症状与 5G 辐射相同"，等等。DeSmog（2020）的研究也表明，许多否认气候变化真实性的人同样也否认冠状病毒的真实性。从语言表述来看，这种否认从轻度的陈述（例如："该病毒有害程度较轻"）到巨大的阴谋（例如："该病毒是一个骗局"）都是存在的，目的是引起人们对冠状病毒出现原因的关注。也就是说，否认"气候变化"真实性描述的语言模式，也同样在破坏着"冠状病毒"的真实性模式。

显然，上述的案例分析中，生态语言学研究者可以从中发挥作用，我们不只是要挖掘不正确的信息表述，还要借助真实性分析的方法以及真实性模式的讨论，揭示出语言背后更深层次的运作机制，这对解决多种全球性的生态环境问题才是有意义的。

> In virtually any situation appeal to the facts, to what really happened and what is only invention, can be a powerful device.
>
> (Jonathan Potter 1996, p. 1)

In 2019 YouGov conducted a survey which asked people in various countries whether they agreed with the description 'The climate is changing and human activity is mainly responsible' (M. Smith 2019). The results showed that 71% of respondents in India agreed, while in the USA 38% agreed, and in Saudi Arabia, only 35% agreed. These respondents are not basing their convictions about whether climate change is caused by humans on direct readings of temperature data or ice core samples, but on the texts to which they have been exposed. Texts (whether written, oral or visual texts) have a dual role — they put forward descriptions such as 'humans cause climate change' and represent these descriptions as true, false, certain or uncertain. In other words, they place descriptions of the world on a spectrum of *facticity*, from absolute truth at one end to absolute falsehood on the other, with a range of levels of uncertainty in between. In doing so, they play a potential role in influencing readers' *convictions*, which are (in this book) stories in people's minds about whether certain descriptions of reality are true, certain, uncertain or false.

As an example, Jem Bendell, a professor of sustainability leadership at the University of Cumbria, is very clear about his own convictions concerning the future of humanity:

- Currently, I have chosen to interpret the information as indicating inevitable collapse, probable catastrophe and possible extinction. There is a growing community of people who conclude we face inevitable human extinction and treat that view as a prerequisite for meaningful discussions about the implications for our lives right now. (ML2:17)

Bendell's convictions range from something he is highly certain about (the collapse of our current civilisation) to something he is much less certain about (total human extinction).

He indicates the strength of his convictions through the adverbs *inevitable, probable* and *possible*. Convictions influence not only how people think and talk, but also how they act. Bendell talks about the need for 'meaningful discussions about the implications for our lives right now' because whether we believe humans are heading towards extinction or not can have a profound influence on what we do each day.

Convictions manifest themselves linguistically in patterns of linguistic devices which represent descriptions of the world on a spectrum from certainly true to certainly false. The Intergovernmental Panel on Climate Change (IPCC), for example, uses language in particular ways to express the facticity pattern 'HUMANS CAUSE CLIMATE CHANGE' IS TRUE:

- Human influence ... is extremely likely to have been the dominant cause of the observed warming since the mid-20th century. (Fifth Assessment Report, EN13:47)

This is not the highest level of facticity since the modal adverb 'extremely likely' is used rather than 'unequivocal', or 'absolutely certain'. If no modals had been used at all then it would have had even higher facticity: 'Human influence *has* been the dominant cause'. On the other hand, the following description from a US conspiracy theorist is about as far *down* on the scale of facticity as it is possible to go:

- The notion of anthropogenic climate change is a fraud — the idea that the planet is getting warmer and that human activity is somehow responsible is a pseudo-scientific fraud, it's a big lie, it's a monstrosity. (Webster Tarpley in the film *The Obama Deception*, ML19:1h:26m)

The facticity is reduced by the vocabulary choice of 'notion' and 'idea' (which are less certain than 'theory' or 'fact'), the adverb 'somehow' (expressing implausibility) and, obviously, the vocabulary choice of 'fraud', 'pseudo', 'lie' and 'monstrosity'. The facticity pattern that this extract, the documentary as a whole, and many other conspiracy theory materials convey is 'HUMANS CAUSE CLIMATE CHANGE' IS CERTAINLY FALSE.

A Canadian free-market think-tank, the Fraser Institute (EN15), conveys a different facticity pattern in one of its reports. The report *Fact, not fiction: an introduction to climate change,* purports to be an objective discussion of climate science but concludes that 'there are considerable uncertainties and scientific debate about the causes of climate change' before offering the advice that 'Canadian policymakers should exercise caution and refrain from imposing unwarranted regulations in response to the overheated rhetoric of alarmists' (EN15:8). The report uses language in various ways to convey the facticity pattern 'HUMANS CAUSE CLIMATE CHANGE' IS UNCERTAIN. The following is just one example:

• While some suggest that current warming is the result of excess emissions of carbon dioxide and other 'greenhouse gasses', there is evidence that at least some climate change is a result of solar activity. (EN15:6)

This represents the description 'current warming is the result of greenhouse gasses' as low facticity by attributing it only to 'some' and using the *quoting verb* 'suggest' to introduce doubts about its reliability. The inverted commas around 'greenhouse gasses' also lower facticity if they are taken as questioning whether there are actually such things as greenhouse gasses. The think-tank then uses the uncertain facticity pattern to try to influence the convictions of policymakers and stop them taking action in response to the threat of climate change. This is hardly a surprise, since the conclusions of industry-sponsored free-market think-tanks are always that government regulation is unnecessary or excessive.

The IPCC AR5 report, the Fraser report, and the documentary *The Obama Deception* are just three among an extremely large number of texts which circulate in society and can influence the convictions of those who are exposed to them. In the case of the IPCC, the choice of modifiers such as 'virtually certain', 'highly likely' or 'exceptionally unlikely' follows a complex institutional process described by Hulme (2009, pp. 84–105). The process involves selection of experts, the elicitation of subjective judgements about their confidence in uncertain future outcomes, considerations of how well constrained the outcomes are by known cause-and-effect processes, how well qualified the scientists are to understand those processes, and the degree of agreement among scientists.

On the other hand, there are very different institutions with a far simpler process for arriving at facticity patterns in the statements they make. Brulle (2014) describes an extensive network of what he calls the 'climate change counter-movement': a web of advocacy organisations, think-tanks and trade associations sponsored by conservative foundations and anonymous industrial donors, which exists to raise doubt about the description that humans are causing climate change. The facticity of the descriptions produced by these organisations is often much higher than those of the IPCC, even if the evidence base is much smaller or non-existent. This has important implications for how the media treat different versions of climate change. As Jones (in BBC Trust 2011) puts it:

Because so much of science involves uncertainty, it is open to attack from those who have never experienced that sensation. Purity of belief makes it easy for denialists to attract the attention of news organisations ... This can lead to undue publicity for views supported by no factual information at all.

The high facticity used by the climate change counter-movement may be one of the reasons why only 38% of people in the US, where the movement is strongest, were found to agree with the description that 'The climate is changing and human activity is mainly responsible'.

Ecolinguistics can analyse texts to show how they build up or undermine key descriptions that are important for the future of humanity — 'climate change is caused by humans' being one of them. What are important are not isolated sentences which build up or undermine facticity but larger patterns which run across multiple texts. It is these larger patterns which have the potential to influence people's convictions. This book uses the terms 'convictions' and 'facticity patterns' in the following ways:

> *Convictions* are stories in people's minds about whether descriptions of the world are true, uncertain or false.
>
> *Facticity patterns* are clusters of linguistic devices which come together to represent descriptions of the world as true, uncertain or false.

Both convictions and facticity patterns are expressed using small capitals in the form 'x' IS CERTAINLY TRUE/TRUE/PROBABLY TRUE/PROBABLY FALSE/FALSE/CERTAINLY FALSE, where 'x' is a particular description of the world (for example, 'CLIMATE CHANGE IS CAUSED BY HUMANS' IS PROBABLY TRUE).

Facticity has been explored in useful ways by a range of disciplines, including discursive psychology (Potter 1996), the sociology of science (Latour and Woolgar 1986; Latour 2013), political discourse analysis (Chilton 2004; Fairclough and Fairclough 2012), and more general discourse analysis (Martin and Rose 2007; van Leeuwen 2008). Jonathan Potter (1996), in his book *Representing Reality: Discourse, Rhetoric and Social Construction,* provides the most comprehensive account of the linguistic devices that speakers and writers use to 'work up the facticity of a version ... to construct a description as a factual account' (p. 112). For Potter, facticity is not about whether a description is actually 'true', but instead about the cluster of linguistic techniques which are used to represent a description *as if* it were 'solid, neutral, independent of the speaker and to be merely mirroring some aspect of the world' (p. 1).

The details of how the facticity of descriptions is worked up or undermined can be analysed by Potter's (1996) combination of social psychology and rhetoric. Among other aspects, Potter considers how people manage *stake*. Participants in a debate may present themselves as neutrally conveying facts which are 'out there', without any particular agenda, while representing their opponents as biased because they have a stake in a particular outcome. One of the most powerful ways of managing stake and increasing facticity is the use of the *repertoire of empiricism* (Potter 1996, p. 150). This is a form of language where conclusions are represented as arriving directly from empirical data (e.g. 'The measurements indicate that...'). Potter (p. 153) describes how:

> The empiricist repertoire provides for descriptions of scientists' actions and beliefs which minimise the involvement of the scientist in constructing and interpreting what is studied. The scientist becomes passive, virtually a bystander ... The empiricist repertoire is a standard device for constructing the out-there-ness of scientific phenomena.

Of course, it is not just scientists who use the empiricist repertoire — it is a standard way of building the facticity of descriptions used by a wide range of participants in social life.

Critical Discourse Analysis provides techniques for analysing the linguistic features that build facticity. These features include: (a) modals such as 'must', 'should' and 'might' which describe how probable a description is (Martin and Rose 2007, p. 53); (b) calls to expert authority and the authority of consensus (van Leeuwen 2008, p. 107); (c) quantifiers such as 'some' or 'many' which 'can be used to gloss over a lack of concrete evidence' (Machin and Mayr 2012, p. 192); (d) hedges such as 'X thinks' or 'X believes' which are 'often used to detract from what others hold to be the case' (Machin and Mayr 2012, p. 189); and (e) presuppositions which construct descriptions as 'taken-for-granted' rather than 'currently at issue or up for discussion' (Martin and White 2005, p. 101). A useful concept is *modality*, which, in Richardson's (2007, p. 59) definition, is the 'degree to which a speaker or writer is committed to the claim he or she is making'. Modality is on a scale from low commitment (e.g. the use of the modals 'might' or 'probably') to high commitment (e.g. the adverb 'certain' or an unhedged declaration 'X is the case').

The following extract, from the textbook *Principles of Microeconomics,* is useful in illustrating how facticity patterns can be built through a chain of increasing modality. The extract describes a fictional bakery owner, Caroline, who is standing as a metonym to describe the behaviour of company owners in general:

- It is conceivable that Caroline started her firm because of an altruistic desire to provide the world with cookies ... More likely, Caroline started her business to make money. Economists normally assume that the goal of a firm is to maximise profit, and they find that this assumption works well in most cases ... Caroline's objective is to make her firm's profit as large as possible. (ET3:260)

The modality gradually increases, from being extremely low (*'conceivable'*) when an altruistic goal of providing the world with cookies is considered, to higher modality ('more *likely*') when the motive of money is considered, to even higher modality ('works well in *most* cases') when the goal is maximising profit, to the highest level of certainty ('Caroline's objective *is...* ') when the goal is making 'profit as large as possible'. In this way the text downplays the possibility that owners of companies want to do something useful for the world, while making the self-centred goal of profit seem to be their obvious motivation. Overall, the facticity pattern can be described as 'HUMANS ARE SELFISH' IS CERTAINLY TRUE.

The example above is just a local pattern in one particular text, but what is important is how neoclassical economics discourse builds up the facticity of the description 'owners maximise profit' widely across the range of documents over which it exerts an influence. If the facticity of a description is high enough and widespread enough, then it can achieve *hegemony*, which 'means achieving a misperception of its arbitrariness ... so that it comes to be seen as transparently reflecting economic realities rather than constructing them in a particular way' (Chouliaraki and Fairclough 1999, p. 5). In other words, the description 'owners maximise profit' could become widely considered to be just the 'way things are', rather than a particular perspective. And, once established, it could justify owners in focusing on increased profits rather than ensuring their company benefits society and the environment.

Within ecolinguistics, facticity patterns have been examined primarily in the area of climate change, which is clearly a key area both in terms of its ecological importance and the strength of opposing views about it. However, there are other areas that have also been examined. Harré *et al.* (1999, p. 85) analyse how a British Nuclear Fuels brochure contains two different 'voices': one of the nuclear industry itself and one of its environmentalist critics. They find that the voice of the environmentalists is represented as 'unreliable, over-optimistic and without the right to make declarations with the authority of science' (p. 86). The other voice, of the nuclear industry, is represented as having 'an unassailable right to make prophecies and to be trusted ... One [voice] has the right to comment on the dangers and the future of nuclear power; the other does not' (p. 86).

British Nuclear Fuels no longer exists and its role has been replaced by the Nuclear Industry Association. The Association represents the environmentalist voice in a very different way from its predecessor. Its website has a page 'Talking Nuclear: who said what?' (ML6) which contains quotes from politicians, energy company owners, scientists and environmentalists. The voices representing environmentalism are named as:

- George Monbiot, Environmentalist. (ML6)
- Lord (Chris) Smith of Finsbury, Chairman, Environment Agency. (ML6)
- Stephen Tindale, former Executive Director, Greenpeace. (ML6)

- Chris Goodall, Green Party Parliamentary candidate. (ML6)

The statements quoted on the website for each of these commentators strongly back the nuclear industry; George Monbiot, for example, is quoted as saying 'Nuclear power is our only workable low-carbon energy source' (ML6). The commentators are not represented as just individuals giving their ideas, but as representatives of environmentalism, the Environment Agency, Greenpeace and the Green Party, respectively, through the use of apposition (i.e., the placing of a noun phrase stating their position immediately after their name). This discursive move manages the issue of stake. By quoting from environmentalists who clearly have no direct financial stake in the future of the industry, the Nuclear Industry Association presents the description that 'nuclear power is beneficial' as a fact independent of its own interest or bias, and accepted now even by those who have traditionally opposed it. The quotations are, of course, carefully selected, and while the Environment Agency does state that 'new nuclear power stations should have a role to play in this country's future energy mix' (PD11), the Green Party and Greenpeace have very different official positions:

- The Green Party is fundamentally opposed to nuclear energy, which we consider to be expensive and dangerous. (PD12)
- Greenpeace has always fought — and will continue to fight — vigorously against nuclear power because it is an unacceptable risk to the environment and to humanity. (EN12)

These examples illustrate two common approaches to undermining the facticity of environmental positions. The first approach represents environmentalists as untrustworthy, unreliable and unscientific. The second represents them as reliable, but carefully selects quotes from environmentalists or former environmentalists who agree with the position being advanced. Either way, the facticity pattern in nuclear industry discourse is, unsurprisingly, 'NUCLEAR POWER IS BENEFICIAL' IS CERTAINLY TRUE.

In another study, Alexander (2008, p. 127) examines 'how the anti-green movement and its "friends" use language to construct the world'. Alexander describes the huge web of industry-funded conservative think-tanks which are linked to environmental scepticism. He describes how these groups use 'simulated rationality' — the use of scientific vocabulary, selected facts and statistics to provide descriptions that are 'plausibly rational to an uninformed listener' but are not based on actual evidence (p. 136). Another aspect that Alexander describes is vocabulary choice — the way that the anti-green movement describes its activities with 'vague, abstract and positive terms such as "common sense", "commitment", "innovative" and "scientific" ... to win approval without providing evidence' (p. 131). On the other hand, the movement uses negative expressions to describe opponents, such as 'nimby' or 'ecoterrorist', thus 'belittling their position'.

Nerlich (2010) examines the reactions to the so-called 'climategate' affair — the leaked emails from scientists at the University of East Anglia that are even now used by sceptics to discredit climate science. Her study analyses blog entries written by climate sceptics in the wake of the leaked emails, and reveals a cluster of metaphors used by the bloggers to undermine the facticity of the accounts of climate scientists. One metaphor, in a variety of forms, was used more than any other: SCIENCE IS RELIGION. Nerlich (p. 432) provides the following example drawn from a sceptic blog entry:

- The Global Warming religion is as virulent and insidious as all mind-bending cults of absolute certitude, and yet it has become mainstream orthodoxy and infallible spirituality faster than any faith-based cult in history.

This quote creates a strong extended metaphor through using five words from the lexical set of religion: 'religion', 'cult', 'orthodoxy', 'spirituality' and 'faith'.

The metaphors that Nerlich found include SCIENTIFIC THEORIES ARE GOSPEL, SCIENTISTS ARE EVANGELISTS OR PRIESTS, SCIENTIFIC DISSEMINATION IS PREACHING, SCIENTIFIC CONFIDENCE IS DEVOTION and SCIENTIFIC PREDICTIONS ARE PROPHECIES. In general, Nerlich describes how the bloggers used the metaphor of CLIMATE SCIENCE IS RELIGION in order to claim 'that the emails show that climate scientists, rather than increasing knowledge, tried to buttress their fabricated system of faith' (p. 428). This 'makes political action impossible, as it undermines the credibility of scientists ... and maintains ... public confusion about climate change' (p. 433). Nerlich describes the paradoxical mixture of claims that sceptics use to undermine the facticity of science: that there is no consensus among scientists; that there is a total consensus, therefore it must be a conspiracy; that scientists are uncertain about climate change, or that scientists are so certain that it is a faith they unquestioningly believe in. This leads to 'a misleading and distorted view of science which deviates from genuine concern over scientific uncertainty' (p. 421).

Particularly valuable for ecolinguistics is research which looks not only at patterns of facticity but also at the result they have on the behaviour of those who are exposed to them. A behavioural response study of this kind was carried out by researchers at the University of Chicago (Bursztyn *et al.* 2020) and described in a report entitled *Misinformation During a Pandemic*. Although the authors did not express it in these terms, the study looked at the convictions 'CORONAVIRUS IS A SERIOUS THREAT' IS TRUE and 'CORONAVIRUS IS A SERIOUS THREAT' IS FALSE. The methodology they used was firstly textual analysis of two Fox News presenters who took different positions on the coronavirus threat towards the beginning of the outbreak. The first presenter, Carlson, had a facticity pattern 'CORONAVIRUS IS A SERIOUS THREAT' IS TRUE. For example, in the following he uses the word 'alarming', and the subordinating conjunction 'even under' to make 27 million deaths appear to be a best-case scenario:

- alarming videos trickling out of China indicate the virus is far from under control
- Even under that scenario [a 0.5% death rate], there would still be 27 million deaths from coronavirus globally. In this country, more than a million would die.

On the other hand, the second presenter, Hannity, had far smaller coverage of coronavirus (which in itself presents a facticity pattern that it is not a serious threat), and downplayed the risk when he did cover it:

- Healthy people, generally, 99 percent, recover very fast even if they contract it. Twenty-six people were shot in Chicago alone over the weekend. You notice there's no widespread hysteria about violence in Chicago.

This implies that the response to coronavirus is 'hysteria', a term with a sexist past that is often used to dismiss threats and encourage inaction. The use of the term here contributes to a facticity pattern of 'CORONAVIRUS IS A SERIOUS THREAT' IS FALSE. The divergence between the presenters was temporary, however, and both converged into treating coronavirus as a very serious threat when it became more obvious that it was. In the meantime, though, Bursztyn et al. (2020, p. 8) discovered a difference in behaviour between the audiences of the two presenters. The audience that frequently watched Carlson washed their hands, cancelled their travel plans and socially distanced more than those who frequently watched Hannity. This resulted in a death rate for those who watched Carlson that was lower than those who watched Hannity.

There are many descriptions related to coronavirus, from 'the virus arises from unhealthy relationships between humans and the natural world' to 'coronavirus symptoms are actually caused by 5G mobile technology' and even 'coronavirus can be cured by injecting bleach'. The degree to which people believe the various descriptions are true, uncertain or false — their convictions about them — will influence how they act in the world, with potentially life or death consequences.

The media, in all its various forms, is one of the key influences of generally held convictions since it can reach such large audiences. An important application of facticity theory in ecolinguistics concerns how the facticity of academic research is transformed when it is reported in the media. For climate change, Hulme (2009, p. 225) writes:

Rather than there being only 'facts' about climate change proclaimed by institutions such as the IPCC — 'facts' received intact by the masses — the circuitry of the media offers spaces and creative potential for social actors to filter, amplify, and rhetoricise these 'facts' in multiple ways.

Richardson (2007, p. 61) provides a useful example of the transformations that can occur in facticity when the media re-express the facts provided by scientists — in this case, conservation scientists. He presents the following extract from the *Daily Express*:

- BAMBI TURNS KILLER: Top environmentalists warned yesterday that a population explosion among British deer is playing havoc with woodland birds ... The British Trust for Ornithology review, carried out for Government wildlife advisers, says that deer are playing a key role in wrecking the habitat for many species.

Richardson notes that the absence of modals such as 'may' or 'might' in '*is* playing havoc' and 'deer *are* playing a key role' makes these categorical assertions — the highest level of facticity, asserting that deer have definitely caused the decline of the birds. This is a facticity pattern of 'DEER HAVE CAUSED BIRD DECLINE' IS CERTAINLY TRUE. The original research that the articles are referring to, however, uses much lower facticity in its claims that deer have caused the decline in woodland birds:

- Intensified grazing and browsing pressure by increasing numbers of deer is very likely to have caused a reduction in habitat quality and contributed to the declines of some woodland birds ... but it should not be concluded that deer are the principal causes of decline in any bird species on a large scale. (EN14:39)

Here the expressions 'very likely', 'contributed to' and 'it should not be concluded' significantly reduce the facticity of the description 'deer cause bird decline'. This facticity pattern is closer to 'DEER HAVE CAUSED BIRD DECLINE' IS POSSIBLY TRUE. Richardson suggests that the *Daily Express* 'chose to single out deer and categorically claim their responsibility purely in order to justify their sensationalist headline!' (p. 62).

It is not just for the sake of sensationalism that the media can transform facticity patterns — it can also be to fit in with the prevailing ideology of the publication. An example of this is *Men's Health* magazine, which uses medical research to build up the facticity of its accounts. From an ecological perspective, one of the most problematic ideologies of the magazine is its promotion of meat and convenience foods as symbols of masculinity, despite their potential negative impacts on both health and the environment.

The following is an example of how the magazine deals with something potentially negative about meat — the fact that it contains carcinogens:

- A world leader in fight against cancer, Dr Dashwood completed his PhD in the UK before hopping across the pond to join Oregon State University. His most recent research, on p. 35, means you can indulge in a rare steak a little more often, without fear of retribution. Bloody heaven we say (MH4:24) ... scientists have discovered an easy way to protect yourself from the harmful effects of a sirloin — eat it with a side of spinach ... Now you can have your steak and eat it. (MH4:35)

This uses the call to the authority of 'Dr Dashwood', mentioning his title, his PhD, his university affiliation and his status as a 'world leader', and expresses the implications of his research with categorical certainty: the research '*means* you can indulge in a rare steak' rather than *suggests* you can; 'scientists *have* discovered an easy way to protect yourself', rather than *may have discovered*; and 'you *can* have your steak' rather than *you may be able to have your steak*. The original research paper that *Men's Health* magazine is referring to expresses the implications of the research in a very different way, however:

- we describe here the first comprehensive screening of miRNAs altered in rat colon tumours induced by a widely consumed dietary carcinogen, PhIP. A systems biology approach coupled with computational modelling and target validation identified key roles for the let-7 family ... Dysregulation of these factors was partially reversed in rats consuming dietary spinach during the post-initiation period. Although the precise mechanisms await further study, the current investigation provides further support for research at the interface of epigenetics, diet, and cancer prevention. (ML5)

This extract has the high modality of the repertoire of empiricism — it is the 'computational modelling' that is the Actor in the process of 'identifying', for example, not the authors, and there is significant use of technical vocabulary. However, the study only claims that dysregulation was 'partially reversed in rats' through mechanisms which 'await further study'. The implication that it is now safe for human males to eat more meat if they have it with spinach is drawn out by *Men's Health* magazine, not the original paper, and expressed with high facticity as a certainty. It is also evaluated highly positively with the expression 'bloody heaven we say' fitting the more general meat-promoting ideology of the magazine.

In another similar example, *Men's Health* draws from research on the impact of drinking tea on the cardiovascular system to conclude, with very high facticity, that junk food is not unhealthy if eaten with a cup of tea:

* EAT JUNK FOOD WITH IMPUNITY ... scientists working at Italy's University of L'Aquila have found that you'll get an instant boost in blood flow with a single cuppa ... So now any time can be burger time, just so long as it's tea time. (MH1:25)

Again, the original press release from the Lipton Institute of Tea which sponsored the study is lower modality, using the words 'depending on', 'suggesting' and 'consistent with', rather than expressing complete certainty:

* A new study conducted at the University of L'Aquila in Italy and supported by the Lipton Institute of Tea, is the first to show that black tea consumption — depending on dose — simultaneously increased blood vessel reactivity and reduced both blood pressure and arterial stiffness, suggesting a cardiovascular health profile that is consistent with maintaining heart health. (ML4)

The authority of medical science is being drawn on to increase facticity, but the facticity is raised far higher than the research it is drawing from. While ecolinguistics cannot determine the exact effect of tea and spinach on human health, it can certainly examine the transformation of the level of certainty between original research articles and commercial lifestyle magazines. In this case, the danger is that the magazine influences its readers to form a conviction in their minds that 'JUNK FOOD IS UNHEALTHY' IS FALSE. This conviction could then guide behaviours, increasing their consumption of products which are potentially unhealthy in excess and are environmentally damaging.

The facticity pattern in *Men's Health* does not just rely on the authority of science, however. The hegemonic masculinity promoted by the magazine emphasises power, but listening to the advice of a more knowledgeable expert could place the reader in a powerless position. Some men may therefore treat the information provided by a trusted friend as a more reliable (and acceptable) source than a distant expert. The language of the magazine itself provides a powerful mixture of calls to the authority of science with the friendly language of the 'buddy'. The voice of the 'buddy' is created through the use of second-person pronouns in '*you* can indulge'; the casual vernacular expressions 'hopping across the pond' (crossing the Atlantic) and 'a cuppa' (a cup of tea); the expletive 'bloody'; and the humorous re-working of the idiom 'now you can have your steak [cake] and eat it'. The following statement from an editor of *Men's Health* magazine (US version) suggests that this is a deliberate strategy:

- We set ourselves apart by providing great, well-researched information with a bit of humour. We are like a buddy filling you in on the latest news, not some pompous know-it-all. (MH9)

This facticity pattern could be described as a 'hybrid' facticity pattern since it relies on two different ways of building up the facticity of its account: the reliability of the scientist due to his/her disinterest, and the reliability of the trusted friend due to his/her loyalty.

A very different area which also uses hybrid facticity patterns is the genre of New Nature Writing. Macfarlane (2013, p. 166) describes how this genre combines poetic language with the high facticity of scholarship from various disciplines:

> [New Nature Writing] folds in aspects of memoir, travel, ecology, botany, zoology, topography, geology, folklore, literary criticism, psycho-geography, anthropology, conservation and even fiction. Most distinctive, to my mind, is its tonal mix of the poetic and the scientific and analytical. *The Snow Geese*, for instance, combines exquisite accounts of geese in flight — 'the flock lifted from the field as a single entity, 10,000 pairs of wings drumming the air, as if people were swatting the dust from rugs' — with an inquiry into the biomechanics of avian migration.

Cowley (2008, p. 9) similarly writes:

> [New Nature writers] share a sense that we are devouring our world, that there is simply no longer any natural landscape or ecosystem that is unchanged by humans. But they don't simply want to walk into the wild, to rhapsodise and commune: they aspire to see with a scientific eye and write with literary effect.

The books can indeed be seen to be a meshwork of lyrical descriptions of nature interjected with high-facticity statements of science and other scholarly areas. However, the lyrical aspects have their own, different form of high facticity. The following two extracts are from Macfarlane's own nature writing in his book *The Wild Places*, and illustrate the two forms of facticity:

- It was then that I saw the glimmering of the water. A line of blinking light — purple and silver — rimming the long curve of the beach. I walked down to the edge, squatted, and waved a hand in the water. It blazed, purple, orange, yellow and silver. Phosphorescence! (NW6:40)
- It is now understood that marine phosphorescence — or, more properly,

bioluminescence — is a consequence of the build-up in the water of minute organisms: dinoflagellate algae and plankton. (NW6:41)

Stenning (2010, p. 19) analyses these examples in her research on the use of science in New Nature Writing. She describes how the second extract uses scientific terminology to add precision to the informal observation in the first quote that the phenomenon was 'phosphorescence'. Stenning points out that technical precision is something that Macfarlane has frequently admired in his critiques of nature writing. Here, his scientific precision comes from using the technical expressions 'bioluminescence', 'organisms' and 'dinoflagellate', as well as the unmodalised 'is a consequence of', and the categorical assertion that 'it is now understood'. This assertion is represented as so certain that the Senser (who it is understood by) does not need to be mentioned.

It might at first be assumed that the facticity of the scientific aspects of New Nature Writing would be high and the more lyrical parts would be low. This, however, is not necessarily the case. The facticity in Macfarlane's more lyrical first quote above is also extremely high — every statement is expressed directly, with no modals such as 'may', 'probably' or 'suggests' to reduce the facticity. The certainty expressed in this quote does not come from calls to the authority of science, but the authority of direct experience. The facticity of the description is backed up by giving the precise details of the event — the specific colours observed, the specific actions involved in the observation, and the specific location of the phenomenon observed. These are all details which are only available to someone who actually participated in this event, and it is in the giving of such details that facticity is built. Potter (1996, p. 3) writes, of a similar example, that 'it is not the general pattern of events so much as the details that makes the story credible. These are the sorts of things that someone who was there to witness events would know'.

The hybrid pattern of scientific or scholarly precision combined with the precision of observed detail is found throughout the works of New Nature Writing examined. The following is another example, from Olivia Laing's *To the River*:

- Isotope hydrology suggests that the trapped fossil water in some of the world's largest confined aquifers is over a million years old ... In comparison, this ditchwater at the river's head was brand new. (NW4:20)
- There was a stinking pond at the edge of the trees, and a tractor waiting for the morning's work. The oats had yet to ripen and everything stood very still. I could hear the faintest trickle of water pattering past roots and tiny stones. (NW4:20)

This shows the use of technical terms from science ('isotope hydrology' and 'confined aquifers') to build facticity in the first example, and the equally high facticity of direct sensory experience in the second. While this example draws from a natural science perspective, Laing elsewhere uses the distinctive vocabulary and grammatical expressions of literary criticism, psychology and history to build facticity.

The New Nature writers peruse the landscape with the eye of someone directly experiencing the reality around them with their senses, but at the same time bring with them the eye of the expert — the scientist or historian who has a different kind of engagement with the world. The bringing together of different facticity patterns is one reason why the writing is powerful: the writers cannot be accused of either being so lost in abstraction that they are disconnected from the world around them, or blind to the larger patterns that underlie the phenomena they observe. What is most important is that the facticity patterns are mixed without one being deemed more correct, proper or superior to the other. The consequences of this hybrid facticity pattern are summed up by Stenning (2010, p. 19) as follows:

> The authors of *Nature Cure*, *The Wild Places* and *Pilgrim* share respect for the empirical method and the precision of scientific language, while remaining sceptical of the claims of dispassionate science and total knowledge of non-human nature. In doing so, they support the role of the imaginatively engaged scientist, and scientifically educated writer.

Facticity in climate change and coronavirus denial

This section will briefly analyse the controversial documentary *The Great Global Warming Swindle* (EN16), which was first broadcast on the UK's Channel 4 in 2007 but remains a popular video on YouTube, with more than a million views in 2018–20. In this documentary there is no uncertainty — the facticity pattern is 'CLIMATE CHANGE IS CAUSED BY HUMANS' IS CERTAINLY FALSE. It conveys this pattern through combining the voice of an offscreen and all-knowing narrator with statements from 17 interviewees, including scientists from a range of disciplines, as well as an economist, a journalist, a politician, a weather forecaster, and a former environmentalist.

The key facticity pattern that runs throughout the documentary is 'CARBON DIOXIDE CAUSES CLIMATE CHANGE' IS CERTAINLY FALSE. The following examples are extracted from different moments in the documentary:

- Clark: CO_2 clearly cannot be causing temperature changes.
- Shaviv: There is no direct evidence which links 20th-century global warming to anthropogenic greenhouse gasses.

- Corbyn: The sun is driving climate change. CO_2 is irrelevant.
- Narrator: There is no evidence at all from earth's long climate history that carbon dioxide has ever determined global temperatures. (EN16)

These are all entirely unmodalised (there are no modals like 'may' or 'perhaps') and the facticity is raised higher by 'clearly' in the first and 'at all' in the last extract. To back up these extremely strong claims, the documentary builds up the authority of its interviewees by describing the plethora of academic titles, awards and respected organisations that they are associated with. To give just two examples:

- Dr Roy Spencer is Senior Scientist for Climate Studies at NASA's Marshall Space Flight Centre. He has been awarded medals for exceptional scientific achievement from both NASA and the American Meteorological Society.
- Patrick Moore is considered one of the foremost environmentalists of his generation. He is co-founder of Greenpeace. (EN16)

There is also the question of 'stake' — if it can be shown that a source has a financial or other motivation for promoting a particular description, then this reduces the facticity of the description. The documentary pre-empts accusations that its interviewees receive payments from the oil and gas industries by including claims from three interviewees that they have received no money:

- Tim Ball: I am always accused of being paid by the oil and gas companies. I've never received a nickel from the oil and gas companies. (EN16)

On the other hand, climate scientists are represented as having a stake in proving that humans cause climate change:

- Spencer: Climate scientists need there to be a problem in order to get funding.
- Christy: We have a vested interest in creating panic because then money will flow to climate science. (EN16)

The environmental movement and the IPCC are also represented as having a stake in the descriptions by emphasising that they are 'political', i.e., they have a cause which goes beyond establishing the facts:

- Moore: The environmental movement, really it is a political activist movement.

- Stott: The IPCC, like any UN body, is political. The final conclusions are politically driven. (EN16)

The people who are putting forward the description that 'HUMANS PLAY A ROLE IN CAUSING CLIMATE CHANGE' are named as 'campaigners', 'political activists', 'government people' or 'peaceniks', who are engaged in a 'moral cause' or 'political cause'. On the other hand, those who claim that humans are *not* causing climate change are never represented as political actors by the documentary, but as 'scientists', 'specialists' and 'thoughtful people', i.e., disinterested observers with no political agenda. To give one example (of many):

- Narrator: Yet, as the frenzy of a man-made global warming grows shriller, many senior climate scientists say the actual scientific basis for the theory is crumbling. (EN16)

One particularly powerful way that the narrator presses home the idea of climate change as a political rather than scientific concept is the use of a *given/new* structure. The following are examples from different moments in the documentary:

- Narrator: By the early 1990s, man-made global warming was no longer a slightly eccentric theory about climate — it was a full-blown political campaign.
- Narrator: It is the story of how a political campaign turned into a bureaucratic bandwagon.
- Narrator: Global warming has gone beyond politics — it is a new kind of morality. (EN16)

In given/new structures, the *given* information is placed on the left-hand side, which represents it as a commonsensical, self-evident, background fact, while the new information on the right is presented as a proposition being put forward (Kress and van Leeuwen 2006, p. 187). Placing controversial information on the left is a way of making it appear much more settled and agreed on than it may actually be. This therefore gives very high facticity to climate change being an 'eccentric theory', a 'political campaign' or 'politics', all of which contribute to the facticity pattern 'HUMANS CAUSE CLIMATE CHANGE' IS CERTAINLY FALSE.

One final way that documentary undermines the facticity of 'humans play a role in causing climate change' is by labelling the description as 'propaganda', 'an alarm', 'orthodoxy', 'lies', 'fantasy', 'a myth', 'an assumption', 'an ideology', 'a farrago' and 'a looney idea'. These nouns themselves contain evaluations of the facticity of descriptions they are applied to within their semantics, all reducing the facticity to various degrees.

Overall, then, the facticity patterns in the documentary push the description 'humans play a role in causing climate change' down to the lowest possible facticity using a number of linguistic techniques, while pulling the alternative description 'climate change is caused by the sun' up to the highest facticity. Rather than draw on the authority of the IPCC, mainstream climate change scientists and environmentalists, the documentary undermines them by representing them as having a financial and political stake in lying about the causation of climate change.

In June 2007, Rive *et al.* (2007) produced a 156-page complaint to Ofcom (the UK's communications regulator) about the documentary. They described how the documentary falsified graphs, misrepresented interviewees' views, used logical fallacies, recycled myths that have clearly been shown to be false, exaggerated the credentials of contributors, failed to state that ten interviewees were sponsored by the oil and gas industry, and, importantly, 'presented contentious opinions as if they were undisputed facts'. They were therefore using analysis of the facticity patterns in the film to criticise the text they were analysing, with the practical aim of resisting it.

Climate change denial has not disappeared in the 13 years since the film came out. Instead it has been kept alive by a network of fossil-fuel industry-funded think-tanks such as the Heartland Institute or the Cato Institute. The slogan of the Heartland Institute is 'Freedom Rising', and their mission is 'to discover, develop, and promote free-market solutions to social and economic problems' (ML17). In practice, promoting 'free-market solutions' often means campaigning against solutions that involve government regulation on industry, including environmental regulation. The Heartland Institute employs Naomi Seibt, a teenage influencer who has been labelled the 'anti-Greta' for presenting diametrically opposing views to Greta Thunberg. In her introductory video on the Heartland Institute website, Seibt states:

- The world is not ending because of climate change ... we are currently being force-fed a very dystopian agenda of climate alarmism that tells that we as humans are destroying the planet ... we at the Heartland Institute want to spread truth about the science behind climate realism which is essentially the opposite of climate alarmism ... I don't want you to panic, I want you to think. (ML26)

This statement is setting up an opposition: on one hand is a 'dystopian agenda', 'alarmism' and 'panic', and, on the other hand, is 'truth', 'science', 'realism' and 'think'. The 'realism' side is attached to the Heartland Institute while the 'alarmism' side is attached to Greta

Thunberg through the intertextual reference 'I don't want you to panic'. This reference echoes but reverses Thunberg's words at Davos: 'I don't want you to be hopeful. I want you to panic' (EN23). In fact, Seibt's comments often parallel Thunberg's, for example:

- I've been called very bad names ... The state of our freedom does not care about my beauty or the lack thereof ... The state of our freedom is an urgent matter right now.... (ML18)

Thunberg has similarly described how people criticise her looks and argued that climate change is an urgent matter that is not about her. However, in Seibt's version, climate change has been substituted by 'the state of our freedom', shifting action away from preventing climate change towards opposing climate regulations. This refocusing is combined with climate change denial in the following extract from a video on Seibt's YouTube channel:

- Climate change, for example, is not really about climate change, it is about the restriction of freedom. If it was about science then people would talk about the science but ... they only talk about panic and ... [a] fight for something that is not even real ... It is an abstract concept and panic only justifies coercion with no rational reasoning behind it. Who are those scientists you say I have to listen to, and do they know the precise make-up of the atmosphere? ... Do they know which other factors contribute to the change in the climate and how much more significant they really are, like for example the Sun? ... All of this is just a bubble of deception because nobody seems to want to really immerse themselves in the research ... And the same goes for the coronavirus ... Do you know how hard it is to distinguish the coronavirus symptoms from symptoms of countless other conditions? ... the truth is always bigger than the popular narrative ... (ML18)

The language choices in this extract reduce the facticity of the description 'climate change is real' through the expressions 'not even real', 'an abstract concept', 'bubble of deception', 'no rational reasoning' and the questioning of whether climate scientists 'know which other factors contribute to the change in the climate and how much more significant they really are like, for example, the Sun'. This question is a powerful rhetorical device because the idea that the Sun plays a much more significant role in climate change than human activity is presupposed by being wrapped up in the question rather than being stated directly, where it would be more open to challenge.

Towards the end of the extract above, Seibt draws parallels between climate change and coronavirus. Another video in her channel sows doubt about official accounts of coronavirus, stating that 'the mortality statistics have been vastly exaggerated', that 'its high infection rate makes it a useful potential bio-weapon', and that 'the coronavirus symptoms are identical [to 5G radiation exposure]' (ML20). In fact, as research by the fact-checking website DeSmog (2020) reveals, many of the same actors who deny climate change also deny coronavirus.

Coronavirus denial ranges along a spectrum from mild statements stating that the virus is not particularly harmful, to conspiracy theories which claim that coronavirus is a hoax created to draw attention away from the actual cause of the symptoms, which is claimed to be 5G. In one of a series of three video interviews (ML22), with view counts in the millions, the conspiracy theorist David Icke argues that:

- This lockdown is stupid, no basis in science. The only reason for it is to destroy the livelihoods of billions of people to create mass control of the many by the few ... But it's not that 5G is creating the virus because I say there is no virus. That's the scam. What I said about 5G is it can produce symptoms similar to what they say the symptoms for COVID-19 are. (ML22)

This is not presented as speculation or conjecture, but instead Icke draws on the authority of virologists and specialists to raise up the facticity of his statements:

- I've spent every waking moment, which has been most of every 24 hours, devouring information from virologists, specialists, doctors all around the world, in America, in Germany, in Austria, Italy, who would never be allowed to get near the BBC or CNN because they are demolishing the official story of this hoax. (ML22)

It is useful to note that elsewhere Icke presents 'bureaucrats, experts, scientists, engineers, technocrats' as part of a cult which is intent on controlling the masses (ML22), while simultaneously relying on his own carefully selected (or invented) group of maverick experts to raise the facticity of his statements. In other words, despite dismissing the views of the overwhelming majority of scientists, Icke never disputes the authority of science itself, which he draws on vigorously in making his statements appear factual. Icke blames the mainstream experts for creating both climate change and coronavirus:

- So, they're phasing out petrol and diesel on this ludicrous idea that humans are causing climate change, which is another one-percent hoax run by ... the same people that are running the computer models of the so-called virus. (ML22)

In both cases the experts are represented as inventing the 'problem' in order to impose their wishes under the cover of providing a 'solution' :

- ...you don't need a real problem, you need the perception of one ... There's a no-problem-reaction-solution called human-caused climate change, which when you break down the facts as opposed to the propaganda is absolutely unsupportable ... And then, we come to current events ... of historic, unprecedented proportions: no-problem-reaction-solution, the global pandemic. (ML22)

In the previous two extracts the description HUMANS CAUSE CLIMATE CHANGE is undermined by the words 'ludicrous idea', 'hoax', 'absolutely unsupportable' and 'propaganda', while the opposite description is simply represented as 'the facts'. The facticity pattern is then transferred from the domain of climate change to the domain of coronavirus, or as Icke puts it, 'the so-called virus'.

What is important about the above examples is that the same linguistic apparatus used to undermine descriptions of the world relating to climate change is also used to undermine coronavirus. As DeSmog (2020) describes:

> The climate science denial machine created by the fossil fuel industry is now a major source of COVID-19 disinformation. Deniers have deployed many of the same tactics they have used to attack climate scientists and delay action to downplay the severity of the coronavirus outbreak and sow distrust in the response efforts of governments, scientists and the medical community — with deadly consequences that are now unfolding before our eyes.

There is a danger that other serious emerging global issues in the future will be treated in the same way: their facticity will be undermined by deniers and conspiracy theorists who present them as a hoax invented by global powers to take away people's freedom. This would not be a problem if it was just a small group of mavericks speculating about far-fetched alternative theories. However, they do not present themselves in this way, but rather as the true voice of science and rationality. And their voices are greatly magnified by the network of industry-sponsored think-tanks that oppose the health and environmental regulations that keep people and the planet safe.

Clearly, ecolinguistics can play a role in countering this kind of misinformation. That role goes beyond simply sifting through evidence and pointing out inaccuracies — which is what Potter (1996, p. 110) would call a 'participant concern'. With the tools of facticity analysis and the concept of evaluations and facticity patterns, ecolinguistics can expose the deeper workings of denial and the agendas behind it as they apply to climate change, coronavirus and other global issues that emerge in the future.

理论延伸

　　本章结合真实性理论，主要聚焦信念和真实性模式两个方面的内容：人们的信念会对其表达语篇或话语的语言模式产生影响；反过来蕴含在语篇或话语中的真实性模式也会反作用于人们的信念。通过分析我们发现，本章的信念和真实性问题实质上可以分别对应哲学领域有关价值判断（value judgement）和事实判断（fact judgement）问题的研究。因此，这个部分我们重点梳理有关价值判断和事实判断的发展脉络，指出二者之间的区别和联系，并列出可进一步阅读的文献。

　　价值判断和事实判断的讨论源自于英国哲学家 David Hume 的观点（黄国文、赵蕊华，2019：135）。1739 年，Hume 在《人性论》（*A Treatise of Human Nature*）第三卷（第一章第一节）中正式提出"是"（事实）与"应该"（价值）的区分问题（Selby & Bigge，1896：244–245；参见万小龙、李福勇，2014），强调事实判断和价值判断的对立，即二元论。

　　所谓事实判断，也有学者将其称为科学判断（谭晓春，2018），指的是人们对事实的客观判断，通常可以用"是……"或者"不是……"的命题来表达。事实判断具有客观实在性，不以人的意志为转移，强调事物的唯一真理，例如："全球气候变暖是由温室效应导致的"的命题。这个命题是一种客观真理，因为"化石燃料燃烧、汽车尾气排放等现象会产生大量的二氧化碳气体（温室气体）"是一种事实情况，会形成温室效应，使得平均温度升高，出现全球气候变暖的现象。价值判断则是基于人们主观的态度或情感表达对事物的判断，具有一定的价值尺度，通常可以用"应该是……"或者"应该不是……"（或"不应该是……"）的命题来表达，用于判断事实的价值属性，例如："气候变化可能会导致生态问题"的命题。这个命题中"可能"一词的使用，流露出该命题的主观性，是说话者的主观表达；意味着如果要想强调该命题是客观事实，需要进一步论证或验证。

　　自 Hume 提出事实判断和价值判断的二元对立之后，许多学者都参与到这一问题的讨论中来（例如：Immanuel Kant 等），促使有关二者的关系问题成为从希腊到现代哲学都在争论的主题（刘复兴，2009）。结合两个概念的定义以及近年来相关学者的研究能够看出，事实判断和价值判断实际上不是绝对对立的，它们之间还存在一定的联系。反对二者对立比较典型的学者是 Jürgen Habermas；20 世纪 70 年代后，Habermas 对事实判断和价值判断的问题进行了拓展，他通过交互主体性的讨论，反对将事实与价值对立起来，而是把它们融合在一起（贾中海，2005；参见刘复兴，2009）。

这样的态度其实一直蕴含在中国哲学中，比如在讨论人与自然关系的问题时，道家学派和儒家学派都在突出"天人合一"的思想；在社会飞速发展的今天，我们也仍然在强调"顺应自然""人与自然和谐共生"的观点（参见余谋昌，2018；余谋昌等，2019）。从另一个角度来讲，这就是我们面对事实判断和价值判断的态度。谭晓春（2018）在谈生态话语的事实判断和价值判断时，特别提出了在中国语境下，"以人为本"的基本假定；良知原则、制约原则和亲近原则所构成的生态哲学观（黄国文，2017）实现了事实判断和价值判断的统一。

有关生态话语和行为分析中"一个假定和三条原则"的内容，读者可进一步参看《论生态话语和行为分析的假定和原则》（黄国文，2017）这篇论文。另外，有意向关注事实判断和价值判断的探讨，或者有想法从生态语言学视角研究有关信念和真实性问题的读者，还可以仔细阅读刘复兴（2009）、孙伟平（2016）、谭晓春（2018）、黄国文和赵蕊华（2019：135–137）等论著。

补充文献

黄国文 . 2017. 论生态话语和行为分析的假定和原则 . 外语教学与研究，（6）：880–889.

黄国文，赵蕊华 . 2019. 什么是生态语言学 . 上海：上海外语教育出版社 .

贾中海 . 2005. 哈贝马斯对罗尔斯事实与价值关系二元论的批判 . 学习与探索，（3）：60–63.

刘复兴 . 2009. 人文社会科学研究中的事实与价值 . 北京师范大学学报（社会科学版），（1）：16–28.

孙伟平 . 2016. 事实与价值：休谟问题及其解决尝试（修订本）. 北京：社会科学文献出版社 .

谭晓春 . 2018. 生态话语的价值判断和科学判断 . 中国外语，（4）：47–53.

万小龙，李福勇 . 2014. 从道义逻辑看"是"与"应该是"的关系 . 华中科技大学学报（社会科学版），（3）：32–36.

余谋昌 . 2018. 生态哲学是生态文明建设的理论基础 . 鄱阳湖学刊，（2）：5–13.

余谋昌，雷毅，杨通进 . 2019. 环境伦理学（第二版）. 北京：高等教育出版社 .

DeSmog. 2020. *COVIDeniers: Anti-science coronavirus denial overlaps with climate denial.* Desmog UK.

Harré, R., Brockmeier, J. & Mühlhäuser, P. 1999. *Greenspeak: A study of environmental discourse.* London: Sage.

Hume, D. 1739. *A treatise of human nature.* (Reprinted from the original edition in three volumes and edited, with an analytical index, by L. A. Selby and M. A. Bigge, 1896, Clarendon Press)

Machin, D. & Mayr, A. 2012. *How to do critical discourse analysis: A multimodal introduction.* London: Sage.

Martin, J. R. & Rose, D. 2007. *Working with discourse: Meaning beyond the clause* (2nd ed.). London: Bloomsbury.

Martin, J. R. & White, P. R. R. 2005. *The language of evaluation: Appraisal in English.* London & New York: Palgrave Macmillan.

Smith, M. 2019. Most people expect to feel the effects of climate change, and many think it will make us extinct. *YouGov*, September 16.

Van Leeuwen, T. 2008. *Discourse and practice.* Oxford: Oxford University Press.

8

ERASURE

在语言学领域，研究者对语篇中的参与者问题是十分关注的，这不只包括话语中具有明显指向的参与者，还包括了那些被隐藏、被背景化、被排除或被删略的参与者。若某个（或某些）参与者在话语中存在系统的缺失情况，则说明对于说话人来说所缺失的参与者是不重要的、无关的，或者是边缘化的或可以边缘化的，这就是话语中的删略现象。删略是一个被广泛应用在社会科学领域的术语，本书中的删略涵盖了通过话语的内容组织、转移人们对参与者或生活领域关注的任何方式，例如：压制、背景化、排除、抽象化，等等。本章以"删略"这个术语为核心探讨语言中的删略现象，具体包括三个部分的内容：（1）理论内涵；（2）删略分析的方法；（3）案例：生态系统评价和可持续发展目标中的删略。

（1）理论内涵。删略模式与评价模式有很多相似之处，但是删略更倾向于将事物评价为不重要的或不值得考虑的，而不是去评价事物的好坏；具体的做法是通过不提及或使用语言策略将其从话语中抹去。本章出现的重要概念有两个："删略"（erasure）和"删略模式"（erasure pattern）。删略指的是人们头脑中有关某个生活领域不重要或不值得考虑的故事（*Erasure* is a story in people's minds that an area of life is unimportant or unworthy of consideration.）。删略模式是一种语言表征，它通过使某个生活领域在语篇中系统性缺失、背景化、扭曲等方式，而将其评价为无关的、边缘化的或者不重要的（An *erasure pattern* is a linguistic representation of an area of life as irrelevant, marginal or unimportant through its systematic absence, backgrounding or distortion in texts.）。

事实上，删略是话语的一种内在属性，几乎所有的话语都存在删略的现象。因为在大部分情况下，说话者在语篇或话语中的描述总是会根据自己的目标或兴趣重点阐释某些因素，而删略一些其他的因素，例如：社会因素在认知信息科学中的删略（Frohmann，1992：365）、白人研究对种族与特权的关注但删略了性别（Ferber，

2007：265），等等。分析者需要站在不同的立场对这些删略的因素进行挖掘；明确指出那些比较重要但在语篇或话语中被删略的因素，并分析所忽略的因素中应该受到关注的群体和原因。因此，这种分析过程和分析方法是非常有价值的。

（2）删略分析的方法。在日常生活的语篇或话语中，发现哪些是被系统删略的事物常常是比较困难的。本书中提出的删略分析方法如下。第一，观察语篇或话语中特定的句子，发现在现实中存在、本该被描述但却被删略的事物，如可以特别关注一些语言形式——被动句、转喻、名物化、下义词等。第二，分析语篇或话语中是否有一种贯穿于整个内容的删略模式，并通过对存在删略模式部分的分析来判断删略的程度（强删略或弱删略）。第三，确定删略的类型，包括空白（the void）、伪装（the mask）、留痕（the trace），然后对删略现象进行评价。其中，空白指的是语篇或话语中完全删略的重要事物；伪装是用扭曲的话语对重要事物的取而代之；留痕涉及删略了语篇或话语中的部分重要事物但还有一部分仍存在其中。

对于这个问题，作者列举了新古典经济学话语中的空白删略、生态经济学话语中的伪装删略等多个典型的例子。这里我们来分析本书中一组关于农业综合企业话语（P187）的例子。这组例子挖掘出了这些话语中，通过隐喻、转喻等方式物化了"动物"的信息。针对这一现象，作者提出要凭借话语中的及物性分析模式来揭示出参与者的成分，探索小句中的描述对生物属性的删略。概括来说，上述例子呈现出多种情况的删略现象，删略了作为生物的"动物"，这与本书的生态哲学观是相反的，不仅会对动物自身的福祉造成影响，还会导致高度集约、破坏环境的饲养技术出现，影响整个生态系统的良性运转。

（3）案例：生态系统评价和可持续发展目标中的删略。生态系统评价与动植物和自然环境的发展是息息相关的。这个小节的案例有两个部分：第一部分，五类典型的生态系统评估报告中的删略；第二部分，联合国可持续发展目标中的删略。

在讨论可持续发展目标中的删略之前，此处研究了五类典型的生态系统评估报告，这些报告是具有很大影响力的话语。该案例分析的主线是考量"动植物"和"自然"在评估报告中的删略程度，激发人们的生态伦理，进而呼吁人们尊重自然。作者分析了评估报告中被删略的"动物"和"植物"的语言形式及其删略的程度和删略的类型。这里面删略的语言形式主要有：用上义词的方式替代物种的名称（比如"鱼"用"资源"这个上义词替代）、依据它们在生态系统中的功能而进行隐喻性或转喻性指代（比如"被捕获的鱼"的表述中忽视了"鱼"的动物属性，将其隐喻删略成"农作物"）。总的来说，这五类报告的整体模式是明确的，但在不同程度上删略了动物、植物、森林、河流和海洋等本该在评估报告中出现的非常重要的因素，因此是需要我们抵制的。

联合国可持续发展目标是更为重要的一份材料，它涉及 2030 年可持续发展的议程（the 2030 Agenda for Sustainable Development），受到世界范围内的决策者、慈善机构、教育机构和各类公司的关注。这个案例中虽然在有些地方承认了动植物的存在和价值，但是也删略了多处本该出现"动植物"的地方，具体的删略方式主要有：抽象化明显、与人类中心主义相关的表述频繁出现等语言特征。

这两个案例给我们的启示是，生态系统评估报告和可持续发展目标都是日常语言，我们在分析过程中既要指出"自然"在这类话语中被删略的事实，还要揭示出实现删略的内在语言机制，帮助话语责任人在今后的报告中更加谨慎地对待删略现象，将"自然"的表述凸显出来。因此，有关凸显的问题成为本书下一章讨论的重点。

> First, erasure is an act of deleting or 'removing something completely' ... A second meaning of erasure is the trace left behind by the attempt to erase. As in writing, erasing something results in marks — physical erasures — that remain on the page.
>
> (Stallmeyer and Dearborn 2012, p. 347)

Linguists give critical attention not only to participants that are explicitly represented in texts, but those who are suppressed, backgrounded, excluded or erased completely from them. A systematic absence or sidelining of certain participants from a text, a discourse, or across multiple discourses tells a story in itself — that they are unimportant, irrelevant or marginal. Rebecca Solnit gives an insightful example of how Native Americans are represented as literally marginal in cowboy movies:

> I grew up on cowboy movies in which Native Americans defending themselves in their homelands were portrayed as invaders galloping into the frame of the camera. The camera stayed with the actual invaders, the white people in covered wagons, and by making them the fixed centre of the movies made them the victims instead of the perpetrators; the stable presence, not the disruptors.
>
> (Solnit 2019)

Language can similarly focus on one group while marginalising others. Solnit gives the example of how Donald Trump spoke of 'the impact on schools and communities and taxpayers' in relation to refugees, which highlights people who are safe and secure while erasing the perspective of those who have lost everything. Trump uses the word 'communities' in a way which excludes refugees, as if they are not part of the community.

Solnit also discusses media representation of homeless people, which often focuses on the annoyance to those with houses while erasing the trauma of those without. She concludes:

> Whenever a story of social conflict breaks, the first question to ask is: whose story is it? Who's been put at the centre? Who does the narrator tell us matters? Whose rights and needs do they dismiss? And what happens if you move the centre?

In the terms used in this book, the key questions are 'who has been made salient in texts?' and 'who has been erased?'

Erasure is a term that has been used in a variety of contexts in social science. Namaste (2000, p. 52) uses the term to describe how transsexual people are erased in texts that represent the world as if there are only two genders:

> Most powerfully, 'erasure' can refer specifically to the very act of nullifying transsexuality — a process whereby transsexuality is rendered impossible ... the use of 'men' and 'women' undermines the very possibility of a transsexual/transgender position. Within this site, transsexuals cannot exist at all.

Ferber (2007, p. 265) claims that whiteness studies, in its concentration on race and privilege, has 'erased' gender; Barnet (2003) argues that technology has been 'erased' in cultural critique; Lutz (1990, p. 611) that women's writing is 'erased' in sociocultural anthropology; and Frohmann (1992, p. 365) that the social dimension is 'erased' in cognitive information science. The term 'erasure', then, is used to indicate that something important, something that we should be giving attention to, has been ignored, sidelined or overlooked within a text or discourse. A poignant example is given by Satya (2019), who noticed that representations of people doing yoga erase black men:

> We can find hundreds of sites on the Internet about Black men being demonised, criminalised, harassed, but when we look for positive healing representation of Black men in the media, we hear crickets. The erasure of Black male healing is toxic for humanity because it implies that Black men don't — and can't — heal. It perpetuates an invisibility surrounding Black male healing. We need to make Black men healing a normalised visual.

Baker and Ellece (2011, p. 40) define 'erasure' as 'a form of exclusion or marginalisation, particularly in relation to identity categories', and 'exclusion' as 'an aspect of social actor representation where particular social actors do not appear in a text or as part of a discourse' (p. 44). Van Leeuwen (2008, p. 29) further divides exclusion into two types: 'suppression', where social actors are entirely absent from a text, and 'backgrounding', when actors are absent from one part of a text but appear later on in the text. Fairclough (2003, p. 139) describes how participants can be absent or backgrounded when situations are described using abstract language that glosses over concrete details. For convenience, this book will use the term 'erasure' to cover suppression, backgrounding, exclusion, abstraction, and, in general, any means by which texts draw attention away from certain participants or areas of life.

When erasure occurs across a text or discourse it forms a pattern very much like an appraisal pattern, except rather than appraising something as *bad*, it appraises it as *unimportant* and generally unworthy of consideration. It does not do this explicitly by stating 'X is unimportant', but implicitly, by failing to mention X or by using linguistic techniques that push X into the background. The following are definitions for the purposes of this book:

> *Erasure* is a story in people's minds that an area of life is unimportant or unworthy of consideration.
>
> *An erasure pattern* is a linguistic representation of an area of life as irrelevant, marginal or unimportant through its systematic absence, backgrounding or distortion in texts.

Erasure, of course, is something intrinsic to the very nature of discourse. In representing and constructing areas of social life, texts and discourses will always be partial, bringing certain elements together into a configuration while leaving out a whole universe of other elements. The concept of erasure only becomes meaningful when an analyst surveys the universe of elements that have been excluded, declares that one of these elements is important, that it is being 'erased' from consciousness, and argues that it should be brought back into consideration. What that 'something important' is depends on the goals and interests of the analyst.

Everett and Neu (2000, p. 18) are concerned with the erasure of people, and specifically certain groups of people, in the discourse of ecological modernisation. This widespread discourse represents environmental problems as solvable through technological innovation without requiring any changes to the structure of society. As Fisher and Freudenburg (2001, p. 702) describe, 'the lynchpin of the argument [is that] environmental problems can best be solved through *further* advancement of technology and industrialization'. Everett and Neu (2000) argue that within the discourse of ecological modernisation 'indigenous and poor peoples' are erased, 'the local' is erased, the 'asymmetric distribution of environmental resources' is erased, and 'linkages between ecology and social relations' are erased:

The 'ideological effect' of ecological modernization is such that the intersection of ecological and social realms is ignored and issues of social justice are effectively erased, despite this discourse's 'radical' or 'critical' aspirations. In other words, ecological modernization is a discourse of the status quo.

(p. 5)

The erasure of people and social justice issues in ecological discourse runs counter to the ecosophy of this book because of the potentially negative impact of environmental measures on vulnerable populations. Bookchin (1988) describes how 'divested of its social core, ecology can easily become a cruel discipline'. If people and social relations are erased, efforts to reduce consumption could force the poorest to consume even less, rather than reducing the overconsumption of the rich. This is doubly unjust since the poor consume fewer resources so are less responsible for environmental damage, but suffer the most from a reduction in already meagre consumption levels.

Schleppegrell (1997, p. 55) more specifically analyses the linguistic features which lead to the erasure of human agents within environmental discourse. She gives the following example from an environmental education report:

- Human-induced changes in the environment, such as pollution, habitat degradation, and the introduction of exotic species, push the limits of nature's resilience and may lead to irreversible environmental damage and biodiversity loss on human time scales.

She analyses this in the following way:

Here environmental problems are presented as caused by *human-induced changes in the environment,* with examples of such problems being *pollution, habitat degradation,* and *the introduction of exotic species.* These are abstractions, realised linguistically as nominalizations which suppress the expression of agency. The grammatical forms require no expressed actor who can be identified as causing these problems.

Nominalisations can be particularly powerful devices of erasure (although their precise impact is the subject of debate — see Martin 2008). Fairclough (2003, p. 114) explains that:

'Destruction' and 'creation' are ... 'nominalisations' — there is a transparent link between 'destruction' and 'people destroy things' ... the conversion of a verb into a noun-like word, and semantically of a process into an entity. Nominalisation ... may involve the exclusion of Participants in clauses.

In Schleppegrell's example, the underlying forms 'X pollutes Y' and 'X degrades Y' have been wrapped up into single nouns (pollution and degradation), allowing the Actor, X, to be erased. Schleppegrell argues that if the key actors responsible for ecological destruction are systematically erased from environmental discourse then the danger is that solutions are sought at the wrong level. For example, campaigns might focus on personal actions such as turning lights off, which will make little difference, rather than targeting the corporations and political institutions most responsible for ecological destruction.

For Berardi (2012, p. 19), the discourse of finance is a key concern since it has become progressively more abstract and has erased the real world of tangible goods and services:

> Finance ... is the culmination of a process of abstraction that started with capitalist industrialisation. Financial capitalism ... has separated the monetary signifier from its function of denotation and reference to physical goods. Financial signs [create] money without the generative intervention of physical matter and muscular work.

McKibben (2006, p. xxiii) states that 'the physical world is no longer as real to us as the economic world ... the Earth has become abstract, and the economy has become concrete'. While the discourse of finance makes 'derivatives', 'options', 'futures', 'indexes', 'swaps', 'shares' and 'securities' salient, it erases physical goods, physical matter, muscular work, material production and the Earth. The consequences, according to Berardi (2012, p. 52), are that 'this digital-financial hyperabstraction is liquidating the living body of the planet and the social body of the workers' community'.

John Berger (2009, p. 21) is concerned with the erasure of animals. In his famous essay *Why Look at Animals?*, Berger states that 'in the last two centuries animals have gradually disappeared. Today we live without them.' There is little doubt that when Berger made this statement, and even more so today, interactions with animals happen increasingly at a distance: mediated by nature programmes, cartoons, logos, museums, books, soft toys and social media with its innumerable videos of amusing animal antics. As Abram (1996, p. 28) puts it, 'we consciously encounter nonhuman nature only as it has been circumscribed by our civilization and its technologies: through our domesticated pets, on the television, or at the zoo ...'

Kahn (2001) is concerned specifically with the erasure of animals in the discourse of wildlife biology. She describes how the language used by scientists shows 'a complete lack of acknowledgement that anything resembling a living, breathing, sentient being is undergoing experimentation', and that 'scientists armed with dart guns and data sheets have been linguistically trained to regard non-humans as non-entities, or at best, lower forms of life ... to be manipulated and controlled' (p. 243). Durham and Merskin (2009, p. 245) are similarly concerned that in animal experimentation 'when animals are seen as pieces and parts of apparatus, the tendency is to treat them as abstract concepts rather than empathise with [their] lived reality'.

Pierson (2005) describes a different form of erasure that occurs in the Discovery Channel's nature programming. Animals are not represented here as objects, but instead anthropomorphised to the extent that the nature programmes become more about human society than the lived reality of animals. Pierson writes:

> The animal world is represented as a highly dramatic realm filled with close-knit families, external conflicts, and intense competitions — in other words, a world not unlike the one inhabited by Discovery's middle-class suburban viewers. For the most part, these representations of the animal world tend to reinforce the dominant social and cultural conceptions of social class in the human world.
>
> (Pierson 2005 p. 771)

The erasure of animals and nature in the prevailing texts that form society is so powerful that Abram (1996, p. 267) claims that 'our organic atonement to the local earth is thwarted by our ever-increasing intercourse with our own signs'. He asks:

> How did Western civilisation become so estranged from non-human nature, so oblivious to the presence of other animals and the earth, that our current lifestyles and activities contribute daily to the destruction of whole ecosystems?
>
> (Abram 1996 p. 137)

Bate (2000, p. 245) also links alienation from nature with ecological destruction: 'a progressive severance of humankind from nature ... has licensed, or at least neglected, technology's ravaging of the earth's finite resources'. Clearly, it is hard to expect people to consider and care about things that are systematically erased from the texts that they deal with in their everyday life.

Analysis of erasure starts with a particular sentence in a particular text, and the observation that something which is present in reality, and could possibly have been represented, has been excluded. The exclusion could be through simply not being mentioned or more actively through linguistic devices such as passives, metonymy, nominalisations and hyponyms. One sentence on its own is not important — what matters is whether there is a pattern of this kind of erasure across the whole text, and, if so, whether this pattern is characteristic of this *type* of text. The erasure pattern does not have to be 'all or nothing' — erasure is a matter of degree, from strong erasure where 'something important' is almost entirely erased from a discourse, to weaker forms of erasure where it is represented only occasionally, or in the background or in a distorted form.

This chapter will examine a number of different types of erasure which will be called (a) *the void*, where 'something important' is completely excluded from a text; (b) *the mask*, where it is erased but replaced by a distorted version of itself; and (c) *the trace*, where something is partially erased but still present. This draws from Baudrillard (1994, p. 6), who contrasts 'a good appearance', where a representation is 'the reflection of a profound reality', with a representation that 'masks and denatures a profound reality'.

In the case of the erasure of the more-than-human world, the 'profound reality' is that of animals, plants, rivers, forests and the physical environment. This reality exists beyond words, but can be represented vividly and concretely through language. Representation can never be perfect, though, since all language ultimately erases. The word 'oak' could never capture the intricate patterns of bark and the particular way the leaves of a real tree move with the wind, but at least is a more vivid representation than, say, 'biotic component'. With a vivid representation 'the image is a reflection of a profound reality'. There are a number of ways that a 'profound reality' can be erased, however. The most obvious of these is through complete absence in a text, which this book calls 'the void'.

An example of 'the void' occurs in the discourse of neoclassical economics, which is frequently accused of failing to consider the ecological embedding of human economies (Williams and McNeill 2005). The standard textbook, *Microeconomics* (ET2), for instance, contains almost no discussion of the dependence on, and effect of, human economic activity on the environment, animals, plants or ecology in its 554 pages, aside from occasional mention of externalities and a brief discussion of what it calls the 'so-called problem of pollution' (p. 491). The following extract from the textbook illustrates the erasure of the natural world:

- It hardly needs pointing out that the goods and services that consumers purchase do not simply materialise out of the blue. In large measure they have to be produced ... The essential fact about production is so obvious that it hardly needs stating: it involves the use of services of various sorts to generate output ... Clearly the manner in which production is organised has important social and political as well as economic aspects. (ET2:169)

In this extract the 'working up of facticity' (Potter 1996) is very strong: '*it hardly needs pointing out ... essential fact ... obvious ... hardly needs stating ... clearly*', as if the discourse was merely pointing out obvious pre-existing truths rather than playing a role in constructing social reality. Something important is missing in this social construction, though: goods are described as produced by 'services' without mention of what is destroyed, harmed or disturbed to make the goods, i.e., the animals, plants and ecosystems used in or affected by production. The term 'production' is nominalised from 'X produces Y', which even in its verb form does not include what is destroyed to make Y. The nominalised expression *production* can therefore erase the natural world without a trace. The list that the textbook gives of the important aspects of how production is organised consists of 'social and political as well as economic aspects'. This erases, by total omission, the ecological aspects of production. If the ecological systems that support life are erased from economics discourse then they cannot be taken into account in economic decisions, with significant implications for how the natural world is treated and exploited.

The macroeconomics textbook ET4 (p. 45) gives a concrete example of production at a bakery:

- The kitchen and its equipment are the bakery's capital, the workers hired to make the bread are its labour and the loaves of bread are its output. The bakery's production function shows that the number of loaves produced depends on the amount of equipment and the number of workers ... doubling the amount of equipment and the number of workers doubles the amount of bread produced.

What is completely missing from this — has been entirely erased — is the wheat that goes into the bread, as well as the plants that the wheat came from, the pesticides and fertilisers used to grow the plants, the fuel used in harvesting and transporting the crop, the water used for irrigation, damage to the topsoil, or any other environmental consideration. Williams and McNeill (2005, p. 8) confirm that the above text is not just an isolated example:

Raw materials used as inputs in the production process, and any other services provided by the natural environment, were omitted from consideration altogether. Amazingly, they still are. First year economics students are still taught in almost all of the currently popular textbooks that businesses manufacture their products using only labour and machines!

More generally, Gare (1996, p. 148) describes how neoclassical economics 'virtually excluded nature from consciousness. The economic process was represented as a circular diagram between production and consumption within a completely closed system'. Keynesian economics does not fare much better, since it 'continued to exclude from consciousness the environmental impact of economic growth and the ways in which the centres of the world-economy are draining off capital and non-renewable resources from the economic peripheries' (Gare 1996, p. 151).

Ecological economics, on the other hand, is a discipline which explicitly challenges the discourse of conventional economics. The textbook *Ecological Economics: Principles and Applications* (NE7) states that:

- To the extent that nature and the environment are considered at all [in conventional economics], they are considered as parts or sectors of the macro-economy ... Ecological economics, by contrast, envisions the macro-economy as part of a larger enveloping and sustaining Whole, namely the Earth, its atmosphere and its ecosystems. (NE7:15)

The discourse of ecological economics is an attempt at 're-minding' — bringing animals, plants and ecosystems back into consideration through statements such as the following:

- We cannot make something from nothing hence all human production must ultimately be based on resources provided by nature. (NE7:67)

Ecological economics is still based on the discourse of economics, however, and tends to bring the natural world into an economic frame rather than placing economics within an ecological frame. The following example is typical:

- The structural elements of an ecosystem are stocks of biotic and abiotic resources (minerals, water, trees, other plants, and animals) which when combined together generate ecosystem functions, or services. The use of a biological stock at a nonsustainable level in general also depletes a corresponding fund and the services it provides. (NE7:107)

The terms 'stocks', 'resources', 'depletes', 'services' and 'funds' combine together to strongly activate the economics frame. The terms 'biotic', 'abiotic', 'ecosystem' and 'biological' activate an ecological frame. However, the economics frame is primary since the economics words form the *head* of noun phrases while the ecological terms are optional *modifiers* (i.e., in the expressions biotic *resources*, ecosystem *services*, and biological *stock* the words in italics are the head and the others the modifiers). As Abram (1996, p. 54) points out, 'to define another being as an inert or passive object is to deny its ability to actively engage us and provoke our senses; we thus block our perceptual reciprocity with that being'.

Treating the living world in the same discursive way as a stock of objects removes what is unique about life, such as consciousness, interaction and interdependence. This could be considered the second type of erasure, 'the mask', where animals and plants have been erased and replaced with a distorted version of themselves (the stock of biological resources).

Another area where the natural world tends to be erased and replaced with a mask is *agribusiness*, and animal product industries in particular. Intensive animal agriculture and the discourses which justify, sustain and construct it, is of particular interest to ecolinguistics because of the scale of negative environmental impacts caused by factory farming (see Appleby 2008). Glenn (2004, p. 72) describes how advertising is used in the external discourse of the animal product industry to erase from consumers' minds the grim conditions that animals are kept in factory farms:

> Advertisements' representations of 'speaking animals' who are selling the end 'products' of the brutal processes they endure in the factory farm system serve ... a dual discursive purpose. The first purpose is to sell products, and the second role is ... to make the nonhuman animal victims disappear.

The 'speaking animal' here is a 'mask' — a distorted version that erases the reality of the animals themselves and the conditions that they are kept in. With anthropomorphic representations like these 'the specificity of the experiences of non-human animals is emptied out and replaced with experiences imported from the human domain' (Herman 2012, p. 101).

To create a system which treats animals inhumanely and is environmentally destructive requires work to be done by agribusiness discourse to erase animals as living beings and focus narrowly on economic factors instead. A key device is metaphor, and the following are stark examples from the 1970s:

- The breeding sow should be thought of as, and treated as, a valuable piece of machinery whose function is to pump out baby pigs like a sausage machine. (Walls Meat Company manager, in Singer 1990, p. 126)
- If the sow is considered a pig manufacturing unit then improved management at farrowing on through weaning will result in more pigs weaned. (US Department of Agriculture, in Singer 1990, p. 126)

These metaphors explicitly encourage the reader to think of pigs as machines and manufacturing units, creating what Fauconnier and Turner (2003) call *conceptual blends*. The resulting pig-machine blend or pig-manufacturing-unit blend is 'a mask' — a distorted version which erases actual pigs as living beings.

The use of explicit metaphors is one way to objectify animals, but there are other, more subtle ways that vocabulary choice is used to represent animals as unfeeling objects. The following examples are from agribusiness handbooks:

- Livestock production in most livestock economies includes bovines (especially cattle), ovines (sheep and goats) and pigs. (AG2:7)
- In the modern poultry industry, producers usually do not own the primary breeding stock (i.e. the parent lines supplying their operation). (AG3:11)
- livestock utilised exclusively for meat production. (AG2:8)

Here animals are 'produced' rather than being born, by 'producers' rather than mothers, and are referred to as 'breeding stock' or 'livestock'. This choice of vocabulary objectifies them since the terms 'produced' and 'stock' are, in their most frequent usage, collated with objects rather than living beings. Another way of turning animals into objects is through metonymy:

- In Georgia, USDA-Georgia has assisted in modernising the red meat slaughtering industry and in establishing new plants. (AG2:48)
- In North America, seven-week-old chickens are classified as broilers or fryers and fourteen-week-old chickens are classified as roasters. (AG3:11)

In these examples, metonymy is used to refer to animals as 'red meat' in the first example, and as cooking methods in the second. This confuses the living, breathing animal with the products their bodies are used to make after death.

A key difference between animals and objects is that animals have intelligence, feelings and mental lives, and act in the world pursuing their own purposes for their own ends. Representing animals as objects erases them as living beings and removes them from the sphere of moral consideration. Importantly, the discourse of agribusiness does this implicitly — there are no statements which explicitly deny that animals have intelligence, feelings or mental lives. However, there are *transitivity* patterns within the discourse which more subtly erase animals as active beings with mental lives.

Transitivity concerns the types of processes that are described in a clause and the participants who play a role in those processes (Halliday 2004, p. 44). *Material processes* are active processes of doing something in the world, while *mental processes* are processes where someone thinks, feels or uses their senses to observe the world. The two main participants in material processes are the *Actor*, who is doing something active, and the *Affected*, who is having something done to them. In mental processes, the most important participant is the *Senser* — the person or animal who is thinking, feeling, seeing, hearing, etc. The patterns of transitivity in a text can help reveal whether animals are being represented actively as beings who do things and think, feel and sense the world around them, or whether they are erased by being represented merely as objects to which something is done.

In the agribusiness document AG3 about poultry farming, birds are only placed in the slot of Actor on four occasions: they 'bleed', 'die', 'require (nutrition)' and 'produce (eggs)'. In other words, they do not do very much. They are *never* in the position of Senser — they are not shown as seeing, hearing, feeling or thinking anything. In five cases, the birds are represented as the Affected, having something done to them by an Actor: producers 'purchase birds' (p. 11), producers 'do not expose birds to predators' (p. 14), biosecurity 'involves isolating birds [and] disposing of dead birds' (p. 16), companies 'buy ... birds' (p. 33), and a company 'processes ... birds' (p. 34). The Actors in these processes are the abstract 'producers', 'biosecurity' and 'company', which avoids representing any direct interactions between humans and birds.

In all of the other cases in AG3, birds are referred to as Affected participants, having something done to them by nameless agents who have been deleted by the use of the passive voice: birds 'are raised' (p. 7), 'are slaughtered' (p. 11), 'are pasteurised' (p. 14), 'are held' (p. 19), 'are transported', 'are killed and disposed of', 'are removed', 'are hung upside-down', 'are shackled', 'are exposed to steam', 'are showered with water', 'are weighed individually', 'are inspected visually', 'are categorised', 'are packed in plastic bags' (p. 20) and 'are sold' (p. 21). This not only erases the birds as living, feeling, sensing beings, it also erases the humans who are harming them. Kahn (2001, p. 242) writes that 'in the passive construction the agent has disappeared — the doer has disconnected — replaced by the deed itself, sterile and isolated, and apparently accomplished without human input'.

In general, the erasure of animals as living beings in agribusiness discourse has the potential to remove moral consideration of animal welfare from the design and running of farming systems. This runs counter to the ecosophy of this book for two reasons. The first and most direct is that it can have an impact on the wellbeing of the animals themselves. The second is that failure to give moral consideration to animals can lead to highly intensive farming techniques which produce high volumes of meat in environmentally destructive ways.

Erasure in ecosystem assessment and the Sustainable Development Goals

Ecosystem assessment is, of course, all about animals, plants and the physical environment. It would seem strange at first to analyse how it erases the natural world, but erasure is not a binary all/nothing phenomenon and can occur to different degrees. Of particular importance is 'the trace' — when discourses represent the natural world but do so in a way which obscures it, leaving a faint trace rather than a vivid image. This section examines five ecosystem assessment reports that are typical of this newly emerging genre before considering erasure in the Sustainable Development Goals.

Ecosystem assessment reports summarise the state of ecosystems to provide information that is useful for policymakers in protecting those ecosystems. The reports examined in this section are as follows (see Appendix for full details):

Ecosystems and Human Well-being: General Synthesis. (EA1)
Ecosystems and Human Well-being: Biodiversity Synthesis. (EA2)
Impacts of Climate Change on Biodiversity, Ecosystems and Ecosystems Services. (EA3)
The UK National Ecosystem Assessment. (EA4)
Mainstreaming the Economics of Nature. (EA5)
Mapping and Assessment of Ecosystems and their Services. (EA6)

These reports represent an influential discourse that potentially shapes how scientists, policymakers and the general public respond to major issues that humanity is facing. The focus of the analysis is the degree to which animals, plants and the natural world are erased in the discourse of the reports. To understand why this is important, it is useful to give quotes from three of the reports themselves:

- Birds of all kinds, butterflies, trees such as oak, beech and birch, mammals such as badgers, otters and seals ... are of great cultural significance and ... undoubtedly have a huge hold over the popular imagination. (EA4:19)
- Recognising value in ecosystems, landscapes, species and other aspects of biodiversity ... is sometimes sufficient to ensure conservation and sustainable use. (EA5:11)
- Ultimately, the level of biodiversity that survives on Earth will be determined not just by utilitarian considerations but to a significant extent by ethical concerns, including considerations of the intrinsic values of species. (EA1:58)

In other words, people are more likely to respect the natural world and work towards preserving it if they value it deeply for its own sake at an ethical level, and they feel strongly about a wide range of familiar species such as butterflies, oaks, badgers and seals. We would therefore expect this outward-facing discourse of ecology to try to encourage respect for the natural world by vividly representing plants and animals in ways which capture people's imagination and stimulate an ethical response.

However, despite the quotations above, and some explicit statements such as 'biodiversity and ecosystems also have intrinsic value' (EA2), the discourse of the reports tends to erase animals, plants and the natural world, turning them into a faint trace that is unlikely to arouse people's imagination or care. The question is whether the discourse paints a picture of humans as part of a living world teeming with a diversity of animals and plants, or a lonely world where humans are surrounded only by 'natural capital', 'biological stock' and 'biomass'; by trees or 'cubic meters of timber'?

Within the reports there are several linguistic ways that animals and plants are erased, ranging from mild to extremely strong forms of erasure. The most vivid representations of nature are the photographs — birds (EA5, EA4), butterflies (EA4, EA2), bees (EA4), fish (EA2), trees (EA5, EA4) and a hippo (EA5), all close-up shots which place the animals within personal space, sometimes with the animals looking out at the viewer in what Kress and van Leeuwen (2006, p. 118) call a 'demand' picture (one which demands a relationship between viewer and subject). The images are two-dimensional and static, so erase some features of the actual animals and trees (as all representations do), but still provide detailed images of individual animals and trees in a photorealistic way, placing the images directly in the minds of viewers.

The statement 'trees such as oak, beech and birch, mammals such as badgers, otters and seals' (EA4:19) also represents trees and animals quite vividly since the species are concretely imaginable (the 'basic' level). Still, nothing about the word 'birch' conveys the myriad of shapes of the actual trees, their colours, smells, textures or the complexity of their forms, so there is (as always) some erasure. These two forms of representation (photographs and basic-level species names) show the minimum amount of erasure, but are actually rare within the documents — the primary ways that animals, plants and the natural world are represented consist of much stronger forms of erasure.

The first form of erasure occurs when superordinates replace the names of species: 'birds' (EA4:23), 'mammals' (EA4:23), and 'amphibians' (EA2:4); then 'animals' (EA2:11); then 'species' (EA3:1); then 'fauna' (EA4:48), right up to 'organisms' (EA2:1). These progressively get more abstract and less imaginable — from 'badger', which brings to mind many characteristics of a particular kind of animal, to 'organism', which erases all but the feature of being alive. Still higher up the ladder of erasure/abstraction are the terms 'bio-diversity' (EA2:1), 'components of biodiversity' (EA2:2), 'assemblages of species' (EA3:1), 'ecological complexes' (EA2:2) and 'ecosystems' (EA5:7). These represent the coming together of a diversity of animals and plants but the imaginable individuals are buried deeply within the abstractions.

Terms such as 'badger', 'mammal', 'species', 'organism', 'fauna' and 'bio-diversity' still remain within the semantic domain of living beings, however, which is as expected since the hyponymy relations are part of the semantics of the words themselves. In other words, it is part of the meaning of the word 'badger' that it is a hyponym of 'animal'. However, as Fairclough (2003, p. 130) describes, texts can set up their own relations of hyponymy 'on the fly', and in doing so can place living beings as co-hyponyms of inanimate objects. The expression 'extraction of timber, fish, water and other resources' (EA3:2) sets up timber, fish and water as equivalent co-hyponyms under the superordinate category of 'resources' — a category which includes both living beings and non-living materials. This erases the distinctiveness of living beings — draining the life out of them by including them in a list of resources along with inanimate objects. The expressions 'soils, air, water and biological resources' (EA5:10), 'terrestrial, marine and freshwater resources' (EA4:20) and 'trade in commodities such as grain, fish, and timber' (EA1:59) carry out a similar function. Even biodiversity is set up as a resource in 'biodiversity and other ecological resources' (EA3:1). The pronoun 'our' is used in the expression 'our ecological resources' (EA3:1) to erase the other life forms we share the planet with by turning them into human possessions rather than beings in their own right. When living beings become 'resources', the entailment is that not using them is a waste and that they should be exploited rather than left to get on with their own lives.

The complex noun phrase 'provisioning services such as food, water, timber and fibre' (EA2:1) erases animals and plants firstly by turning them into co-hyponyms of 'provisioning services', and secondly by burying them within mass nouns (food, timber and fibre). They are still there, but only as a trace. The process of 'massification' is a strong form of erasure, so trees become 'timber' (EA4:7), then 'fuel wood' (EA5:17), then 'cubic meters of timber' (EA5:12), then 'wood biomass' (EA4:18), and at the top level of erasure biomass becomes merely a modifier in '27 million tonnes per year of ... biomass imports' (EA4:38). When trees, plants and animals are represented in mass nouns, they are erased, becoming mere tonnages of stuff.

Another massification term is 'natural capital'. The expression 'forests and living coral reefs are critical components of natural capital' (EA5:7) starts off with the concretely imaginable forests and reefs but then turns them into the unimaginable mass term 'capital', which later becomes 'stocks of natural capital' (EA5:7). EA5 is explicitly about the economics of ecosystems, so it is not surprising that it draws from the discourse of ecological economics mentioned above. However, the other documents also contain similar expressions, e.g. 'the value of the UK's natural capital is not fully realised' (EA4:47), 'natural capital assets' (EA2:6), 'natural capital declaration' (EA6:11) and 'maintaining ecosystem capital stocks' (EA6:31). The discourse of economics has spilled out into the ecological realm to become one of the primary ways that these reports describe the living world.

There are also representations which contain traces of animals and plants by mentioning the places where they live, but not the dwellers themselves: 'Urban greenspace amenity' (EA4:51) includes trees and plants as the merest of traces in the 'green' of 'greenspace'. The terms 'living and physical environments' (EA4:4) and 'environmental resources' (EA5:20) represent animals and plants as part of an all-encompassing environment surrounding humans rather than existing in their own right. The expressions 'a biome's native habitat' (EA2:2), 'the diversity of benthic habitats' (EA2:8) and 'aquatic habitat types' (EA4:10) represent what Philo and Wilbert (2000) call 'beastly places', though without the beasts. Likewise, the expression 'seasonally grazed floodplains' (EA4:23) contains just a trace of animals, for who else is doing the grazing? And a hint of plants, for what else is being grazed?

Another way that animals and plants are erased is through being referred to metonymically by the function they are serving within an ecosystem: 'pollinators', 'primary producers', 'dispersers' or the slightly more vivid 'pollinating insects' (EA4:19). Fish are erased through taking the place of a modifier in noun phrases such as 'fish catch' (EA1:103), 'fish stocks' (EA1:6), 'fishing technology' (EA4:55), 'fish consumption' (EA1:103) and 'fish production' (EA1:17). When fish are modifiers of other nouns, they have been pushed to the periphery, the clause being about something else. And the erasure is taken even further with the expression 'fisheries' (EA2:5), where the fish themselves remain in the morphology of the word, but just a trace within a large commercial operation. Fish are also erased by metaphor in the expression 'commonly harvested fish species' (EA2:3) or 'the fish being harvested' (EA1:15), since they are made equivalent to crops rather than being treated as animals.

The overall pattern across the reports is clear: there are visual illustrations and vivid expressions towards the top of the hierarchy of erasure (e.g. badgers, oaks, otters) but these are few and far between. For the most part the reports erase the animals, plants, forests, rivers and oceans, even though they are what the reports are all about. Four of the five reports acknowledge that people are encouraged to protect the natural world if they find intrinsic value within it, but an expression like 'ecosystem structural elements such as biomass' (EA3:1) contains only the faintest trace of the natural world, and no hint of intrinsic value.

Ecosystem assessment reports are important because they are read by policymakers and can influence political decision-making. However, perhaps even more important are the United Nations Sustainable Development Goals (SDGs), because they are used not only by policymakers but also by a wide range of charities, educational institutions and corporations across the world. Chapter 3 has already described how the primary framing of the SDGs is economic, with a focus on 'inclusive, sustainable and sustained growth'. A key question is whether the natural world appears at all in the SDGs, and if it does then is it displayed prominently and visibly or is it erased?

Born (2019) is concerned that the central focus on human wellbeing of the goals 'clearly reinforces a paradigm of human exceptionalism, and therefore positions animals as resources to which humans are entitled'. Certainly, the 2030 Agenda for Sustainable Development (EN2) which lays out the goals does start with the words 'This Agenda is a plan of action for people, planet and prosperity', with people first. Under the heading for 'people' it states: 'ensure that all human beings can fulfil their potential in dignity and equality and in a healthy environment'. Under the heading for 'planet' it states:

- We are determined to protect the planet from degradation, including through sustainable consumption and production, sustainably managing its natural resources and taking urgent action on climate change, so that it can support the needs of the present and future generations. (EN2:2)

Animals, plants, forests and rivers are in there somewhere, but deeply buried in the 'planet', 'environment' and 'natural resources', while the purpose of protecting the planet is explained only in terms of the needs of present and future generations (of humans, presumably). The natural world appears, but only as the vaguest of traces. Born notes that 'although there are 17 goals, only three of them (Goals 12, 14, and 15) mention animals at all, and even then, animals are described as mere resources ... animals as living beings are essentially erased from the picture'. Some examples of this erasure from goals 12, 14 and 15 are as follows:

- 12.2: By 2030, achieve the sustainable management and efficient use of natural resources.
- 14.7: By 2030, increase the economic benefits ... from the sustainable use of marine resources.
- 14.c: Enhance the conservation and sustainable use of oceans ...
- 15.1: By 2020, ensure the conservation, restoration and sustainable use of terrestrial and inland freshwater ecosystems and their services, in particular forests, wetlands,

mountains and drylands.

- 15.5: Take urgent and significant action to reduce the degradation of natural habitats, halt the loss of biodiversity and, by 2020, protect and prevent the extinction of threatened species.
- 15.6: Promote fair and equitable sharing of the benefits arising from the utilisation of genetic resources.
- 15.7: Take urgent action to end poaching and trafficking of protected species of flora and fauna. (EN2)

The first thing to note about this is the abstraction: 'flora', 'fauna', 'species', 'biodiversity' and 'ecosystems'. The more concrete terms 'forests' and 'mountains' are present but their vividness is diminished because the restoration is in terms of the 'use' of their 'ecosystems and services'. Utilisation is a strong theme, with 'natural resources', 'marine resources', 'oceans', 'terrestrial and inland freshwater ecosystems' and 'genetic resources' all being framed in terms of use or 'sustainable use'. Placing the modifier 'sustainable' in front of 'use' may be an improvement, but it still reproduces the same utility framing.

The anthropocentrism is very strong; for example, the following extract only calls for protection of human health from chemicals without explicitly mentioning the health of other species:

- We will reduce the negative impacts of urban activities and of chemicals which are hazardous for human health and the environment ... (EN2:9)

Quantitative analysis is also useful in revealing anthropocentrism. According to analysis conducted by Elena Valvason (personal correspondence), there are 44 different words in the 2030 Agenda for Sustainable Development which refer to humans ('people', 'women', 'farmers', etc). Some of these words appear frequently, so the total number of mentions of humans is 274 in total. In other words, there are 44 *types* (i.e., distinct words) and 274 *tokens* (instances) which refer to humans.

On the other hand, there are only 6 distinct words that refer to animals ('species', 'wildlife', 'animals', 'fauna', 'fish', and 'livestock') in the 2030 Agenda, and they appear only 14 times in total. Similarly, there are only seven words that refer to plants ('species', 'plant', 'flora', 'forest', 'plants', 'seed', 'seeds') and they also appear only 14 times. While the words for people include detailed information such as employment, age and gender (e.g., 'teacher', 'youth', 'woman'), the words for plants and animals are all abstract ('fauna', 'species', etc.). Table 8.1 gives the full information on the specific words that refer to humans, animals and plants, along with their rank and frequency. The anthropocentrism can be most clearly seen in the pie charts of Figure 8.1. which summarise this information. This analysis is just of one document, but *corpus-assisted ecolinguistics* is an emerging area with great potential to discover patterns across large numbers of texts (Poole 2016, 2017, 2022).

Tokens in the 2030 Agenda for Sustainable Development

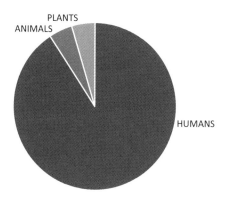

Types in the 2030 Agenda for Sustainable Development

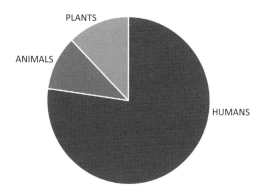

FIGURE 8.1 Tokens and types for humans, animals and plants in the 2030 Agenda for Sustainable Development

Although rare, there are occasional statements in the 2030 Agenda which extend the goals to include consideration of other species, in a way which aligns closely with the ecosophy of this book:

- [a world] in which humanity lives in harmony with nature and in which wildlife and other living species are protected. (EN2:4)
- We envisage a world free of poverty, hunger, disease and want, where all life can thrive. (EN2:4)

TABLE 8.1 Relative rank, type and raw frequency of terms describing humans, animals and plants in the 2030 Agenda for Sustainable Development, produced by Elena Valvason (personal correspondence)

Rank	Type	Frequency	Rank	Type	Frequency
Humans					
1	people	64	23	refugees	3
2	women	32	24	representatives	3
3	girls	15	25	workers	3
4	children	12	26	adults	2
5	persons	12	27	individuals	2
6	peoples	11	28	leaders	2
7	child	10	29	president	2
8	youth	10	30	workforce	2
9	poor	9	31	families	1
10	communities	8	32	girl	1
11	men	8	33	herders	1
12	generation	6	34	infants	1
13	migrants	6	35	learners	1
14	boys	5	36	newborns	1
15	humanity	5	37	organizers	1
16	population	5	38	participants	1
17	community	4	39	person	1
18	family	4	40	producers	1
19	citizens	6	41	soldiers	1
20	farmers	3	42	teacher	1
21	fishers	3	43	teachers	1
22	generations	3	44	woman	1
Animals			**Plants**		
1	species	7	1	species	7
2	wildlife	3	2	plant	2
3	animals	1	3	flora	1
4	fauna	1	4	forest	1
5	fish	1	5	plants	1
6	livestock	1	6	seed	1
			7	seeds	1

There is abstraction in the quotations above such as the terms 'wildlife', 'other living species' and 'all life', but at least other species are represented as worthy of protection for their own sake rather than for narrow anthropocentric or economic goals. The document even uses the metaphor of 'Mother Earth', to call for protection and care for the Earth as a whole:

- we reaffirm that planet Earth and its ecosystems are our common home and that 'Mother Earth' is a common expression in a number of countries and regions. (EN2:13)

It is interesting that the metaphor is distanced from the writers of the report through just pointing out that it is a common expression rather than one which the writers necessarily agree with. Other metaphors, such as the one which represents developing countries as lagging behind on a journey, are just expressed directly without this kind of hedging, for example:

- As we embark on this great collective journey, we pledge that no one will be left behind ... And we will endeavour to reach the furthest behind first. (EN2:3)

Overall, there are very occasional places in the 2030 Agenda where the existence and value of plants and animals is acknowledged, while the overall pattern is one of erasure where they are represented as existing only as resources for efficient utilisation by humans. These goals are translated into many different languages and spread around the world, even to countries where the traditional culture gives great salience and value to nature.

The language of ecosystem assessments and the 2030 Agenda for Sustainable Development is, in Heidegger's terms, 'ordinary language'. As Garrard (2012, p. 35) explains:

> Heidegger was dismissive of everyday chatter because it discloses both language and beings to us as mere instruments of our will; disposable words correspond to a world of disposable stuff. Worse still, things may emerge as mere resources on call for our use when required, so that a living forest may show up as merely a 'standing reserve' of timber (*Bestand*), no longer trees but just lumber-in-waiting.

The point of ecolinguistic analysis is not only to point out that the natural world *has* been erased in discourses such as ecosystem assessment, but also to show *how* it has been erased. Knowledge of the detailed linguistic mechanisms of erasure can help those who are responsible for the discourse to reverse the erasure and represent the natural world more saliently in future reports. Garrard (2012, p. 34) describes Heidegger's view as follows:

> Thus responsible humans have an implicit duty to let things disclose themselves in their own inimitable way, rather than forcing them into meanings and identities that suit their own instrumental values. One of the crucial modes of proper letting be or unhindered disclosure of being is poetry.

理论延伸

贯穿于本章的核心理论内容是语篇或话语中的删略问题。不过，此处我们并非简单地将"删略"作为一个理论来梳理，而是倾向于将"删略"视为一种语言使用现象，一种近乎所有话语中都存在的语言现象。因为任何话语都是具有价值取向的，都以显性或隐性的方式，表达或隐含特定的价值准则（黄国文，2020）；人们通过语言建构客观世界的现实，表达对客观世界识解的过程（Halliday，1995/2006：13）。当人们在语言表达的过程中，重视某个方面的同时就会不自觉地删略其他一些方面。所以，既然删略主要通过语言来实现，那要研究有关语言中的删略问题势必要与其他的理论结合来分析，如前面章节讨论过的话语分析、框架理论、隐喻理论等理论（故事）。结合本章的内容，这个部分我们重点补充几个在前面章节的理论延伸部分未详细介绍、但对于本章的删略研究十分重要的概念或理论。

第一，及物性系统。及物性系统是系统功能语言学研究中的一个重要概念，属于概念元功能的内容。系统功能语言学既是一门普通语言学，又是一门适用语言学（Halliday，2009；辛志英、黄国文，2010）。作为普通语言学，系统功能语言学的最终目标是对人类语言意义的功能描述和解释，发现语言中的普遍规律和特征；而作为适用语言学，它还强调语言的实践性，将系统功能语言学用于解决与语言有关的问题（黄国文，2017）。从这个角度来看，及物性系统属于系统功能语言学的普通语言学部分，我们当前关注的生态语言学（韩礼德模式，即系统生态语言学，见 Halliday，2007）属于系统功能语言学的适用语言学部分；及物性系统和系统生态语言学的根源都是系统功能语言学，强调系统功能语言学中的不同方面，所以将及物性系统用于分析生态语言学中的语言现象是顺理成章的。

系统功能语言学有三个元功能，即概念功能（经验功能和逻辑功能）、人际功能和语篇功能（Halliday，1994/2000）。及物性系统是概念功能（经验功能）中的重要组成部分，用于描述整个小句的内容，主要包括过程、参与者成分和环境成分等。参与者成分指的是小句中的施事、受事、载体、属性等内容；过程指的是小句中的物质过程、关系过程、言语过程、心理过程、行为过程和存在过程。本章与此相关的部分主要是小句中的参与者角色问题，按照何伟和魏榕（2017）的说法，从生态语言学的角度，小句的参与者成分可以分成生命体和非生命体两个部分。对小句中的参与者角色进行分析，能够根据参与者角色的类型和功能，判断出某个特定内容在话语中的删略现象。有关及物性系统的内容以及系统功能语言学的其他方面，尤其是与生态语言学的结合方面，读者可参考黄国文和辛志英（2012）、何伟和魏榕（2017）、何伟和张瑞杰（2017）、黄国文（2017）、何伟和耿芳（2018）、何伟和马宸（2020）、黄国文和陈瑜敏（2021）等论著。

第二，概念转喻（conceptual metonymy）。转喻和隐喻之间既有区别，又存在一定的联系。根据 Lakoff & Turner（1989：103）的观点，转喻和隐喻的一个明显区别是：隐喻涉及的是两个概念域，而转喻只涉及一个概念域。试比较本书中的两个例子："产仔母猪应该被想象成（或被当作）是一种很有价值的机器"（P186）和"十四周龄大的鸡被归类为烤肉鸡"（P187）。简单来说，第一个例子将"猪"（第一个概念域）隐喻为"机器"（第二个概念域）；第二个例子是使用烹饪方法的转喻（只有一个概念域），将"活生生的鸡"与"鸡做成的产品"联系起来。

有关隐喻的理论背景补充，在前面第 4 章已经进行了详细的讨论，在此则重点关注转喻的问题。转喻在话语的删略现象中具有重要的位置；在认知语言学视角下，转喻（metonymy）指的是一种基本的认知手段，在人类的推理过程中意义重大；鉴于转喻的概念本质，认知语言学中将其称为概念转喻（Lakoff & Johnson，1980/2003；参见李福印，2008：145）。在具体的实例中，转喻和隐喻经常是无法清晰地分离的，出现了类似于来自转喻的隐喻（metaphor from metonymy）、隐喻中的转喻（metonymy within metaphor）、隐喻中的非转喻化（demetonymisation inside a metaphor）和转喻中的隐喻（metaphor within metonymy）等四种现象（Goossens，2003；参见陈道明，2016：111–113）。需要进一步了解转喻问题的读者可参看李福印（2008）、陈道明（2016）、申奥和梅德明（2018）等论著。

最后，上下义词语的使用也能够对语言中的删略现象产生影响。上下义关系研究在系统功能语言学中属于衔接问题。衔接主要包括照应、替代、省略、连接和词汇衔接（Halliday & Hasan，1976：29）。本章所运用的内容主要是词汇衔接中的复现（reiteration）手段。上义词通常更具概括性，能够对所覆盖的下义词进行概括；下义词则表达得更为具体，是对上义词的具体阐释和表述。有关语篇的衔接问题以及语篇的连贯问题，读者可深入阅读朱永生和严世清（2001：66–95）、黄国文（2011）、姜望琪（2012：127–182）、何伟和郭笑甜（2020）等论著。

生态语言学中的删略现象涉及的内容非常多，我们在此无法一一列举，对这个角度感兴趣的读者可以从自己的学术背景和研究兴趣出发，关注其中删略现象的具体层面。到目前为止，对本书作者提出的删略问题直接应用在生态语言学领域的研究较少，读者可选择从 Stibbe（2012）的专著等研究成果中探索出可研究的思路。

补充文献

陈道明 . 2016. 认知语言学理论与语言实例 . 北京：社会科学文献出版社 .

何伟，耿芳 . 2018. 英汉环境保护公益广告话语之生态性对比分析 . 外语电化教学，（4）：57–63.

何伟，郭笑甜 . 2020. 语言系统的复杂性与语篇功能的体现方式 . 当代修辞学，（1）：39–49.

何伟，马宸 . 2020. 生态语言学视角下的主位系统 . 中国外语，（4）：23–32.

何伟，魏榕 . 2017. 国际生态话语之及物性分析模式构建 . 现代外语，（5）：597–607.

何伟，张瑞杰 . 2017. 生态话语分析模式构建 . 中国外语，（5）：56–64.

黄国文 . 2011.《论语》的篇章结构及英语翻译的几个问题 . 中国外语，（6）：88–95.

黄国文 . 2017. 从系统功能语言学到生态语言学 . 外语教学，（5）：1–7.

黄国文 . 2020. 思政视角下的英语教材分析 . 中国外语，（5）：21–29.

黄国文，陈瑜敏 . 2021. 系统功能语言学十讲 . 上海：上海外语教育出版社 .

黄国文，辛志英 . 2012. 系统功能语言学研究现状和发展趋势 . 北京：外语教学与研究出版社 .

姜望琪 . 2012. 语篇语义学 . 黄国文，辛志英主编 . 系统功能语言学研究现状和发展趋势 . 北京：外语教学与研究出版社，127–182.

李福印 . 2008. 认知语言学概论 . 北京：北京大学出版社 .

申奥，梅德明 . 2018. 概念隐喻和转喻互动下非透明英语习语的认知研究 . 西安外国语大学学报，（3）：29–34.

辛志英，黄国文 . 2010. 系统功能类型学：理论、目标与方法 . 外语学刊，（5）：50–55.

朱永生，严世清 . 2001. 系统功能语言学多维思考 . 上海：上海外语教育出版社 .

Ferber, A. 2007. Whiteness studies and the erasure of gender. *Sociology Compass*, (1): 265–282.

Frohmann, B. 1992. The power of images: A discourse analysis of the cognitive view point. *Journal of Documentation*, (4): 365–386.

Goossens, L. 2003. Metaphtonymy: The interaction of metaphor and metonymy in expressions for linguistic action. In R. Dirven & R. Pörings (Eds.), *Metaphor and metonymy in comparison and contrast*. Berlin: Mouton de Gruyter, 349–371.

Halliday, M. A. K. 1994/2000. *An introduction to functional grammar* (2nd ed.). London: Arnold / Beijing: Foreign Language Teaching and Research Press.

Halliday, M. A. K. 1995/2006. Language and the reshaping of human experience. In J. Webster (Ed.), *The language of science, Vol. 5 in The collected works of M. A. K. Halliday*. London: Continuum, 7–23.

Halliday, M. A. K. 2007. Applied linguistics as an evolving theme. In J. Webster (Ed.), *Language and education, Vol. 9 in The collected works of M. A. K. Halliday*. London: Continuum, 1–19.

Halliday, M. A. K. 2009. Methods—techniques—problems. In M. A. K. Halliday & J. Webster (Eds.), *Continuum companion to systemic functional linguistics*. London: Continuum, 59–86.

Halliday, M. A. K. & Hasan, R. 1976. *Cohesion in English*. London: Longman.

Lakoff, G. & Johnson, M. 1980/2003. *Metaphors we live by*. Chicago: University of Chicago Press.

Lakoff, G. & Turner, M. 1989. *More than cool reason: A field guide to poetic metaphor*. Chicago: University of Chicago Press.

Stibbe, A. 2012. *Animals erased: Discourse, ecology and reconnection with the natural world*. Middleton: Wesleyan University Press.

9

SALIENCE

章节导读

　　本章的主要内容与第 8 章的联系十分紧密，二者可以看作是同一枚硬币的两个侧面。从目前的文献看，主流语言学通常更加关注语言在人际交流互动中的作用，而对于维系人类赖以生存的生态系统的作用常常出现删略的情况，但这一点恰恰是人类和社会的可持续发展中至关重要的因素。因此，作者提请人们要在主流语言学的研究中关注生态系统的删略现象，以凸显的语言方式呈现出这一要点，最终使得该凸显内容能够在某种文化群体的头脑中普遍形成。这个过程实质上也是生态语言学研究的凸显方式。就第 9 章来说，作者将视角聚焦在凸显问题的讨论上，所覆盖的内容如下：（1）理论内涵；（2）凸显分析的方法；（3）案例：新自然文学中的凸显。

　　（1）理论内涵。许多生态环境和自然文学类的写作都特别关注关于"地方"（place）和"住所"（dwelling）的讨论，这类语篇或话语能够唤起人们对其他物种和生态环境的尊重和关怀。但是，在很多其他类型的话语中经常会删略掉这些非常重要的因素。本书所举的例子是纪录片《皮革的地狱》（*Hell for Leather*）（P205）。这个例子描绘的是廉价皮革生产背后的代价，这种活动在生活中常被忽视。不过在该纪录片中，当地居民在镜头里讲述皮革厂的污染对他们健康的影响，并特写了一名妇女手臂上的皮肤病变。这里居民自述的话语配上具体而生动的镜头画面构成了凸显模式，给观众以深刻的印象。观众接触这样的话语内容，不仅是在提醒自己关注这一被删略掉的重要情境；同时，这些问题也会凸显在他们的脑海中，无法忽视。

　　本章涉及的核心术语有三个——"提醒"（re-minding）、"凸显"（salience）和"凸显模式"（salience pattern），结合上面例子的分析，作者明晰了这几个概念。"提醒"的定义是：明确呼吁人们对某一特定语篇或话语中被删略的重要生活领域进行关注，并要求对其重新考量（explicitly calling attention to the erasure of an important area of life in a particular text or discourse and demanding that it be brought back into consideration）。

"凸显"是指人们头脑中的故事，将某个生活领域视为重要的或值得关注的（a story in people's minds that an area of life is important or worthy of attention）。凸显模式讲的是通过具体、明确、生动的语言或视觉描绘方式，将某个生活领域呈现为值得关注的对象（a linguistic or visual representation of an area of life as worthy of attention through concrete, specific and vivid depictions）。

（2）凸显分析的方法。凸显的方法有很多种表现形式，其基本方式是通过一系列的语言特征形成的模式构成凸显模式，突出语篇或话语中特定的参与者。所以在凸显分析时要注重挖掘其中的语言特征（焦点、活力、抽象水平、及物性和隐喻等），揭示出某个生活领域中生动具体的凸显模式。具体哪些领域应该在语篇或话语中得以凸显，主要是由分析者的生态哲学观决定的。从本书作者的生态哲学观来看，语篇或话语中需要凸显的内容有：人类赖以生存的生态系统、人类之外的福祉和自然系统、过度消耗引发的生态破坏等与生态环境保护有关的话语。作者在这个部分分析了多个典型的语篇，这里以其中一个语篇为例进行讨论——以凸显模式质疑生物多样性补偿的问题（P211）。在这个例子中，George Monbiot 使用了一系列的语言对比手段建立了一种生动的凸显模式，凸显的是史密斯树林（Smithy Wood）的破坏情况。一方面，使用了个体化（individualisation）的语言形式突出个体的独特性和不可替代性——古树林的名字（史密斯树林）、树种名字（橡树）、橡树的具体描述（弯曲的、有裂缝的、矮小的）等；另一方面，也使用到了同质化（homogenisation）的语言形式减少此处个体的独特凸显程度，间接指向提倡生物多样性补偿的人——将"自然"形容成"可替代的""没有意义的""没有内在价值的""可取代的"，以形成鲜明的对比。概括来看，Monbiot 表达的思想是：史密斯树林不可替代，它既有意义，又存在很大的内在价值。

此外，凸显在可视化分析（visual analysis）中也是最为常用的，也可以体现在多模态的文本中（Kress & van Leeuwen，2006：210）。这种凸显手法不单单是通过语言模式建立起来的，还包括了附有文字的视觉图像模式，以明示想要凸显的目标实体。本小节分析的纪录片《皮革的地狱》（P205）就是一种典型的多模态凸显，图文并茂、生动形象，能够产生良好的效果。

（3）案例：新自然文学中的凸显。这一小节是案例分析环节，作者通过分析新自然文学（New Nature Writing）中的英国学派（UK school），研究这类语篇是以怎样的语言模式凸显出"动植物"和"自然世界"的。新自然文学语篇能够较好地关注被忽视的重要事物，用可持续的方式看待人类与非人类世界的相互关系和相互作用。这类语篇无论是对生态系统评估报告、生物学教程等存在删略重要信息内容的优化，还是对自然系统的意义和内在价值的凸显，都有着不可估量的作用。新自然文学的具体案例是选取的七部作品（P219）。总结下来，作者归纳出，新自然文学凸显了自然系统的语言模式，主要采用主动化、感官意象、个性化、基层分类和明喻等方式向我们传达了"自然是十分重要的，值得我们去关注"的故事；但与此同时，"人类"在文中也没有被删略。这样的凸显模式与本书的生态哲学观是完全符合的。

> We can be ethical only in relation to something we can see, feel, understand, love, or otherwise have faith in.
>
> (Aldo Leopold 1979, p. 214)

Much environmental, ecological and nature writing focuses on 'place' and 'dwelling' — a sense of rootedness in local community and environment. There are many reasons for this — the wellbeing gained from time spent in local nature as an alternative to the empty promises of consumerism; the building of local communities which can fulfil their needs in ecologically beneficial ways such as sharing; the direct understanding of natural systems that can be gained through close observation and attention to the living world around us; and the kindling of care for other species and the environment. And yet ecological philosopher Val Plumwood points out that discourses of place often erase something of great importance — what she calls the 'shadow lands'. In her own words:

> Ideals of dwelling [encourage] us to direct our honouring of place towards an 'official' singular idealised place consciously identified with self, while disregarding the many unrecognised, shadow places that provide our material and ecological support ... An ecological re-conception of dwelling has to include a justice perspective and be able to recognise the shadow places, not just the ones we love, admire or find nice to look at. So ecological thought ... must ... reflect on how nice (north) places and shadow (south) places are related, especially where north places are nice precisely because south places are not so nice.
>
> (Plumwood 2008)

What Plumwood is doing here can be called *re-minding*. She is surveying the discourse of place-based ecological writing, noticing that something of great importance has been erased, calling attention to this erasure, and demanding that the 'shadow places' be brought back to mind. What she does not do, however, is to give vivid depictions of the 'not so nice' places in the South to directly bring these places to mind. In Plumwood's text, the shadow places remain in shadow.

In a very different kind of text, the Ecologist Film Unit shines a light on the shadow places in the documentary *Hell for Leather* (EN17). The documentary investigates 'the shocking human cost of cheap leather', vividly depicting the pollution produced by tanneries in Bangladesh and the impact it has on local people's health. In one scene, blue polluted water is shown running out of a factory into open drains in a village as an unseen narrator states:

- Untreated tannery effluent fills the stagnant drains around Hazaribagh and the stench of chemicals is overwhelming. (EN17)

Local people are shown describing the health problems this has caused them, with a close-up shot of skin lesions on a woman's arm. Through a *salience pattern* of concrete and vivid images of sights, sounds and smells, the documentary brings the suffering of people in the South to the attention of the viewers. If viewers are frequently exposed to texts such as this, the *salience* of the shadow lands in their minds may increase and they may become less likely to overlook them.

On the one hand, then, is *re-minding,* which is an explicit call for something that has been erased to be brought back to attention, and on the other there is the more direct building of salience in people's minds through vivid and concrete depiction. The following are definitions for the purposes of this book:

Re-minding — explicitly calling attention to the erasure of an important area of life in a particular text or discourse and demanding that it be brought back into consideration.

Salience — a story in people's minds that an area of life is important or worthy of attention.

Salience pattern — a linguistic or visual representation of an area of life as worthy of attention through concrete, specific and vivid depictions.

The concept of salience is most often used in visual analysis, where Kress and van Leeuwen describe it as 'the degree to which an element draws attention to itself due to its size, its place in the foreground or its overlapping of other elements, its colour, its tonal values, its sharpness of definition and other features' (Kress and van Leeuwen 2006, p. 210). Patterns of visual features like these come together in pictures to give prominence to particular entities in the picture. In the same way, patterns of linguistic features can come together to form salience patterns which represent particular participants prominently in a text.

By analysing a range of linguistic features, including focus, vitality, levels of abstraction, transitivity, and metaphor, it is possible to reveal salience patterns which represent an area of life vividly and concretely. If these patterns are widespread, they can build up the salience of an area in individual people's minds or more widely in the minds of multiple people within a culture. The ecosophy of the analyst will determine what areas of life *should* be made more salient. For the ecosophy of this book these include the ecosystems that life depends on; the local more-than-human world which people can experience directly and gain wellbeing and understanding of natural systems; and the ecological destruction in faraway places caused by overconsumption in local ones.

Ecolinguistics itself is a form of re-minding in the sense that it calls attention to the erasure of the ecosystems that life depends on within the discourse of mainstream linguistics, and asks that they be considered. Ecolinguists point out that mainstream linguistics, in its focus on the role of language in human-human interaction, has erased the interaction of humans with the larger ecosystems that support life. What ecolinguistics tends not to do (and this book is no exception) is to concretely, specifically and vividly represent the natural world in ways that bring it into the minds of the readers. There is an exception, however, in the work of David Abram. In *The Spell of the Sensuous,* Abram explicitly describes how our bodily and sensual embedding within the more-than-human world has been erased through the abstractions of writing and technology. In his own words:

Caught up in a mass of abstractions, our attention hypnotised by a host of human-made technologies that only reflect us back to ourselves, it is all too easy for us to forget our carnal inherence in a more-than-human matrix of sensations and sensibilities.

(Abram 1996, p. 22)

He calls for writing which brings our attention back to the more-than-human world that we have forgotten:

There can be no question of simply abandoning literacy, of turning away from all writing. Our task, rather, is that of taking up the written word, with all of its potency, and patiently, carefully, writing language back into the land. Our craft is that of releasing the budded, earthly intelligence of our words, freeing them to respond to the speech of the things themselves — to the green uttering-forth of leaves from the spring branches ... Finding phrases that place us in contact with the trembling neck-muscles of a deer holding its antlers high as it swims toward the mainland, or with the ant dragging a scavenged rice-grain through the grasses.

(Abram 1996, p. 274)

Within this call for a different form of writing there is a salience pattern which itself brings the more-than-human world into the minds of the readers. There is the concrete and specific lexical set drawn from nature: 'leaves', 'branches', 'deer', 'antlers', 'ant' and 'grasses'. The specificity of the 'neck-muscles of a deer' and 'the ant dragging a scavenged rice-grain' creative vivid images which counter the abstractions of environmental discourse — 'fauna', 'biomass', 'ecosystem components', etc. And finally, the deer and the ant are represented actively as doing something in the world for their own purposes. All this creates strong and vivid images in the minds of those who read it, building up a salience pattern to counter the abstraction and erasure of the more-than-human world in so many texts that we come across in everyday life.

In his later work, *Becoming Animal,* Abram seeks 'a new way of speaking, one that enacts our interbeing with the earth ... A style of speech that opens our senses to the sensuous' (Abram 2010, p. 3). His book strives 'to discern and perhaps to practice a curious kind of thought, a way of careful reflection that no longer tears us out of the world of experience in order to represent it' (p. 34). Linguistically, this is achieved in multiple ways, one of which is an interesting form of metonymy:

- Massive animals and small animals, hoofed ones and clawed ones, antlered and quilled and bright-feathered ones, finned and tentacled and barnacled ones, all steadily dwindling down to a few members before they dissolve entirely into the fever dreams of memory. (p. 288)

The metonymies here turn characteristic parts of animals into adjectives and use them to represent whole classes of animals. To get an idea of how vivid this is, it is useful to compare it to a more abstract description such as the following from the WWF:

- The rapid loss of species we are seeing today is estimated by experts to be between 1,000 and 10,000 times higher than the natural extinction rate. These experts calculate that between 0.01 and 0.1% of all species will become extinct each year. (EN18)

The difference is that the expressions 'species' and 'extinction rate' are abstract, while 'hoofs', 'claws', 'antlers', 'quills', 'feathers', 'fins', 'tentacles' and 'barnacles' cause imaginable frames to come into the mind of readers. Lakoff's (2014) famous book *Don't Think of an Elephant* made the point that hearing the word 'elephant' will trigger a frame consisting of our image of an elephant and all the knowledge we have about elephants. Likewise, the word 'antler' triggers the frame of 'deer' — a concrete image that a word like 'species' cannot summon up. In addition, the expression 'dwindling down to a few members' focuses on the individuals themselves rather that the more abstract 'species' they belong to.

In general, the more abstract the description is, the less salient the entities being described. Abstraction in itself is not a problem — indeed it is a necessary tool in responding to the global and diffuse nature of the challenges we face. What is a problem is if there is so much abstraction that the concrete reality of individuals and their lives, deaths and wellbeing is forgotten. As Wendell Berry (in Foltz 2013, p. 21) points out, we need ways of writing that overcome the abstraction of terms like 'organisms':

> We are using the wrong language ... We have a lot of genuinely concerned people calling upon us to 'save' a world which their language simultaneously reduces to an assemblage of perfectly featureless and dispirited 'ecosystems', 'organisms', 'environments', 'mechanisms' and the like. It is impossible to prefigure the salvation of the world in the same language by which the world has been dismembered and defaced.

According to embodied cognitive theory (Johnson 1987; Lakoff and Johnson 1999; Lakoff and Wehling 2012a), meaning is based in the body, and terms that relate to actual or potential bodily experience have much more power to invoke images and emotions than more abstract terms. Finding a new form of language which does not 'dismember and deface' the world requires use of terms that invoke bodily experience. Lakoff and Wehling (2012a, p. 42) describe how:

> The word *environment* is an abstract category. There is no one clear image that comes to mind when hearing it. Contrast this with the words *forest, soil, water, air* and *sky*. They bring clear imagery to mind. We have all seen the sky, touched water, breathed air and walked in forests.

Abram (1996, p. 268) puts this somewhat more eloquently as:

> The earth ... discloses itself to our senses not as a uniform planet inviting global principles and generalisations, but as this forested realm embraced by water, or a windswept prairie, or a desert silence.

Importantly, Lakoff and Wehling (2012a, p. 41) describe how, among the possible levels of concreteness and abstraction, there is a particular level which is most imaginable — the 'basic level':

> Words have the most powerful effect on our minds when they are ... basic level
> ... Basic-level words activate imagery in our mind; for example, the basic-level
> word *chair* evokes an image of a chair; the more general, or superordinate-level,
> word *furniture* does not evoke a specific image. Basic-level words activate motor
> programs in our brain as part of our speech comprehension; the word *cat*, for example
> evokes motor programs that have to do with prototypical interaction with cats, such as
> petting them. The word *animal* activates no such motor programs. In short, basic-level
> concepts are the most powerful and effective in communication due to their connection
> to the body and the way that aspects of their meaning are integrated.

Basic-level representations are therefore the most salient, with a word like 'orangutan'
evoking a clear, salient image, while superordinates such as 'mammal', 'animal', 'organism',
or 'fauna' are more abstract and difficult to imagine. Descriptions which are more specific
than the basic level are not necessarily more salient — for example, few people have the
specialist knowledge for terms such as 'Sumatran orangutan' or 'Bornean orangutan' to
give a more vivid image than just 'orangutan'.

One important form of abstraction is *impersonalisation*. Fairclough (2003, p. 150)
describes how:

> Impersonal representation ... can dehumanise social actors, take the focus away
> from them as people, represent them ... instrumentally or structurally as elements of
> organisational structures and processes. The opposite extreme to impersonalization is
> naming — representing individuals by name.

This is clearly focused on humans, but animals too can be represented instrumentally as
elements of organisational structures and processes. An example is the way that pigs are
represented in the *Pork Industry Handbook* (AG1) with modifiers that signify their role
in the organisation rather than anything about them personally. There are 'nursery pigs',
'grower pigs', 'farrowing pigs', 'feeder pigs', 'finisher pigs', 'carry-over sows', 'cull
sows', 'market hogs' and 'slaughter hogs' (AG1:146, 6, 83, 12, 123). In addition, pigs are
impersonalised through expressions which treat them as a mass rather than individuals, for
example, when their death is described as the 'volume slaughtered' (AG1:141) rather than
'number slaughtered'. This form of impersonalisation gives very low salience to animals,
potentially helping to justify an environmentally damaging and inhumane farming system.

On the other hand, if we turn to a different and less ecologically destructive form of
farming, we see a very different form of language. The following example is from the
Harmony Herd, a free-range pork producer based in Wales:

- We have two Boars — Pumba and Naughty Nigel. Pumba is a gentle giant, and loves his ears being scratched, but don't get between him and his food! Nigel is slightly shy, although not when it comes to his wives! (AG4)

Here pigs are given high prominence through being named as individuals. Although this does stray into anthropomorphism, it is far harder to imagine treating a pig badly if he is *personalised* by being named 'Nigel' as opposed to a 'cull pig' whose only function in life is depicted as dying.

Naming is just one aspect of *individualisation*, where individuals are represented as unique and irreplaceable, as opposed to *homogenisation*, where individuals are indistinguishable parts of a larger group or mass. In the extract above, the boars are individualised by describing their own personal character (gentle, shy) and likes (loves his ears being scratched) rather than generalised characteristics of the species or breed. A contrasting example of homogenising language is the following from the British Pig Association, which describes the general physical characteristics of a particular breed of pig:

- The Gloucestershire Old Spot is a large meaty animal with a broad and deep body and large hams. Its white coat has large clearly defined black spots. (AG5)

In this description the combination of definite and indefinite articles 'The X is a Y' treats individuals as if they were identical, since the physical characteristics described apply to all members of the breed. The importance of homogenising language is that it reduces the salience of the individual as a unique being, and instead represents them as one of a set of equivalents. A Gloucestershire Old Spot can always be replaced, but there will never be another Nigel or Pumba.

Charles Eisenstein's book *Sacred Economics* explores the cultural tendency towards homogenisation — the way that increasingly houses, possessions, animals, plants and people are seen as replaceable functional units rather than having value in themselves:

Mass-produced, standardised commodities, cookie-cutter houses, identical packages of food, and anonymous relationships with institutional functionaries all deny the uniqueness of the world.

(Eisenstein 2011, p. xvi)

Eisenstein makes the case that unless we start seeing the uniqueness and value in objects and living beings we will not care about them, and will ultimately destroy them. He uses the word 'sacred' to describe the value of something that is unique:

And what is the sacred? ... A sacred object or being is one that is special, unique, one of a kind. It is therefore infinitely precious; it is irreplaceable.

(Eisenstein 2011, p. xv)

Language which increases the salience of individual people, animals, plants, forests or rivers can help resist the tendency towards homogenisation. It can build, in Eisenstein's sense of the word, a sense of 'sacredness'.

In the following example, *Guardian* columnist George Monbiot uses a particular salience pattern to argue against biodiversity offsets (attempts to compensate for the destruction of nature in one area by building new nature sites in another area). He takes up the specific case of an ancient woodland threatened by developers:

- On the outskirts of Sheffield there is a wood which, some 800 years ago, was used by the monks of Kirkstead Abbey to produce charcoal for smelting iron ... the company that wants to build the service station ... is offering to replace Smithy Wood with '60,000 trees ... planted on 16 hectares of local land close to the site'. Who cares whether a tree is a hunched and fissured coppiced oak, worked by people for centuries, or a sapling planted beside a slip-road with a rabbit guard around it? ... But this is the way it's going now: everything will be fungible, nothing will be valued for its own sake, place and past and love and enchantment will have no meaning ... Costing nature tells us that it possesses no inherent value; that it is worthy of protection only when it performs services for us; that it is replaceable. (EN20)

Monbiot creates a series of contrasts here. On one side is a set of terms that indicate homogeneity: nature is seen as 'fungible', as having 'no meaning', 'no inherent value' and 'replaceable'. This viewpoint is indirectly ascribed to those proposing biodiversity offsets. The offset itself is accordingly represented with low individuality. It does not have a name, it is just '60,000 trees', with each tree being a 'sapling' rather than a specific species of tree, and the place being the generic 'beside a slip road', which could be anywhere in the country. On the other hand, the ancient woodland it is intended to replace has a specific name (Smithy Wood); the example tree is of a specific species (oak); the tree is individualised by three adjectives (hunched, fissured and coppiced); the place is in a specific location (outskirts of Sheffield); and it has a specific history (used by monks). All of this shows that Smithy Wood is not fungible, it has meaning and inherent value and is irreplaceable.

Through individualisation, Monbiot builds up a pattern of language that makes Smithy Wood highly salient — something to notice and care about — while he reduces the salience of the proposed biodiversity offset. His point is not just about Smithy Wood, but about biodiversity offsetting and the economic valuation of nature in general, with the high salience of the wood giving far more vividness to the argument than if it had just been conducted in abstract terms.

In addition to personalisation and individualisation, salience can be built up by foregrounding participants in clauses. Van Leeuwen (2008, p. 33) describes how people (or members of other species) can be foregrounded in language by *activation*:

> *Activation* occurs when social actors are represented as the active, dynamic forces in an activity, *passivation* when they are represented as 'undergoing' the activity, or 'being at the receiving end of it'. [Activation] may be realised by ... transitivity structures in which activated social actors are coded as actor in material processes, behaver in behavioural processes, senser in mental processes, sayer in verbal processes, or assigner in relational processes ... [when activated] the social actor in question is most clearly foregrounded.

Participants are activated when they are represented as doing, thinking, feeling or saying things rather than having things done to them. The last chapter discussed how chickens are represented in the poultry industry with very low activation — as the Affected participants having something done to them. In the agribusiness handbook examined (AG3:20), chickens were represented using the passive voice: chickens 'are hung upside-down', 'are shackled', 'are exposed to steam', 'are showered with water', and 'are weighed individually'. Interestingly, animal rights texts frequently have a similar erasure pattern, to the extent that Tester (1991, p. 196) claims that within the animal rights movement 'the animals are nothing more than objects to which something is done'. An example of this pattern from the website of People for the Ethical Treatment of Animals (PETA) is as follows:

- In the United States, more than 7 billion chickens *are killed* for their flesh each year, and 452 million hens *are used* for their eggs ... At the slaughterhouse, their legs *are forced* into shackles, their throats *are cut*, and they *are immersed* in scalding-hot water. (EN19, emphasis added)

All of the verbs here are in the passive with the chickens as the Affected participant, a remarkably similar pattern to the agribusiness handbook. While this form of representation is useful in highlighting the ways that animals are treated in the industrial farming system, it does not necessarily encourage respect for the animals as living, breathing beings with goals, purposes and mental lives.

Passivated representations are not, however, the only linguistic pattern used by animal rights organisations. In the same text, PETA writes:

- chickens *are* inquisitive, interesting animals who *are* as intelligent as mammals such as cats, dogs, and even some primates. They *are* very social and *like* to *spend* their days together, *scratching* for food, *taking* dust baths, *roosting* in trees, and *lying* in the sun. (EN19, with verbs emphasised)

In this extract, chickens are in the position of the subject of all the verbs. They are the Actors of the material processes of 'scratching', 'taking', 'roosting' and 'lying', which shows them leading their own lives for their own purposes. They are the Sensers of the mental process 'like', which represents them as beings who have a mental life, which is further emphasised by the adjectives 'inquisitive' and 'intelligent'. The linguistic pattern activates the chickens, foregrounds them, and makes them salient in the minds of the readers, telling a story that they are important and worthy of consideration. The hope (as far as the ecosophy of this book is concerned) is that increasing the salience of domestic animals in the minds of people across a culture could increase the pressure on agribusiness to treat animals more humanely and encourage consumers to purchase less environmentally damaging meat.

IMAGE 9.1   Veal farm in the Netherlands © CIWF/Martin Usborne

In multimodal texts, salience patterns are built up not just through language but also through the visual images that accompany the words. Visual images are a particularly powerful way of building up or decreasing salience since they position the viewer within a scene, making them look at a subject from a particular angle and perspective (literally and metaphorically). Images 9.1–9.5 are from *Compassion in World Farming* and illustrate how the medium of photography can give salience to domestic animals in different ways.

Image 9.1, of intensive veal farming in the Netherlands, represents the calves with very low salience. There are a large number of animals depicted, with no individuals standing out in any way; the calves are not actively engaged in doing anything and do not look at the viewer. There is a long, narrowing perspective with identical pens of animals going all the way back into the distance, representing homogeny rather than individuality. The viewer is looking down at the calves, a high *camera angle* which suggests powerlessness of the subjects. This, then, is an illustration of how calves are conceptualised in the agribusiness industry, *en mass*e as 'livestock' rather than unique individuals with intrinsic worth.

Image 9.2, in contrast, highlights the plight of one individual animal caught within this system of farming. The white calf is given high salience through: (a) being the only animal pictured; (b) the contrast with the darker background; (c) the close-up of his face; (d) his central position; and (e) through his eyes looking out at the viewer. Kress and van Leeuwen call pictures where the eyes meet those of the viewer 'demand pictures' since they demand a relationship between the subject and the viewer, making the subject highly notice-able and salient. However, taking away from the salience is the fact that the calf is passivated by being depicted as not only doing nothing, but unable to do anything.

IMAGE 9.2 Calf in veal farm in the Netherlands © CIWF/Martin Usborne

IMAGE 9.3   Sheep in transporter truck © Compassion in World Farming

Image 9.3 is similar to 9.2 in being a demand picture, but in this case the blurred bodies in the background and the visual context of the transport truck highlight that this sheep is one individual within a mass of others awaiting the same fate. The shot is close, and as Kress and van Leeuwen (2006, p. 124) point out, the closer the shot, the more intimate the relationship depicted between viewer and subject. The camera angle is level, implying equality and suggesting empathy, as opposed to image 9.2 where the high angle looking down on the calf suggests sympathy.

Images such as 9.1, 9.2 and 9.3 are passivated depictions since they do not place the animals in active roles leading their own lives but rather having something done to them (i.e., an Affected role). They are important in highlighting the way that animals are treated as objects by industrial farming, but do not necessarily encourage respect for animals as beings with mental lives who are living their own lives for their own purposes.

Images 9.4 and 9.5 are very different, however. These images do not show animals as replaceable components of a huge industrial process, or as suffering and powerless, but as activated and salient individuals. The chickens in Image 9.4 are depicted against a natural background which suggests freedom, and from a low camera angle, making them appear powerful. Their eyes are looking intently at something just off-camera, which is an activated position of being a Senser in the mental process of looking. In Image 9.5, the expression on the face of the pig suggests she is also in the role of Senser, but this time of a mental process of enjoyment. In this way the animals are depicted saliently, as beings actively living and enjoying their lives.

Images 9.6 and 9.7 are from the Compassionate Farming Education Initiative and are useful in illustrating how words and images can work together to give salience. In Image 9.6, the words 'I' and 'someone' in the expression 'I am someone' both give salience to the turkey as an individual, while the close-up shot, central position, blurred background, and eye looking out to the viewer do the same visually.

IMAGE 9.4   Chickens © Compassion in World Farming

IMAGE 9.5   Pig in mud © CIWF/Martin Usborne

Image 9.7 makes sophisticated use of *visual simile*, which is a subtype of visual metaphor. Forceville (2016, p. 247) describes how:

In this subtype, the target is saliently compared to a source, which it resembles in one way or another. This can be done visually by various means: for instance by juxtaposing target and source, by presenting them in the same form or posture [or] by depicting them with the same attention-drawing colour...

IMAGE 9.6   I am someone © CFEI

IMAGE 9.7   Live and Let Live © CFEI

In this case, the target domain consists of pig, cat, elephant, cow and chicken families, which are being compared to the source frame of a human family. The simile is triggered because each of the images is 'in the same form or posture' — a child snuggling with their mother. The simile is, therefore, ANIMAL FAMILIES ARE JUST LIKE HUMAN FAMILIES. The text performs something very similar by using the words 'the mother/child bond', 'every family' and 'all love' in a way which includes both the human families and animal families. The simile is implicit, but clearly animals are the target domain since that is what the message is about, while the human family is there as a source frame to be a point of comparison. In all the embedded photos (aside from the cats) there are eyeline vectors between parent and child, indicating a relationship between the two. The text specifies and emphasises that relationship with the words 'love' and 'bond'.

The power of Image 9.7 is partly in its logic (logos): viewers are likely to accept the premise that human families deserve to be together in freedom and peace; they may (or may not) accept the simile that animal families are just like human families, and therefore may (or may not) accept the logical conclusion that they should give animals freedom and peace through becoming vegan. Much more powerful than the logic, however, is the emotion (pathos), achieved through making the animals and their mother/child bond highly salient.

In general, then, photography can use various visual techniques to give high or low salience to animals. While low-salience photographs of animals suffering *en masse* in factory farming systems are useful for highlighting how the animals are harmed, high-salience images can encourage respect for animals as individuals with mental lives who are actively engaged in living life for their own purposes and have loving relationships with others. While the impact on viewers can never be guaranteed, images such as these have the potential to encourage viewers to rethink their relationship with animals and reduce behaviours which harm them and the environment.

Salience in new nature writing

This section will investigate the patterns of language that New Nature Writing uses to give salience to animals, plants and the more-than-human world in general. Making the more-than-human world salient is essential for the ecosophy of this book for several reasons. Firstly, the ecosophy considers the wellbeing of all species, and if only humans have salience then the needs of others may be overlooked.

Secondly, the continuing survival and wellbeing of humans depends on interconnection with larger living systems. These systems need to be salient so that human impact on them is taken into consideration when making decisions. Thirdly, there is the mental health and wellbeing that people can get from connection with nature — a deep sense of contentment that does not require vast amounts of consumption. As Kathleen Jamie (in Crown 2012) remarks, 'and when we do that — step outdoors, and look up — we're not little cogs in the capitalist machine. It's the simplest act of resistance and renewal'. Fourthly, natural systems provide a model of sustainability. In the absence of humans they are productive, require inputs only from sunlight and biogeochemical cycles, and produce no waste. Direct interaction with and observation of the more-than-human world can help gain the understanding of natural systems necessary to model human societies along similar lines. Hall (2014, p. 302) writes:

> Many people find in their interaction with domesticated and wild animals a profound sense of fulfilment which counteracts the restless quest to acquire material goods ... When our yearning for connection with other living beings is satisfied, the hunger to consume is lessened and we gain a deep, bodily sense of belonging and attunement to the natural world. And that is one of the conditions, as well as a goal, of sustainability.

This section will examine how texts use language to build up the salience of the natural world in the minds of readers, with the aim of revealing specific linguistic techniques that could be applied in a wide range of areas. The techniques could help ecosystem assessment reports, biology textbooks or charity campaigns present animals and plants not just as stocks of resources, automatons or suffering objects, but as important and worthy of attention in their own right.

The reason for choosing the UK school of New Nature Writing is that, as Lilley (2013, p. 18) describes, these works pick out 'the hidden detail in the everyday, to illuminate what is overlooked and in doing so, to see the interrelationships between the human and the non-human differently'. The particular works of New Nature Writing examined are Jim Crumley's *Brother Nature* (NW1), William Fiennes's *The Snow Geese* (NW2), Kathleen Jamie's *Findings* (NW3), Olivia Laing's *To the River: A Journey Beneath the Surface* (NW4), Richard Mabey's *Nature Cure* (NW5), Robert Macfarlane's *The Wild Places* (NW6) and Esther Woolfson's *Field Notes from a Hidden City: An Urban Nature Diary* (NW7).

The starting point is the representation of starlings. Starlings, like human migrants, can sometimes get a hard time in the tabloid press in the UK. The *Daily Mail* reports how:

- A cul-de-sac is being drenched in bird droppings after it was invaded by a flock of more than 20,000 starlings. Like a scene from Alfred Hitchcock's thriller *The Birds*, the huge swarm turns the sky black each dawn and dusk as they prepare to feed or roost for the night. (ML8)

The terms 'flock' and 'swarm' reduce the salience of individuals, representing the birds as a single mass, with the word 'invaded' giving negative appraisal to this mass. Esther Woolfson, in her *Field Notes from a Hidden City,* counters this kind of representation by focusing on a single starling, and giving him the highest possible salience by naming him. She writes:

- The starling I personally knew was Max ... I think of the nature of his character, the exquisite sweetness of his evening solos as well as the extraordinary beauty of the bird, the gilded feathers, the neatness of wing as he flew ... (NW7:55)

By describing the characteristics of an individual, rather than a generalised list of characteristics of a particular kind of bird, Woolfson is representing him as unique rather than replaceable. Further than that, she takes this individualisation and applies it back to the larger flock, encouraging readers to see starlings as a collection of individuals rather than a mass:

- ... After I got to know him, I'd look anew each evening at the cloud of swirling starlings, understanding that each one of them was as Max was. Knowing increased my amazement at their individuality, at the magical coordination of their movement, the singular, transcendent beauty of this turning, sweeping cloud of birds. (NW7:55–56)

Starlings, then, become salient not because of the nuisance of their droppings but as individuals, and are appraised positively through the terms 'magical', 'beauty' and 'transcendent'.

Naming of individual animals is rare in New Nature Writing, but the use of the pronouns 'he', 'she', 'his', and 'her' for animals is common and gives them salience by representing them in a more personalised way than the pronoun 'it'. The following are examples:

- Once in my wood I had a face-to-face meeting with a female muntjac deer ... We got to about 10 feet from each other and then just stared. I looked into her large eyes and at her humped back and downpointed tail ... She looked at my eyes ... (NW5:21)
- She [a grizzly bear] raised her head above the tops of the fireweed and sniffed and stared ... We watched each other. I don't know what she thought. I revered her ... (NW1:6)
- Whatever he was, this bird was beautiful. His new, fresh feathers were lavender and navy, shading to a fine line of black towards the tips of his wings, his eyes bright and watching. (NW7:7)

These three examples also contain the mental processes 'staring', 'watching', 'thinking' and 'looking', with the animals as Sensers. This activates the animals, foregrounding them and giving them salience as conscious beings.

Animals are also frequently activated by being represented as Actors of material processes, i.e., as involved in purposeful activity. In one paragraph, Mabey uses fourteen processes to describe the flight of kites, all of them (except for one) material processes with the birds as the Actor:

- Then they [kites] lifted up, flexed, soared ... They glided towards me — no hurry, just riding the wind, sliding across the eddies. They came close ... They were sporting over the villages, lifting on gusts that took them sailing clean over cottages ... arcing across the hedges ... I watched one close to as it turned into the wind. It raised its wings ... and gathered the air in, folded it into itself. (NW5:114)

In a different context, Mabey (2008) stated that:

Our language, our syntax, our whole terms of reference with regard to the world beyond us are those of occupation ... can we go 'post-colonial' ... to respect the autonomy and agendas of what David Abram calls the 'more-than-human world'.

By using syntax that represents the birds as Actors, Mabey is putting this into practice by vividly representing the autonomy and agendas of the birds.

In most cases, animals and plants are referred to at the basic level — the level that conveys the most vivid images. Among the wide range of animals that authors encounter there are:

Peregrines, ospreys, peewits, cranes, salmon, ravens, herons, gannets, corncrakes, minke whales, snow geese, bald eagles, Canada geese, grizzly bears, badgers, kites, rats, nightingales, magpies, beavers, whooper swans, otters, golden eagles, swifts, larks, hares, deer, and sparrows.

Abstract terms like 'mammal', 'reptile', 'fauna' and 'organism' are sometimes used in New Nature Writing since it is a multi-voiced genre that frequently mixes scientific and personal observation. However, the more concrete and vivid basic-level terms are by far the most common. With some exceptions such as grizzly bears encountered in the USA, the animals and plants described tend to be ordinary ones that readers are likely to come across in their everyday lives. By giving salience to these animals and plants in their writing, the writers model a way of paying close attention to the natural world which readers could adopt in their daily encounters with nature.

Another linguistic feature that can build up prominence and is common in New Nature Writing is what can be called a *sense image*. For the purposes of this book, *sense image* can be defined as a description of how an external entity impacts on the senses. It is a subjective description of what is seen, heard, smelled, touched or tasted rather than an objective description of what, or who, is there. Sense images encourage the reader to imagine being in the scene described by the author and view what the author is viewing for themselves, leading to strong prominence for what is being described.

Tim Ingold (2011, p. 72) describes how, in the language of the Koyukon of Alaska, the actual names of animals reflect what you would characteristically see or hear them doing:

> Animals, likewise, are distinguished by characteristic patterns of activity or movement signatures, and to perceive an animal is to witness this activity going on, or to hear it. Thus, to take a couple of illustrations from Richard Nelson's wonderful account of the Koyukon of Alaska, *Make Prayers to the Raven*, you see 'streaking like a flash of fire through the undergrowth', not a fox, and 'perching in the lower branches of spruce trees', not an owl ... The names of animals are not nouns but verbs.

It would be impossible to change the names of animals to sense images like this in English, but New Nature writers produce a similar effect when they refer to animals and plants through describing what they see. Macfarlane (NW6:33), for instance, writes 'I could make out the shapes of seals moving through the water' rather than 'there were seals moving through the water'. This places himself in the position of observer, interactively engaging with the world through his senses. Similarly, in the following quotations, Fiennes refers to birds by their observable shapes:

- Deer bounded along the stubble edge as geese returned to their roosts from grain fields: smudges and specks of geese above the low sun. (NW2:93)
- Rooks had colonised the chestnuts, sycamores and limes, and when the trees were bare you could see the thatched bowls of their nests lodged in the forks, and black rook shapes perched in the heights. (NW2:8)
- [of a pair of peregrines] She is bigger, and more brown. His back was the colour of slate roofs after rain. What you see when they swivel their heads round is the white of their cheeks. (NW3:30)

The expressions 'smudges and specks of geese above the low sun' and 'rook shapes perched in the heights' show the more-than-human world as it manifests itself to the human observer. The use of the pronoun 'you' together with the verb 'see' in the last two examples places the reader directly into the scenes, encouraging them to imagine themselves seeing the nests, rooks and peregrines.

In another example, Kathleen Jamie creates a sense image by describing the light that bounces off the underside of a peregrine and then giving details of what the light revealed:

- He [a peregrine] flew in an easy loop, and when the sunlight glanced his undersides they were pale and banded like rippled sycamore. (NW3:30)

The cover of the book that this came from, *Findings*, provides a visual image which is remarkably similar to the linguistic sentence (Image 9.8). The peregrine on the cover is presented actively as flying and given salience through its central position and its contrast to the monochrome blue sky. The photo has high photo-realism — it looks very much as you would expect to see the scene in reality, with the viewer positioned on the ground, looking up at the bird. The underside of the peregrine is lit clearly, and the viewer can see the details of the bands on the wings. The combination of sense image in the text and visual image on the cover creates very high salience and models close observation of the natural world.

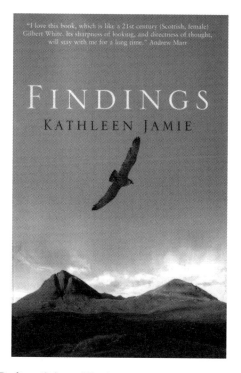

IMAGE 9.8 *Cover of Findings* © Sort of Books

Another device that can build salience, and is widespread across New Nature Writing, is simile. The following are examples:

- The water brightens to something like tinfoil. (NW1:24)
- Three wading birds moved forwards together in a line, swinging their beaks from side to side in arcs as they advanced, like a team of metal detectors. (NW6:39)
- He lifted first one yellow talon then the other, like one who has chewing gum on his shoe. (NW3:32)
- Two young crows ... began to circle each other playfully, each keeping a steady distance from the other, like opposing magnets, or kings on a chessboard. (NW6:111)
- Blossom issues out of them and fills the tree slowly, like a dancehall on Saturday night. (NW3:33)

These similes use concrete, imaginable images from everyday life and superimpose them on a scene from nature, placing a detailed and precise image in the minds of viewers that it would be hard to create in other ways. In this way, they build the salience of the more-than-human world, although ironically they do so by drawing on images from the human world.

There is, of course, a danger that the image from the human world is stronger in people's minds than the images of nature — that, for instance, in reading the last example above, the reader thinks more about a dancehall than the falling blossoms. This would be a partial erasure of the more-than-human world rather than an increase in its salience. There are examples, however, of similes which draw from nature to describe the more-than-human world, for example:

- I look up to see a badger on the shore. I see it emerge from the shoreline trees the way an otter emerges from a Hebridean sea. (NW1:21)
- The mountain stretches like a waking wolf, bares its long, blue shoulder. (NW1:24)
- The day as laden with warmth as a bee bowed down with the burden of pollen. (NW1:28)

Examples such as these have a double impact in increasing the salience of the more-than-human world, both of the subject being described and the area of life being drawn on for the description.

Overall, New Nature Writing uses a number of techniques, including activation, sense images, personalisation, basic-level categories and simile, to give salience to the more-than-human world. It therefore tells the story that nature is important and worthy of consideration. Importantly, however, it does this without erasing humans. As Smith (2013,

p. 6) explains:

> One of the problems with such a term as 'The New Nature Writing' is that it does not seem to acknowledge the fact that the desecration it is endeavouring to counter is as much cultural as it is natural, that it is precisely *cultures of nature* that are under threat, cultures without which it becomes increasingly hard to care, both for and about, the non-human world around us ... [New Nature writers] are concerned with how this cluster of islands and ecological niches is related in complex ways to human communities of the local, regional and even national and global ways of life that are lived out across and within them.

Ecology, in the sense that the term is used in this book, consists of the life-sustaining relationships of humans with other humans, other organisms and the physical environment. To move towards more sustainable ways of living, none of these elements can be overlooked — not humans (particularly those most vulnerable to ecological destruction), nor other organisms, nor the physical environment, nor the relationships among them. If there are areas of life which have been erased or neglected then ecolinguistics can help identify linguistic strategies for building up their salience, both in texts and, eventually, in the minds of people within the culture.

理论延伸

凸显是上一章删略的对立面，也就是人们在语言表达中突出展示的那个方面。所以，凸显也是一种语言现象，需要与其他的理论内容结合研究。换句话说，我们在上一章的理论延伸处所补充的内容（及物性系统、概念转喻和上下义词语使用等）对本章的研究也是同样适用且同样重要的。此外，本章还特别分析了许多其他的凸显方式，供读者在研究中参考。这个部分我们以本章使用的一种典型的凸显方式——多模态话语分析（multimodal discourse analysis）为例，重点梳理多模态话语分析理论的脉络及其在话语凸显研究中的作用。虽然本部分是以多模态话语分析理论为例的，但我们不仅仅是在强调多模态话语分析是话语凸显过程中最重要的一种方式，而是通过全面展示一种话语凸显研究的发展情况，说明有效的凸显过程中的要素和形式。目的是让读者清楚话语凸显是表达意义的一种有效路径，并以此尝试更多有效的方式去研究生态语言学中的凸显问题。

关于话语分析的发展情况，我们已经在前面第 2 章的理论延伸部分进行了阐述，感兴趣的读者可参看本书第 2 章末尾的内容。这里我们将重点放在"多模态"和"多模态话语分析"的讨论上。"多模态"实际上指的是研究视角和意义表达方式，它强调人们在交际中不应单单靠语言这个模态来沟通交流，而是要实现语言与多种其他的交际模式共同作用，例如：声音、图像、手势、音乐、色彩等非语言模式。概括来说，多模态是由一种以上的社会符号进行编码而实现意义的文本（李战子，2003）。通过对多模态话语的分析，揭示出话语中的意义表达，特别是话语中凸显的内容，让人们能够全方位地理解话语表达者的意图。

随着信息技术的不断进步，多模态话语分析的研究于 20 世纪 90 年代在西方国家开始兴起。Kress & van Leeuwen（1996/2006）在《阅读图像》（*Reading Images*）这本专著中首次研究视觉语法的问题，推动了多模态话语分析研究在西方的发展，出现了多项研究成果（Kress & van Leeuwen，2002；Jewitt，2004；Lemke，2009）。2003年，中国学者开始关注多模态话语分析（李战子，2003），随后国内许多学者开始了多模态话语分析的研究（如胡壮麟，2007；王红阳，2007；朱永生，2007；陈瑜敏，2008；韦琴红，2009；张德禄，2009；李战子、陆丹云，2012；程瑞兰、张德禄，2016）。鉴于多模态话语分析是跨学科的，也就是需要将它与其他的语言学理论，甚至是社会学、心理学、人类学、符号学等其他非语言学学科的内容结合起来研究。就多模态话语分析的理论基础而言，比较引人注目的是从系统功能语言学的视角出发进行研究的（李战子，2003；张德禄等，2015；张德禄，2018）；近年还出现了以认知语言学为代表的其他语言学理论作为多模态话语分析的理论基础的研究成果（张德禄、郭恩华，2013；高佑梅，2014；王振华、瞿桃，2020），这表明多模态话语分析研究的路径是多样的。

无论从系统功能语言学，还是从其他语言学理论去分析多模态话语，对本章的意义在于，只要能够发现话语中的凸显内容，就是有价值的分析。有关凸显的有效方式还有可视化分析（夏蓉、杨金海，2021）、隐喻（见本书第 4 章）等多种途径。但是，目前在国内从生态语言学视角聚焦凸显问题的研究成果比较少，我们见到的只有何伟（2018）、何伟和魏榕（2018）在谈生态话语分析时提及了多模态话语分析的部分内容。感兴趣的读者可以以上述路径和文献为基础进行思考，努力通过各种手段探讨生态语言学中的凸显问题，将有利于可持续发展的生态要素凸显出来。

补充文献

陈瑜敏 . 2008. 奥运电视公益广告多模态评价意义的构建 . 北京科技大学学报（社会科学版），（3）：108–114.

程瑞兰，张德禄 . 2016. 多模态语篇模态协同模式跨学科研究 . 外语电化教学，（5）：3–8.

高佑梅 . 2014. 语言符号"非任意性"研究：认知语言学框架下的多模态语言分析 . 天
　　津：南开大学出版社 .

何伟 . 2018. 关于生态语言学作为一门学科的几个重要问题 . 中国外语，（4）：1,
　　11–17.

何伟，魏榕 . 2018. 话语分析范式与生态话语分析的理论基础 . 当代修辞学，（5）：
　　63–73.

胡壮麟 . 2007. 社会符号学研究中的多模态化 . 语言教学与研究，（1）：1–10.

李战子 . 2003. 多模式话语的社会符号学分析 . 外语研究，（5）：1–8.

李战子，陆丹云 . 2012. 多模态符号学：理论基础、研究途径与发展前景 . 外语研究，
　　（2）：1–8.

王红阳 . 2007. 卡明斯诗歌"l(a"的多模态功能解读 . 外语教学，（5）：22–26.

王振华，瞿桃 . 2020. 多模态语篇的评价研究：过去、现在与未来 . 外国语，（6）：
　　42–51.

韦琴红 . 2009. 视觉环境下的多模态化与多模态话语研究 . 北京：科学出版社 .

夏蓉，杨金海 . 2021. 基于 CiteSpace 的语言距离跨学科研究分析与展望 . 外语界，（2）：
　　90–96.

张德禄 . 2009. 多模态话语分析综合理论框架探索 . 中国外语，（1）：24–30.

张德禄 . 2018. 系统功能理论视阈下的多模态话语分析综合框架 . 现代外语，（6）：
　　731–743.

张德禄，郭恩华 . 2013. 多模态话语分析的双重视角——社会符号观与概念隐喻观的
　　连接与互补 . 外国语，（3）：20–28.

张德禄等 . 2015. 多模态话语分析理论与外语教学 . 北京：高等教育出版社 .

朱永生 . 2007. 多模态话语分析的理论基础与研究方法 . 外语学刊，（5）：82–86.

Jewitt, C. 2004. Multimodality and new communication technologies. In K. L. O'Halloran
　　(Ed.), *Multimodal discourse analysis*. London & New York: Continuum, 184–195.

Kress, G. & van Leeuwen, T. 1996. *Reading images: The grammar of visual design*.
　　London: Routledge.

Kress, G. & van Leeuwen, T. 2002. Colour as a semiotic mode: Notes for a grammar of
　　colour. *Journal of Visual Communication*, (3): 343–368.

Kress, G. & van Leeuwen, T. 2006. *Reading images: The grammar of visual design* (2nd
　　ed.). London: Routledge.

Lemke, J. L. 2009. Multimodal genres and transmedia traversals: Social semiotics and the
　　political economy of the sign. *Semiotica*, (173): 283–297.

10

NARRATIVES

章节导读

　　叙事是描述我们信奉和践行的故事中最有说服力的一种形式，因为叙事所阐释的故事是结构相对完整的一系列事件的集合；它能够将事件的因果联系在一起并传递给读者，以较深刻的方式渗透到他们的生活中去。就生态问题来看，叙事重要的是能够采用鼓舞人心、令人难忘的方式传达道德规范，并归咎责任，提高读者的生态意识。因此，本章作为书中的最后一个故事，主要围绕叙事的问题展开，具体从三个方面推进：（1）理论内涵；（2）叙事分析的方法；（3）案例：自我中心论、生态中心论和起源叙事。

　　（1）理论内涵。虽然不同领域的研究者对"叙事"（narrative）这一术语的用词是不一样的，但通常的做法是相似的，主要从特定的文本体现中将叙事的基础结构分离出来。本书使用"叙事结构"（narrative structures）这一术语来表示联系事件与事件之间的基本框架，它的定义是：人们头脑中的一系列故事，这些故事是在逻辑上具有相关性的事件（*Narrative structures* are stories in people's minds which involve a sequence of logically connected events.）。其中，事件在逻辑上的联系可以是明确的，也可以把这一过程留给读者，让读者以推理的方式进行判断。例如：书中关于 Greta Thunberg 演讲的例子（P231），其叙事结构包括两个具有逻辑关系的事件（"不说话""说话的理由"），并且是按顺序发生的。

　　Thunberg 在另一篇演讲（P232）中再次使用了相同的叙事结构，不过在词语选择和细节表达上使用了不同方式，本书中将这个内容称为"叙事文本"（narrative texts）。"叙事文本"是本章另一个非常重要的术语，它主要描述基础的叙事结构所显现出来的文本；它是一种明确的口头讲述、书面作品或其他的表现形式，叙述一系列在时间和逻辑上相关的事件（A *narrative text* is a specific oral telling, written work, or other expressive form, which recounts a series of temporally and logically connected events.）。叙事文本会补充一些对事件发展不是特别重要的细节，但这些细节对整个叙事的意义表达是十分重要的，揭示着整个叙事的来龙去脉。本书采用"叙事"这个术语来指代叙事结构和它在叙事文本中的体现，以实现术语的统一。

（2）叙事分析的方法。揭示工业社会中流传的叙事问题并塑造出人类与自然世界之间的关系是生态语言学的关键任务之一；而更有必要的任务是要为那些破坏性的叙事寻找新的可替代性叙事。其探索方法主要有两种：第一种，新的可替代叙事可以是对主流叙事重述的全新叙事，但这个新的叙事必须要与原始叙事一样生动，才能够推动其广泛传播，以代替原始叙事；第二种，可以从多年来世界各地的传统文化和土著文化的口头叙事中汲取精华，讲述当前世界面临的生态问题。一旦我们发现了有益性的叙事，就应该对其进行宣传，把它融入教育、政治、政策或有关活动的话语中，为提供新的可信奉和践行的故事做准备（Jones & McBeth，2010；Gersie *et al.*，2014；Molthan-Hill *et al.*，2020）。

由于叙事结构是认知的，所以它不仅仅可以通过语言表达，也可以用其他方式（例如：视觉图像、手势或音乐等）表现出来。下面来看本书中的一个例子——Nanson 讲述的《旅鸽》（*The Passenger Pigeon*）的故事（P238）。这个例子的叙事结构包括：第一，时间序列（"早期的欧洲定居者"来到"现在"）；第二，数字序列（"大量的旅鸽"开始到"没有旅鸽存在"结束）；第三，逻辑序列（以因果关系的方式解释旅鸽数字下降的原因）。在描绘的过程中，不仅有叙事语言将旅鸽的灭绝过程表达得生动形象（例如：使用一系列与"kill"有关的动词），同时还有语调、停顿、手势、眼神交流和观众的互动等策略融入其中，增强了叙事的生动程度，唤醒了人们对旅鸽甚至是鸟类的同情，并进一步警醒人们不要重复过去的生态破坏性事件。

（3）案例：自我中心论、生态中心论和起源叙事。这个部分通过大量的多模式叙事案例探讨有关人类中心主义（anthropocentrism）、生态中心主义（ecocentrism）以及起源叙事（origin narratives）的问题，具体的案例内容包括：世界主要宗教的创世叙事，科学、小说和电影的起源叙事，传统神话叙事，世界各地的土著文化等。通过叙事案例的分析作者发现，关于宇宙起源与生命的叙事，会影响我们对人与人、人与其他物种、人与整个物理环境之间的关系以及自身行为的思考和改良。因此，这类案例对生态语言学的研究至关重要。

我们以其中一个案例为线索来分析其中的内在价值，即 2020 年 1 月世界经济论坛（World Economic Forum）上发表的题为《我们必须将以自我为中心的领导转变为以生态为中心的领导，以保护我们的星球》（"We must move from egocentric to ecocentric leadership to safeguard our planet"）的文章（P240）。该案例从地球面临的困境开始讲起，按照"问题—解决方案"的路径连接了两类事件：当前发生的事件（以自我为中心的实践）和未来发生的事件（以生态为中心的实践）。除了语言文字外，这个案例还以图片对比（P242，图 10.1a）的形式表达了叙事的内容，并通过箭头将两个事件的顺序连接在一起，其内涵和寓意生动形象，视觉效果好，画面感十足。

此外，这个案例还有另一个版本的图片对比（P243，图 10.1b）。这种叙事方式虽没有图 10.1a 直观，但它所蕴含的信息更为全面；比如：语言表达中"over"一词的反复使用，与人类中心论的图片相吻合；而话语"for evolution and for life"的表述，其意义是"所有生命形式是平等的"，匹配了生态中心论的图片。这个以生态为中心的叙事过程是从生命和宇宙起源的深层叙事中汲取的，这种方式能够在人类对待其他物种和整个物理环境的过程中产生很大的作用，值得我们进一步探究。

The novella *Son of the Thundercloud* (NR1) tells of a time when people forgot their traditional stories:

- When I first came to live here the earth was green and fertile ... There were storytellers who went all over the land telling stories to the people, and spreading joy and hope ... But when the storytellers were killed, one after another, the people slowly forgot what they had been told ... and allowed their minds to accept the darkness. So the drought came as a result of people rejecting the joyful stories and accepting the dark stories. (NR1:43–44)

The novella is by Easterine Kire, an award-winning author from the Angami ethic group in Nagaland, North East India. It is easy to see the joyful stories in the extract above as the traditional narratives of oral cultures that pass on knowledge to future generations about how to live sustainably in the local environment (Abram 1996), and the dark stories as the stories of industrial civilisation that cause people to be overtaken by greed and destroy the environment.

Son of the Thundercloud draws on Naga legends and presents these traditional narratives in a form that speaks to current generations about the ecological issues we are facing (Das 2019). It is a rich, mythic tale that makes use of a modified form of the classic 'hero's journey' structure (Bloom and Hobby 2009) in which the main character, Pele, is forced to leave his village due to drought and famine, and begin a journey of discovery and transformation. There is one theme which links together all the events on the journey: water, 'the purest form of life you can find' (NR1:141). At the start there is a terrible drought that lasts hundreds of years; then rapid ecological restoration when the rain returns. There is a river the villagers call 'mother' because it provides food; a 'monster rainstorm that ruined houses and fields' (p. 140), and the son of the thundercloud himself who was conceived by a raindrop. The tale links water with the fertility and flourishing of humans and ecosystems, with climate change and with culture. And it has a clear message, that when traditional culture is ignored, and people are greedy or filled with hate, ecological disaster will occur. What makes the book so powerful is that it is structured as a *narrative* — a sequence of events which links causes with consequences and conveys messages for readers to draw out and infuse into their own lives.

Narrative is the most powerful form of story that this book describes. As Dahlstrom points out, narratives offer benefits in 'motivation and interest, allocating cognitive resources, elaboration, and transfer into long-term memory. As such, narrative cognition is thought to represent the default mode of human thought, proving structure to reality' (Dahlstrom 2014, p. 13615). Narratives can weave together characters, events and locations, ascribe intentions and motivations, link causes with effects, actions with consequences, and, importantly for ecological issues, convey ethics and ascribe blame. And they can do all this in ways that are inspiring, moving and memorable.

The terms *narrative, story, plot, fabula, narration* and *text* are used in different ways by different theorists, but it is common practice to separate the underlying structure of a narrative from its manifestation as particular texts. For the purposes of this book, the term *narrative structure* is used to represent the basic scaffold of events and connections between them:

> *Narrative structures* are stories in people's minds which involve a sequence of logically connected events.

Like the other kinds of story in this book, narrative structures are considered to be cognitive (Herman 2003), existing in the minds of individuals. They can also be widespread across the minds of multiple people as social cognition and play a role in shaping dominant worldviews. The term 'sequence' implies that the events have a temporal connection, and 'event' implies a location and characters who take action or have experiences (Toolan 2001). The logical connections may be explicit, or it may be left for readers to infer them in a process of narrative reasoning.

Narrative structures can be very simple. The following words by Greta Thunberg are based on a structure which contains just two events:

- A year and a half ago, I didn't speak to anyone unless I really had to, but then I found a reason to speak. (EN24)

The events occur in a sequence and are logically connected through the opposition of not speaking, and then having a reason to speak (i.e., climate change). In another speech, Thunberg uses the same narrative structure again, but with different words and slightly different details:

- Later on I was diagnosed with ... selective mutism. That basically means I only speak when I think it is necessary. Now is one of those moments. (EN25)

Every word of this, aside from 'I' and 'speak', is different, but it is still drawing on the same underlying structure of events and connections. This book uses the term *narrative texts* (following Bal 2017) to describe the texts that underlying structures manifest themselves in:

> A *narrative text* is a specific oral telling, written work, or other expressive form, which recounts a series of temporally and logically connected events.

There are many types of narrative text, and Cohan and Shires (1988, p. 53) list only some of them: 'novels, short stories, and films ... also newspapers, advertisements, histories, myths, letters, anecdotes, jokes, popular entertainments and public ceremonies'. Being cognitive rather than linguistic, narrative structures can also manifest themselves in other modes too, for example in visual images, gestures or music. For convenience (and to follow the convention), the term *narrative* is used in this book to refer to both narrative structures and to their manifestation in narrative texts.

Narrative structures can be simple, or they can be incredibly complex and intricate. They can appear transiently for a moment and then be forgotten or can be repeated so often that they echo across cultures and history. There is a particular narrative which folklorists call ATU328 'The Boy Steals the Ogre's Treasure'. Using phylogenetic analysis, da Silva and Tehrani (2016) traced this narrative 'deep into Indo-European prehistory', going back several thousand years and appearing across a number of European cultures. The common fairy tale *Jack and the Beanstalk* has a structure which fits this narrative.

This book will indicate narrative structures using small capitals, e.g., JACK AND THE BEANSTALK. This is just a label (what Lakoff 1993, p. 209 calls a 'mnemonic') to stand for a cognitive structure. The structure is the basic framework of temporally and logically connected events that someone who 'knows the story' keeps in their minds. Of course, there can be different versions of a narrative, and memories are never perfect, so there is likely to be variation in the exact details that are stored in people's minds. Nonetheless, it is possible to discuss *prototypical* narrative structures.

The prototypical narrative structure JACK AND THE BEANSTALK starts with Jack and his mother, poor and forced to sell their cow to survive. Jack instead exchanges the cow for magic beans, incurring the wrath of his mother who throws the beans out of the window. They grow into a huge beanstalk, which Jack climbs and finds a giant who plans to eat him. Jack steals the giant's treasure, kills him, becomes extremely rich and lives happily ever after. This is an abridged summary of the sequence of events contained in the narrative structure, and particular narrative texts will fill in the details. The narrative texts could be particular books, films, or live storytelling performances, although, as Hanne (1992) points out, the written forms are very different from the oral traditions that stretch through time. Joseph Jacobs's 1892 written text starts and ends as follows:

- [start] There was once upon a time a poor widow who had an only son named Jack, and a cow named Milky-White. (NR2:53)
- [end] Jack and his mother became very rich, and he married a great princess, and they lived happy ever after. (NR2:58)

The narrative text adds details which can be considered 'satellite' in the sense of not being crucial to the unfolding tale (Cohan and Shires 1988, p. 55). It does not matter what name the cow has, or whether Jack marries a princess or not, whereas 'kernel' events such as the growth of the beanstalk are essential to the progression of the narrative. The satellite elements, however, can be 'very important for the meaning and overall impact of the narrative', and can give 'a work its power and significance' (Abbott 2008, p. 23).

Of particular importance for ecolinguistics are the underlying messages or morals within narratives which can be extracted, taken outside the narrative itself, and applied to everyday life. These are called *narrative entailments* here and are considered part of the narrative structure in the same way that metaphorical entailments are part of the metaphorical structure.

In fairy tales, the narrative entailments are sometimes drawn out explicitly by the text. For example, *The Hare and the Hedgehog* states: 'The moral of this story is ... that no one, no matter how great he may be, should permit himself to jest at anyone beneath him' (Grimm 2011, p. 764). More often, though, the entailment is implicit, with hints and clues for messages readers should take away with them. As Merchant (2014, p. 78) points out, 'imagery found in a culture's literature can play a normative role within the culture. Controlling images operate as ethical restraints or as ethical sanctions — as subtle "oughts" or "ought not's"'.

Andrew Lang's version of *Jack and the Beanstalk* includes a fairy who gives a strong hint for the entailment readers should take away with them. The fairy tells Jack the following:

- You showed an inquiring mind, and great courage and enterprise, therefore you deserve to rise; and when you mounted the Beanstalk you climbed the Ladder of Fortune. (NR4:142)

The verticality metaphor (Cian 2017) here maps 'climbed' to 'enterprise'; 'rising' to 'success'; and 'ladder' to 'fortune' in a way that entrenches dominant stories of individual enterprise as a path to material gain.

While some entailments are explicitly drawn out and others are more subtly hinted at, readers can draw out entailments for themselves from any part of a narrative. In JACK AND THE BEANSTALK there are potential entailments that it is acceptable to steal from and harm people who are physically different and evil, that money brings happiness, etc. The potential narrative entailments available for the reader to draw out can be judged against the ecosophy of the analyst. The ecosophy of this book calls for wellbeing for all, and redistribution from rich to poor so that all can meet their needs as overall consumption massively decreases. There *is* redistribution in this narrative, but it is only from previously rich to newly rich, leaving the poverty of Jack's neighbours untouched and erased as an issue. As always, it is important to view the reader as being critical — able to selectively draw out entailments for themselves, and able to accept or reject entailments that the text is explicitly or subtly encouraging them to take.

McLaren (2002, p. 89) uses the expression 'the narratives we live by', which are the 'stories we tell ourselves about ourselves, stories which shape both the terror and ecstasies of our world'. He argues that 'if narratives give our lives meaning we need to understand what those narratives are and how they have come to exert such an influence on us' because 'narratives can become politically enabling of social transformation'. He therefore proposes a pedagogy he calls 'critical narratology' which involves a questioning of 'society's treasured stock of imperial or magisterial narratives' (p. 91).

A critical narratology would not attempt to ban cultural narratives such as JACK AND THE BEANSTALK — something which would be as undesirable as it is impossible. Instead it would encourage critical awareness of the potential entailments of narratives and compare them with those of alternative narratives. One alternative narrative to JACK AND THE BEANSTALK is found in the children's book *What Jill Did While Jack Climbed the Beanstalk* (NR5). In this narrative, Jack has a sister, who also received magic beans. Except in this version she planted them and reaped an enormous field of bean plants. The family had enough to eat and shared the food with their friends and neighbours. This overcomes the negative entailments of the traditional narrative by promoting enterprise which works for the good of the wider community rather than for individual financial gain. In terms of verticality, it celebrates staying close to the productive soil of the ground, and it promotes the horizontality of sharing. Rebecca Solnit's alternative telling of Cinderella, *Cinderella Liberator,* also ends with a similar message when the cruel sisters realise that:

- There is always enough for everyone, if you share it properly ... There is enough food, enough love, enough homes, enough time, enough crayons, enough people to be friends with each other. (NR6)

Entailments that promote sharing resonate with the ecosophy of this book since they can promote both wellbeing and staying with environment limits through conserving resources. While retellings of dominant narratives do have important liberatory and ecological potential, Crowley and Pennington (2010) also describe how there are pitfalls of being overly prescriptive or reconfirming rather than truly subverting the original stereotypes. And, of course, whatever the new version of the story is, it will need to be as vivid, engaging and captivating as the original if it is to become popular and spread its alternative message.

Another possibility in the search for new narratives to live by is the use of traditional storytelling techniques to craft new narratives that are designed to speak to the ecological issues that the world is currently facing. An example is the *Knock at the Door* collection of short stories which contains dozens of 'modern folk tales for troubling times' (NR7). These narratives help the reader envisage the changes we need to make to move beyond 'an economic system that drives inequality, crushes the spirit and corrodes our ecological life support' (NR7:11). Philip Pullman, in the foreword to the series, writes:

Stories are one of the most ancient and most effective ways of making sense of the world ... The human imagination is profoundly important, and when it turns to exploring the problems we human beings find when we try to live a good life in a world we seem to be simultaneously destroying, there is nothing more valuable or worth encouraging.

One of these modern folk tales, *The Magician's House* by Jan Dean, provides a useful demonstration of the powerful coming together of metaphor and narrative. In this tale, the main character, Genet, signs a contract with a magician to work for a year and a day lighting fires in his house in exchange for her heart's desire. The house is small, and the work is easy. However, the house suddenly starts growing exponentially and Genet must work harder and harder to light the fires in all the new rooms that keep appearing. It grows so much that it starts to cover the Earth and the warmth from its fires melts the ancient ice at the poles. After her time is up, Genet tries to leave the house, with the last words of the tale being 'But she could not. For now the house was all there was' (NR7:17).

In this narrative, there is a clear sequence of logically connected events occurring over a year and a day; from the signing of the contract, to the house repeatedly doubling in size, to Genet trying to leave at the end with nowhere to go. The impact of the house in melting ice at the poles is one of the clues that the narrative is not just a tale about a magician's house but a metaphor for the growth of industrial civilisation and its encroachment on the natural world. It illustrates exponential growth on a finite planet in a vivid way by simplifying complex processes occurring over long timescales into the structure of a simple sequence of easily imaginable events.

The metaphor of THE MAGICIAN'S HOUSE can be analysed in exactly the same way as a normal metaphor, except that instead of a source frame there is a *source narrative* which structures the target domain of industrial growth. Within the metaphor, Genet maps onto exploited workers, the house maps onto industrial civilisation and the melting of the poles by the fires of the house maps onto anthropogenic climate change. The metaphor conveys an entailment that the exponential growth of industrial civilisation destroys life on the planet. Narrative and metaphor often work together in this way, and a 'binocular' focus on the intermingling of these two linguistic devices has been fruitfully explored in a series of works by Michael Hanne (Hanne 2011; Hanne and Kaal 2018).

Narrative structures are the bare bones of logically connected events occurring in a sequence, but it is narrative texts which flesh out the details and make them come alive. If narrative texts are vivid and powerful enough then listeners can feel that they are vicariously living out the events. Annette Simmons describes how 'personal experience delivers deep understanding that allows true empathy', with the example of putting an investor to work in a sweatshop in a developing country before asking him to insist on better working conditions for his suppliers. But where personal experience is unfeasible, narrative texts can provide the next best thing, to the extent that Simmons defines story as 'a reimagined experience narrated with enough detail and feeling to cause your listeners' imaginations to experience it as real' (Simmons 2015, p. 22).

One power that narrative has is the ability to allow people to imagine the lived experience of not only other humans but also other species. As Herman describes:

> Narrative can be viewed as a resource for modelling the richness and complexity of what it is like for nonhuman others, and hence as a means to underscore what is at stake in the trivialisation — or outright destruction — of their experiences.
>
> (Herman 2012, p. 101)

Narratives can therefore be extremely effective in giving salience to elements of the natural world which are so often erased in contemporary discourse. The book *Being Salmon, Being Human* by Martin Lee Mueller provides an excellent example of giving salience to the lived experience of animals. The preface defines a clear goal: 'We are in the midst of a systemic ecocide ... This is the time to abandon humanity-as-separation and to aid forth the emergence of entirely different stories to live by' (Mueller 2017, p. xiii). Mueller contributes to the search for new stories to live by, firstly by critiquing industrial representations of salmon:

> Biomass is how fish farms define what a salmon is. [Biomass] is a stand-in for a concrete equation: Living beings equal flesh; flesh equals mass; mass equals numbers; numbers equal economic performance.
>
> (Mueller 2017, p. 33)

He then draws from indigenous folktales about salmon, such as the Native American tale *Salmon Boy,* in the search for narratives that can help us rethink our relationship with the natural world. *Salmon Boy* (NR8) is a mythical tale of a boy who breaks an agreement with the salmon, causes them harm, but is nonetheless rescued from drowning by the salmon and treated with kindness as an honoured guest in their underwater village. On return to his community, he calls on the villagers to treat the salmon with respect. Mueller says of the tale that it 'opens the listener's experience to being embedded within a living Earth teeming with agency' (Mueller 2017, p. 186). He describes how the salmon in the tale assume the role of elders, helping the boy into his maturity by making him aware of the consequences of his actions on other beings. This, Mueller concludes, makes it inconceivable to think of salmon as 'resources' or 'stock'. In general, the combination of temporal and logical connections in narratives, together with vivid imagery, offers great power to link ecological destructive behaviour with its negative impacts on the world, and in doing so convey entailments that promote pro-environmental behaviour.

In addition to drawing from indigenous tales, Mueller writes his own micronarratives to contribute to the shift towards new stories to live by. One of them, *Being Salmon,* traces the journey of a female salmon from her birth in a freshwater stream to her emergence into the ocean. The moment that she first encounters saltwater is captured vividly as follows:

- She pays attention to the others. Her eyes, her tongue, her lateral line, her muscled fin ... the confluence of her senses flowing back and forth between her nervous system, the others and the encompassing river ... Her shuddering muscles, her fins, her scales, the whizzing network of her nerves — her entire pulsating body was strangely on edge:

salt! (NR9:133)

The writing pays close attention to both the mental and embodied experience of the salmon, helping the reader to empathise with the thoughts, feelings and bodily sensations of another being. There is the mental process of 'attending to', the lexical set of body parts, and, most effectively, the present continuous verbs *flowing (back and forth), shuddering, whizzing,* and *pulsating* which vividly capture the rhythm of bodily life processes. The importance of this kind of writing in creating empathy beyond the human world is described well by Herman (2012, p. 100):

> In stories figuring the moment-by-moment experiences of non-human animals, narrativity emerges from the attempt to imagine how a different kind of intelligent agent constitutes the world — and from using this imaginative engagement to prompt, in turn, a rethinking of the relationship between human and non-human experiences.

Oral storytelling is particularly powerful because the narrative texts it creates include not only words but intonation patterns, gestures and interactions with audience and place. As Nanson (2011, p. 146) describes:

> In the storytelling moment a web of connections is woven between the storyteller and the audience, and among the audience and between them and the place where they are. If the place is outdoors then a connection is made with whatever aspects of nature are manifest there.

Although oral storytelling has been eclipsed by writing in industrial societies, there is a growing number of oral storytellers who are using their craft to challenge the dominant stories of industrial civilisation and promote more ecologically beneficial stories to live by (Gersie *et al.* 2014; Molthan-Hill *et al.* 2020). Nanson describes how these storytellers use oral tales to 'bridge the ravine of modern society's alienation from nature and to counterbalance the logic of economic self-interest with values rooted in ecology, community and compassion' (Nanson 2021).

One of Nanson's narratives is *The Passenger Pigeon*, an extinction tale that attempts to create empathy for its main character, which is an entire species. The tale begins as follows:

- The passenger pigeon was once the most abundant bird on earth. It's possible that forty per cent of all the birds in North America were passenger pigeons. The early

European settlers were amazed to see such enormous flocks, hundreds of kilometres long and containing literally thousands of millions of birds. (From the transcript provided in NR10:114)

The narrative continues by describing a series of events in which the birds were hunted and killed in an increasingly mechanised way. It finishes with:

- Until there was just one left. They called her Martha ... She died on 1 September 1914 at 1pm. With her death the passenger pigeon, which had once been the most abundant bird on earth, became extinct. Martha's body was ... stuffed and put on display in a glass case. She remains in the collections of the Museum of National History to this day. (NR10:116)

The bare bones of the narrative structure consist of: (1) a temporal sequence of events from the arrival of the European settlers to the present day; (2) a numerical sequence that starts with vast numbers of birds and ends with none; and (3) a logical sequence of causality which explains why the numbers went down. The narrative text, however, goes beyond the bare bones to convey the events vividly in ways that evoke empathy for the birds and caution against repeating the ecological disasters of the past.

It can be hard to create vivid images of something as abstract as extinction, but Nanson draws on the testimony of the naturalist John J. Audubon who witnessed the flocks first-hand. The similes and sense images in sight, sound and smell in the following passage allow listeners to imaginatively witness the events as if they were there:

- He [Audubon] said the sky was literally full of birds and the noonday sun was darkened as if by an eclipse. Their droppings fell from the sky like snow and the noise of so many beating wings overwhelmed his senses ... The smell in there was incredible ... the sound as they landed in the trees was like thunder, their wooing calls were like the ringing of bells ...

The narrative text represents the reduction in the numbers of birds through a lexical set of killing verbs: *killed, hunted, destroyed, slaughtered, obliterated, shot* and *shot down*, which all imply a deliberate action. It also includes a lexical set of technologies involved in the operation, including *guns, nets* and *a primitive kind of machine gun* as the direct implements; *the telegraph* as a way of coordinating the activity; and *railways* to bring the birds to market. These lexical sets, along with the word *mechanised*, trigger a technological frame and associate it with killing and extinction. In this way the narrative challenges the dominant story in industrial countries of technological progress as an unmitigated good. As Nanson puts it, 'my presentation of the story, in both structure and delivery, implies a mourning of this creature's loss and a challenge to the mode of development that necessitates such a loss' (Nanson 2014, p. 144).

The aspect of the narrative text that is most likely to evoke empathy is how it ends: with a focus on the last passenger pigeon, Martha. She is individualised and given salience by her name, by the details of her life (where and when she was born and how long she lived) and by the unusual precision of the timing of her death — '1 September 1914 at 1pm'.

In addition to the words, the oral performance of this narrative text includes features of intonation, pauses, gestures, eye contact and interaction with the audience. Nanson describes how he pauses after the words 'That was the last time anyone shot — or saw — a wild passenger pigeon' to mark that point in history, and then pauses even more emphatically after 'one by one the captive birds died' (Nanson 2014, p. 146).

The power of extinction narratives such as this is that they can condense an abstract process that takes place over a long duration and make it vivid by allowing the listener to imaginatively experience concrete key events and feel empathy for an entire species. As Heise (2016, p. 5) points out, 'biodiversity, endangered species, and extinction are primarily cultural issues, questions of what we value and what stories we tell'.

In conclusion, revealing the narratives that circulate within industrial societies and shape relationships between people and the natural world is one of the key tasks of ecolinguistics. Even more important is the search for new narratives to live by, which could be newly written or could be drawn from the oral narratives of traditional and indigenous cultures around the world — cultures which have lived sustainably in place for hundreds or thousands of years. As Machiorlatti (2010, p. 62) describes, 'many traditional oral narratives of indigenous people are a direct reflection of their worldview that all creation is interconnected, with vast cyclical fluctuations and expressions of life, relationship, transformation and renewal'. Once beneficial narratives have been found they can be promoted in themselves and woven into the discourses of education, politics, policy or campaigning to provide new stories to live by (Jones and McBeth 2010; Gersie *et al.* 2014; Molthan-Hill *et al.* 2020).

Ego, eco and origin narratives

In January 2020, an unusual article was published by *World Economic Forum* entitled 'We must move from egocentric to ecocentric leadership to safeguard our planet' (NR11). The narrative in this article starts with the trouble the planet faces. It then identifies the cause — deep-seated stories which see humans as 'separate, dominant and superior to nature', and nature as 'a commodity to buy, sell, extract and exploit'. Finally, it identifies a solution for the future, where leaders adopt 'an ecocentric mindset whereby we are grateful to and revere nature, rather than consider ourselves superior to it'. The narrative uses a problem/solution structure to link two classes of event, one taking place currently (egocentric leadership practices) and one in the future (ecocentric practices). In doing so, it provides a rare voice within mainstream economics arguing for the intrinsic value of the natural world.

Alongside the text of this article there is a diagram which expresses the narrative in a visual form: on the left a pyramid with humans at the top and other animals below, and on the right a circle with humans in amongst the other animals. In fact, this diagram is a common internet meme, appearing on many websites in slightly different forms, one of which is reproduced in Image 10.1.

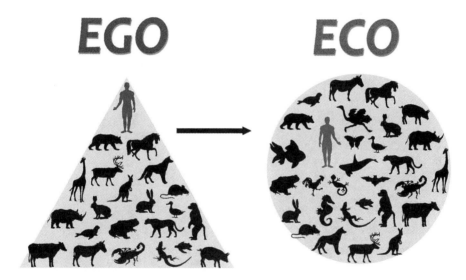

IMAGE 10.1 Ego and Eco meme.

The visual design of Image 10.1 is a classic given/new structure (Kress and van Leeuwen 2006, p. 180), where the *given* on the left is what the viewer is assumed to be familiar with, the already existing state of affairs. The *new,* on the right, is the 'issue', the 'point', a newly occurring or desired state of affairs. The *given* in this meme is the word EGO and the figure of the pyramid, representing the anthropocentric story of hierarchy which currently underpins industrial civilisation. The *new* is the word ECO and the circle, representing the desired ecological form of civilisation for the future. The position of the human on the top of the pyramid follows the verticality metaphor of UP IS SUPERIOR, a logic which the circle on the right subverts by not having any animal fully above the others. The arrow between the two is, in Kress and van Leeuwen's (2006, p. 45) terms, a *vector,* and it instantiates a visual narrative by linking two events in a sequence. Even without the arrow, however, it is still a narrative representation because given/new structures provide both temporal and logical connections.

IMAGE 10.1a   Ego and Eco meme variation 1

Different versions of the meme can be discovered by using the search term 'eco ego meme' in image search engines. Sometimes the meme appears with two further images below it which show a destroyed Earth with dry deserts on the left, and a green Earth with flourishing trees and animals on the right (Image 10.1a). This is visual narrative that gives a similar message to 'We must move from egocentric to ecocentric leadership to safeguard our planet'. In another version (Image 10.1b), the meme appears with a quote from Genesis 1:26 on the left below the pyramid that reads:

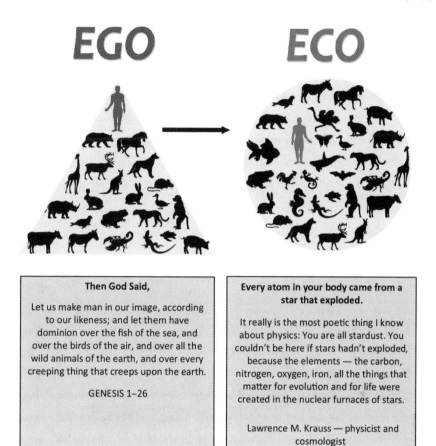

IMAGE 10.1b   Ego and Eco meme variation 2

- [let humans] have dominion over the fish of the sea, and over the birds of the air, and over all the wild animals of the earth, and over every creeping thing...

The repeated word 'over' here performs the same verticality metaphor as the physical location of the human at the top of the pyramid. On the right-hand side, below the circle, is a quote from a physics professor, Lawrence Krauss:

- Every atom in your body came from a star that exploded ... all the things that matter for evolution and for life ... were created in the nuclear furnaces of stars...

The *theme* of this second quote, in Halliday's (2013, p. 88) sense of 'the point of departure', is anthropocentric — the atoms of the reader's body. However, the expression 'for evolution and for life' implicitly includes all forms of life equally, as all arise from stars. When the meme includes quotes from scriptures and scientists it is drawing from deep-seated narratives about the origin of life and the Universe that potentially play a powerful role in shaping how people relate to other species and the physical environment. These deeper narratives are worthy of further exploration.

In the narrative of the creation myth in Genesis 1, there is a clear series of events, which occur in temporal order, with an enumeration of days emphasising the temporality. To summarise briefly: the first event is God creating heaven and Earth; then light and the first night and day; then sky and waters on the second day; then land and sea, then grass, herbs and trees on the third day; then the Sun, Moon and stars on the fourth day; then ocean creatures and birds on the fifth day. On the sixth day, God creates land animals; then humans in his image; then God grants humans dominion over animals and the Earth. He then gives humans seed-bearing plants and fruit trees to provide food; and gives green plants to other creatures for food.

The narrative structure is fleshed out in different narrative texts in different ways, from the original Hebrew version and thousands of translations in hundreds of languages, to the same underlying structure appearing in plays, films or picture books. The following two versions of Genesis 1:28 are examples of this:

- New International version: 'fill the Earth and subdue it. Rule over the fish in the sea and the birds in the sky and over every living creature that moves on the ground.'
- King James version: 'replenish the earth, and subdue it: and have dominion over the fish of the sea, and over the fowl of the air, and over every living thing that moveth upon the Earth'.

These are describing the same narrative structure using different but synonymous lexemes (fill/replenish; rule/have dominion; birds/fowl; living creature/ living thing; ground/Earth).

As with all narratives, there are a range of different narrative entailments that can be drawn out and emphasised. It would be possible to draw out an entailment of human exceptionalism from the temporal sequence where humans were created last (i.e., with narrative end-focus); the fact that they were the only beings created in the image of God; and were the only beings given dominion over the rest of creation. In a classic paper, Lynn White (1967) argued that 'Christianity is the most anthropocentric religion the world has ever seen' because 'God planned all of this explicitly for man's benefit and rule; no item in the physical creation had any purpose save to serve man's purposes' (p. 1205). White contrasts the creation narrative with earlier pagan narratives of nature spirits who must be considered and placated. He concludes 'by destroying pagan animism, Christianity made it possible to exploit nature in a mood of indifference to the feelings of natural objects' (p. 1205).

Unsurprisingly, White's strong views led to great amount of debate in the more than half a century since he expressed them (LeVasseur and Peterson 2017). Charles Camosy (2017) expresses a very different opinion:

> Genesis 1 and 2 are among the best pro-animal texts we could ever imagine there being. Nonhuman animals and humans are created on the same day of creation. Both share the breath of life. God commands humans to eat plants ... It is true that in the biblical narrative God gives Noah and his descendants (limited) permission to eat meat, though this notably occurs after sin enters the order of creation.

The key entailments that Camosy implicitly draws out are: (a) that humans and animals are equal, since both share the breath of life and were created on the same day; and (b) that Christians should eat plant-based foods. In ecolinguistic terms, Camosy is describing Genesis as a *beneficial* narrative in the sense that it promotes plant-based lifestyles, while White is describing it as a *destructive* narrative that promotes human exceptionalism. Both, however, share the same aim of promoting ecological awareness.

On the other hand, Tony Abbott, former prime minister of Australia, used the creation narrative for a very different goal: climate change denial. In a speech to the *Global Warming Policy Foundation* in 2017, he reiterated his earlier assertion that the settled science of climate change was 'absolute crap'. He described climate change as a new religion, 'sacrificing our industries and our living standards to the climate gods' because societies have 'forgotten the scriptures about man created in the image and likeness of God and charged with subduing the earth and all its creatures' (Abbott 2017). This is an illustration of how stories may exist deep in the background of cultures and be brought back to the surface in different ways to serve ecologically beneficial or destructive goals.

There are, of course, a vast number of creation myths from across the world to explore. Alida Gersie's book *Earthtales: Storytelling in Times of Change* (NR15) is a useful resource because it brings together stories and myths from indigenous and traditional communities that speak to ecological issues, and describes ways that the narratives can be used practically in education to open up new ways of thinking. The book begins with *How the Earth Was Made*, a retelling of a Cheyenne creation myth. The myth bears some similarities to the Genesis creation story: there is a creator, the great spirit Maheo, who starts with nothing in darkness but then creates salty water, then fish, then birds that live on the water. However, it departs from Genesis because the birds are not just passively 'created' but play an activated role. They are Sayers of verbal processes, speaking with Maheo, asking for land to make a nest. They are then activated further by being agents of materials processes of 'flying', 'finding', 'diving', 'swimming' and bringing things back as they help Maheo create the land. Eventually they find mud, and the giant Grandmother turtle offers her back to place the mud on, and this became the land. After that, Maheo creates humans, and only after that the land animals. The giving of agency to the birds and turtle and placing the creation of humans in the middle, rather than the end of the sequence, gives humans a more humble place in nature than narratives where humans are created last or appear to be the pinnacle of evolution. As Gilderhus (1994) puts it, in the Genesis story 'God is separate and has no creative assistance from his creatures. God is sacred' whereas in the Cheyenne narrative 'all creatures share in the process of creation which makes all things sacred' (p. 70).

Scientific narratives of the origins of the Universe are just as open to critical analysis because the history of the Universe is vast, and they will necessarily select particular events to focus on. The 'big bang' is an obvious starting point, but from then the Universe expands in all directions for 14 billion years, so the narrative may narrow to a particular solar system, a particular planet, and the evolution of a sequence of increasingly complex lifeforms. Of particular interest is where the narrative stops. Does it close with the emergence of particular classes of animals, of modern human beings, or of human civilisation? Or does it close with the ecological destruction caused by humans and the hope of a more ecologically sensitive form of civilisation in the future?

One example narrative, *Big Bang to Civilization* (NR12), which appeared on the website *Live Science*, makes the start and end points very clear in its title. After the 'big bang' it describes the following events: the formation of the stars, the solar system, organic molecules, Eukaryotic life, a period when 'dinosaurs ruled the Earth', and then a meteor strike which destroyed them. Following this is the passage:

- But the small furry mammals that burrowed underground survived. They had been living in the shadows of the dinosaurs all along, but with the dinosaurs gone they could now thrive and grow in size. They became the new rulers of the Earth. Eventually the mammalian lineage evolved into primates, then apes, then hominids, and finally the Homo lineage that produced human beings. (NR12)

The words 'had been', 'now', 'became', 'new', 'eventually', 'then' and 'finally' are all temporal markers, linking the events into a sequence. The expression 'the mammalian lineage evolved into primates' erases the many other classes of mammals aside from primates that evolved after the dinosaurs, and the sequence of events presents human beings as being the last species of all to evolve. In addition to this, the expression 'rulers of the Earth' sets up a natural hierarchy, which, by implication, has humans at the top by the end. The words 'ruled' and 'rulers' echo the wording of some versions of the Genesis story.

If an origin narrative stops with the evolution of modern humans then there is a danger of an entailment being drawn out that humans are the final species to evolve in a chain of increasingly sophisticated and 'better' organisms — indeed, the *Big Bang to Civilization* text states: 'It seems that the humans living in East Africa who survived the Toba event were a new and *better* version of Homo sapiens' (NR12, emphasis added). An educational project from the University of California (Berkeley 2020) specifically counters the drawing of entailments such as these by setting up the metaphor EVOLUTION IS A LADDER (another verticality metaphor), but then replacing it with the less hierarchical EVOLUTION IS A TREE:

> It is tempting to see evolution as a grand progressive ladder with Homo sapiens emerging at the top. But evolution produces a tree, not a ladder — and we are just one of many twigs on the tree.

After the appearance of humans, *Big Bang to Civilization* describes the emergence of early and modern forms of civilisation. However, it tries to prevent readers from drawing out the entailment that modern civilisation is the crowning achievement of the universe by giving a selective list of characteristics that gives it an overall negative appraisal: 'centralized government and power, military forces and warfare, institutionalised religion, patriarchy, monetary systems, poverty, large-scale agriculture, trade networks, and empire' (NR12). It ends with 'But is this model [civilisation] still serving us well, or is humanity ready for something new, the next Great Leap?' This rhetorical question clearly implies that it is time to move from current industrial civilisation to something new, compensating for some of the hierarchical entailments of the narrative.

The Emmy award-winning documentary *Journey of the Universe* provides a different science-based narrative about the origins of the Universe. It ends with an extremely concise narrative that summarises the whole film:

- These deep discoveries of science are leading to a new story of the Universe. It's a story that can be summarised in a single sentence. Over the course of 14 billion years hydrogen gas transformed itself into mountains, butterflies, the music of Bach, and you and me, and these energies coursing through us may indeed renew the face of the Earth.

(NR13)

Although short, there is a lot to analyse in this text. Firstly, the facticity is raised by the first sentence which makes the story of the Universe appear to arise directly from the discoveries of science without an intermediate agent crafting it. Secondly, the activated characters are 'hydrogen gas' and 'energies', which locates the force of creation in the physics of the Universe rather than a deity. This force is described as being channelled *through* humans, which goes beyond ecological identity to what we could call a 'universal identity' or 'cosmic identity', where humans are an integral part of the Universe. The other characters in the narrative are passivated and presented in a clear order — firstly 'mountains', which can be seen a metonym standing for the physical environment; then 'butterflies' standing for 'animals'; then the 'music of Bach' standing for cultural achievement; and, finally, 'you and me', standing for humans. The choice of a western composer, Bach, gives a Eurocentric aspect to the narrative, and the sequence ends with the human. However, the agency in the last sentence is not human agency but the agency of the physical Universe working through humans, and the end-focus is on ecological action that can preserve life on Earth. This potentially leads to entailments which encourage ecologically beneficial actions. The narrative in a sentence here is just a tiny part of the film which gives a much fuller narrative; and, as well as the film, there is a corresponding book, a website, a TED talk and an online course. In this way the narrative can be both complex and multimodal.

A similar project, the *Deep Time Walk*, provides yet another mode — a mobile phone app which takes the listener on a journey in a quite literal sense. This is how the app is described:

- Deep Time Walk is a 4.6 km walking audio history of the living Earth. This unfolding takes you from 4,600 million years ago to the present day, with each metre you walk representing 1 million years. [From the narration by] a Fool and a Scientist you learn how our planet evolved over this vast stretch of time ... (NR14)

In addition to the app, the Deep Time Walk project offers a field kit for people to lead their own walks, which provides a resource for the creation of their own local and culturally contextual narratives.

As the listener walks, the app measures the distance they have travelled and describes the corresponding events from the timeline of Earth's history, using a commentary written by Stephan Harding and Peter Oswald (NR14). The commentary is structured as a conversation between two characters, the Scientist and the Fool. Just before embarking on the walk, the Fool explains:

Human Population 7.6bn —— | —— Industrial Revolution
Human Population 100m —— | —— Axial Age
Great Pyramids / Stonehenge —— | —— First writing, history begins

Human Population 2m —— | —— Agricultural Revolution
| —— End of last ice age
| —— Bow and arrow
| —— Domestication of animals
Modern humans in N. America —— | —— Clay pottery
| —— Fish hooks
| —— First houses
| —— Woven textiles
Modern humans in Europe —— | —— Clay hearths

| —— Cave art

| —— Bone/ivory flutes for music

Modern humans in Australia ——
Modern humans in South Asia —— | —— Sewing needles

Modern humans in Near East —— | —— Bone arrow heads

Symbolic culture and language —— | —— Oldest drawing on rock flake
| —— Jewellery

| —— Bone harpoons

Scale: 1cm=10,000 years

IMAGE 10.2   Time and distance. © The Deep Time Walk

- We'll walk four thousand six hundred metres,

  Four thousand six hundred million years,

  From the explosion from which the Earth came,

  to the present moment.

  We can take one other person with us,

  That's you listener. Come with us. Walk with us. (NR14)

These words align the physical distance with the span of time and map both dimensions onto the start and end events of the narrative. The direct address and imperatives reach out to the listener and bring them into the narrative. One of the most powerful aspects of the experience is that 200 years of industrial civilisation normally seems like a long time but is only the final 0.2 mm of the 4.6 km walk. This helps brings salience to the fact that life, which took so long to develop, is being destroyed in just the briefest flash of geological time.

The final hundred thousand years is represented with a visual metaphor of a ruler published by the Deep Time Walk (reproduced as Image 10.2). The ruler is a reference to the original deep time walks led by Stephan Harding in person along the south Devon coast. Right at the end of the walk Harding places a yellow tape measure on the ground and then describes facts such as there being 12mm since the last ice age, 5 mm since Stonehenge was built, and only 0.2 mm since the industrial revolution.

The expressions 'living Earth' and 'our planet evolved' in the description of the Deep Time Walk frame the planet as an organism — a framing which occurs frequently during the narrative. At one particular point, 2.7 billion years ago (or 1.9 km of walking), a key event occurs which triggers the framing: 'the birth of Gaia'. From this point the commentary uses the expression 'lady Gaia' and the pronoun 'she' to personify the Earth. Much later in the narrative text, after the evolution of humans, the Scientist laments that human consciousness lacks 'Gaia's gift for favouring her own survival', lacks self-regulation, and is wrecking the Earth. Towards the end of the narrative the Scientist addresses Gaia directly with a second-person pronoun: 'If we wound you, it is us that dies ... there is no gap between us at all, we are the same thing!' The narrative therefore builds towards an entailment of a planetary ecological identity — that humans are not just a part of nature but part of a living planet that was born and evolved as an organism. And that we are in danger of destroying this organism and, in doing so, destroying ourselves.

A key question is whether there is any empirical evidence that alternative origin narratives, and the worldviews they correspond to, influence people's actions. A study by Taylor *et al.* (2019) conducted statistical analysis which compared 328 informants' religious beliefs (through the lens of theistic beliefs and views of evolution) and beliefs about the place of humans in the world (through the lens of humility) with their environmental behaviours (focusing on food, transport and energy use). The authors came to the following conclusion:

> Those who hold anthropocentric and monotheistic religious views, and express low levels of environmental, religious, and cosmic humility, are less likely to engage in pro-environmental behaviours than those who maintain views ... that are ecocentric, Organicist/Gaian, pantheistic, animistic, and that in general reflect humility about the human place in the world.

Although the study had limitations and more research is required, it does at least suggest a correlation between views and behaviour — in other words, the stories in people's minds influence not only how they think and talk but also act. And in this case, the more humble views of humans' place in the Universe were correlated with positive treatment of the environment.

This section could only touch briefly on a few narratives — there is a vast amount of multimodal material to be explored, from creation stories of the major world religions, to the origin stories of science, of fiction and film, and to the myths of traditional and indigenous cultures across the world. Clearly, narratives about the origin of the Universe and life can influence how we think about our relationship with each other, other species and the physical environment and how we act, so they are of great importance for ecolinguistics.

理论延伸

叙事理论（narrative theory）是贯穿于本章分析的理论基础，也被称为叙事学（narratology）。由于叙事的问题是很多人文社会科学领域共同关注的内容，不断被应用在文学、语言学、社会学、人类学，甚至是心理学、经济学、法学等更加广泛的研究领域中，因此叙事理论的跨学科属性也是非常明显的。将叙事理论引入生态语言学研究进行讨论，既是一种可行的尝试，也进一步丰富了生态语言学的理论内容。

自古以来，有关叙事问题的研究就是一个重要的话题，如柏拉图（Plato）划分了叙事要素——模仿（mimesis）和叙事（diegesis），亚里士多德对情节（plot）问题的描述，等等（唐伟胜，2003）。不过，作为一门学科的叙事学，直到20世纪60年代末，受到法国结构主义和俄国形式主义的影响才形成。1969年，法国结构主义符号学家、文艺理论家Tzvetan Todorov首次提出了叙事学的概念，将其定义为"关于叙事作品的科学"（Todorov，1969：132；参见陈桂琴，2010）。这使得叙事理论逐渐取代了传统的小说理论，成为文学研究中的一个议题（华莱士·马丁，2018）。

在中国，我们自己的叙事传统和叙事理论一直存在，但是未受到足够的重视，目前发展出来的叙事理论是在西方的影响下出现的（申丹、王丽亚，2010：1）。1979年，袁可嘉发表了《结构主义文学理论述评》的文章，将结构主义文学理论（包括叙事学）研究引入中国，成为新时期第一篇介绍该主题的较有影响力的文章（施定，2003）。随后，国内很多学者开始关注叙事学的研究。20世纪90年代中期出现了"叙事学热"的现象（陈桂琴，2010）。但早期国内的叙事学研究主要是从西方的叙事理论出发的，而对中国自己的叙事理论研究得较少。随着叙事学在中国的持续推进，国内也开始了建设本土化叙事理论的步伐（施定，2003）。到了20世纪90年代末，"叙事"

一词的意义出现了广泛扩展的现象，即"叙事转向"（the narrative turn）（莫妮卡·弗卢德尼克，2007：40）。"叙事转向"的发展将原本仅应用在小说研究中的叙事学扩展到非文学文本的解释，这个现象也就是由经典叙事学研究向后经典叙事学的转变。

近20年来，随着叙事学"认知转向"（the cognitive turn）的出现，语言学家也开始重视叙事理论的意义，推动了叙事理论在语言学研究中的应用（莫妮卡·弗卢德尼克，2007：40–47）。同时，跨学科趋势的不断发展，叙事理论与语言学的结合研究也成为一种新的研究路径，与生态语言学的结合更是非常重要的一步。当前，中国叙事学的发展有一个主要的目标是要挖掘中国传统的叙事故事，复兴中国传统的叙事理论，并将国内有价值的叙事传统推向世界（万晓蒙、李亚飞，2018）。这些叙事故事就包括了那些与生态环境有关的叙事，这样的叙事对生态语言学研究是必不可少的，对人们生态哲学观、生态话语乃至生态素养的形成颇有裨益。

不同学科的学者对生态叙事问题的探究已经取得了一定的成果，读者可选择性地阅读刘卫英（2013）、马特（2019）、张泽兵（2019）、王蕾和张月（2020）等学者的文章。但是目前还几乎没有从生态语言学角度讨论叙事问题的研究，因此本书的作者在第二版中新增添"叙事理论在生态语言学研究中的价值"（P230–251）的内容也与此现象有关。对这一研究角度感兴趣的读者可参考上面其他领域研究者的相关论著，并进一步阅读申丹（1998，2009，2013，2020）、谭君强（2008）、申丹和王丽亚（2010）、傅修延（2014）、Shen（2014）、华莱士·马丁（2018）等学者的论著内容，努力从叙事学的理论层面探索出一条生态语言学研究的叙事道路。

补充文献

陈桂琴.2010.国内叙事学研究发展述评.外语学刊，（6）：135–137.

傅修延.2014.从西方叙事学到中国叙事学.中国比较文学，（4）：1–24.

华莱士·马丁.2018.当代叙事学.伍晓明，译.北京：中国人民大学出版社.

刘卫英.2013.还珠楼主大鸟意象的生态叙事及其渊源.中南民族大学学报（人文社会科学版），（6）：127–130.

马特.2019.论加里·斯奈德的后现代城市建构与生态叙事.外国文学研究，（4）：75–88.

莫妮卡·弗卢德尼克.2007.叙事理论的历史（下）：从结构主义到现在.詹姆斯·费伦，彼得·J.拉比诺维茨编.当代叙事理论指南.申丹等，译.北京：北京大学出版社，40–47.

申丹.1998.叙述学与小说文体学研究.北京：北京大学出版社.

申丹.2009.关于叙事学研究的几个问题.中国外语，（5）：60–65.

申丹 . 2013. 关于叙事 "隐性进程" 的思考 . 中国外语，（6）：1，12.

申丹 . 2020. 修辞性叙事学 . 外国文学，（1）：80–95.

申丹，王丽亚 . 2010. 西方叙事学：经典与后经典 . 北京：北京大学出版社 .

施定 . 2003. 近 20 余年中国叙事学研究述评 . 学术研究，（8）：129–132.

谭君强 . 2008. 叙事学导论——从经典叙事学到后经典叙事学 . 北京：高等教育出版社 .

唐伟胜 . 2003. 范式与层面：国外叙事学研究综述——兼评国内叙事学研究现状 . 外国语，
（5）：60–66.

万晓蒙，李亚飞 . 2018. 对话前沿 回归本土——2017 年中国叙事学研究述论 . 当代外
语研究，（6）：119–125.

王蕾，张月 . 2020. 讲好 "中国故事" 的生态叙事研究——基于纪录片《影响世界的
中国植物》的分析 . 中国电视，（7）：84–88.

袁可嘉 . 1979. 结构主义文学理论述评 . 世界文学，（2）：291–309.

张泽兵 . 2019. 生态叙事的理论与实践——关于傅修延先生的生态叙事研究 . 鄱阳湖学
刊，（4）：26–30.

Gersie, A., Nanson, A. & Schieffelin, E. (Eds.). 2014. *Storytelling for a greener world: Environment, community and story-based learning*. Stroud: Hawthorn Press.

Jones, M. & McBeth, M. 2010. A narrative policy framework: Clear enough to be wrong. *Policy Studies Journal*, (2): 329–353.

Molthan-Hill, P., Baden, D., Wall, T., Puntha, H. & Luna, H. (Eds.). 2020. *Storytelling for sustainability in higher education: An educator's handbook*. London: Routledge.

Shen, D. 2014. *Style and rhetoric of short narrative fiction: Covert progressions behind overt plots*. London: Routledge.

Todorov, T. 1969. *Grammaire du décameron*. Mouton: The Hague.

11

CONCLUSION

　　本书运用了系统功能语言学、话语分析、认知语言学、身份理论、叙事学等多种理论，旨在揭示出我们信奉和践行的故事。其中一个重要的方面是，作者根据自己的生态哲学观判断所分析的故事，批评、抵制那些与本书生态哲学观相悖的故事，并努力寻找新的可替代性故事。第11章是全书的总结，作者基于当前世界面临的生态问题，警醒我们要重新思考社会的发展定位，抛弃旧的、不合理的故事，践行能使生态崛起、万物复苏、保护生态的新故事。本章主要谈到三个问题：（1）本书中生态语言学的定义；（2）生态语言学的理论发展；（3）不同领域研究者的贡献。

　　（1）本书中生态语言学的定义。学术研究在巩固或挑战社会主流故事方面作用显著，兴起了许多与生态相关的交叉学科。其中，与生态相关的人文社会科学有着相同的出发点——尽管平等与人类福祉极为重要，但无论我们站在什么样的立场，都不能忽视其他物种和更广泛的物理环境的存在。由此，本书给出了生态语言学最新的明确定义：生态语言学研究的是有关语言在人类、其他物种和物理环境之间的生命可持续互动中的作用（*Ecolinguistics* is the study of the role of language in the life-sustaining interactions of humans with other species and the physical environment.）。这个概念告诉读者，语言学研究不仅仅要考虑语言和社会语境中的语言使用，还要将语言放在更广泛的生态系统中进行考量。

　　（2）生态语言学的理论发展。生态语言学研究在早期主要聚焦在英语和其他语言的语法问题上，探讨特定的语法特征是怎样支撑或导致生态破坏行为的（如Halliday，1990/2003；Goatly，2001；Mühlhäusler，2001等）。但实际上，通过改变语言本身来促进生态有益的行为是不现实的。因此，学者们探索出了一条用语言来讲述有关世界不同故事的道路。这也是本书的重点，即用语言使用、表达方式和语言学特征来建构我们信奉和践行的故事。这种做法的假定是，语言不仅仅反映现实，而且主动构建现实（Halliday，1990/2003）。语言所构建的现实和我们接触的故事不仅影响我们的所思所想，也最终影响我们的行为。

本书在第2章至第10章共讲述了九个类型的故事，这些故事之间不是完全无关的，它们存在着各种各样的内在联系。例如：书中对《太阳报》（The Sun）上的新闻标题分析（P259）就包含了几种类型的故事——意识形态、评估、隐喻、身份、删略和叙事。从研究的理论意义和实践价值看，生态语言学研究的作用是为更高层次的道德目标服务的，而不仅仅是关注研究本身。正是如此，才能让生态语言学以更好的方式把生命可持续发展理念延续给子孙后代，也延伸到与其他物种和物理环境有关的生态系统中去。

（3）不同领域研究者的贡献。作者在最后这个部分汇集了来自不同领域的研究者在生态环境问题研究方面做出的贡献。他们都在根据自己的学习或工作生活背景，审视、评判着我们信奉和践行的生态故事。另外，生态语言学鼓励研究者要特别关注世界各地的传统文化和土著文化，挖掘这些文化中的生态智慧，补充我们信奉和践行的可替代性新故事，这也是生态语言学研究的一个重要发展方向。目前巴西和中国已经在此方面有所建树，例如：巴西的生态系统语言学（ecosystemic linguistics）（do Couto，2018）、中国的和谐话语分析（Huang & Zhao，2021）。在全书的末尾，本书作者呼吁未来有更多领域的研究者在生态语言学研究领域做出自己的贡献，共同成就这一伟大事业（The Great Work）。

The pandemic has given us an unprecedented chance to rethink society and leave behind some of the stories that contribute to inequality and ecological destruction. Arundhati Roy (2020) expresses this eloquently:

> Whatever it is, coronavirus has made the mighty kneel and brought the world to a halt like nothing else could. Our minds are still racing back and forth, longing for a return to 'normality', trying to stitch our future to our past and refusing to acknowledge the rupture. But the rupture exists. And in the midst of this terrible despair, it offers us a chance to rethink the doomsday machine we have built for ourselves. Nothing could be worse than a return to normality.

The scale of change required goes far beyond small technical fixes such as more efficient cars. It requires the emergence of a different kind of society, based on different stories. If we fail and return to 'normal' after the pandemic, then we face ecological devastation and possible systemic collapse. However, even if current forms of society collapse we still need new stories to survive by as the Earth becomes increasingly hostile to human life and the lives of countless other species. We need new stories to allow ecological societies to emerge from the ruins and for all forms of life to thrive as far as possible.

In their teaching, research and outreach activity, academic disciplines play a role in entrenching or challenging the dominant stories of society. What has changed over the last thirty years or so is that many academics have realised that their discipline is overlooking the life-sustaining ecosystems that humans and human societies are embedded in. This has consequences for both the accuracy of the discipline and its ability to contribute to reinventing society along more ecological lines. We have therefore seen the emergence of ecopsychology, ecocriticism, ecofeminism, ecopoetics, ecohistory, environmental communication, ecosociology and, eventually, ecolinguistics. The central point of these ecological humanities and social science subjects is that while equality and human wellbeing is of great importance we must not forget about other species and the physical environment, both for their own sake and because human life depends on them.

One way of defining ecolinguistics in a way that matches the common goal of all the ecological humanities subjects is:

Ecolinguistics is the study of the role of language in the life-sustaining interactions of humans with other species and the physical environment.

Of course, it would be possible to express the definition in other words, but what is essential is that language is considered not just in isolation or within a purely social context, but in the context of the wider ecosystems that life depends on. Any form of linguistic enquiry can be adapted to be a form of ecolinguistics if it considers this wider context, from language interaction studies which look at the loss of traditional environmental knowledge as English spreads around the world, to rhetorical studies which look at the persuasive power of advertising.

This book used theories from cognitive linguistics, discourse analysis and identity theory with an aim of revealing the stories we live by, judging those stories according to an ecosophy, resisting stories which oppose the ecosophy, and contributing to the search for new stories to live by. This is just one of the tasks of ecolinguistics, but an important one. After all, as Ben Okri (1996, p. 33) describes:

Stories can destroy civilisations, can win wars, can lose them, can conquer hearts by the millions ... can re-shape the psychic mould of a people, can re-mould the political and spiritual temper of an age.

It is the ecosophy which makes the analysis ecolinguistic, since by definition ecosophies must consider both humans and the more-than-human world. However, the ecosophy used in this book is just one particular ecosophy, and each analyst will bring their own ecosophy to bear in their analysis and use their own constellation of theories and sources of data. There are therefore as many kinds of 'ecolinguistics' as there are researchers, but all are united in taking into consideration and protecting the ecosystems that life depends on.

This concluding chapter describes how the form of ecolinguistics in this book moves away from a focus on the grammar of the language itself towards a focus on how language is used to tell stories about the world. It discusses possibilities for moving beyond some of the limitations of discourse analytic work and brings together some of the voices in the book into a final 'gathering'.

Theory

Ecolinguistics, in its early days, often focused on the grammar of English and other languages, describing how particular grammatical features encourage ecologically destructive behaviour. Halliday (2001, p. 103) describes how certain aspects of grammar 'conspire ... to construe reality in a certain way ... that is no longer good for our health as a species'. The first is that mass nouns like 'soil' and 'water' are unbounded, giving a story of abundance rather than limitation of supply. The second is that opposites have a positive (unmarked) pole, with 'bigger' and 'growth' being more positive than 'smaller' or 'shrinkage', making economic growth appear attractive. The third is that the use of the pronoun 'who' vs 'what' divides the world falsely into conscious beings (humans and to some extent their pets) and non-conscious beings (other species). Chawla (2001, p. 121) similarly claims that 'the language habits of fragmenting the mass, quantifying intangibles and imaginary nouns, and perceiving time in terms of past, present and future are factors in our inability to perceive the natural environment holistically'.

Goatly (2001, p. 213) too focuses on the level of grammar and argues that modern scientific theory demands a grammar which does not simplistically separate Actors (who do things) from Affected participants (who have things done to them). This separation is out of step with the radical interconnected nature of the world that modern science reveals. Actors, he points out, are also affected by their actions: car drivers, for example, are actors in driving a car but they are also affected by the pollution and climate change that they are contributing to.

Mühlhäsler (2001, p. 36) describes how languages such as Aiwo contain semantic distinctions that are useful in dealing with environmental issues. Aiwo has a prefix 'ka', for instance, which signals entities 'which are, for most of the time, inert but are liable to sudden dramatic changes of behaviour'. It may be useful if, in English, the words 'landfill', 'nuclear power station' or 'certain chemicals' could similarly be labelled with a prefix like this. However, he stops short of calling for the English language to be re-engineered along the lines of Aiwo: 'I do not wish to claim that such distinctions should be introduced into English ... by acts of planning' (p. 37). Indeed, the concept of 'language planning' to change the English Language itself is a controversial one. Smith (1999, p. 233) writes that 'there is ... something Orwellian about the concept of "language planning" which sometimes imparts a managerialist overtone to [some ecolinguists'] agenda. Just who is to determine what language is appropriate and hence what world we will live in?' Indeed, a decree that in English 'landfill' must now be called 'ka-landfill' to emphasise its volatile nature would most likely be met with derision.

Even if language planning to change the grammar of the English language were desirable, it is not at all clear that it is possible. It is inconceivable that we could change English to remove the past tense, or stop clauses from separating out participants into Actor and Affected, or turn 'water' into a count noun. Halliday (2001, p. 196) concludes that 'you cannot co-opt the grammar ... neither can you engineer it. I do not think ... language professionals ... can plan the inner layers of grammar; there is an inherent antipathy between grammar and design.'

While it may be impractical to change the language of English itself to encourage more ecologically beneficial behaviour, what *is* possible is to use the English language, however imperfect or flawed, to tell different *stories* about the world. Instead of attempting to turn 'growth' into a marked (negative) term, it is easier to drop the story that GROWTH IS THE KEY GOAL OF SOCIETY and replace it with other stories, e.g. WELLBEING IS THE KEY GOAL OF SOCIETY. The focus of this book, therefore, has been on how the linguistic features of the English language are combined together and *used* to construct the stories we live by. This shifts the question from 'How can we change the language itself?' to 'How can we use the linguistic features of the language to convey new stories to live by?'

The term *stories we live by* is based on Lakoff and Johnson's (1980) book *Metaphors We Live By,* which gave a radically new perspective on the role of metaphors in our lives. Metaphors are not, they argued, mere rhetorical flourishes used to make texts more vivid, but a fundamental part of our conceptual system. They write:

> The concepts that govern our thought are not just matters of the intellect. They also govern our everyday functioning, down to the most mundane details. Our concepts structure what we perceive, how we get around in the world and how we relate to other people. Our conceptual system thus plays a central role in defining our everyday realities.

> (Lakoff and Johnson 1980, p. 3)

It is at the level of conceptual system that this book has focused. If our conceptual system influences how we act in the world, then it can encourage us to protect or destroy the ecosystems which life depends on. The key insight of Lakoff and Johnson's theory is that metaphors are shared across the minds of multiple people in a culture and therefore have important consequences for how large numbers of people think. More generally, Social Representation Theory (Rateau *et al.* 2012) explains how not just metaphors but a range of ideas, attitudes, perceptions, evaluations, and beliefs exist across the minds of multiple individuals in social groups.

This book has taken Lakoff and Johnson's idea of *metaphors we live by* and extended it to the more general *stories we live by*, which include *ideologies, frames, metaphors, evaluations, identities, convictions, erasure, salience* and *narratives*. Although it is impossible to look into people's minds and directly observe these cognitive structures, it is possible to analyse the characteristic patterns of language which arise from them. There are three levels: *stories*, which are cognitive structures in people's minds; the *stories we live by*, which are shared across the minds of large numbers of people; and *linguistic manifestations*, which are the patterns of language which arise from the underlying stories. Importantly, these stories influence not only how we think and talk, but ultimately how we act.

The nine types of story should not be thought of as separate and distinct since there are various ways that they interact. The following examples of headlines from *The Sun* newspaper contain several types of story:

- HUMAN TIDE Turkish President Erdogan repeats threat to flood Europe with refugees. (ML13: 15/10/2019)
- Huge hike in number of migrants flooding UK. (ML13: 28/8/2014)
- THE TIDAL wave of poorer European migrants heading to Britain is going to soar. (ML13: 22/9/2014)
- Fears of new migrant influx as 100 refugees arrive in Calais. (ML13: 1/7/2017)
- CRISIS POINT Moment migrants storm Kent beaches as more than 270 descend on Britain in a WEEK. (ML13: 31/08/2019)

There is clearly a nationalist, anti-immigration ideology in these examples. The ideology manifests itself in certain features, primarily the IMMIGRANTS ARE WATER metaphor, which is triggered by the words *tide, flood, flooding, tidal wave, influx,* and *storm.* Hansen and Machin (2018:118) describe a similar example of a headline in the right-wing newspaper, the *Daily Mail:* 'Britain will be scarcely recognisable in 50 years if the immigration deluge continues'. They describe how the metaphor of 'deluge' creates an image of rainfall that overspills and causes damage. The metaphors set up a negative appraisal pattern since 'flood', 'tidal wave' and 'storm' are dangerous. The pattern is intensified by the negative prosody of the words 'threat', 'hike', 'fears' and 'crisis' (the word 'hike' has negative prosody because it is usually associated with something unwelcome, e.g., a 'hike in prices').

At the same time, these headlines create identities, firstly through selecting the term 'migrant', and then by homogenising individuals who have their own life history as an undifferentiated mass through the flooding metaphor and the enumeration of total numbers. And these headlines are part of a larger narrative that is common in right-wing newspapers: that huge numbers of migrants are entering the country, taking jobs from residents, overcrowding services, drawing benefits, committing crimes and generally damaging society. The narrative erases the countries that people are coming from, the environmental destruction that they faced there and the host country's culpability in that destruction. It also erases the contribution that people coming from overseas make to the host country.

Underlying just these few headlines, then, there are ideologies, evaluations, metaphors, identities, erasure and narratives. Ecolinguistic analysis can reveal how these stories combine together in ways that could influence people to be less welcoming of environmental refugees, and less likely to take responsibility for the ecological damage that caused refugees to leave their homes in the first place. Once the stories (and the linguistic techniques for creating those stories) are revealed, then ecolinguists can resist the stories by producing critical analyses and making them available for campaigners and educators to use. There are organisations like *Stop Funding Hate* which encourage consumers to boycott corporations that advertise in newspapers that represent refugees and other oppressed groups negatively (SFH 2020).

As well as critical analysis of damaging dominant stories, ecolinguistics also has an important role to play in positive analysis of beneficial stories and the linguistic techniques that can be used to convey them. An example of this is the video *You Clap for Me Now* (ML25), produced by Sachini Imbuldeniya, which was published on social media during the coronavirus lockdown. In the video, key workers of different races and with accents from different countries take it in turns to say the following:

- So it's finally happened. That thing you were afraid of. Something's come from overseas and taken your jobs. Made it unsafe to walk the streets. Kept you trapped at home. A dirty disease ... you clap for me now, you cheer as I toil, bringing food to your family, bringing food from your soil, propping up your hospitals, not some foreign invader — delivery driver, teacher, life saver. Don't say go home ... (ML25)

This begins with words that trigger the narrative that the right-wing press has promoted over the years — 'come from overseas', 'taking your jobs' and 'made it unsafe'. However, the words 'a dirty disease' restructure the narrative to make the disease the invader rather than the migrants, with the migrants recast as key workers and life savers. The visuals frame migrants as individuals and essential workers rather than a homogenous flood of benefit scroungers. This is achieved through having just one person in shot at a close distance, speaking directly to the viewer with eye contact, wearing characteristic work clothing and being in a typical work setting. In this way, the video values and gives salience to people who are often demonised and erased in the mainstream press. As Bruno Latour puts it:

> We should remember that this idea of framing everything in terms of the economy is a new thing in human history. The pandemic has shown us the economy is a very narrow and limited way of organising life and deciding who is important and who is not important.
>
> (Latour in Watts 2020)

Ironically, *The Sun* published this video on its website alongside a hugely positive article about it entitled 'My brave mum risked everything flying across world to save NHS — and inspired our coronavirus hit *You Clap for Me Now*' (ML7). It is ironic since the video challenges the exact story that headlines in the newspaper have conveyed over the years. Of course, where a newspaper like *The Sun* does use positive forms of language which convey beneficial stories then it is useful to point this out and use it as a direction for the newspaper as a whole to head towards in the future.

Critical Discourse Analysts are sometimes accused of consciously or unconsciously selecting data in order to make a political point (Breeze 2013), a criticism which can equally be applied to ecolinguists. There is certainly a danger, for example, of just choosing the most negative headlines from *The Sun* to highlight its underlying nationalistic ideology, while overlooking other stories which may be more positive. The example above, though, shows the potential value of highlighting positive stories as well as negative ones. It may be easier to engage with the producers of a discourse if the linguistic features which convey positive stories are covered first, with encouragement to use them more frequently (see Macgilchrist 2007); then, after that, moving on to features which convey destructive stories and recommending change. Bartlett (2018, p. 138) emphasises the importance of strategic engagement with producers of discourse, taking into account the specific social conditions and linguistic practices that influence the uptake of alternative discourses.

In a similar vein, it would be easy to focus only on the way that the Sustainable

Development Goals tell the story that other species are resources with no intrinsic value. There is no doubt that this is the primary story about the natural world that is conveyed by the goals and is one that needs calling out. However, dotted here and there are statements which convey a different story, e.g., 'We envisage a world free of poverty, hunger, disease and want, where all life can thrive.' It is valuable to comb through texts carefully looking for expressions which tell the opposite story from the ones which are immediately obvious, as these provide a starting point for change.

Breeze (2013) points out another criticism of Critical Discourse Analysis which can also apply to ecolinguistics: that analysts are naïe in assuming that a particular discourse will determine people's thinking directly. She writes:

> It is uncontroversial to assume the existence of a significant relationship between discourse and people's view of reality. However, it is equally obvious that in a globalised world people are exposed to many different discourses, and that they learn to navigate them, ignoring many, accepting some, rejecting others.
>
> (Breeze 2013, p. 508)

This is an important statement as in it lies the hope of ecolinguistics to make a difference in the world. There is no need to assume that audiences are passive recipients of the messages contained in the discourses they are exposed to — some will accept the messages and some will be critical and reject them. The aim ecolinguistics is to encourage people to be *more* critical, and reject or accept discourses based not just on personal or social considerations but ecological ones too. In other words, ecolinguistics can encourage people to do what they already do, which is being critically discerning about the stories they choose to live by, but with the aid of linguistic analysis to help expose and gain awareness of the stories that surround them, and an ecosophy to evaluate those stories against.

For this reason, it is important that ecolinguistics does not remain a narrow academic field focused on publications in journals and monographs but reaches out to a wider audience and attempts to infuse critical awareness within mainstream education and discourse producers of all kinds. It would be useful if weather forecasters thought carefully about how they describe a misty day — as unpleasant 'murk' to be avoided by staying at home watching advertising on TV, or as an enchanting atmosphere for exploring local nature. Or if writers of biology textbooks thought carefully about the words they choose to describe animals and considered whether they were representing them as assemblages of body parts or as individuals who are leading their lives for their own purposes. And it would be good to see school children being critical of the representations of the natural world in their textbooks and experimenting with new ways of describing the world in their creative writing.

While it is important to keep ecolinguistics accessible for multiple audiences, it is also important to think carefully about how systematic and rigorous ecolinguistic enquiry is. Widdowson (2008, p. 173) makes the point:

> It seems reasonable to be critical of ... *discourse analysis,* where it appears not to conform to the conventions of rationality, logical consistency, empirical substantiation, and so on that define authority. It seems to me that the promotion of the critical cause by persuasive appeal at the expense of academic rigour deflects critical attention from the academic shortcomings of CDA ...

There is a danger, however, that an increased focus on rationality, logical consistency and empiricism distracts attention away from the original purpose of critical scholarship. Nichols and Allen-Brown (1996, p. 228) describe how critical theory arose as an attempt to balance rational, scientific approaches with moral perspectives, based on the view that:

> Modern social crises ... are related to the intrusion of overly rational (scientific, analytical, technological), instrumental, means-ends philosophies that detract from reflection on our ultimate ends — ends related to good and bad, right and wrong.

For the most part, critical studies are based on a moral framework of care, compassion and empathy with oppressed people. In a classic paper, van Dijk (1993, p. 252) characterises Critical Discourse Analysts as follows:

> Their hope, if occasionally illusory, is change through critical understanding. Their perspective, if possible, is that of those who suffer most from dominance and inequality. Their critical targets are the power elites that enact, sustain, legitimate, condone or ignore social inequality and injustice. That is, one of the criteria of their work is solidarity with those who need it most. Their problems are real problems, that is, the serious problems that threaten the lives or well-being of many ...

Ecolinguistics similarly works towards wellbeing and social justice for humans, but extends the care to future generations, other species and the physical environment. While it is essential for studies to be valid, systematic and rigorous, this is for the sake of better serving these higher ethical goals rather than being an end in itself.

Ecolinguistic analyses in general are likely to receive criticism from two directions: on one hand for being overly technical, rational and instrumental in ways which fail to encourage care for the victims of ecological destruction. And, on the other hand, for being politically, emotionally and ideologically driven at the expense of objective, empirical enquiry. The two aspects of compassion and rigour should not, however, be seen as mutually exclusive, and ecolinguistic studies will need to combine them to be both academically valid and true to the ethical spirit of the enquiry.

The gathering

This book has focused squarely on a key overarching issue of our time: the survival and wellbeing of humans and other species at a time when the systems that support life are increasingly eroded by human activity. It has explored how linguistics can play a role in addressing this issue. To this end, this book brought together multiple voices from different areas of life into what can be called a 'gathering'.

From one direction come those who can be called 'visionary ecologists' — those who realise that the issues we face bring into question the fundamental stories that we live our lives by. Charles Eisenstein (2013, p. 14), for example, writes:

> We desire to transcend the Story of the World that has come to enslave us, that indeed is killing the planet ... We are like children who have grown out of a story that once enthralled us, aware now that it is only a story ... We need a Story of the People — a real one, that doesn't feel like a fantasy — in which a more beautiful world is once again possible ... We do not have a new story yet. Each of us is aware of some of its threads, for example in most of the things we call alternative, holistic or ecological today. Here and there we see patterns, designs, emerging parts of the fabric. But the new mythos has not yet formed. We will abide for a time in the 'space between stories'. It is a very precious — some may say sacred — time.

These visionary ecologists describe how the current stories we live by are contributing to increasing inequality and environmental destruction, and they call for change.

Coming from a different direction are Critical Discourse Analysts, cognitive scientists, identity theorists and rhetoric scholars who all, in one way or another, show how the specific forms of language that we use reflect the underlying stories we live by. Their research provides practical tools for interrogating language to expose the stories and explain how they work.

From yet another direction come ecological philosophers: ecofeminists, deep ecologists, social ecologists, political ecologists, dark mountaineers, transitioners and cornucopians. Some of these are more welcome at the gathering than others, but all need their perspectives to be considered. Critical reading of the work of philosophers such as these informs the ecosophy that analysts use to judge stories as beneficial, destructive or ambivalent.

Coming from multiple directions are the voices of those who wrote or spoke the texts being analysed: neoclassical economists, industrial agriculturalists, journalists, politicians, environmentalists, nature writers, haiku poets, writers from traditional and indigenous cultures around the world, and many more. Some of these voices could be accused of perpetuating the destructive stories we live by, some praised for helping to bring new stories into being. But they are not heroes or villains; instead, all are potential contributors to the task of re-writing and re-speaking the world.

Finally, there are the ecolinguists who analyse texts, reveal the stories we live by, judge these stories based on their ecosophy, and contribute to the search for new stories to live by.

The constraints of the pages of this book mean that the gathering is small. There are far more visionary ecologists, linguists, ecological philosophers, authors and ecolinguists whose voices need to be heard. In particular, there is the wisdom in traditional and indigenous societies across the world that can be drawn from in the search for new stories to live by. This is possible because ecolinguistics is an intensely international movement, with strong activity across countries in all continents. There are many ecolinguists in Brazil and China in particular who are developing ecolinguistics in important directions.

For many years, scholars in Brazil have been working on Ecosystemic Linguistics, a form of ecolinguistics centred on linguistic ecosystems. Linguistic ecosystems consist of 'a people (P), whose members live in their territory (T) and communicate according to the usual way of communicating in their community (L)' (do Couto 2018, p. 150). The ecosystemic analysis of discourse, as do Couto describes, 'bases itself on the preservation of life on earth and on an avoidance of suffering' (p. 156).

More recently, in China, scholars have developed Harmonious Discourse Analysis (Huang 2018; Huang and Zhao 2019). This approach is unique because it is strongly rooted in traditional Chinese philosophies of harmony, particularly the three Confucian principles of conscience, proximity and regulation (Huang 2017, p. 880). Huang and Zhao (2021, p. 16) describe how in Harmonious Discourse Analysis, 'by examining language-related ecological problems in discourse, we aim to present the various relations of humans with other ecological participants and to promote harmonious relations via language'. The importance of Harmonious Discourse Analysis is that it provides an example of ecolinguistics travelling across the world and being reinvented in line with the culture, philosophy and ecology of the place it has arrived in.

Ultimately, the hope is for ecolinguists across the world to gather together with visionary ecologists, linguistic scientists, ecological philosophers and storytellers of all kinds to contribute to what Thomas Berry called 'The Great Work'. The Great Work is no less than the 'task of moving modern industrial civilisation from its present devastating influence on the Earth to a more benign mode of presence' (p. 7).

补充文献

do Couto, H. 2018. Ecosystemic linguistics. In A. Fill & H. Penz (Eds.), *The Routledge handbook of ecolinguistics*. London: Routledge, 149–162.

Goatly, A. 2001. Green grammar and grammatical metaphor, or language and myth of power, or metaphors we die by. In A. Fill & P. Mühlhäusler (Eds.), *The ecolinguistics reader: Language, ecology, and environment*. London: Continuum, 203–225.

Halliday, M. A. K. 1990. New ways of meaning: The challenge to applied linguistics. *Journal of Applied Linguistics*, (6): 7–16. (Reprinted from *On language and linguistics, Vol. 3 in The collected works of M. A. K. Halliday*, pp. 139–174, by J. Webster, ed., 2003, Continuum)

Huang, G. W. & Zhao, R. H. 2021. Harmonious discourse analysis: Approaching peoples' problems in a Chinese context. *Language Sciences*, 85: 1–18.

Mühlhäusler, P. 2001. Talking about environmental issues. In A. Fill & P. Mühlhäusler (Eds.), *The ecolinguistics reader: Language, ecology, and environment*. London: Continuum, 31–42.

APPENDIX

Sources of data

This appendix proves details of the sources of the data analysed in this book. Throughout this book, data are referred to using tags consisting of two letters and two numbers, e.g. ET5:7. The two letters refer to a type of data, e.g. ET = economic textbooks, MH = *Men's Health* magazine. The two numbers give further information such as a specific book or edition of a magazine, and the page number. The list below is in alphabetical order of the tag.

AG: Agribusiness documents

AG X:Y where X = report number and Y = page number, except AG1 where Y = fact sheet number

AG1   PIH, 2002. *Pork industry handbook CD-ROM edition.* Lafayette: Purdue University Press.

AG2   FAO, 2009. *Agribusiness handbook: Red meat.* Food and Agriculture Organisation of the United States.

AG3   FAO, 2010. *Agribusiness handbook: Poultry, meat and eggs.* Food and Agriculture Organisation of the United States.

AG4   HH, 2014. *Our Welsh wild boar herd.* Harmony Herd.

AG5   BPA, 2014. *The Gloucestershire Old Spots.* British Pig Association.

EA: Ecosystem assessment reports

EA X:Y where X=report and Y=page number

EA1   MEA, 2005. *Ecosystems and human well-being: General synthesis.* Millennium Ecosystem Assessment.

EA2   MEA, 2005. *Ecosystems and human well-being: Biodiversity synthesis.* Millennium Ecosystem Assessment.

EA3   NCA, 2012. *Impacts of climate change on biodiversity, ecosystems and ecosystem services: Technical input to the 2013 National Climate Assessment.* United States Global Change Research Program.

EA4   NEA, 2011. *UK National Ecosystem Assessment: Synthesis of the key findings.* United Kingdom National Ecosystem Assessment.

EA5   TEEB, 2010. *Mainstreaming the economics of nature.* The Economics of Ecosystems and Biodiversity.

EA6   EC, 2013. *Mapping and Assessment of Ecosystems and their Services.* European Commission.

EN: Environmental articles, reports, films and websites

EN X:Y where X=source Y=page number (where available)

EN1   Blight, G. 2012. 50 months to save the world. *The Guardian*, 1 October.

EN2   UN, 2015. *Transforming our world: The 2030 Agenda for Sustainable Development.* United Nations.

EN3   CRed, 2005. *Carbon saving hints and tips.* Low Carbon Innovation Centre.

EN4   Huhne, C. 2013. Typhoon Haiyan must spur us on to slow climate change. *The Guardian.* 17 November.

EN5   Specter, M. 2012. The Climate Fixers. *The New Yorker*, 14 May.

EN6   Greer, J. 2013. *The long descent: A user's guide to the end of the industrial age.* Gabriola Island, BC: New Society Publishers.

EN7   Bates, A. 2006. *The Post Petroleum Survival Guide and Cookbook: Recipes for Changing Times.* Gabriola Island, BC: New Society Publishers.

EN8   Hopkins, R. 2011. *Might peak oil and climate change outlive their usefulness as framings for Transition?* Transition Network.

EN9   Hopkins, R. 2011. Tale of transition in 10 objects. *Permaculture magazine*, 70: 13–16.

EN10   SAS, 2014. *Sustainable guide to surfing.* Surfers Against Sewage.

EN11   FM, 2014. *Biodiversity and Conservation: The Web of Life.* The Field Museum.

EN12   GP, 2014. *End the nuclear age.* Greenpeace.

EN13   IPCC, 2015. *Climate Change 2014 Synthesis Report.* Intergovernmental Panel on Climate Change.

EN14   Vanhinsbergh, D., Fuller, R. & Noble, D. 2003. *A review of possible causes of recent changes in populations of woodland birds in Britain.* British Trust for Ornithology.

EN15   Schneider, N. 2008. Facts, not fiction. *Fraser Forum*, April: 6–8.

EN16   Durkin, M. (director). *The Great Global Warming Swindle.* Original version broadcast on 8 March 2007 on Channel 4, UK.

EN17   Wickens, J. 2008. *Hell for Leather.* The Ecologist.

EN18   WWF, 2014. *How many species are we losing?* WWF.

EN19   PETA, 2014. *Chickens used for food.* People for the Ethical Treatment of Animals.

EN20   Monbiot, G. 2014. Can you put a price on the beauty of the natural world? *The Guardian*, 22 April.

EN21   Solnit R. 2014. Call climate change what it is: Violence. *The Guardian*, 7 April.

EN22   Kyriakides, R. 2008. *Arctic ice cover is reducing, how this will affect the climate and hope for the future.* Robert Kyriakides's Weblog.

EN23   Thunberg, G. 2019. Speech at the World Economic Forum in Davos.

EN24   Thunberg, G. 2019. Speech at UN Climate Change Conference, Madrid.

EN25   Thunberg, G. 2020. TEDx Stockholm speech.

ET: Economics Textbooks

ETX:Y where X=book & Y=page number

ET1   Pindyck, R. & Rubinfeld, D. 2012. *Microeconomics* (8th ed.). London: Pearson.

ET2   Estrin, S., Dietrich, M. & Laidler, D. 2012. *Microeconomics* (6th ed.). London: Pearson.

ET3   Mankiw, G. 2011. *Principles of Microeconomics* (6th ed.). Nashville: South-Western.

ET4   Mankiw, N. 2003. *Macroeconomics* (5th ed.). New York: Worth Publishing.

ET5   Sloman, J. & Jones, E. 2011. *Economics and the Business Environment* (3rd ed.). London: Prentice Hall.

HK: Haiku Anthologies

ML X:Y where X=anthology name Y=page number

HK1   Addiss, S., Yamamoto, F. & Yamamoto, A. 1996. *A haiku garden: The four seasons in poems and prints.* Tokyo: Weatherhill.

HK2   Addiss, S., Yamamoto, F. & Yamamoto, A. 1998. *Haiku people, big and small: In poems and prints.* Tokyo: Weatherhill.

HK3   Yamamoto, A. 2006. *A haiku menagerie: Living creatures in poems and prints.* Tokyo: Weatherhill.

HK4   Addiss, S. & Yamamoto, F. 2002. *Haiku landscapes: In sun, wind, rain, and snow.* Tokyo: Weatherhill.

HK5   Bowers, F. 2012. *The classic tradition of haiku: An anthology.* New York: Dover Publications.

HK6   Lanoue, D. 2014. *Haiku of Kobayashi Issa.*

MH: Men's Health magazine

MHX:Y where X=edition and Y=page no

MH1   MH. 2013. *Men's Health.* UK edition. March.

MH2   MH. 2013. *Men's Health.* UK edition. January/February.

MH3   MH. 2012. *Men's Health.* UK edition. December.

MH4   MH. 2012. *Men's Health.* UK edition. November.

MH5   MH. 2012. *Men's Health.* UK edition. July.

MH6   MH. 2012. *Men's Health.* UK edition. October.

MH7   MH. 2012. *Men's Health.* UK edition. January/February.

MH8   MH. 2014. *Cover Model.* Men's Health Magazine (website).

MH9   Stump. B. 1999. *Men's Health editor recaps annual survey. CNN* edition.

ML: Miscellaneous

ML X:Y where X=source Y=page number (unless otherwise specified)

ML1   Achbar, M. & Abbott, J. (directors). *The Corporation.* Big Media Picture Corporation.

ML2   Bendell, J. 2018. *Deep adaptation: A map for navigating climate tragedy.* IFLAS Occasional Paper.

ML3   A corpus of UK travel advertisements and UK newspaper travel sections.

ML4   BM, 2009. New research suggests drinking as little as one cup of black tea per day may help maintain cardiovascular function and heart health. *BioMedicine.*

ML5   Parasramka, M., Dashwood, W., Wang, R., Abdelli, A., Bailey, G., Williams, D., Ho, E. & Dashwood, R. 2012. MicroRNA profiling of carcinogen-induced rat colon tumours and the influence of dietary spinach. *Molecular nutrition & food research*, 56(8), 1259–1269.

ML6   NIA. 2014. *Talking Nuclear — who said what?* Nuclear Industry Association.

ML7   Pocklington, R. 2020. Hero's calling. *The Sun*, 20 April.

ML8   Brady, T. 2014. Street covered in thousands of bird droppings after flock of starlings swarm area like scene from The Birds. *Daily Mail*, 27 February.

ML9   BBC. 2014. Jaguar posts record sales figures. *BBC Online News,* 12 January.

ML10   BBC. Transcribed extracts from videos of BBC national and local (South West) weather forecasts between 2017 and 2019.

ML11   Finely, R. 2020 quoted in Weston, P., 2020 'This is no damn hobby': The 'gangsta gardener' transforming Los Angeles. *The Guardian*, 28 April.

ML12   BBC. 2013. *What makes us human? BBC*, 4 July.

ML13   A corpus of articles from the *Sun Newspaper.*

ML14   SF. 2014. *Celebrate what's on your plate!* Slow Food UK.

ML15   Schumacher, E. F. 1993. *Small is beautiful: A study of economics as if people mattered.* London: Vintage.

ML16   Orr, D. 2004. *Earth in mind: On education, environment, and the human prospect. 10th anniversary edition.* Washington, DC: Island Press.

ML17   The Heartland Institute.

ML18   Seibt, N. *The truth waits for no-one.* YouTube video.

ML19   Jones, A. (director). 2009. *The Obama Deception.* Alex Jones Productions.

ML20   Seibt, N. *Five grams of corrina.* YouTube video.

ML21   Brummer, A. 2019. Brexit 'will not damage UK's status in the world'. *The Daily Mail*, 26 December.

ML22   Icke, D. David Icke interviewed by Brian Rose on London Real TV on March 18, April 19, and May 3 2020.

ML23   A corpus of advertisements from newspapers from the *Sun on Sunday* and the *Daily Star on Sunday.*

ML24   A corpus of articles from *Ethical Consumer Magazine.*

ML25   Imbuldeniya, S. (director). *You clap for me now.*

ML26   Seibt, N. *Introduction.* Heartland Institute.

ML27   A corpus of UK news articles appearing on 21 January 2014 in response to the IMF raising the UK economic growth forecast.

NE: New economics books and reports

NEX:Y where X=book or report and Y=page number

NE1   Jackson, T. 2011. *Prosperity without Growth.* London: Routledge.

NE2   Raworth, K. 2018. *Doughnut economics: Seven ways to think like a 21st-century economist.* London: Random House.

NE3   Shah, H. 2005. *Wellbeing and the environment.* New Economics Forum.

NE4   CBS, 2012. *A short guide to gross national happiness.* Centre for Bhutan Studies.

NE5   Eisenstein, C. 2011. *Sacred Economics.* Berkeley: Evolver Editions.

NE6   de Graaf, J., Wann, D. & Naylor, T. 2005. *Affluenza: The all-consuming epidemic.* San Francisco: Berrett-Koehler.

NE7   Daly, H. & Farley, J. 2004. *Ecological economics: Principles and applications.* Washington, DC: Island Press.

NE8   Kennedy, R. 1968. *Remarks of Robert F. Kennedy at the University of Kansas March 18, 1968.* John F. Kennedy Presidential Library & Museum.

NR: Narrative texts

NWX:Y where X = book or webpage and Y = page number if available

NR1   Kire, E. 2016. *Son of the thundercloud.* Delhi: Speaking Tiger.

NR2   Jacobs, J. 2003. *English fairy tales.* Boston: Adamant Media Corporation.

NR4   Lang, A. 1948. *Red fairy book.* Longmans, Green.

NR5   Zlotkowski, E. 2016. *What Jill did while Jack climbed the beanstalk.* Boston: E. Zlotkowski.

NR6   Solnit, R. 2020. *Cinderella liberator: A fairy tale revolution.* New York: Random House.

NR7   Simms, A. ed., 2016. *There was a knock at the door: 23 modern folk tales for troubling times.* New Weather Institute.

NR8   'Salmon Boy', narrative in Mueller (2017), p. 185–186.

NR9   'Being Salmon', narrative in Mueller (2017), p. 133–136.

NR10   'The Passenger Pigeon', transcript of an oral story in Nanson (2001), p. 114–116.

NR11　Vijayakumar, S. & Seetal, R. 2020. *We must move from egocentric to ecocentric leadership to safeguard our planet.* World Economic Forum.

NR12　Briggs, R. and 2013, 2020. Big bang to civilization: Ten amazing origin events. *Livescience website.*

NR13　Kennard, D. & P. Northcutt (directors). 2011. *Journey of the Universe.* New York: Shelter Island.

NR14　*Deep time walk: A new story of the living earth* [mobile app]. Transcript published in book form as Harding, S. & P. Oswald. 2017. *Deep time walk: The fool and the scientist.* Deep Time Walk CIC.

NR15　Gersie, A. 1992. *Earth-tales: Storytelling in times of change.* London: Green Print.

NR16　Standing Bear, L. 2006 (originally published in 1933), *Land of the Spotted Eagle.* Lincoln: Bison Books.

NW: New Nature Writing

NWX:Y where X = book Y = page number

NW1　Crumley, J. 2007. *Brother nature.* Dunbeath: Whittles Publishing.

NW2　Fiennes, W. 2003. *The snow geese.* London: Picador.

NW3　Jamie, K. 2005. *Findings.* London: Sort of Books.

NW4　Laing, O. 2011. *To the river: A journey beneath the surface.* Edinburgh: Canongate Books.

NW5　Mabey, R. 2006. *Nature cure.* London: Pimlico.

NW6　Macfarlane, R. 2009. *The wild places.* London: Granta Books.

NW7　Woolfson, E. 2013. *Field notes from a hidden city: An urban nature diary.* London: Granta Books.

NW8　Yates, C. 2012. *Nightwalk: A journey to the heart of nature.* London: William Collins.

PD: Political documents

PDX:Y where X=document number and Y=page no. where relevant

PD1　Truman, H. 1949. *Inaugural Address.* The American Presidency Project.

PD2　WCED. 1990. *Our common future.* Oxford University Press.

PD3

PD4　UK Govt. 2011. *Mainstreaming sustainable development.* UK Government.

PD5　Everett, T., Ishwaran, M., Paolo, G. & Rubin, A. 2010. *Economic growth and the environment.* DEFRA.

PD6　BIS. 2012. *Benchmarking UK competitiveness in the global economy.* Department for Business, Innovation and Skills. Economics Paper no. 19.

PD7　UK Govt. 2014. *Red Tape Challenge.* United Kingdom Government.

PD8　Gilchrist, K. 2019. *Response to climate change is the true test for global leaders.* CNBC.

PD9   US Govt. 2006. *United States Code 2006 by Congress and House Office of the Law Revision.* US Government.

PD10   Johnson, B. 2020. Quotes in article: There is such a thing as society, says Boris Johnson from bunker. *The Guardian*, March 29.

PD11   EA. 2014. *New Nuclear Power Stations.* Environment Agency.

PD12   GPY. 2014. *Energy.* The Green Party.

PD13   BNP. 2016. *Immigration Crisis Leaflet.* The British Nationalist Party.

PD14   BNP. 2018. *Labour reveal plan to open immigration floodgates to Britain* by Henry Watts, February 22. The British Nationalist Party.

PD15   BNP. 2019. *BNP Chairman Adam Walker responds to the New Zealand terror attack,* March 15. The British Nationalist Party.

PD16   BNP. 2020. *What is Real Nationalism,* by James Caterill, March 14. The British Nationalist Party.

PD17   Lucas, C. 2020. Social media speeches by Caroline Lucas.

PD18   Johnson, B. 2013. The 2013 Margaret Thatcher Lecture. *Centre for Policy Studies.*

PD19   BNP. 2016. Greater London Authority Manifesto.

GLOSSARY

This glossary gives brief descriptions of the linguistics terms used in the book. In linguistics, terms are often used in a variety of different ways by different authors, so what is presented here is a description of the specific way in which this book uses the terms. The descriptions are intended to be concise and indicative rather than comprehensive.

Activation（主动化）：　Participants are activated when they are represented as doing, thinking, feeling and saying things, rather than having things done to them; useful in investigating which participants are foregrounded in a text.

Actor（动作者）：　A participant in a clause who is *doing* something active; useful in analysing which participants are represented as actively involved in living their own lives for their own purposes.

Affect（情感）：　In appraisal patterns, expressions of affect represent participants as feeling a certain way towards something (e.g. delighted by X or devastated by X).

Affected（受影响的）：　A participant in a clause who is having something done to them; useful in analysing which participants are represented as powerless.

Ambivalent story（中性故事）：　A story which only partially accords with the ecosophy of the analyst (e.g. it is seen as having mixed benefits and drawbacks in encouraging people to protect the ecosystems that life depends on).

Antonymy（反义关系）：　A semantic relationship where two expressions have opposite meanings or are represented *as if* they have opposite meanings; useful in seeing how a text sets up relationships of difference.

Apposition（同位语）：　The equating of two concepts by placing them immediately after each other in a sentence, usually separated by commas (e.g. 'Rachel Carson, the founder of the environmental movement, wrote ...').

Appraisal pattern（评价模式）： A cluster of linguistic features which come together to represent an area of life as good or bad.

Appraising item（评价项）： A word or expression which is used to shed a positive or negative light on someone or something (e.g. in *He welcomed the good news,* both 'welcomed' and 'good' are appraisal items which give positivity to 'the news').

Attitudinal terms（态度术语）： Terms such as *best* or *excellent* which represent a positive attitude towards what they describe in all contexts.

Beneficial story（有益性故事）： A story which accords with the ecosophy of the analyst (e.g. it is seen as encouraging people to protect the ecosystems that life depends on).

Camera angle（摄影角度）： A high camera angle in a photograph is one where the camera is high up, looking down on the subject, whereas a low angle looks up at the subject. The camera angle can represent the subject as powerful (low angle) or powerless (high angle).

Collocation（搭配）： When words frequently appear in proximity to each other in texts (e.g. the words *alleviate* and *poverty*).

Conceptual blend（概念混合）： A new concept created through the combination of two or more other concepts during thought processes.

Connotation（内涵）： The associations that a word brings to mind in addition to its direct meaning (e.g. champagne connotes luxury).

Conviction（信念）： A story in people's minds about whether a particular description is true, uncertain or false.

Critical discourse analysis（批评话语分析）： A form of linguistics which brings together social theory and detailed linguistic analysis to investigate how language structures society, often with a focus on relationships of power and oppression.

Cultural evaluations（文化评估）： Evaluations that are widespread across the minds of multiple individuals in a culture.

Demand picture（需求图像）： A visual image where a participant is looking out at the viewer, as if demanding a relationship with them.

Destructive story（破坏性故事）： A story which opposes or contradicts the ecosophy of the analyst (e.g. it is seen as encouraging people to destroy the ecosystems that life depends on).

Discourse（话语）： The characteristic way that a particular group in society uses language, images, and other forms of representation (e.g. the discourse of neoclassical economists, environmentalists, or New Nature writers).

Ecolinguistics（生态语言学）： The study of the role of language in the life-sustaining interactions of humans, other species and the physical environment.

Ecosophy（生态哲学观）： An ecological philosophy, i.e. a set of values concerning the ideal relationship of humans with each other, other species and the physical environment. Analysts use their own ecosophy to judge stories as beneficial, ambivalent or destructive.

End-focus（末尾焦点）： The extra importance given to an item through its location at the end of a clause or narrative.

Entailment（蕴涵）： A statement X entails another statement Y if Y is necessarily true when X is true (e.g. *The corporation committed a crime* entails that *The corporation acted illegally*).

Erasure pattern（删略模式）： A linguistic representation of an area of life as irrelevant, marginal or unimportant through its systematic absence or distortion in text.

Erasure（删略）： A story in people's minds that an area of life is unimportant or unworthy of attention.

Evaluations（评估）： Stories in people's minds about whether an area of life is good or bad.

Extrinsic value（外在价值观）： Where value is placed on goals such as profit, status, fame, winning competitions or other self-serving goals which, *in themselves*, make no contribution to the common good.

Facticity pattern（真实性模式）： A cluster of linguistic devices which come together to represent a description of the world as true, uncertain or false.

Facticity（真实性）： The degree to which a description is presented as a certain and established truth (e.g. through the use of high modality, calls to authority, or the repertoire of empiricism).

Frame chaining（框架链）： A process where a frame is repeatedly modified over time, resulting in a frame that is very different from the original.

Frame modification（框架修改）： The modification of an existing frame to create a new frame that carries some of the structure and characteristics of the old one but also some differences.

Frame（框架）：　A packet of knowledge about an area of life. Frames are brought to mind through trigger words (e.g. 'steering wheel' will bring to mind the frame of a car).

Framing（构架）：　A story which uses a package of knowledge about one area of life (a frame) to structure how another area of life is conceptualised (e.g. CLIMATE CHANGE IS A PROBLEM).

Given/new（已知信息/新信息）：　An information structure where certain information is presented as if already known to the reader, while other information is presented as conveying something previously unknown. In English, 'given' information is typically presented first in a sentence followed by 'new' information, and visually, given information is presented on the left, with new information on the right.

Head（中心词）：　The main word in a phrase, for example the noun in a noun phrase or the adjective in an adjectival phrase.

Hegemony（霸权地位）：　The exercising of power through acquiescence (e.g. by convincing people that a harmful ideology is 'just the way things are' rather than one viewpoint among other possible viewpoints).

Homogenisation（同质化）：　The representation of individual entities as indistinguishable parts of a larger group, crowd or mass.

Hyponymy（上下义关系）：　A semantic relationship where several words are represented as equivalent by virtue of all being examples of the same thing (e.g. in the expression *commodities such as fish, grains and timber* the hyponyms *fish*, *grains* and *timber* are represented as being equivalent in as much as all are *commodities*).

Identity（身份）：　A story in people's minds about what it means to be a particular kind of person, including appearance, character, behaviour and values.

Ideology（意识形态）：　A belief system about how the world was, is, will be or should be, which is shared by members of a group.

Impersonalisation（非人格化）：　The act of representing a social actor as a replaceable member of a category rather than a unique individual.

Individualisation（个体化）：　The representation of an entity as a single, unique individual.

Ingroup and outgroup（内群和外群）：　An 'ingroup' is a group that an individual identifies as being a member of, while an outgroup is one they do not identify as belonging to.

Intertextuality（互文性）: When texts draw from previous texts, either borrowing extracts directly or using similar phrasing and patterns of language use.

Intrinsic values（内在价值观）: Where value is placed on goals such as alleviating poverty, contributing to the wellbeing of others, protecting the environment, or other altruistic goals which, *in themselves,* contribute to the common good.

Kernel elements（内核元素）: Elements which cannot be left out of a narrative without altering its basic structure.

Language system（语言系统）: The linguistic units available as part of a language and the rules for how they can be combined together to form meaningful utterances.

Lexical set（词汇集）: A set of words which are all drawn from the same semantic domain (e.g. *cook, boil, ingredients* and *recipe* are all part of a lexical set of cooking).

Lexicalisation（词汇化）: The way that a particular concept is put into words (e.g. in English certain kinds of meat are lexicalised differently from the corresponding animal as in cow/beef, pig/pork).

Liminal state（阈限状态）: In identity theory, a person is in a liminal state when they feel the identity they once had no longer applies to them but have not yet found a new identity to replace it.

Marked（有标记）: In contrasting pairs like happy/unhappy or honest/dishonest the marked term is the one with the prefix (e.g. un- or dis-). In general, marked terms tend to have a more negative meaning than unmarked ones.

Mask（伪装）: A form of erasure where an entity has been omitted from a text or discourse and replaced by a distorted version of itself.

Material process（物质过程）: An active process of doing something.

Mental process（心理过程）: A process of thinking, feeling or sensing.

Metaphor（隐喻）: The use of a frame from a specific, concrete and imaginable area of life to structure how a clearly distinct area of life is conceptualised (e.g. CLIMATE CHANGE IS A ROLLERCOASTER).

Metaphorical entailment（隐喻蕴涵）: A statement about the target domain that arises from knowledge of the source domain. X metaphorically entails Y if, when a particular metaphor is applied, Y is necessarily true when X is true (e.g. if a

CORPORATIONS ARE PEOPLE metaphor is applied then 'people have rights' in the source frame metaphorically entails that 'corporations have rights' in the target domain).

Metaphorical reasoning（隐喻推理）： The use of knowledge from the source frame in reasoning about the target domain (e.g. in the source frame of 'machines', there is the knowledge that *machines have no feelings*. If this is carried over to the target domain of 'pigs' by a PIGS ARE MACHINES metaphor, then it can lead to the metaphorical entailment *pigs have no feelings*).

Metonymy（转喻）： Calling something not by its own name but by something associated with it (e.g. cooking method for type of chicken in *broiler* or *roaster*).

Modality（情态）： The level of certainty expressed by the speaker about the truth of a statement, typically through the use of modal auxiliaries (*can, could, may, might, must, ought, shall, should, will,* or *would*) or adverbs (*probably, arguably*).

Mode（模式）： A medium of expression such as language, visual images, music or film.

Modifier（修饰语）： An optional element in a phrase which influences the meaning of the head of the phrase (e.g. in *biotic component*, the word 'biotic' is the modifier and adds further information about 'component', which is the head).

Morphology（形态）： The units of meaning available in a language and the rules that govern how they combine together to form words.

Narrative（叙事）： This term is used for both a narrative structure or a narrative text (see below)

Narrative entailments（叙事蕴涵）： Messages or morals which can be drawn out of a narrative and applied to real life. Texts can explicitly encourage the reader to draw entailments (e.g. 'The moral of this story is ...'), can subtly hint at entailments, or the reader can selectively draw them out for themselves.

Narrative structure（叙事结构）： A story in people's minds which involves a sequence of logically connected events. The term 'sequence' implies that the events have a temporal connection, and 'event' implies a location and characters who act or have experiences.

Narrative text（叙事文本）： A specific oral telling, written work or other expressive form, which recounts a series of temporally and logically connected events. Narrative texts are the linguistic manifestations of underlying narrative structures.

Nominalisation（名词化）： A noun phrase which can be thought of as derived from an underlying process (e.g. *destruction* derives from *X destroys Y*); useful in investigating erasure since both X and Y can be omitted in the nominalised form.

Participants（参与者）： The living beings, physical objects or abstract entities that appear in a clause or image.

Passivation（被动化）： Participants are passivated when they are represented as having something done to them rather than actively doing or thinking things; useful in investigating which participants are backgrounded in a text.

Passive voice（被动语态）： A grammatical form such as 'Y is destroyed by X' as opposed to the active voice 'X destroys Y'; useful in investigating the erasure of participants since the passive voice allows the participant X to be omitted.

Personalisation（个体化）： When a social actor is represented as a unique individual through being named or vividly described; useful for investigating salience.

Phenomenon（现象）： The participant that is seen, heard, felt or otherwise perceived as part of a mental process (e.g. in *I saw the owl,* 'the owl' is the Phenomenon).

Phonology（音韵）： The units of sound that are available in a language and the rules that govern how they come together in speech.

Photo-realism（照相写实主义）： A photo-realistic image is one which looks as it normally would if an observer was viewing the phenomenon in real life. Images with low photo-realism may encourage the viewer to search for a symbolic meaning behind the image.

Positive discourse analysis（积极话语分析）： Analysis aimed at finding inspirational forms of language which can convey beneficial new stories to live by.

Presupposition（预设）： The representation of a proposition as an obvious, taken-for-granted, background fact about the world.

Process（过程）： A part of a clause which represents the activities or relationships that participants are involved in, such as *being, doing, having, sensing, behaving* or *saying*. Usually, the process corresponds to the verb (e.g. in 'X destroys Y', the process is *destroying*), but see also nominalisation.

Prosody（韵律）： Semantic prosody is the positivity or negativity that words take on due to other words they are typically used with (e.g. *commit* has negative prosody because it tends to be collated with *crime* or *murder*).

Quoting verbs（引用动词）： Verbs used to introduce direct or indirect quotes, which can also convey the writer's attitude to the quotes (e.g. *said, confessed, admitted, boasted*).

Re-framing（重构）：The act of framing a concept in a way that is different from its typical framing in a culture.

Re-minding（提醒）：Explicitly calling attention to the erasure of an important area of life in a particular text or discourse, and demanding that it be brought back into consideration.

Repertoire of empiricism（实证方式）：Ways of writing which increase facticity by representing conclusions as being derived directly and impartially from data (e.g. 'Measurements indicate that ...').

Salience（凸显）：A story in people's minds that an area of life is important or worthy of attention.

Salience pattern（凸显模式）：A linguistic or visual representation of an area of life as worthy of attention through concrete, specific and vivid depictions.

Satellite elements（卫星元素）：Elements of a narrative text which can be altered or removed without affecting the basic structure of the narrative.

Sayer（说话者）：The participant who is speaking or sending out a message as part of a verbal process (e.g. in *She called out,* 'she' is the Sayer).

Self-identity（自我身份）：An evolving story people tell themselves and others about what kind of person they are.

Senser（感知者）：A participant in a clause who is thinking, feeling or sensing something; useful in analysing which participants are represented as beings with mental lives.

Shot size（景别）：In visual images, shot size is the size of a subject compared to the size of the frame. Close-up shots, where the subject is large, can indicate close relationships between the viewer and the subject, while long shots can indicate both physical and emotional distance.

Social cognition（社会认知）：Shared values, belief systems or stories in the minds of multiple individuals across a society.

Source domain（源域）：The general area from which a source frame is drawn (e.g. the source frames of 'robot' and 'calculator' both belong to the source domain of 'machines'); useful in searching for more general patterns that underlie a range of metaphors or framings.

Source frame（源框架）： The area of life which is being drawn from to provide words and structures in a metaphor or framing (e.g. in CLIMATE CHANGE IS A TIME BOMB the source frame is 'a time bomb').

Stake（利害关系）： When a participant has an interest in a particular outcome occurring (e.g. the fossil fuel industry has an interest in climate change legislation being weakened).

Story（故事）： A cognitive structure in the minds of individuals which influences how they think, talk and act. Types of story include ideologies, metaphors, framings, identities, evaluations, convictions, erasure, salience and narrative.

Story we live by（我们信奉和践行的故事）： A story in the minds of multiple individuals across a culture.

Subject position（主体地位）： A role in society, usually with a label attached (e.g. mother, manager, doctor, patient) and a set of social expectations for how a person in that role should speak, dress and behave.

Suppression（压制）： The omission or backgrounding of a particular participant in a clause (e.g. the clause *The chickens were slaughtered* suppresses the actor who carries out the killing).

Synonymy（同义关系）： A semantic relationship where two expressions have very similar meanings, or are used in a text *as if* their meanings were very similar; useful in seeing how a text sets up relationships of equivalence.

Target domain（目标域）： The area of life that is being structured in a framing or metaphor (e.g. in CLIMATE CHANGE IS A TIMEBOMB the target domain is 'climate change'). The target domain is what is being described using terms drawn from the source frame.

Theme（主位）： In functional grammar terms, the *theme* is the entity that is first mentioned in a clause and is seen as the 'point of departure', i.e., the main thing that the clause is about. The rest of clause is the *rheme*, which provides more information about the theme.

Trace（留痕）： A form of erasure where an entity is represented in a text or discourse but is obscured or backgrounded.

Transitivity（及物性）： The arrangement of participants and processes in a clause.

Unmarked（无标记）： In contrasting pairs like happy/unhappy or honest/dishonest the unmarked term is the one without the prefix. In pairs such as high/low where there is no prefix, the unmarked term is the one used in a neutral question (e.g. 'how *high* is the tower?'). In general, unmarked terms tend to have a more positive meaning than marked ones.

Vector（矢量）： In visual analysis, a vector is an arrow or line within an image which implies action or changes from one state to another. Where eyes are depicted, an 'eyeline vector' follows the line of gaze.

Verbal process（言语过程）： A process which involves speaking, writing or communicating.

Vitality（活跃度）： The degree to which a metaphor has the potential to bring vivid and concrete images of the source frame into the mind of a hearer; useful for establishing how influential a metaphor is likely to be.

Void（空白）： A form of erasure where an entity is entirely absent from a text or discourse.

REFERENCES

Abbott, H. P. 2008. *The Cambridge introduction to narrative*. Cambridge: Cambridge University Press.

Abbott, T. 2017. Daring to doubt. *Global Warming Policy Foundation*.

Abram, D. 1996. *The spell of the sensuous: Perception and language in a more-than-human world*. New York: Pantheon.

Abram, D. 2010. *Becoming animal: An earthly cosmology*. New York: Pantheon.

Adams, C. 2010. *The sexual politics of meat: A feminist-vegetarian critical theory*. 20th Anniversary edn. New York: Continuum.

Adams, C. & Gruen, L. 2014. *Ecofeminism: Feminist intersections with other animals and the earth*. London: Bloomsbury.

Alcott, B. 2005. Jevons' paradox. *Ecological Economics, 54* (1), 9–21.

Alexander, R. 2008. How the anti-green movement and its "friends" use language to construct the world. In M. Döing, H. Penz & W. Trampe (Eds.), *Language, signs, and nature: Ecolinguistic dimensions of environmental discourse*. Tübingen: Stauffenburg, 127–142.

Alexander, R. 2009. *Framing discourse on the environment: A critical discourse approach*. New York: Routledge.

Alexander, R. 2018. Investigating texts about environmental degradation using critical discourse analysis and corpus linguistic techniques. In A. Fill & H. Penz (Eds.), *The Routledge handbook of ecolinguistics*. London: Routledge, 196–210.

Appleby, M. 2008. Eating our future: The environmental impact of industrial animal agriculture. *World Society for the Protection of Animals*.

Armon, J. (Ed.). 2019. *Prioritizing sustainability education*. New York: Routledge.

Baker, P. & Ellece, S. 2011. *Key terms in discourse analysis*. New York: Continuum.

Baker, S. 2006. *Sustainable development*. London: Routledge.

Bal, M. 2017. *Narratology: Introduction to the theory of narrative*. Toronto: University of Toronto Press.

Barnet, B. 2003. The erasure of technology in cultural critique. *Fibreculture Journal*, 1.

Barrows, A. 1995. The ecopsychology of child development. In T. Roszak, M. Gomes & A. Kanner, (Eds.), *Ecopsychology: Restoring the earth, healing the mind*. San Francisco: Sierra Club Books, 101–110.

Barthel, D. 1992. When men put on appearances: Advertising and the social construction of masculinity. In S. Craig (Ed.), *Men, masculinity, and the media*. London: Sage.

Bartlett, T. 2012. *Hybrid voices and collaborative change: Contextualising positive discourse analysis*. London: Routledge.

Bartlett, T. 2018. Positive discourse analysis. In J. Flowerdew & J. E. Richardson (Eds.), *The Routledge handbook of critical discourse studies*. London: Routledge, 133–147.

Bate, J. 2000. *The song of the earth*. Cambridge: Harvard University Press.

Baudrillard, J. 1994. *Simulacra and simulation*. Ann Arbor: University of Michigan Press.

Bendell, J. 2018. Deep adaptation: A map for navigating climate tragedy. *IFLAS Occasional Paper*.

Benton-Short, L. 1999. *Environmental discourse and practice*. Oxford: Blackwell.

Benwell, B. & Stokoe, E. 2006. *Discourse and identity*. Edinburgh: Edinburgh University Press.

Berardi, F. 2012. *The uprising: On poetry and finance*. Los Angeles: Semiotext(e).

Berger, J. 2009. *Why look at animals?* London: Penguin.

Berkeley. 2020. Trends in evolution. *Understanding Evolution*.

Berman, T. 2001. The rape of mother nature: Women in the language of environmental discourse. In A. Fill & P. Mühlhäsler (Eds.), *The ecolinguistics reader: Language, ecology, and environment*. London: Continuum, 258–269.

Berry, T. 1988. *The dream of the earth*. San Francisco: Sierra Club Books.

Blackmore, E. & Holmes, T. (Eds.). 2013. *Common cause for nature: Values and frames in conservation*. Machynlleth: Public Interest Research Centre.

Bloom, H. & Hobby, B. 2009. *The hero's journey*. New York: Infobase Publishing.

Bloor, M. & Bloor, T. 2007. *The practice of critical discourse analysis: An introduction*. London: Routledge.

Bookchin, M. 1988. The population myth. *Green Perspectives*, 8.

Bookchin, M. 2005. *The ecology of freedom: The emergence and dissolution of hierarchy*. Oakland: AK Press.

Born, P. 2019. A future that is big enough for all of us: Animals in sustainability education. In J. Armon (Ed.), *Prioritizing sustainability education*. New York: Routledge, 187–201.

Boulding, K. 1966. The economics of the coming spaceship earth. In H. Jarrett (Ed.), *Environmental quality in a growing economy*. Baltimore: Johns Hopkins University Press, 3–14.

Breeze, R. 2013. Critical discourse analysis and its critics. *Pragmatics*, 21 (4), 493–525.

Brewer, J. & Lakoff, G. 2008. Comparing climate proposals: A case study in cognitive policy. *The Rockridge Institute*.

Bringhurst, R. 2008. *The tree of meaning: Language, mind, and ecology*. Berkeley: Counterpoint.

Brulle, R. 2014. Institutionalizing delay: Foundation funding and the creation of U.S. climate change counter-movement organizations. *Climatic Change, 122* (4): 681–694.

Bunting, M. 2007. We need an attentiveness to nature to understand our own humanity. *The Guardian*, 30 Jul.

Bursztyn, L., Rao, A., Roth, C. & Yanagizawa-Drott, D. 2020. *Misinformation during a pandemice*. BFI Working Paper 2020–44, University of Chicago.

Cachelin, A., Norvell, R. & Darling, A. 2010. Language fouls in teaching ecology: Why traditional metaphors undermine conservation literacy. *Conservation Biology, 24* (3): 669–674.

Camosy, C. 2017. Why all Christians should go vegan. *Washington Post*.

Carson, R. 2000. *Silent spring*. London: Penguin.

Charlton, E. 2019. New Zealand has unveiled its first "wellbeing" budget. *World Economic Forum*.

Chawla, S. 2001. Linguistic and philosophical roots of our environmental crisis. In A. Fill & P. Mühlhäsler (Eds.), *The ecolinguistics reader: Language, ecology, and environment*. London: Continuum, 109–114.

Chilton, P. 2004. *Analysing political discourse: Theory and practice*. London: Routledge.

Chilton, P. & Schäfner, C., 2011. Discourse and politics. In T. van Dijk (Ed.), *Discourse studies: A multidisciplinary introduction*. London: Sage, 303–330.

Chilton, P. Crompton, T., Kasser, T., Maio, G. & Nolan, A., 2012. *Communicating bigger-than-self problems to extrinsically-oriented audiences*. Woking: WWF UK.

Chomsky, N. 2006. *Language and mind*. Cambridge: Cambridge University Press.

Chouliaraki, L. & Fairclough, N., 1999. *Discourse in late modernity: Rethinking critical discourse analysis*. Edinburgh: Edinburgh University Press.

Cian, L. 2017. Verticality and conceptual metaphors: A systematic review. *Journal of the Association for Consumer Research, 2* (4): 444–459.

Cohan, S. & Shires, L. 1988. *Telling stories: A theoretical analysis of narrative fiction*. New York: Routledge.

Connell, R. 1996. Teaching the boys: New research on masculinity, and gender strategies for schools. *Teachers College Record, 98* (2): 206–235.

Connell, R. 2005. *Masculinities* (2nd ed.). Berkeley: University of California Press.

Cook, G. 2004. *Genetically modified language: The discourse of arguments for GM crops and food*. London: Routledge.

Cook, G. & Sealey, A. 2018. The discursive representation of animals. In A. Fill & H. Penz (Eds.), *The routledge handbook of ecolinguistics*. London: Routledge, 311–325.

Costanza, R., Kubiszewski, I., Giovannini, E., Lovins, H., McGlade, J., Pickett, K., Ragnarsdóttir, K.V., Roberts, D., De Vogli, R. & Wilkinson, R. 2014. Development: Time to leave GDP behind. *Nature, 505* (7483): 283–285.

Courtenay, W. 2002. Behavioural factors associated with disease, injury, and death among men: Evidence and implications for prevention. *International Journal of Men's Health, 1* (3): 281–342.

Cowley, J. (Ed.). 2008. *Granta 102: The new nature writing*. London: Granta Publications.

Cox, J. 2012. *Environmental communication and the public sphere* (3rd ed.). London: Sage.

Crompton, T. 2010. *Common cause: The case for working with our cultural values*.

Crompton, T. & Kasser, T. 2009. *Meeting environmental challenges: The role of human identity*. Godalming: WWF-UK.

Croney, C. & Reynnells, R. 2008. The ethics of semantics: Do we clarify or obfuscate reality to influence perceptions of farm animal production? *Poultry Science, 87* (2): 387–391.

Crowley, K. & Pennington, J. 2010. Feminist frauds on the fairies? Didacticism and liberation in recent retellings of "Cinderella". *Marvels & Tales, 24* (2): 297–369.

Crown, S. 2012. Kathleen Jamie: A life in writing. *The Guardian*, 6 Apr.

da Silva, S. & Tehrani, J. 2016. Comparative phylogenetic analyses uncover the ancient roots of Indo-European folktales. *Royal Society Open Science, 3* (1): 150645.

Dahlstrom, M. F. 2014. Using narratives and storytelling to communicate science with nonexpert audiences. *Proceedings of the National Academy of Sciences, 111* (Supplement 4): 13614–13620.

Daly, H. & Cobb, J. 1994. *For the common good: Redirecting the economy toward community, the environment, and a sustainable future* (2nd ed.). Boston: Beacon Press.

Darier, E. (Ed.). 1999. *Discourses of the environment*. Oxford: Blackwell.

Darnton, A. & Kirk, M. 2011. Finding frames: New ways to engage the UK public in global poverty. *Bond*.

Das, S. 2019. Language ecology in the mythic narrative of Esterine Kire's *Son of the Thundercloud*. In K. Maiti and S. Chakraborty (Eds.), *Global perspectives on eco-aesthetics and eco-ethics: A green critique*. London: Rowman & Littlefield, 137–144.

Deane-Drummond, C. 2008. *Eco-theology*. London: Darton, Longman and Todd.

DeSmog 2020. *COVIDeniers: Anti-science coronavirus denial overlaps with climate denial*. Desmog UK.

Dewi, N. & Perangin-Angin, D. 2020. Of landscapes and animals: an ecosophical analysis of Pagu folktales. *Jurnal Arbitrer, 7* (1): 10.

Díaz, S. *et al.* 2019. Pervasive human-driven decline of life on Earth points to the need for transformative change. *Science, 366* (6471).

do Couto, H. 2018. Ecosystemic linguistics. In A. Fill & H. Penz (Eds.), *The Routledge handbook of ecolinguistics*. London: Routledge, 149–162.

Drengson, A. & Inoue, Y. (Eds.). 1995. *The deep ecology movement: An introductory anthology*. Berkeley: North Atlantic Books.

Durham, D. & Merskin, D. 2009. Animals, agency and absence: A discourse analysis of institutional animal care and use committee meetings. In S. McFarland & R. Hediger (Eds.), *Animals and agency: An interdisciplinary exploration.* Leiden: Brill.

Eick, G. 2013. Dakota/Lakota progressive writers: Charles Eastman, Standing Bear, and Zitkala Sa. In Pro*ceedings of the 10th Native American Symposium.* Durant: Southeastern Oklahoma State University.

Eisenstein, C. 2011. *Sacred economics: Money, gift, and society in the age of transition.* Berkeley: Evolver Editions.

Eisenstein, C. 2013. *The more beautiful world our hearts know is possible.* Berkeley: North Atlantic Books.

Ekins, P., Hillman, M. & Hutchison, R. 1992. *Wealth beyond measure: An atlas of new economics.* London: Gaia Books.

Everett, J. & Neu, D. 2000. Ecological modernization and the limits of environmental accounting? *Accounting Forum,* 24 (1), 5–29.

Fairclough, N. 1992a. *Discourse and social change.* Cambridge: Polity Press.

Fairclough, N. 1992b. *Critical language awareness.* London: Longman.

Fairclough, N. 2003. *Analysing discourse: Textual analysis for social research.* London: Routledge.

Fairclough, N. 2014. *Language and power* (3rd ed.). London: Routledge.

Fairclough, N. & Fairclough, I. 2012. *Political discourse analysis.* New York: Routledge.

Fauconnier, G. & Turner, M. 2003. *The way we think: Conceptual blending and the mind's hidden complexities.* New York: Basic Books.

Ferber, A. 2007. Whiteness studies and the erasure of gender. *Sociology Compass, 1* (1): 265–282.

Fiddes, N. 1991. *Meat, a natural symbol.* London: Routledge.

Fill, A. & Mühlhäsler, P. 2001. *The ecolinguistics reader: Language, ecology, and environment.* London: Continuum.

Fillmore, C. & Baker, C. 2010. A frames approach to semantic analysis. In B. Heine & H. Narrog (Eds.), *The Oxford handbook of linguistic analysis.* Oxford: Oxford University Press, 313–340.

Finke, P. 2018. Transdisciplinary ecolinguistics. In A. Fill & H. Penz (Eds.), *The Routledge handbook of ecolinguistics.* London: Routledge, 406–419.

Fisher, A. 2013. *Radical ecopsychology: Psychology in the service of life* (2nd ed.). Albany: State University of New York Press.

Fisher, D. & Freudenburg, W. 2001. Ecological modernization and its critics: Assessing the past and looking toward the future. *Society & Natural Resources, 14* (8): 701–709.

Foltz, B. 2013. *The noetics of nature: Environmental philosophy and the holy beauty of the visible.* Oxford: Oxford University Press.

Forceville, C. 2016. Pictorial and multimodal metaphor. In N.-M. Klug & H. Stökl (Eds.), *Handbuch Sprache im multimodalen Kontext.* Berlin: De Gruyter.

Forencich, F. 1992. Homo carcinomicus: A look at planetary oncology. *Trumpeter, 9* (4): 142–145.

Foucault, M. 2013. *Archaeology of knowledge.* London: Taylor & Francis.

Foust, C. & O' Shannon Murphy, W. 2009. Revealing and reframing apocalyptic tragedy in global warming discourse. *Environmental Communication: A Journal of Nature and Culture, 3* (2): 151–167.

Frohmann, B. 1992. The power of images: A discourse analysis of the cognitive viewpoint. *Journal of Documentation, 48* (4): 365–386.

Furtwangler, A. 1997. *Answering chief Seattle*. Seattle: University of Washington Press.

Gare, A. 1996. *Nihilism inc.: Environmental destruction and the metaphysics of sustainability*. Como, NSW: Eco-Logical Press.

Gare, A. 2002. Human ecology and public policy: Overcoming the hegemony of economics. *Democracy & Nature, 8* (1): 131–141.

Garrard, G. 2012. *Ecocriticism* (2nd ed.). London: Routledge.

Garrard, G. (Ed.). 2014. *The Oxford handbook of ecocriticism*. Oxford: Oxford University Press.

Gauntlett, D. 2002. *Media, gender, and identity: An introduction*. London: Routledge.

Gavriely-Nuri, D. 2012. Cultural approach to CDA. *Critical Discourse Studies, 9* (1): 77–85.

Gersie, A., Nanson, A. & Schieffelin, E. (Eds.). 2014. *Storytelling for a greener world: Environment, community and story-based learning*. Stroud: Hawthorn Press.

Giddens, A. 1991. *Modernity and self-identity: Self and society in the late modern age*. Stanford: Stanford University Press.

Gilderhus, N. 1994. The art of storytelling in Leslie Silko's "ceremony". *The English Journal, 83* (2): 70–72.

Giles, D. & Close, J. 2008. Exposure to "lad magazines" and drive for muscularity in dating and non-dating young men. *Personality and Individual Differences, 44* (7): 1610–1616.

Glenn, C. 2004. Constructing consumables and consent: A critical analysis of factory farm industry discourse. *Journal of Communication Inquiry, 28* (1): 63–81.

Glotfelty, C. 2014. What is ecocriticism? *Association for the Study of Literature and Environment*.

Goatly, A. 2000. *Critical reading and writing: an introductory coursebook*. London: Routledge.

Goatly, A. 2001. Green grammar and grammatical metaphor, or language and myth of power, or metaphors we die by. In A. Fill & P. Mühlhäsler (Eds.), *The ecolinguistics reader: Language, ecology, and environment*. London: Continuum, 203–225.

Goffman, E. 1974. *Frame analysis: An essay on the organization of experience*. New York: Harper & Row.

Goojisho. 2020. *Goojisho Japanese-Japanese dictionary*.

Gorz, A. 1993. Political ecology: Expertocracy versus self-limitation. *New Left Review, 202*: 55–67.

Grant, A. 2013. Does studying economics breed greed? *Psychology Today*.

Greenfield, J., O' Connell, S. & Reid, C. 1999. Fashioning masculinity: Men only, consumption and the development of marketing in the 1930s. *Twentieth Century British History, 10* (4): 457–476.

Grimm, B. 2011. *The complete Grimm's fairy tales*. New York: Knopf Doubleday Publishing Group.

Hall, K. 2014. The forgotten tongue. In A. Gersie, A. Nanson, & E. Schieffelin (Eds.), *Storytelling for a greener world: Environment, community and story-based learning*. Stroud: Hawthorn Press, 294–303.

Halliday, M. 2001. New ways of meaning: The challenge to applied linguistics. In A. Fill & P. Mühlhäsler (Eds.), *The ecolinguistics reader: Language, ecology, and environment*. London: Continuum, 175–202.

Halliday, M. 2013. *Halliday's introduction to functional grammar* (4th ed.). London: Routledge.

Hanne, M. 1992. Peasant storytelling meets literary theory: The case of la finta nonna. *The Italianist, 12*: 42–58.

Hanne, M. 2011. The binocular vision project: An introduction. *Genre, 44* (3): 223–237.

Hanne, M. & Kaal, A. A. (Eds.). 2018. *Narrative and metaphor in education: Look both ways*. London: Routledge.

Hansen, A. & Machin, D. 2018. *Media and communication research methods*. New York: Macmillan.

Harding, S. 2010. Gaia theory and deep ecology. In M. Van Eyk McCain (Ed.), *GreenSpirit*. London: John Hunt, 36–49.

Harré, R., Brockmeier, J. & Mühlhäser, P. 1999. *Greenspeak: A study of environmental discourse*. London: Sage.

Haugen, E. 1972. *The ecology of language*. Stanford: Stanford University Press.

Hearst. 2020. *Men's health magazine*.

Heise, U. K. 2016. *Imagining extinction: The cultural meanings of endangered species*. Chicago: University of Chicago Press.

Henning, B. 2011. Standing in livestock's "long shadow": The ethics of eating meat on a small planet. *Ethics & the Environment, 16* (2): 63–93.

Herman, D. (Ed.). 2003. *Narrative theory and the cognitive sciences*. Stanford: CSLI Publications.

Herman, D. 2012. Towards a zoonarratology: Storytelling and species difference in animal comics. In M. Lehtimäi, L. Karttunen & M. Mäelä (Eds.). *Narrative, interrupted: The plotless, the disturbing and the trivial in literature*. Berlin: De Gruyter, 93–121.

Hiscock, G. 2012. *Earth wars: The battle for global resources*. Hoboken: Wiley.

Hopkins, R. 2008. *The transition handbook: From oil dependency to local resilience*. Dartington: Green Books.

Huang, G. W. 2017. Lun shengtai huayu he xingwei fenxi de jiading he yuanze / One assumption and three principles for ecological analysis of discourse and behaviour. *Waiyu Jiaoxue yu Yanjiu / Foreign Language Teaching and Research, 6*: 880–889.

Huang, G. W. 2018. Cong shengtai piping huayu fenxi dao hexie huayu fenxi / From eco-critical discourse analysis to harmonious discourse analysis. *Zhongguo Waiyu / Foreign Languages in China, 4*: 39–46.

Huang, G. W. & Zhao, R. H. 2019. *Shenme Shi Shengtai Yuyanxue / What is ecolinguistics*. Shanghai:

Foreign Language Education Press.

Huang, G. W. & Zhao, R. H. 2021. Harmonious discourse analysis: Approaching peoples' problems in a Chinese context. *Language Sciences, 85*: 1–18.

Hulme, M. 2009. *Why we disagree about climate change: Understanding controversy, inaction and opportunity*. Cambridge: Cambridge University Press.

Ihlen, Ø. 2009. Business and climate change: The climate response of the world's 30 largest corporations. *Environmental Communication: A Journal of Nature and Culture, 3* (2): 244–262.

Ingold, T. 2010. Footprints through the weather-world: Walking, breathing, knowing. *Journal of the Royal Anthropological Institute, 16* (s1): 121–139.

Ingold, T. 2011. *Being alive: Essays on movement, knowledge and description*. London: Routledge.

Inman, P. 2013. Economics students aim to tear up free-market syllabus. *The Guardian*, 24 October.

IPCC. 2018. Global warming of 1.5°C. IPCC.

Johnson, M. 1983. Metaphorical reasoning. *The Southern Journal of Philosophy, 21* (3): 371–389.

Johnson, M. 1987. *The body in the mind: The bodily basis of meaning, imagination, and reason*. Chicago: University of Chicago Press.

Jones, M. & McBeth, M. 2010. A narrative policy framework: Clear enough to be wrong. *Policy Studies Journal, 38* (2): 329–353.

Kahan, D. 2012. Why we are poles apart on climate change. *Nature, 488* (7411): 255.

Kahn, M. 2001. The passive voice of science: Language abuse in the wildlife profession. In A. Fill & P. Mühlhäsler (Eds.), *The ecolinguistics reader: Language, ecology, and environment*. London: Continuum, 232–240.

Kendall, G. 2007. What is critical discourse analysis? *Forum: Qualitative Social Research, 8* (2).

Keulartz, J. 2007. Using metaphors in restoring nature. *Nature & Culture, 2* (1): 27–48.

Killingsworth, M. 2005. From environmental rhetoric to ecocomposition and ecopoetics. *Technical Communication Quarterly, 14* (4): 359–373.

Kingsnorth, P. & Hine, D. 2009. *The Dark Mountain Project manifesto*.

Klein, A. 1993. *Little big men: Bodybuilding subculture and gender construction*. Albany: State University of New York Press.

Knickerbocker, S. 2012. *Ecopoetics: The language of nature, the nature of language*. Amherst: University of Massachusetts Press.

Knight, C. 2010. The discourse of "encultured nature" in Japan: The concept of *satoyama* and its role in 21st-century nature conservation. *Asian Studies Review, 34* (4): 421–441.

Koller, V. 2009. Brand images: Multimodal metaphor in corporate branding messages. In C. Forceville & E. Urios-Aparisi (Eds.), *Multimodal metaphor*. Berlin: Mouton de Gruyter, 45–71.

Korten, D. 2006. *The great turning: From empire to Earth community*. San Francisco: Berrett-Koehler.

Kowalski, R. 2013. Sense and sustainability: The paradoxes that sustain. *World Futures: The Journal of General Evolution, 69* (2): 75–88.

Krementsov, N. & Todes, D. 1991. On metaphors, animals, and us. *Journal of Social Issues, 47* (3): 67–81.

Kress, G. 2010. *Multimodality: A social semiotic approach to contemporary communication*. London: Routledge.

Kress, G. & van Leeuwen, T. 2006. *Reading images: The grammar of visual design* (2nd ed.). London: Routledge.

Kurz, T., Donaghue, N., Rapley, M. & Walker, I. 2005. The ways that people talk about natural resources: Discursive strategies as barriers to environmentally sustainable practices. *British Journal of Social Psychology, 44* (4): 603–620.

Lakoff, G. 1993. The contemporary theory of metaphor. In A. Ortony, (Ed.), *Metaphor and thought*. Cambridge: Cambridge University Press, 202–251.

Lakoff, G. 2014. *Don't think of an elephant!: Know your values and frame the debate: the essential guide for progressives*. White River Junction: Chelsea Green.

Lakoff, G. 2006. *Thinking points: Communicating our American values and vision (a progressive's handbook)*. New York: Farrar, Straus and Giroux.

Lakoff, G. 2010. Why it matters how we frame the environment. *Environmental Communication: A Journal of Nature and Culture, 4* (1): 70–81.

Lakoff, G. & Johnson, M. 1980. *Metaphors we live by*. Chicago: University of Chicago Press.

Lakoff, G. & Johnson, M. 1999. *Philosophy in the flesh: The embodied mind and its challenge to Western thought*. New York: Basic Books.

Lakoff, G. & Wehling, E. 2012a. *The little blue book: The essential guide to thinking and talking Democratic*. New York: Free Press.

Lakoff, G. & Wehling, E. 2012b. The power to make metaphor into law. *RSN*.

Larson, B. 2011. *Metaphors for environmental sustainability: Redefining our relationship with nature*. New Haven: Yale University Press.

Latour, B. 2013. *An inquiry into modes of existence: An anthropology of the moderns*. Cambridge: Harvard University Press.

Latour, B. & Woolgar, S. 1986. *Laboratory life: The construction of scientific facts*. Princeton: Princeton University Press.

Leopold, A. 1979. *A sand county almanac and sketches here and there*. Oxford: Oxford University Press.

LeVasseur, T. & Peterson, A. (Eds.). 2017. *Religion and ecological crisis: The "Lynn White thesis" at fifty*. New York: Routledge.

Lilley, D. 2013. Kathleen Jamie: Rethinking the externality and idealisation of nature. *Green Letters, 17* (1): 16–26.

Lindströ, K. 2019. Classic and cute: Framing biodiversity in Japan through rural landscapes and mascot characters. *Popular Communication, 17* (3): 233–251.

Locke, T. 2004. *Critical discourse analysis*. London: Continuum.

Lomborg, B. 2001. *The skeptical environmentalist: Measuring the real state of the world*. Cambridge: Cambridge University Press.

Lovelock, J. 2004. Something nasty in the greenhouse. *Atmospheric Science Letters, 5* (6): 108–109.

Lovelock, J. 2006. *The revenge of Gaia: Earth's climate in crisis and the fate of humanity*. New York: Basic Books.

Lovelock, J. 2009. *The vanishing face of Gaia: A final warning*. New York: Basic Books.

Loy, D. 2010. *The world is made of stories*. Boston: Wisdom Publications.

Lutz, C. 1990. The erasure of women's writing in sociocultural anthropology. *American Ethnologist*, (4): 611.

Lynch, T. 1998. "A path toward nature": Haiku's aesthetics of awareness. In P. Murphy (Ed.), *Literature of nature: An international sourcebook*. Chicago: Fitzroy Dearborn, 116–125.

Mabey, R. 2008. Nature and nation. *Youtube*.

Macfarlane, R. 2013. New words on the wild. *Nature, 498*: 166–167.

Macgilchrist, F. 2007. Positive discourse analysis: Contesting dominant discourses by reframing the issues. *Critical Approaches to Discourse Analysis Across Disciplines, 1* (1): 74–94.

Machin, D. & Mayr, A. 2012. *How to do critical discourse analysis: A multimodal introduction*. London: Sage.

Machiorlatti, J. 2010. Ecocinema, ecojustice, and indigenous worldviews. In P. Willoquet-Maricondi (Ed.), *Framing the world: Explorations in ecocriticism and film*. Charlottesville: University of Virginia Press, 62–80.

Macy, J. & Johnstone, C. 2012. *Active hope: How to face the mess we're in without going crazy*. Novato: New World Library.

Manji, F. & O'Coill, C. 2002. The missionary position: NGOs and development in Africa. *International Affairs, 78* (3): 567–583.

Martin, J. 2004. Positive discourse analysis: Solidarity and change. *Revista Canaria de Estudios Ingleses, 49*: 179–200.

Martin, J. 2008. Incongruent and proud: De-vilifying "nominalization". *Discourse & Society, 19* (6): 801–810.

Martin, J. 2014. *Politics and rhetoric: A critical introduction*. London: Routledge.

Martin, J. & Rose, D. 2007. *Working with discourse: Meaning beyond the clause*. London: Bloomsbury.

Martin, J. & White, P. 2005. *The language of evaluation: Appraisal in English*. New York: Palgrave Macmillan.

Martusewicz, R. Edmundson, J. & Lupinacci, J. 2011. *Ecojustice education: Toward diverse, democratic, and sustainable communities*. New York: Routledge.

McBay, A., Keith, L. & Jensen, D. 2011. *Deep green resistance: Strategy to save the planet*. New

York: Seven Stories Press.

McCarron, B. 2017. *Factory farming in Asia: Assessing investment risks*. London: FAIRR.

McCracken, E. 1993. *Decoding women's magazines: From Mademoiselle to Ms*. New York: St. Martin's Press.

McIntosh, A. 2004. *Soil and soul: People versus corporate power*. London: Aurum.

McKibben, B. 2006. *The end of nature*. New York: Random House.

McLaren, P. 2002. *Critical pedagogy and predatory culture: Oppositional politics in a postmodern era*. London: Routledge.

McLoughlin, L. 2000. *The language of magazines*. London: Routledge.

Merchant, C. 2014. *Earthcare: Women and the environment*. London: Routledge.

Messersmith-Glavin, P. 2012. Between social ecology and deep ecology: Gary Snyder's ecological philosophy. In S. Elkholy (Ed.), *The philosophy of the beats*. Lexington: University Press of Kentucky.

Mey, J. 2018. The pragmatics of metaphor: An ecological view. In A. Fill & H. Penz (Eds.), *The Routledge handbook of ecolinguistics*. London: Routledge, 211–226.

Meyer, J. & Land, R. 2005. Threshold concepts and troublesome knowledge (2): Epistemological considerations and a conceptual framework for teaching and learning. *Higher Education, 49* (3): 373–388.

Midgley, M. 2011. *The myths we live by*. New York: Routledge.

Mieder, W. 2009. *"Yes we can": Barack Obama's proverbial rhetoric*. New York: Peter Lang.

Milstein, T. 2009. "Somethin' tells me it's all happening at the zoo": Discourse, power, and conservationism. *Environmental Communication: A Journal of Nature and Culture, 3* (1): 25–48.

Milstein, T. & Dickinson, E. 2012. Gynocentric greenwashing: The discursive gendering of nature. *Communication, Culture & Critique, 5* (4): 510–532.

Milstein, T., Littlejohn, S. & Foss, K. 2009. Environmental communication theories. In S. Littlejohn & K. Foss (Eds.), *Encyclopaedia of communication theory*. Los Angeles: Sage, 344–349.

Minsky, M. 1988. A framework for representing knowledge. In A. Collins & E. Smith (Eds.), *Readings in cognitive science: A perspective from psychology and artificial intelligence*. San Mateo: Morgan Kaufmann, 156–189.

Molinsky, A., Grant, A. & Margolis, J. 2012. The bedside manner of homo economicus: How and why priming an economic schema reduces compassion. *Organizational Behaviour & Human Decision Processes, 119* (1): 27–37.

Molthan-Hill, P., Baden, D., Wall, T., Puntha, H. & Luna, H. (Eds.). 2020. *Storytelling for sustainability in higher education: An educator's handbook*. London: Routledge.

Moser, S. & Dilling, L. 2011. Communicating climate change: Closing the science-action gap. In J. Dryzek, R. Norgaard & D. Schlosberg (Eds.), *Oxford handbook of climate change and society*. Oxford: Oxford University Press, 161–174.

Mueller, M. L. 2017. *Being salmon, being human: Encountering the wild in us and us in the wild.* White River Junction: Chelsea Green Publishing.

Mühlhäsler, P. 2001. Talking about environmental issues. In A. Fill & P. Mühlhäsler (Eds.), *The ecolinguistics reader: Language, ecology, and environment.* London: Continuum, 31–42.

Mühlhäsler, P. 2003. *Language of environment, environment of language: A course in ecolinguistics.* London: Battlebridge.

Müller, C. 2008. *Metaphors dead and alive, sleeping and waking: A dynamic view.* Chicago: University of Chicago Press.

Naess, A. 1995. The shallow and the long range, deep ecology movement. In A. Drengson & Y. Inoue (Eds.), *The deep ecology movement: An introductory anthology.* Berkeley: North Atlantic Books, 3–10.

Naish, J. 2009. *Enough: Breaking free from the world of excess.* London: Hodder.

Namaste, V. 2000. *Invisible lives: The erasure of transsexual and transgendered people.* Chicago: University of Chicago Press.

Nanson, A. 2011. *Words of re-enchantment: Writings on storytelling, myth, and ecological desire.* Stroud: Awen Publications.

Nanson, A. 2014. Jumping the gap of desire. In A. Gersie, A. Nanson & E. Schieffelin (Eds.), *Storytelling for a greener world: Environment, community and story-based learning.* Stroud: Hawthorn Press, 141–151.

Nanson, A. 2021. *Storytelling and ecology: Empathy, enchantment and emergence in the use of oral narrative.* London: Bloomsbury.

NEF. 2008. Five ways to well-being: The evidence.

NEF. 2020. *Happy planet index.*

Nerlich, B. & Jaspal, R. 2012. Metaphors we die by? Geoengineering, metaphors, and the argument from catastrophe. *Metaphor and Symbol, 27* (2): 131–147.

Nerlich, B. 2010. "Climategate": Paradoxical metaphors and political paralysis. *Environmental Values, 19* (4): 419–442.

Nerlich, B., Hamilton, C. & Rowe, V. 2002. Conceptualising foot and mouth disease: The socio-cultural role of metaphors, frames and narratives. *Metaphorik. de, 2*: 90–108.

Nichols, R. & Allen-Brown, V. 1996. Critical theory and educational technology. In D. Jonassen (Ed.), *Handbook of research for educational communications and technology.* New York: Macmillan, 226–252.

NZ Government. 2017. *Innovative bill protects Whanganui River with legal personhood.* New Zealand Government.

Okri, B. 1996. *Birds of heaven.* London: Phoenix.

Oktar, L. 2001. The ideological organization of representational processes in the presentation of us and them. *Discourse & Society, 12* (3): 313.

Ooi, V. 2017. A corpus-based linguistic profile of marine humanities discourse. *Journal of global and area studies, 1* (2): 83–109.

Orr, D. 1992. *Ecological literacy: Education and the transition to a postmodern world.* Albany: State University of New York Press.

Peterson, A. 2001. *Being human: Ethics, environment, and our place in the world.* Berkeley: University of California Press.

PHE. 2018. *Heatwave mortality monitoring: Summer 2018.* London: Public Health England.

Philo, C. & Wilbert, C. 2000. *Animal spaces, beastly places.* London: Routledge.

Pierson, D. 2005. "Hey, they're just like us!": Representations of the animal world in the discovery channel's nature programming. *Journal of Popular Culture, 38* (4): 698–712.

Plumwood, V. 2007. Human exceptionalism and the limitations of animals. *Australian Humanities Review,* 42.

Plumwood, V. 2008. Shadow places and the politics of dwelling. *Australian Humanities Review,* 44.

Poole, R. 2016. A corpus-aided ecological discourse analysis of the Rosemont Copper Mine debate of Arizona, USA. *Discourse and Communication, 10* (6): 576–595.

Poole, R. 2017. Ecolinguistics, GIS, and corpus linguistics for the analysis of the Rosemont Copper Mine debate. *Environmental Communication, 12* (4): 525–540.

Poole, R. 2022. *Corpus-assisted ecolinguistics.* London: Bloomsbury.

Poore, J. & Nemecek, T. 2018. Reducing food's environmental impacts through producers and consumers. *Science, 360* (6392): 987–992.

Potter, J. 1996. *Representing reality: Discourse, rhetoric and social construction.* London: Sage.

Rateau, P., Moliner, P., Guimelli, C. & Abric, J. 2012. Social representation theory. *Handbook of theories of social psychology, 2*: 477–497.

Raymond, C., Singh, G., Benessaiah, K., Bernhardt, J., Levine, J., Nelson, H., Turner, N., Norton, B., Tam, J. & Chan, K. 2013. Ecosystem services and beyond: Using multiple metaphors to understand human-environment relationships. *BioScience,* (7): 536.

RE. 2014. *Rethinking economics.*

Richardson, J. 2007. *Analysing newspapers: An approach from Critical Discourse Analysis.* New York: Palgrave Macmillan.

Ridley, M. 2010. *The rational optimist: How prosperity evolves.* New York: Harper.

Rive, N., Jackson, B. & Rado, D. 2007. Complaint to Ofcom regarding *The great global warming swindle.*

Robbins, P. 2012. *Political ecology: A critical introduction.* Hoboken: John Wiley & Sons.

Robertson, M. 2014. *Sustainability principles and practice.* London: Routledge.

Roccia, M. 2019. Changing lives and professional practice: A report on the impact of Ecolinguistics. *Language & Ecology.*

Romaine, S. 1996. War and peace in the global greenhouse: Metaphors we die by. *Metaphor and*

Symbolic Activity, 11 (3): 175–194.

Roy, A. 2020. The pandemic is a portal. *The Financial Times*, 3 April.

Russill, C. 2010. Temporal metaphor in abrupt climate change communication: An initial effort at clarification. In W. L. Filho (Ed.), *The economic, social and political elements of climate change.* London: Springer, 113–132.

Sachs, W. 1999. *Planet dialectics: Explorations in environment and development.* London: Zed Books.

Sachs, W. (Ed.). 2010. *The development dictionary: A guide to knowledge as power* (2nd ed.). London: Zed Books.

Salvi, R. & Turnbull, J., 2010. Appraisal theory as a methodological proposal for stylistic analysis. *Textus, 23*: 103–138.

Satya. 2019. Radical self care: Black men healing. *Afropunk*, 3 June.

Savran, D. 1998. *Taking it like a man: White masculinity, masochism, and contemporary American culture.* Princeton: Princeton University Press.

Schleppegrell, M. 1997. Agency in environmental education. *Linguistics and Education, 9* (1): 49–67.

Schö, D. 1993. Generative metaphor: A perspective on problem setting in social policy. In A. Ortony (Ed.), *Metaphor and thought.* Cambridge: Cambridge University Press, 167–163.

Schultz, B. 2001. Language and the natural environment. In A. Fill & P. Mühlhäsler (Eds.), *The ecolinguistics reader: Language, ecology, and environment.* London: Continuum, 109–114.

Sedlaczek, A. 2016. Representation of climate change in documentary television: Integrating an ecolinguistic and ecosemiotic perspective into a multimodal critical discourse. *Language & Ecology*, 1–19.

Selby, D. 2008. Degrees of denial: As global heating happens should we be educating for sustainable development or sustainable contraction? In J. Satterthwaite, M. Watts & H. Piper (Eds.), *Talking truth, confronting power.* Stroke: Trentham Books, 17–34.

Semino, E. 2008. *Metaphor in discourse.* Cambridge: Cambridge University Press.

SFH. 2020. *Stop funding hate.*

Shields, F. 2019. Why we're rethinking the images we use for our climate journalism. *The Guardian.*

Simmons, A. 2015. *Whoever tells the best story wins: How to use your own stories to communicate with power and impact* (2nd ed.). New York: Amacom.

Singer, P. 1990. *Animal liberation* (2nd ed.). London: Random House.

Skutnabb-Kangas, T. & Harmon, D. 2018. Biological diversity and language diversity: Parallels and differences. In A. Fill & H. Penz (Eds.), *The Routledge handbook of ecolinguistics.* London: Routledge, 11–25.

Smith, A. 2019. Some indigenous communities have a new way to fight climate change: Give personhood rights to nature. *Mother Jones.*

Smith, J. 2013. An archipelagic literature: Re-framing "the new nature writing". *Green Letters, 17* (1): 5–15.

Smith, M. 1999. Greenspeak (book review). *Environmental Politics, 8* (4): 231.

Smith, M. 2019. Most people expect to feel the effects of climate change, and many think it will make us extinct. *YouGov*, September 16.

Solnit, R. 2019. Trump's anti-immigrant rhetoric shows the danger of misplaced empathy. *The Guardian*, 25 October.

Stallmeyer, J. & Dearborn, L., 2020. *Erasure and appearance*. In P. Daly & T. Winter (Eds.), *Routledge handbook of heritage in Asia*. London: Routledge, 46–362.

Stenning, A. 2010. *Literary illumination: A study in the use of celebratory narratives in Nature Cure by Richard Mabey, The Wild Places by Robert Macfarlane, and Pilgrim at Tinker Creek by Annie Dillard*. Unpublished MA thesis: Colchester: University of Essex.

Stevens, P. 2012. Towards an ecosociology. *Sociology, 46* (4): 579–595.

Stibbe, A. 2012. *Animals erased: Discourse, ecology, and reconnection with the natural world*. Middletown: Wesleyan University Press.

Stiglitz, J. 2003. *Globalization and its discontents*. London: Penguin.

Stiglitz, J., Fitoussi, J. & Durand, M. 2020. *Measuring what counts: The global movement for well-being*. New York: The New Press.

Sullivan, K. 2013. *Frames and constructions in metaphoric language*. Amsterdam: John Benjamins.

Sutton, P. 2007. *The environment: A sociological introduction*. Cambridge: Polity.

Suzuki, D. 1970. *Zen and Japanese culture*. Princeton: Princeton University Press.

Tannen, D. (Ed.). 1993. *Framing in discourse*. Oxford: Oxford University Press.

Taylor, B., Wright, J. & LeVasseur, T., 2019. Dark green humility: Religious, psychological, and affective attributes of proenvironmental behaviours. *Journal of Environmental Studies and Sciences, 10*: 41–56

Taylor, S. 2020. Instagram post.

Tester, K. 1991. *Animals and society: The humanity of animal rights*. London: Routledge.

Thomashow, M. 1995. *Ecological identity: Becoming a reflective environmentalist*. Cambridge: MIT Press.

Toolan, M. 2018. *Making sense of narrative text*. London: Routledge.

Toolan, M. J. 2001. *Narrative: A critical linguistic introduction*. London: Routledge.

Trainer, T. 2011. The simpler way perspective on the global predicament. *Post Carbon Institute*.

Trampe, W. 2018. Euphemisms for killing animals and for other forms of their use. In A. Fill & H. Penz (Eds.), *The Routledge handbook of ecolinguistics*. London: Routledge, 325–341.

UNEP. 2019. Global environmental outlook 6. UNEP.

Väiverronen, E. & Hellsten, I. 2002. From "burning library" to "green medicine" the role of metaphors in communicating biodiversity. *Science Communication, 24* (2): 229–245.

van Dijk, T. 1993. Principles of critical discourse analysis. *Discourse & Society, 4* (2): 249–283.

van Dijk, T. 1998. *Ideology: A multidisciplinary approach*. London: Sage.

van Dijk, T. 2009. *Society and discourse: How social contexts influence text and talk*. Cambridge: Cambridge University Press.

van Dijk, T. (Ed.). 2011. *Discourse studies: A multidisciplinary introduction* (2nd ed.). London: Sage.

van Leeuwen, T. 2008. *Discourse and practice*. Oxford: Oxford University Press.

Verhagen, F. 2008. Worldviews and metaphors in the human-nature relationship: An ecolinguistic exploration through the ages. *Language & Ecology*.

VHEMT. 2014. *The voluntary human extinction movement*.

Watts, J. 2020. Bruno Latour: "this is a global catastrophe that has come from within". *The Observer*, 6 June.

Wheaton, B. 2007. Identity, politics, and the beach: Environmental activism in *Surfers Against Sewage*. *Leisure Studies, 26* (3): 279–302.

White, L. 1967. The historical roots of our ecologic crisis. *Science, New Series, 155* (3767): 1203–1207.

White, P. 2004. Subjectivity, evaluation and point of view in media discourse. In Coffin, C., Hewings, A. & O' Halloran, K. (Eds.), *Applying English grammar*. London: Hodder Arnold, 229–246.

Widdowson, H. 2008. *Text, context, pretext: Critical issues in discourse analysis*. Hoboken: John Wiley & Sons.

Williams, J. & McNeill, J. 2005. *The current crisis in neoclassical economics and the case for an economic analysis based on sustainable development*. Rochester: Social Science Research Network.

Witt, J. 2011. What is the basis for corporate personhood? NPR.

Yeager, P. 2009. Science, values and politics: An insider's reflections on corporate crime research. *Crime, Law & Social Change, 51* (1): 5–30.